The Routledge Companion to Accounting Communication

One of the prime purposes of accounting is to communicate. However, to date, this fundamental aspect of the discipline has received relatively little attention. *The Routledge Companion to Accounting Communication* represents the first collection of contributions to focus on the power of communication in accounting.

The chapters have a shared aim of addressing the misconception that accounting is a purely technical, number-based discipline. They highlight the use of narrative, visual and technological methods to communicate accounting information. The contents comprise a mixture of reflective overview, stinging critique, technological exposition, clinical analysis and practical advice on topical areas of interest such as:

- The miscommunication that preceded the global financial crisis
- The failure of sustainability reporting
- The development of XBRL
- The cutting of clutter

This volume has an international coterie of contributors, including a communication theorist, a 'Big Four' practitioner and accounting academics. It provides an eclectic array of expert analysis and reflection. The contributors reveal how accounting communications represent, or misrepresent, the financial affairs of entities, thus presenting a state-of-the-art assessment on each of the main facets of this important topic. This book will be of interest to a wide range of readers, including postgraduate students in management and accounting; established researchers in the fields of accounting and communications; and accounting practitioners.

Lisa Jack is Professor of Accounting at the University of Portsmouth Business School, UK. Her research interests encompass performance measurement, accounting in food-supply chains and management control. She is the author of *Benchmarking in Food and Farming: Creating Sustainable Change* (Gower, 2009), as well as several research papers, book chapters and CIMA reports.

Jane Davison is Professor of Accounting at Royal Holloway, University of London, UK. Her research interests include visual and narrative perspectives on accounting. She is widely published in major international journals. She is co-editor of several journal special issues, co-founder of the *in*Visio research network and associate director of the Bangor Centre for Impression Management in Accounting.

Russell Craig is Professor of Accounting at Victoria University, Australia. His main research interests include financial reporting, international accounting and the accountability discourse of executives. He is the co-author of *CEO-Speak: The Language of Corporate Leadership* (McGill Queens University Press, 2006) and over 150 research papers, research monographs and book chapters.

Routledge Companions in Business, Management and Accounting

Routledge Companions in Business, Management and Accounting are similar to what some publishers call 'handbooks', i.e. prestige reference works providing an overview of a whole subject area or sub-discipline, and which survey the state of the discipline including emerging and cutting-edge areas. These books provide a comprehensive, up-to-date, definitive work of reference which can be cited as an authoritative source on the subject.

One of the key aspects of the Routledge Companions in Business, Management and Accounting series is their international scope and relevance. Edited by an array of well-regarded scholars, these volumes also benefit from teams of contributors which reflect an international range of perspectives.

Individually, Routledge Companions in Business, Management and Accounting provide an impactful one-stop-shop resource for each theme covered, whilst collectively they represent a comprehensive learning and research resource for researchers, postgraduates and practitioners.

Published titles in this series include:

The Routledge Companion to Fair Value and Financial Reporting
Edited by Peter Walton

The Routledge Companion to Nonprofit Marketing
Edited by Adrian Sargeant and Walter Wymer Jr

The Routledge Companion to Accounting History
Edited by John Richard Edwards and Stephen P. Walker

The Routledge Companion to Creativity
Edited by Tudor Rickards, Mark A. Runco and Susan Moger

The Routledge Companion to Strategic Human Resource Management
Edited by John Storey, Patrick M. Wright and David Ulrich

The Routledge Companion to International Business Coaching
Edited by Michel Moral and Geoffrey Abbott

The Routledge Companion to Organizational Change
Edited by David M. Boje, Bernard Burnes and John Hassard

The Routledge Companion to Cost Management
Edited by Falconer Mitchell, Hanne Nørreklit and Morten Jakobsen

The Routledge Companion to Digital Consumption
Edited by Russell W. Belk and Rosa Llamas

The Routledge Companion to Identity and Consumption
Edited by Ayalla A. Ruvio and Russell W. Belk

The Routledge Companion to Public–Private Partnerships
Edited by Piet de Vries and Etienne B. Yehoue

The Routledge Companion to Accounting, Reporting and Regulation
Edited by Carien van Mourik and Peter Walton

The Routledge Companion to International Management Education
Edited by Denise Tsang, Hamid H. Kazeroony and Guy Ellis

The Routledge Companion to Accounting Communication
Edited by Lisa Jack, Jane Davison and Russell Craig

The Routledge Companion to Accounting Communication

Edited by Lisa Jack, Jane Davison and Russell Craig

LONDON AND NEW YORK

First published 2013
by Routledge
2 Park Square, Milton Park, Abingdon, Oxon OX14 4RN

Simultaneously published in the USA and Canada
by Routledge
711 Third Avenue, New York, NY 10017

Routledge is an imprint of the Taylor & Francis Group,
an informa business

British Library Cataloguing in Publication Data

A catalogue record for this book is available from the British Library

Library of Congress Cataloging in Publication Data

The Routledge companion to accounting communication /
edited by Lisa Jack, Jane Davison and Russell Craig.
pages cm. — (Routledge companions in business, management and
accounting)
Includes bibliographical references and index.
ISBN 978-0-415-61714-7 (hbk.) — ISBN 978-0-203-59349-3 (ebook)
1. Communication in accounting. I. Jack, Lisa.
HF5625.5.R68 2013
657.01'4—dc23
2012044452

ISBN: 978-0-415-61714-7 (hbk)
ISBN: 978-0-203-59349-3 (ebk)

Typeset in Bembo
by Cenveo Publisher Services

Printed and bound in Great Britain by
TJ International Ltd, Padstow, Cornwall

Contents

Contents

Figures

Tables

Contributors

Joel Amernic is Professor of Accounting at the University of Toronto's Rotman School of Management. His research interests include topics such as the accountability language of top management, financial reporting and accounting education. He has published extensively and has also received the Canadian Academic Accounting Association's outstanding accounting educator award.

José L. Arquero is the editor of the *Spanish Journal of Accounting, Finance and Management Education*. Since obtaining an extraordinary doctoral award at the University of Seville with a thesis focused on accounting education, he has published several papers with Trevor Hassall and John Joyce in the *European Accounting Review, Accounting Forum, Accounting Education* and other journals.

Niamh M. Brennan is Michael MacCormac Professor of Management and Academic Director of the Centre for Corporate Governance at University College Dublin. She has published on financial reporting, corporate governance and forensic accounting, including best paper/article awards from the *British Accounting Review, Accounting, Auditing & Accountability Journal* and *Accountancy Ireland*.

Frank Clarke is Professor Emeritus at the University of Newcastle (Australia) and Honorary Professor of Accounting at the University of Sydney. His books include (with Professor Graeme Dean) *Corporate Collapse: Accounting, Regulatory and Ethical Failure* and *Indecent Disclosure: Gilding the Corporate Lily*, and (with Professors Graeme Dean and Murray Wells) *The Sydney School of Accounting: The Chambers Years*.

Russell Craig is Professor of Accounting at Victoria University, Melbourne. His main research interests include financial reporting, international accounting and the accountability discourse of executives. He is the co-author of *CEO-Speak: The Language of Corporate Leadership* (2006) and over 150 research papers, research monographs and book chapters.

Christine Cooper is Professor of Accounting at Strathclyde University and co-editor of *Critical Perspectives on Accounting*. Her research is concerned with the economic, political and social impact of accounting. This has produced publications in diverse arenas including social and environmental accounting, gender, privatization, deskilling of accountants and book-keepers, insolvency and accountability.

Jane Davison is Professor of Accounting at Royal Holloway, University of London. Her research interests include visual and narrative perspectives on accounting. She is widely published in major international journals, co-editor of several journal special issues, co-founder of the *in*Visio research network and associate director of the Bangor Centre for Impression Management in Accounting.

Graeme Dean is Honorary Professor of Accounting at the University of Sydney. He was sole editor of *Abacus* from 1994 to 2009. He has published several books and books of readings. With Frank Clarke he has traced ideas about the development of accounting for inflation and their transportation from European to Anglo-American countries, and examined asset valuation and auditing issues through the lens of company failures.

John Richard Edwards is Research Professor of Accounting at Cardiff Business School. Book publications include *The History of Financial Accounting* (1989) and joint authorship of *The Priesthood of Industry: The Rise of the Professional Accountant in British Management* (1998), *The Routledge Companion to Accounting History* (2009) and *A History of Management Accounting: The British Experience* (2012).

José María González is a Doctor Contracted in Accounting at the University of Seville as well as a Visiting Research Fellow of Sheffield Hallam University. Specific research interests include social aspects of management accounting and repercussions of the implementation of the European Higher Education Area on accounting education.

Trevor Hassall is Professor of Accounting Education at Sheffield Hallam University. His research interests include the development of vocational and personal skills in undergraduate and professional accountants and the barriers to skills development. He has produced extensive publications in professional and refereed accounting and education journals and several book chapters.

John Hitchins is a partner at PricewaterhouseCoopers and leads the Global Accounting Consulting Services division. He has 36 years' experience working with leading global and UK financial services companies on corporate reporting, governance and controls. He is a member of the IFRS Advisory Council which works with the IASB to provide input to its programme from a range of stakeholder perspectives.

Lisa Jack is Professor of Accounting at University of Portsmouth Business School. Her research interests encompass performance measurement, accounting in food supply chains and management control. She is the author of the book *Benchmarking in Food and Farming: Creating Sustainable Change* (Gower, 2009) as well as several research papers, book chapters and CIMA reports.

John Joyce is Professor of Management Accounting Education at Sheffield Hallam University. He has published extensively in professional and refereed journals. His interests include the approaches to learning of accounting students, vocational skills for accountants, skills development and apprehensions.

Joanne Locke is Professor of Accounting at the Open University in the UK. Her research interests are in digital reporting, enterprise resource planning systems and standardization. She has been researching XBRL for over ten years.

Doris M. Merkl-Davies is a Reader in Accounting and Deputy Director of the Centre for Impression Management in Accounting Communication (CIMAC) at Bangor University. Her research focuses on corporate narrative reporting and impression management. She received the Mary Parker Follett Best Paper Award from *Accounting, Auditing & Accountability Journal* in 2011.

Markus J. Milne is Professor of Accounting at the University of Canterbury, New Zealand. His research over the past 20 years has focused on corporate social and environmental reporting, including critiques of corporate attempts to address the triple bottom line and (un)sustainability.

In 2009 he received the Mary Parker Follet Award for the best paper in *Accounting, Auditing & Accountability Journal*.

Lee Parker is Professor of Accounting at the University of South Australia. He is an extensively published qualitative researcher whose research covers strategy and management control, accounting and management history, social and environmental accounting, corporate governance and accounting communication. He is joint founding editor of *Accounting, Auditing & Accountability Journal*.

Paolo Quattrone is Professor of Accounting and Management Control at IE Business School, Madrid, and also holds academic posts at the Universities of Manchester, Carlos III (Madrid) and Oxford. His research spans the history of administrative practices in religious orders to information and management control technologies in large organizations.

Abhi Rao is the Director of the College of Business Communications Center at Iowa State University. His research interests include writing in the disciplines, writing across the curriculum, writing-centre theory and practice, and multimodal communication pedagogy. Other research interests include qualitative research methodologies and ethnography in communication studies.

Sue Ravenscroft is the Roger P. Murphy Professor of Accounting at Iowa State University. Her research interests in accounting education include ethics, meta-cognitive processes and developing communication skills. Other research interests include corporate social responsibility and the conceptual foundations of accounting theory.

Wally Smieliauskas is Professor of Accounting at the University of Toronto's Rotman School of Management. He has published research on a variety of auditing, accounting and education issues, and his audit textbook (with Kathryn Bewley) *Auditing: An International Approach* is in its 6th edition.

Laura Taylor is a senior manager in PricewaterhouseCoopers' Global Accounting Consulting Services division. Laura has 14 years' experience with PwC and has worked with a variety of high-profile companies. In recent years she has advised clients and practice staff on technical matters, including IFRS, UK GAAP, company law and corporate governance.

Theo van Leeuwen is Professor of Media and Communication and Dean of the Faculty of Arts and Social Sciences at the University of Technology, Sydney. He has published extensively in the areas of critical discourse analysis, social semiotics, visual communication and multimodality. His books include *Discourse and Practice* (Oxford University Press, 2008), *Global Media Discourse* (with David Machin, Routledge, 2008) and *The Language of Colour* (Routledge, 2010). He is a founding editor of the journal *Visual Communication*, published by Sage.

Foreword

The contemporary business landscape is distinguished from its predecessors by concerns about efficiency, calculation and predictability. Despite its shortcomings, accounting has become a key technology for mediating uncertainty and promoting rational management. The hand of accounting is visible in every nook and cranny. It influences not only wages, dividends, pensions, prices and corporate taxes, but also the provision of healthcare, education, policing, street cleaning and even the size of a portion of potato fries that you might buy at your local burger bar.

Accounting information is communicated to interested parties through a variety of channels, such as annual reports, social responsibility reports and the internet, and using a variety of mediums, including narratives, pictures, graphs and charts. The language used in these mediums is worthy of closer study because it remains highly value-laden and has serious consequences. For example, payments to providers of human capital are described as 'costs' or burdens. The description invokes the logic that in pursuit of efficiency wages should be reduced. Towards that end companies create monitoring systems to discipline labour. In the absence of effective resistance, the portrayal of workers as burdens can lead to loss of spending power available to workers. Soon we have the spectre of empty high-street shops, social strife and economic recessions. In contrast, payments to providers of capital, such as dividends, are portrayed as rewards and the logic is that these should be maximized. This logic supports transfers of wealth from workers to capital and is one of the major reasons for social antagonisms.

Accounting communication is valued because it gives visibility to things. Thus, it enables us to talk about wages, dividends and some selected assets and liabilities. However, it also creates invisibilities. For example, the focus on wages and salaries is detached from the impact on workers. What might the consequence of wage freezes and reductions be for workers, their families, level of social security payments, tax revenues, government debt, or even the demand for the company's own product and services? Such issues call for a closer study of the communicative capacity of accounting and provide opportunities for shaping future developments.

Accounting uses immense organizational, regulatory and human resources. Around the world some 2.5 million professionally qualified accountants are involved in the production of reams of documents. Nearly 320,000 of these are to be found in the UK. Yet a steady stream of corporate scandals reminds us that despite the huge investment in economic surveillance, good systems of corporate governance, transparent and honest accounts and good accountability have remained somewhat elusive.

The above provides a brief glimpse of the challenges facing the way accounting information is produced, consumed, regulated, represented and communicated. It is a pleasure to welcome this book. The chapters by various authors seek to delineate the field of inquiry about accounting. They go beyond conventional logics and provide a deep and critical perspective on a dominant social technology.

Professor Prem Sikka
University of Essex
October 2012

Acknowledgements

We are indebted to our respective universities (University of Portsmouth, Royal Holloway University of London and Victoria University, Melbourne) for allowing us the time and giving us support in completing this volume. We particularly thank Terry Clague (Routledge) and Stephen Walker (University of Cardiff) for their good advice in the initial stages of the project, and Prem Sikka (University of Essex) for his ongoing support and counsel. We are grateful to our chapter authors for agreeing to contribute to the volume and for their responsiveness to our editorial suggestions. The enduring patience and expert technical advice of the staff at Routledge – Alexander Krause and the rest of the production team – together with the support of Teresa Plummer (The Admin Agency) have been invaluable. We offer special thanks to Philip Johnson at Royal Holloway for technical advice. Finally, we extend a heartfelt and collective 'thank you' to many colleagues over the years who have fostered and encouraged our interest in accounting communication.

Lisa Jack, Jane Davison and Russell Craig

Part 1
The landscape

1

The power of accounting communication

Lisa Jack, Jane Davison and Russell Craig

> [A]ccounting is as much about communication as it is to do with measurement. No matter how effective the process of accounting quantification, its resultant data will be less than useful unless they are communicated adequately.
>
> *(Lee, 1982: 152)*

In compiling this companion volume the shared view we have of accounting communication is one that implies a broad-ranging process of creating and sharing meaning. Thus, it should be unsurprising that the following chapters are a diverse collection. They reflect growing interest in the processes and media that accountants use to communicate accountability information and to represent (and mis-represent) the financial positions of entities. The chapters contain many suggestions for making accounting communications more effective and less biased. They vary in tone and nature by including a mixture of reflective overview, stinging critique, technological exposition, clinical analysis and practical advice. The contributors assess accounting communication from a wide variety of perspectives, including those focusing on pedagogy, discourse analysis and argument theory. The views presented range from mainstream orthodoxy to radical critique.

Our chapter contributors are preponderantly accounting academics. However, we also have contributors from the practising arm of the accounting profession and from the academic wing of the communication studies discipline. The contributors canvass a wide variety of accounting communications research by drawing variously on aspects of accounting history, management accounting, financial reporting, accounting education, auditing and accountability discourse.

An important motivation for this companion volume is reflected in the observation by Hitchins and Taylor in Chapter 14 that 'good communication, both internal and external, is critical to a company's success ... *it is not just about the numbers*' (italics applied). Thus, a major purpose is to address the misconception among accounting practitioners, academics and students, and the public that accounting is a purely technical and number-based discipline. Accordingly, chapter contributors highlight the importance of words, language and rhetoric in accounting communication. They draw attention to the need for all who practise, research or otherwise engage with accounting to recognize the complexity and malleability of language; and to acknowledge the extent to which the accessibility and transparency of language as a conduit of objective truth is easy to compromise. Contributors emphasize the need for alertness to the potential for accounting messages to be moulded by language and communication media to make those messages incoherent and ambiguous.

This volume begins with a historical overview of research in accounting communication. Then Part 2 explores theory and practice relating to the presentation of accounting reports, including discussion of such matters as discourse, imagery and metaphor. The general intent is to highlight how accountants can be influenced by, and can attempt to influence others, into accepting messages communicated about entities. Part 3 focuses on the means of communication used by entities and discusses attendant issues. Part 4 explores clarity of meaning in audited financial reports, both from an academic and from a practitioner point of view. In particular, the final chapter offers a strong critique of the taken-for-granted socio-political context that shapes accounting communication.

The landscape

In the opening chapter of Part 1 Lee Parker seeks to 'whet our appetite' for research and practical action in accounting communications by reviewing the accounting communications research landscape. He explores a selection of the key research subjects addressed since the 1970s: accounting report readability, Internet communication, visual and graphical communication, impression management, and the concerns of the profession and academe for accounting communication skills. Parker analyses the progress and impact of this research, and outlines several vanished and emergent agendas of accounting communications research. He laments the 'almost total neglect by accounting researchers of internal organizational communication processes'. Such neglect, in his view, is remarkable 'given the pervasiveness of accounting communications and their myriad forms within organisational life'.

Frank Clarke, Graeme Dean and John Richard Edwards draw upon the corpus of the scholarly life's work of the eminent Australian academic Professor Ray Chambers to illustrate the importance for accountants to develop better communication skills in order that they can better 'tell it as it is'. They illustrate their chapter with examples of 'bad communication' in the prelude to the unexpected collapses and financial difficulties of several large companies in the global financial crisis of 2007–09. In particular, they focus on mark-to-market accounting and recent 'accounting miscommunications of the kind Chambers wanted to avoid'. Chambers is revealed as a 'true wordsmith' with a deep commitment to meticulously proper use of language, tight logic and conclusions that 'could clearly and exclusively be drawn from the preceding argument'. In particular, Clarke et al. highlight Chambers' 'desire to rid accounting of loose terminology and to achieve recognition of accounting as a communication language [that will] reduce entropy when one receives financial signals from financial reports'.

A variety of media: beyond numbers

Various tools can help to analyse the language used in accounting communication. Theo van Leeuwen uses critical discourse analysis to illustrate that when 'actions are changed into words, transformations occur'. He argues that 'Discourses select what actions will be represented, transform actions through the way they are worded, and add *motives* to actions – purposes, justifications and value judgments'. Van Leeuwen uses a corporate annual report to demonstrate the presence of four distinctly inherent discourses: accounting, finance, public relations and legal.

Jane Davison highlights the relevance of visualization to accounting. She reveals how 'the visual' exists in various media, and how it takes numerous forms: pictures, photographs, graphs, charts, diagrams, sketches, typography, colour, film, video, logos, cartoons, web pages and architecture. She argues that, as with words, visual images are not transparent, but are powerful impression-management devices. They direct our thought processes and carry important messages regarding professional identity and business leadership.

Joel Amernic outlines the richness and importance of metaphor in accounting, illustrating his argument with the specific example of an IASB exposure draft. He draws on Postman (1996) to stress that like other rhetorical devices 'metaphor is not an ornament. It is an organ of perception.' As such, it plays an important role in shaping accounting discourse. Accountants need to be more sensitive to this role.

Paulo Quattrone investigates the historical roots of rhetoric and memory in the Renaissance. He argues that rhetoric is more than an art of persuasion. Rather, rhetoric is a rational device classifying and ordering thinking through mental images that are often visual. He analyses contemporary balanced scorecards from this perspective.

Niamh Brennan and Doris Merkl-Davies discuss the use of accounting narratives for impression management purposes, for example through favourably presenting an entity's annual performance. Subtle strategies to do this include manipulation of reading ease, deployment of rhetorical devices, over-emphasis or under-emphasis of good or bad news, and the attribution of poor results to external factors beyond an entity's control.

Contemporary and professional issues

Change in organizational and social contexts bring new communications challenges for accounting practitioners. The expectations of users are raised. Thus, in attempts to accommodate expectations and to justify results and actions, there is a danger accountants will overload their communications with inadequate and misleading, albeit possibly well-intentioned, narrative. The inadequate nature of accounting communications and the changing face of communications technology is discussed by several following contributors.

Markus Milne assesses the development and effectiveness of environmental and sustainability reporting. Despite the increasingly widespread availability of social and environmental reports, he argues we should be dissatisfied with the results. He poses the challenging question: 'If all organizations were to practise as so-called leading sustainability reporters do, would we be any closer to living on a planet that could sustain us (humans) and other species?' If not, then he contends that all of the communication poured out voluntarily by companies amounts to no more than 'sustain-a-babbling': they do not constitute fair reports on environment and social practice by which organizations should be held accountable.

An important issue for accountants is how they resolve or ameliorate their difficulties in communicating well. Trevor Hassall, José Acquero, John Joyce and José González report on their examination of communication apprehension among accounting students. Disconcertingly, their general conclusion is that 'current accounting courses have little effect on students' levels of communication apprehension and therefore their communication skills development'. This invites us to ponder where and how accountants should acquire the communication skills they need.

Sue Ravenscroft and Abhi Rao review the concerted efforts made in the USA to improve the writing skills of students. They describe the experience of some US accounting schools that have instituted initiatives to improve the writing, thinking and learning skills of students. These initiatives have had disappointing results. Ravenscroft and Rao argue for a keener appreciation by accountants and accounting educators of the important role of writing.

Lisa Jack and Joanne Locke draw attention to the underappreciated potential of computerised information systems (and, to a lesser extent, social networking media) in accounting communication, a point covered also by John Hitchins and Laura Taylor in Chapter 14. They recognise that electronic information systems within organisations drive how data are collected, processed and disseminated; and that electronic technology can enhance and constrain communications between accountants and an entity's stakeholders, including other managers. Jack shows that growing reliance on screen-based communications has implications for the way in which accountants think and work. She notes that, increasingly, the role of management accountants is more likely to be about the creation and maintenance of computer interfaces. Accountants need to recognise verbal and paper communications are affected by the growing presence of on-screen, non-verbal business intelligence systems and associated algorithms.

Locke explores another aspect of the impact of technology on accounting practice. She describes the development of eXtensible Business Reporting Language (XBRL) and speculates that XBRL might be the 'killer app' to replace paper-based reporting. Locke draws attention to the emergence of XBRL in government and business – particularly in regulatory filings in the USA and in the UK that use proforma templates and tag information in XBRL. Locke introduces us to developing perspectives of how a disciplined computer language might be used to enhance or impair accounting communication.

Construction of meaning

The final three chapters draw from different disciplines to enhance understanding of problems and solutions to vexing issues in accounting communication. Accounting practitioners John Hitchins and Laura Taylor are involved in the UK Financial Reporting Council's initiative to 'cut clutter' in financial reports. They aver that 'Many annual reports are hard to navigate and contain immaterial or repetitive disclosures.' Hitchins and Taylor outline the features of the integrated reporting model developed by PriceWaterhouseCoopers and present case studies of what they regard to be good reporting practice. They contend that good reporting is 'concise and transparent and provides sufficient detail to demonstrate the quality and sustainability of a company's position and performance'.

Wally Smieliaukas explores how the formal analysis of arguments can justify fair presentation claims by auditors and financial report preparers. He argues strongly that principles-based accounting requires an ability to reason and to communicate. Thus, skill in argumentation is conceived as a vital ingredient in communicating accounting information successfully.

In the final chapter, Christine Cooper adopts a critical perspective to argue that by drawing on social constructionism and the symbolic nature of language, accounting communications can be exposed as part of the means by which current economic systems are legitimated and maintained. Cooper provides examples of misrepresentations that were influential in recent global financial crises. Her analysis provides an interesting and insightful counterpoint to the perspective of Clarke et al. regarding the presentation of fair value accounting and future economic cash flow valuations in balance sheets. Cooper provides an important salutary message on which to conclude this introductory chapter, and perhaps to adopt as a tacit *leitmotif* for this companion volume: 'Accounting in *communicating* a social, political and economically determined reality has the power to *construct* a biased reality.'

References

Lee, T.A. (1982). 'Chambers and Accounting Communication', *ABACUS*, 18(2): 152–165.
Postman, N. (1996). *The End of Education*, New York: Vintage Books.

2

The accounting communication research landscape

Lee Parker

Introduction

One of the most crucial elements of the accounting and accountability process, accounting communication has been a phenomenon of interest to accounting researchers particularly, but not exclusively, over the past 40 years. Nonetheless, they have represented but a very small cohort amongst the overwhelming majority of accounting researchers who have paid this issue little attention. Intuitively, it remains the case that if accounting communication is ineffective in constructing its messages, reaching its target audiences, and communicating message encoders' intended meanings to decoders and maintaining feedback loops then the exercises of measurement, calculative sophistication, standards promulgation and management control systems serve little point. Yet despite its 'minority group' research culture, the corpus of research literature in this field has steadily grown both in volume and, more importantly, in subject-matter reach.

Notably, the accounting communication research literature has exhibited advances and retreats in some of its focal subject areas over time. Some of these trends have probably reflected changes in the accounting communication environment while others appear to result from the waxing and waning of researcher interest and attention. This has resulted in some earlier areas of focus almost disappearing from the literature. Against this, the range of more recently emerging issues engaging accounting communication researchers has been considerable.

This chapter offers a 'grand tour' of the accounting communication research landscape, offering perspectives on work largely conducted since the early 1970s. In doing so, it will examine the key research subjects that have been addressed, offer critiques of their progress and impact, and explicate both vanished and emerging areas of communication research. This period of research has of course witnessed significant changes in the accounting environment, including the emergence of the global economy and the internet, the commercialization and privatization of public-sector enterprises in many countries and the pervasive deregulation of financial markets, as well as significant national and international economic and financial crises. Reflecting and participating in this context, accounting communication research has embraced a raft of issues ranging across corporate and accounting report readability, internet communication, visual and graphical communication, impression management and obfuscation, and accounting communication skills.

From dormancy to disappearance

It is instructive to first address accounting communication subject areas that have previously enjoyed various levels of researcher attention but have more recently languished. These include the subjects of intra-organizational accounting communication, corporate financial reporting to private investors, simplified corporate annual reporting to employees, highlight statements in annual reports and pictics.

Intra-organizational accounting communication

The question of patterns, processes and conditioners of accounting communications within organizations has been largely neglected by accounting researchers over the past 40 years. Given accounting's centrality in organizational life and functioning, this is quite remarkable. Management accounting researchers just do not seem to have identified it as an important aspect of their craft that deserves attention. At best, assorted concepts of communication have been incorporated along with other variables by positivist researchers attempting to test models predicting various definitions of performance. Examples of this can be found in studies by Chenhall and Morris (1995) and Chen et al. (2006). Rather than focussing on the nature and role of the accounting communication process itself, it has instead been simply treated as a stereotyped functional variable in a shopping list of potential independent variables seeking to explain and predict performance. Any published accounting research papers focussing upon the accounting communication process itself within organizations are extremely rare. Some early examples include Parker's (1978) paper on communication processes and the accountant's communication role within the corporate budgetary system. This was a literature-based review and reflection drawing largely on the preceding organizational behaviour literature rather than any prior accounting research, essentially because it was simply unavailable. The closest to any accounting researcher attention to organizational communication processes can, for example, be found in Dirsmith and Covaleski's (1985) study of communication and mentoring processes in public accounting firms. This relates to organizational communication in an accounting setting, however, rather than accounting communication *per se*. They found that informal communication played a limited role in informing public accounting firm members of the status and operations of politics and power within their firm, but that it was employed in socializing firm members and in performing audit tasks.

While a comprehensive search of the published accounting and management research literatures will possibly be able to reveal further examples of intra-organizational accounting communication studies, their scarcity nonetheless remains evident. The reasons for this lacuna are unclear and can only be subject at this stage to speculation. On the one hand it is tempting to attribute primary cause to accounting researchers reflecting their 'facts and figures' stereotype and thereby ignoring communication. However, this is likely to be a simplistic interpretation, when the more communication-disposed interdisciplinary accounting research community has been active for more than three decades. Yet research into management accounting communication patterns, strategies, processes, influences and impacts on organizational functioning offers the prospect of contributing to both the management and accounting literatures. The potential ramifications for knowledge and practice span our approaches to and management of organizational strategy, corporate governance and management decision-making, through to the role of the management accountant.

Reporting to private investors

The 1970s saw a veritable explosion of accounting research study surveys of annual report users, particularly 'unsophisticated' private investor recipients of corporate annual reports. These surveys mostly focussed upon private investors' usage and understanding of these reports. Examples included studies across the USA, UK, Australia and New Zealand, authored by Foy (1973), Baker and Haslem (1973), Lee and Tweedie (1975), Chenhall and Juchau (1976), Wilton and Tabb (1978), Winfield (1978), Most and Chang (1979), Worthington (1979), Cumpstone et al. (1980) and Hines (1981). Their respondents exhibited profiles that shared some common features, including a significant proportion of well-educated over-50-year-old investors. While some surveys (e.g. Chenhall and Juchau, 1976; Most and Chang, 1979) found a heavy reliance on corporate annual reports, other researchers (e.g. Baker and Haslem, 1973) discovered that approximately 50 per cent of investors declared stockbrokers and financial advisors to be their most important source of financial information about their investee companies. Overall, between 66 and 91 per cent of private investors *claimed* to read the annual reports they received (Foy, 1973; Wilton and Tabb, 1978; Worthington, 1979; Cumpstone et al., 1980). However, these surveys also revealed that only between 5 and 26 per cent of these investors read annual reports thoroughly; even then, the narrative chairman's and directors' report was most widely read, with financial statements being much less inspected by private investors.

Beyond annual-report readership there arose the question of private-investor understanding of what they read. Lee and Tweedie (1975) and Cumpstone et al. (1980) found that while between 70 and 90 per cent of these investors claimed to understand the financial information they read, when subject to comprehension tests, their actual comprehension was much less than they had perceived. Nonetheless, investors declared that future-oriented information was of the greatest importance to their decision-making; these included general business conditions, earnings, dividends and management quality (Parker, 1986, 1988a).

Communication research into accounting report readership in the 1970s and 1980s essentially identified two major audience groups: the sophisticated institutional investors and security analysts, versus the financially unsophisticated private shareholder. Studies quickly identified the problems of, first, private-investor information overload as they struggled to deal with annual reports and related corporate information they received, and, second, of the content of these documents being primarily targeted towards sophisticated financial analysts (Parker, 1981). Neilson and Lind (1971) had earlier suggested that corporations did not reach the private investors because of the complexity of financial information being conveyed in the annual report, the potentially differential requirements and abilities of private investors (compared to institutional investors and financial analysts), the intent of the annual report as a sophisticated investor relations vehicle, and the focus of reported financial information upon technical accounting standards.

Critically reviewing these studies across the 1970s, Parker (1981) concluded that the private investor was generally apathetic towards corporate annual reports, particularly their financial information content, and that there appeared to be a trend towards their bypassing the annual report in favour of other more accessible/understandable sources of corporate financial information. Further causes of private investor apathy may be attributable to the increasing sophistication and complexity of capital markets, the rise of superannuation and investment funds as the predominant private-investor investment vehicle, and the proliferation of the number and complexity of accounting standards and their accompanying impacts on financial information being disclosed.

Searches of the accounting research literature reveal a pronounced decline and virtual disappearance since the early 1980s of investigations into investor, and particularly private-investor annual-report access and usage and related strategies for communicating with them. The reasons for this may reflect some of the capital-market complexity factors mentioned above, as well as the rise to prominence among accounting and finance researchers of a belief in the efficient markets hypothesis, the more recent dominance of financial reporting research by the finance paradigm, and an accompanying shift towards finance-based stock-price market response research more readily conducted through data bases accessed from the researcher's desk. At least for the time being, the private investor appears to be of little consideration for the accounting researcher.

Reporting to employees

The presentation of simplified annual reports and financial statements to corporate employees has a far longer history than most accounting researchers realize. Indeed, many of today's accounting researchers would be totally unaware that this phenomenon ever took place. The practice and its associated professional and research literatures date back to the 1920s and earlier. The most comprehensive analysis of this practice and its associated discourse has been presented by Lewis et al. (1984a) in their study of the relevant literature from 1919 to 1979; they identified a number of phenomena characterizing this practice. First, they pointed to a distinct rise and fall in frequency of publications concerning this practice over their 60-year study period; second, the vast majority of publications occurred before the end of the 1970s in North America, although interest in the UK and Australia and New Zealand became prominent in the 1970s. One of the earliest signs of interest from the British accounting literature can be found in Parker's (1976) monograph published by the Institute of Chartered Accountants in England and Wales, outlining the aims of the practice, its format and positioning in the corporate information and disclosure system, technical presentation challenges, and likely employee usage. The monograph concluded with a proposed conceptual framework and further research agenda. Following relocation to Australia, Parker (1977) also published a paper assessing similar developments and prospects in Australia, pointing to the rise of industrial democracy pressures and innovations in Australia, which reflected those already in motion in Europe and related developments in social responsibility accounting. His research found a sizeable number of leading companies in Australia that had embarked on the provision of financial reports to employees through media, including special purpose year-end reports to employees, simplified financial statements in the annual report issued to employees, commentaries on corporate accounts in the staff journal, audio-visual presentations to employees and employee seminars.

Given accounting researchers' unfamiliarity with this practice and its related publishing discourse, Parker (1988b) published an edited book of selected publications on this subject, covering its early beginnings in the 1920s and 1930s, the rationales and methods advocated for this form of reporting, case studies and surveys of actual practice, assessments of employee interest levels, and this form of reporting in its industrial-relations context. It evidences the writings of early executives and other report producers who pioneered this practice, as well as requirements of employees, critiques by observers and the findings of researchers in this field.

The theme of reporting to employees was also taken up by other British and 'Down Under' researchers in the 1970s and early 1980s. They included Hussey and Craig (1979), Lyall (1981) and Purdy (1981), who undertook an empirical interview study of UK corporate executives. In addition, Lewis et al. (1984b) offered a proposition-based research framework for further investigating employee receipt and interest in this type of report. Researchers into this practice advanced a range of causal influences to explain periods of high-frequency activity both in practice and the related literature. These included the application of new workplace technology, corporate-merger activity, economic recession (or fears of its imminence), groundswells of anti-union sentiment or response to union pressure (Purdy, 1981; Lewis et al., 1984a). Lewis et al. (1984a) suspected that a prime driver was that of management's desire to tell its own story regarding events that had or were about to affect the organization directly to their employees.

Yet again, however, this subject has virtually disappeared from the accounting research literature from the mid-1980s onwards and the reasons are once more open to speculation and debate. The last decade of the twentieth century and the first decade of the twenty-first century witnessed significant industrial, commercial and governmental shifts in these developed countries. The pressure or motivation for this practice and any related research agendas was wound back by such developments as the commercialization and privatization of the public sector, trends towards small government, workforce casualization, declining trade-union membership, large corporate and manufacturing industry relocations to developing countries, capital markets' exponential developments in sophistication and complexity, and shifts towards capital intensive rather than labour intensive organizations. The question of whether the practice of financial information provision tailored to employees will re-emerge remains purely speculative.

From the common to uncommon

In the 1980s particularly, the production of a highlights statement in the annual report became increasingly commonplace. This took the form of a one- or two-page summary of key operational and financial issues and events, along with summary operating and financial statistics for the financial year. They typically included narratives, tables, graphs, charts and diagrams as presentation strategies and tended to be located at the beginning of an annual report, variously badged as "Highlights", "Financial and Operating Highlights", "Financial Summary", "Year in Review", "At a Glance" or "Selected Financial Data". Most often, declared items tended to include income, sales, earnings per share and dividends per share (Parker, 1986; Parker et al., 1989). Considered the most detailed study of the phenomenon appeared in Parker's (1986) monograph for the Institute of Chartered Accountants in England and Wales. From a sample of companies listed in the UK and USA, their reports and highlights statements were examined in some detail with respect to location, length, presentation formats, focus of content, key themes, data types, comparative figures, change data and other information types contained therein. Comparisons of results were made with respect to corporate profile characteristics and country.

What is notable with respect to this particular and fairly common form of financial disclosure and communication is that the literature evidences very little of such detailed analysis. More recently, some studies do refer to highlight statements, but only in the sense of listing them as part of an extended set of variables being employed in empirically examining internet-based financial reporting (Ettredge et al., 2001; Marston, 2003; Fisher et al., 2004). There appears to have been little recent attention paid to the actual phenomenon itself by accounting researchers, even though it appears to still be a practice found in corporate internet reporting. Thus for researchers, highlight statements appear to be a communication issue that has never really attracted their attention or registered its potential significance.

A further uncommon form of potential financial communication is that of pictics. These are simple line-drawn facial representations of corporate financial performance with different elements of facial expression representing trends in performance. For example, a financially healthy and profitable company might be represented with large smiling face, bright eyes and strong slanting eyebrows. A financially distressed company might be represented with worried frown, sad eyes and downcast expression (Parker et al., 1989). This form of pictorial representation was first proposed as a simplified means of presenting financial data by Moriarty (1979); however, it was championed in the accounting literature most notably by Smith and Taffler (1984, 1996). They put forward this presentation method and explored its potential application through empirical experiments of representing actual published corporate financial results over time in this schematic fashion. They argued that the evidence suggested that pictics are processed faster than traditional forms of financial representation, by report users of varying financial sophistication. Hence, they contended that the development could be a useful decision tool, even for bankers and investment analysts, although they anticipated some potential levels of resistance by both corporations and report users.

Beyond Smith and Taffler, however, pictics appear to have attracted virtually no attention from accounting researchers and have not been visible in the accounting research literature of recent years. With researchers conditioned to avoid normative or policy/practice subjects in pursuit of the quasi-scientific 'ideal' research methodology for publication in many highly rated academic journals, the experimentation and application challenges that pictics require may be a major disincentive to emerging scholars. They may prefer to study what already exists in practice, rather than take on the challenge of developing new practices.

Contemporary priorities

Having examined accounting communication issues of earlier periods in the accounting research literature, ongoing contemporary issues of concern deserve further attention. These include the profession and academe's concerns with accounting communication skills, the question of accounting and annual report readability, and the subjects of visual communication and internet communication that have been steadily gathering momentum.

The ongoing issue of accounting communication skills

This has been an enduring issue for both accounting teachers and researchers and has shown no signs of waning in the literature. At the heart of this issue are concerns about employers' communication skills expectations of accounting and business degree graduates and the extent to which there is a gap between those expectations and graduates' actual skills (Kermis and Kermis, 2010). Examples of studies addressing this issue include Stowers and White (1999) and Sriram and Coppage (1992) in the USA, and Gray (2010) and Gray and Murray (2011) in New Zealand. The US-based studies revealed that accounting employers place high priority on accounting graduates' communication skills, particularly written, but that there continues to be a significant shortfall in graduates' actual skills compared to employers' expectations. In addition, Gray (2010) and Gray and Murray (2011) have paid particular attention to accountants' oral communication skills. Again they have found major shortfalls in accounting graduates' oral communication skills when compared against the accounting profession employer requirements. Listening, advising and explaining skills figured strongly in employers' assessments of graduates' weaknesses. In further teasing out employer expectations, Jones (2011) conducted survey research that revealed basic writing mechanics and effective documentation were the communication skills most demanded, while computer-based communication skills (other than email) were not as valued as accounting graduates might presume.

From the accounting graduate provider perspective, the variety of research agendas is illustrated by the following study examples. As early as the late 1980s, May and May (1989) had surveyed colleges and universities to ascertain what strategies they were employing to improve accounting students' and graduates' communication skills. The majority of respondents offered undergraduate students a general business communication course, with approximately 10 per cent providing a communication course tailored to accounting majors. In the 1990s, Simons et al. (1995) studied accounting students' apprehension (fear) of communication (written and oral), finding them to exhibit higher levels of apprehension towards both forms of communication than other business majors. Interestingly, they found a statistically significant higher level of apprehension towards oral communication amongst female students than male. Yet another research agenda is signalled by Davidson (2005) in his examination of introductory accounting textbooks published in the USA over a 100-year period, which found decreasing sentence complexity but increasing word complexity. He suggested that some causal factors may include increasing complexity of accounting standards, a growing technical accounting language, as well as stylistic changes in written English over time. Linking to some of the study subjects discussed above, Davidson argues that simplification of textbook narratives may carry inherent risks of simplifying students' mental models in a complex and demanding business environment, as well as deskilling students' communication abilities.

Thus, accounting communication skills remain a longstanding issue of demonstrated importance to accounting employers, students, educators and graduates alike. To this end accounting researchers have paid this issue ongoing attention. This has particularly been the province of accounting education researchers publishing in educational and communication research journals.

Accounting report readability

The readability of narrative texts has been a subject of interest to researchers generally as far back as the 1940s. Readability is concerned with a passage of text and the level of reading difficulty it presents and readability measures have been developed with the aim of predicting textual reading ease and subsequently communicative effectiveness to a target audience (Courtis, 1986; Lewis et al., 1986; Smith and Taffler, 1992). A variety of measurement systems have been promulgated and applied to this question, including the Dale–Chall formula (1948), the Flesch formula (1948), the Fog formula (1952), the Lix formula (1968), the Kwolek formula (1973) and the Fry graph (1977). In varying combinations, they attempt to measure and factor into their scores the number of words, sentences, 'unfamiliar' words, syllables, polysyllabic words, 'hard words' and 'big words (>6 letters)' (Lewis et al., 1986). Dale–Chall was based on a list of 3000 words best known to North American children aged 8 years. Flesch was developed to assess primary school children and later adult reading materials (Lewis et al., 1986; Clatworthy and Jones, 2001). Fog, Kwolek and Fry were all developed with similar aims to Flesch. Lix was designed to assess readability across multiple languages (Lewis et al., 1986; Smith and Taffler, 1992).

Associated with readability has been researchers' concern with understandability. Critics have argued that a text measured as easy to read may still not be well understood, due to a range of factors including the reader's background, prior knowledge, interest and reading ability (Jones, 1997). Thus, readability and understandability may not necessarily be indissolubly linked. The most prominent measure of understandability is the Cloze test, developed in 1953 by Wilson Taylor. This test deletes a number of words from a passage of text at random or fixed intervals so that readers are required to reconstruct the text by inserting the deleted words (Lewis et al., 1986; Smith and Taffler, 1992; Clatworthy and Jones, 2001).

Tests of readability have been applied to accounting documents and reports over many years by accounting researchers. The most widely used over time has been the Flesch formula (Clatworthy and Jones, 2001). Examples of readability assessment from the many accounting studies undertaken include assessments of corporate financial reports to employees (Lewis et al., 1986), failed and non-failed company chief executive reports (Smith and Taffler, 1992), multilingual annual reports (Courtis, 1995; Courtis and Hassan, 2002), chairman's statements (Clatworthy and Jones, 2001), risk reporting (Hewaidy, 2007; Linsley and Lawrence, 2007) and accounting textbook readability (Plucinski et al., 2009). In their review of the empirical accounting research literature in this field, Jones and Shoemaker (1994) found that readability studies addressed the questions of how difficult annual reports are to read, differences in reading difficulty between different types of annual report as well as between different sections of the annual report, changes in annual report reading difficulty over time, and any associations between readability and other factors. Overall, they reported studies concluding that annual reports are generally scored as difficult or very difficult to read, and that their readability has declined over time, that readability and understandability are linked, and that the majority of the population would not be able to understand the annual report. Merkl-Davies and Brennan's (2007) review of the field concurs with this assessment, reporting that research studies have found annual report narratives to be difficult to read, and such reading difficulty attributed to two factors: managerial manipulation and bad writing.

Nonetheless, the limitations inherent in currently available approaches to assessing readability and understandability have been clearly identified. For example, word and sentence difficulty may oversimplify the assessment of readability, assumptions of linear relationships between reading age and increasing word and sentence length may be suspect, reading motivation and speed may influence readability and understandability, society and education levels have changed since many of these measures were developed, and the Cloze measure's validity and precise meaning has been subject to criticism (Lewis et al., 1986; Jones, 1997; Clatworthy and Jones, 2001). Despite such limitations and related critiques, readability research in the accounting discipline has continued its momentum, examples of which can be found in Courtis and Hassan (2002), Johnson et al. (2002), Rutherford (2003), Courtis (2004b), Hewaidy (2007), Sun (2007) and Li (2008).

The blossoming of the visual

Visual communication research in accounting represents an, albeit slow, awakening amongst accounting researchers to the predominantly visual business and accounting world that we now inhabit (Preston et al., 1996; Davison and Warren, 2009). Until the recent past we have been almost entirely fixated upon narrative text and numbers as focal communication vehicles, while our environment over the past 30 years has become increasingly dominated by visual communication through the media of film, television, internet and digital photography. Information is increasingly being purveyed and accessed visually, through laptop computers, mobile phones, electronic tablets and more. This has somewhat belatedly triggered two streams of research agenda: accounting representations and its messages created and transmitted via the visual image, and the use of the visual image as an accounting and management research tool.

Research into accounting-related representations and messages conveyed visually through annual reports and advertising has been particularly emergent from a special sub-theme issue of *Accounting, Organizations and Society* (1996, vol. 21, no. 1) and a special visual issue of *Accounting, Auditing & Accountability Journal* (2009, vol. 22, no. 6). Across the accounting research literature on this subject area, the variety of study foci is quite striking and probably reflects the first explorations of a small coterie of researchers commencing studies in this area. Preston et al. (1996) examine the multiple layers of meaning implicit in annual-report images, spanning the transparently intended corporate message, a less evident but still discernible indicator of institutional and social relations, evasion of criticism by displacing reality with imagery, and the constituting of different types of realities. Campbell et al. (2009) analysed human representations in 210 annual reports issued by 14 companies, finding a rise in the totality of human facial representation over time, offering a reassuring image of the faces of people within the organization about whom stakeholders should theoretically care despite a climate of self-interested economic pursuit. In some senses a related project is undertaken by Matilal and Höpfl (2009), who considered the annual report footnote disclosures by Union Carbide India Ltd. involving the corporate and legal impacts of the Bhopal gas tragedy that occurred in India in 1984. The company's ignoring of the human cost is contrasted against photographic-based accounts of the tragedy.

Other researchers have examined the forms of visual imagery and visualization employed in corporate annual reports. Graves et al. (1996) examined visual effects presented in reports, including colour pictures, gloss paper and novel formats as forms of rhetoric asserting the 'truth' of financial and other claims as well as social constructs. Courtis (2004a) analysed annual report use of colour, finding it more frequently employed when profitability either increased or decreased, some colours being specifically related to more or less favourable attributions. His preliminary conclusions were that when employed in annual reports, colour is not simply neutral with respect to its effects. Justesen and Mouritsen (2009) conducted a case study based on annual reports, interviews and field observations, finding that both in organizational functioning and the annual report representing them visualizations are juxtaposed with operational, marketing and accounting calculations, mutually interacting and superimposed. They serve to co-ordinate the organization's activities, and act as much more than mere window dressing.

Visual accounting research has also addressed the role of visual imagery in portraying interpretations of accounting and accountants, conveying representations of intangibles and intellectual capital excluded from traditional accounting reports and other documentation (Davison, 2011). Baldvinsdottir et al. (2009) investigated accountants' changing image as represented in software advertisements, revealing them as portraying a responsible and rational professional in the 1970–1980s period, an action-oriented person in the 1990s and a more hedonistic person post-2000, thereby raising accompanying concerns about implications for accountants' perceived trustworthiness. A further theme pursued by some visual researchers has been that of visual branding effects. McKinstry (1996) conducted a longitudinal case study of one company's annual reports over more than 60 years, finding it being increasingly employed as a public-relations document (post-1980). Davison (2009) examined visual representations by a UK building society, finding it to employ visual-branding techniques to represent its intangible assets, particularly its corporate brand, which is not possible or permitted under accounting standards. Davison (2010) has also examined visual portraits of the business élite, arguing them to be carefully constructed and complex representations of intellectual knowledge, organizational brand capital and social assets not easily represented in conventional accounting terms.

The second stream of the visual research agenda, the use of the visual image as an accounting and management research tool, has scarcely begun to break the surface in the accounting research literature. Warren (2005) and Parker (2009) have individually and together (Warren and Parker, 2009) begun to advocate the use of photo-voice or photo-elicitation as a promising research methodology for providing alternative perspectives on and insights into accounting subjects. This takes the form of empowering research subjects through variously involving them in photographic based interviews that can take the forms of auto driving, reflexive photography, photo-voice and photo-elicitation. In generic terms, these methodologies involve from historical to contemporary photographs that have some bearing upon the subject under investigation. Contemporary photographs may have been guided or taken by interviewees and in all cases subjects are interviewed about their impressions, interpretations and stories from the photographs by unstructured or semi-structured interview. This research design aims to penetrate and unpack worlds and issues otherwise ignored, or silenced by traditional research methodologies. Warren and Parker (2009) signal, for example, its potential ability to assist in unpacking accountants' identity perception and construction processes.

One further aspect of the visual research agenda has been championed by two leading accounting researchers, Vivien Beattie and Michael Jones: the contribution of graphs to corporate financial reporting. Their synthesis of graphical research in accounting published in *Journal of Accounting Literature* provides the most comprehensive overview of this field currently available (Beattie and Jones, 2008). They see companies communicating via graphs due to their ability to present information flexibly, to summarize complex information, to attract reader attention, to appeal to readers' visual instincts, to communicate to sophisticated and unsophisticated report users, and to be memorable. Thus, they report from their multiple studies that in many countries more than 80 per cent of top companies use graphs in their annual reports. Much of the research into corporate use of graphs has been concerned with evidence of their role in impression management. This can take the forms of selectivity (biased selection of favourable items), measurement distortion (graphical representation disproportionate to underlying numbers) and presentational enhancement (manipulation of graphical features such as colour and shape to emphasize chosen features) (Beattie and Jones, 2008). The information most frequently graphed in annual reports is sales, profit, earnings per share and dividends per share (Beattie and Jones, 1997, 1999, 2008). Research over the past 20 years has produced consistent evidence of the use of graphs by corporations for the purpose of impression management. This has been found in the UK, USA, Australia, France, Germany and the Netherlands. The overall agenda appears to be one of attempting to induce favourable reader impressions of reported corporate financial performance via the three strategies outlined above (Beattie and Jones, 1992, 1997, 1999, 2000a, 2000b, 2002). Less financially sophisticated report users appear to be at greatest risk from this practice (Beattie and Jones, 2002). One exception to this overall trend has been uncovered by Mather et al. (2000), who found a corporate tendency to unfavourably manipulate performance impressions for initial public offering (of shares) documents which Beattie and Jones (2008) suggest may simply exhibit a cautionary approach to performance representations and predictions being implied by companies seeking to raise capital funds.

When reflecting upon the corpus of visual accounting communication research overall, it becomes evident that, in general, accounting researchers have been remarkably blind to the visual turn in accountants' everyday and business worlds and to the increasingly aesthetic economy in which accounting operates, where the act of presenting corporate brand, image, services and employees generates revenue in and of itself. Enmeshed in their obsession with constructing research designs that emulate the 'hard' sciences, accounting researchers may be missing the opportunities presented for original contributions to knowledge occasioned by experimenting with the messier, less structured arts and social-science disciplines that may better capture the human and social dimensions of the accounting world. This offers prospects for researching accountants themselves, corporate and accounting profession image, imagery that surrounds accounting and images of accountability (Davison and Warren, 2009). As Brown (2010) argues, accounting and the visual are inextricably intertwined as we are challenged to investigate and develop our accountings of the visual, for the visual and by the visual. She offers visual cultural studies as a basis for innovative new accounting research that pays attention to how accounting is implicated in the shaping of social practices and their environments by imagery.

The pervasive internet

The arrival of the internet on the societal and business scene has had far-reaching and pervasive effects on how the processes of business, government and community are conducted. The impact on accounting has been no less significant. Yet again, it is remarkable how slow accounting researchers have been to direct their inquiring gaze towards what has been the greatest change to their immediate professional environment in the last 100 years. Just as in some other 'minority group' areas of accounting communication research, there is only a small group of accounting scholars internationally who have been addressing the many facets of this phenomenon. Nonetheless, as Gallhofer and Haslam (2006) point out, the implications for accounting are significant, both positively and negatively spanning disclosure, regulation and audit practices.

From a reporting and disclosure perspective, the range of internet-related issues and research questions is almost infinite. Research conducted to date has included interview studies of corporate financial reporter intentions with respect to financial reporting via the internet. These reveal interest in provision of some announcements and information not previously provided, and in timelier uploading of reports. However, the internet reporting appears to be dominated by provider prerogatives, with a decided 'push' rather than consultative 'pull' from stakeholders driving what is reported. Some evidence of potential addressing of inequities in provision of different types of information to different classes of stakeholders does appear evident nevertheless (Gowthorpe, 2004). Further research also suggests that auditors, regulators, corporations and report users anticipate that the major challenge for financial reporting in the internet environment will be the balancing between standardization and customization of report design and content. Issues anticipated in connection with internet reporting include commercial confidentiality, information reliability, information overload, and audit and regulatory risks (Jones and Xiao, 2004). Studies of corporate internet reporting to date have also found that the potential for internet-based reporting to improve corporate pension schemes' disclosure has not been yet been significantly realized (Paisey and Paisey, 2006a, 2006b). The timeliness of corporate reporting via the internet has been studied and revealed as significant with respect to directors' experience and independence (the latter being a negative association) (Abdelsalam and Street, 2007). One group of researchers has attempted to develop a disclosure quality index for corporate reporting via the internet (Hanafi et al., 2009).

Some research on auditing and regulatory implications has also begun to emerge. Lymer and Debreceny (2003) reported on the need for regulatory guidance to auditors with respect to the implications for themselves and their audit function of internet-based financial reporting. Also in relation to this issue, Baker (2006) has examined the consensus-driven discourse between the US Securities Exchange Commission and the US Financial Accounting Standards Board with respect to regulating internet financial reporting. As Jones and Xiao (2004) find, auditors may face a conflict of interest between focussing upon enhanced assurance or professional self-protection in relation to the audit of internet reports. This raises the question of their probable attitude to and support for innovative internet reporting developments. Regulators too, they argue, face tensions between their traditional desire to monitor and control standardized reporting and accountability, while at the same time facilitating better disclosure across heterogeneous report users. Associated with these issues of audit and regulation come the questions of internet report content trustworthiness. Cho et al. (2009), for example, studied user trust in corporate website disclosures, finding that the richness of the website communications (characterized by extent of responsive feedback, multiple cues, use of language/numbers) positively enhanced trust in a website and its information, but not in the company's honesty, sincerity and truthfulness. Barrett and Gendron (2006) have also examined the auditor's attempts to establish their own trustworthiness in the internet domain and found this to be a particularly challenging task which, in today's world of trust building, still required some form of or replacement for face-to-face relationships.

Accounting researchers have begun to contemplate the emancipatory potential of internet reporting. This has notably emerged in a special internet reporting theme issue of *Accounting, Auditing & Accountability Journal* (2006, vol. 19 no. 5). The editors of that issue call for further research into the economic, social and political implications of this development, particularly through critical and interpretive lenses (Gallhofer and Haslam, 2006). Researchers do see an emancipatory potential for addressing issues and audiences through the internet not previously possible, but with accompanying threats and limitations along the road. Organized forms of counter-accounting, producing critical, alternative reports on corporate activities and impacts, loom large on their agenda (Gallhofer et al., 2006; Sikka, 2006).

Finally, we can detect slight glimmerings of accounting and business researcher interest in the emergence of social media. Examples can be found in the work of Kaplan and Haenlein (2010) who outline the concept and classify social media with a view to informing corporations contemplating its use. Fong (2011) provides a recent study of strategic management accounting processes in the start-up of a social network service company. What will be interesting to watch is the growth of attention to social media amongst accounting researchers. Will they lag behind this development to the same degree that many have failed to address the rise of the internet? Time will tell.

Accounting and audit firm communication

Patterns and effectiveness of public accountant and auditor communication to clients, regulators and other stakeholders would seem to be matters of considerable professional importance and therefore subject to researcher curiosity. However, that appears not to have been the case. Yet some examples of studies in this area do date back as far as the 1980s. For example, Bailey III et al. (1983) report the results of their study of the effects of audit report wording changes on recipient message perceptions, finding an absolute difference in recipients' perceptions. Golen et al. (1997) also investigated the auditor–client communication relationship, revealing the presence of communication barriers including credibility, conflict and hostility factors. Koski et al. (2004) examined the impact of communication on the relationships between the accounting firm and its clients, finding effective communication techniques produced improved client satisfaction and reduced conflict between the firm and its clients.

More recently, Stone (2011a, 2011b) has investigated communications between small public accounting firms and their small business owner–manager clients. In one of his papers he examined the readability of accounting firm letters, decision support documents and newsletters to these owner–manager clients, finding that their easier readability and the inclusion of non-financial information improved the prospects of effective firm–client communication. Formal accounting reports and documents exhibited more difficult levels of readability and less client interest (Stone, 2011a). He also examined the effect of small business managers' objectives and their preferred methods of accountants' advisory communicating with them, finding that small business managers preferred direct contact with their accountants and verbal communications (Stone, 2011b). Formal documents were regarded by their clients more as supplementary to accountants' direct personal communications. Furthermore, Stone discovered that these small business owners and managers had personal objectives that went beyond the purely financial objectives of their business, and these needed to be addressed by accountants who wished to communicate effectively with them. Employing interview methodology, Stone (2012) has also examined the communicative effectiveness of accounting firm newsletters in relating to small business managers, finding that this popular form of accounting firm communication is ineffective in developing client relationships. His study found that clients could not relate their own personal needs and circumstances to newsletters' technicality, impersonality and generality.

This small sample of studies demonstrates the need and potential for further research into the issue of communications between public auditors, accounting firms and their clients. The justification returns once again to the opening themes of this chapter, namely that accounting and audit calculations, reports and regulations serve little purpose if they are not effectively communicated to their intended audiences.

Aiming to impress

Impression management and obfuscation have emerged as related themes of significant accounting communication researcher interest, especially over the past decade or so. Hooghiemstra (2000) defines impression management as corporate attempts to influence people's perceptions of their organization by using self-presentational devices that try to control the images the company projects. Thereby the company aims to manipulate or manage outsiders' impressions of its profile and performance (Merkl-Davies and Brennan, 2007). Strategies that may be employed include acclaiming positive events to reinforce their positive perception by others. This may be done by claiming entitlements when seeking credit if responsibility is unclear and by enhancements when the corporate credit is clear so the desirability of the event itself is emphasized. On the other hand, where events may be perceived negatively, accounting may be employed as a remedial tactic in offering excuses or justifications (Hooghiemstra, 2000).

Brennan et al. (2009) have developed a composite impression management score based on quantitative and qualitative data, which can be used in assessing corporate narrative disclosures. Having developed this score, they applied it to 21 corporate disclosure examples, finding that impression management is pervasive in corporate financial communications. They observed its forms to generally manifest themselves as exaggerated positive information and minimized or ignored negative information. Further examples of studies revealing impression management at work include Ogden and Clarke's (2005) privatized UK water-company annual reports dealing with customer service, which found them employing sustained assertive and defensive impression management tactics. They can also be found in Aerts' (2005) examination of attributional statements in a large sample of Belgian companies, which revealed self-serving tendencies that were influenced by contextual factors. While he found listed companies to show higher levels of defensiveness in explaining negative accounting results, the overall attributional defensiveness across all his sample companies appeared to be low to moderate. Leventis and Weetman (2004) have also reported that companies in experiencing higher visibility through dual language reporting tend to engage in greater degrees of voluntary disclosure, possibly with a view to emphasizing their prestige and to attract foreign investors.

While studies appear to have detected considerable evidence that corporate impression management does indeed occur, the evidence for them engaging in obfuscation is much less persuasive. Obfuscation involves obscuring the supposedly intended message in order to distract or confuse the readers (Courtis, 2004b). Courtis sees obfuscation as a form of impression management employing techniques such as esoteric vocabulary, irrelevant information and long sentences with complex grammatical structures, highly variable reading ease and convoluted arguments. Such tactics may be employed to disguise unfavourable results and calm reader anxiety by softening the appearance of changes, or may simply represent an unwitting failure in report construction and composition. However, findings of corporate obfuscation are inconsistent both within reports examined and between studies. Textual complexity does not appear to be maliciously employed to mask poor financial results, levels of executive compensation, good or bad news in the annual report (Rutherford, 2003; Courtis, 2004b; Smith et al., 2006; Linsley and Lawrence, 2007; Laksmana et al., 2011; Bayerlein and Davidson, 2012).

Merkl-Davies and Brennan (2007) provide the most comprehensive review and critique of impression-management research to date. They conclude that, so far, researchers have been unable to ascertain whether investors are susceptible to impression management by reporting corporations.

However, they do suggest that results may indicate that investors potentially are initially suscep-tible, but on receipt of further information, subsequently revise their perceptions of corporate profile and performance.

Let's communicate

This grand tour of the accounting communication research literature cannot do justice to its subjects in the space of one chapter. Instead, what has been offered is a selective sweep across some of the literature's significant themes, both past and present. Some of these remain with us as vibrant areas of inquiry and practice. Others have withered on the vine, either through chang-ing environmental circumstances or researchers' apparent disinterest. The crucial questions con-cern the future direction which the accounting communication research agenda should take.

Researchers in this field have paid varying degrees of attention to the theories which can usefully inform our endeavours and provide broader scope opportunities for effective research design as well as deeper insights into the data we collect. Theories available and employed to date have included agency theory, signalling theory, legitimacy theory, stakeholder theory, institutional theory, media richness theory, mass communication theory, visual culture, critical theories and more (Parker, 1982; Gallhofer and Haslam, 2006; Merkl-Davies and Brennan, 2007; Cho et al., 2009; Brown, 2010). Given the rich and expanding tapestry of communica-tion media and pathways open to accountants and organizations, accounting communication research can only be empowered by searching for and innovating in a wider raft of theories derived from other disciplines. To understand and critique the communication process, we need as many lenses as are capable of opening up our vision and our horizons.

It must be said that the almost total neglect by accounting researchers of internal organiza-tional communication processes is remarkable, given the pervasiveness of accounting commu-nications and their myriad forms within organizational life. Both management accounting and accounting communication researchers have an obligation to put this area at the front of their agendas.

What are we to do about employees and private investors? There was a period when their needs and responses were a significant issue in the accounting-research literature. Lamentably, that is no longer the case. Have the complexities of global capital markets and the casualization of labour moved them to the wings while institutional investors and analysts have taken centre stage? The commodification, casualization and marginalization of labour by technological, social and political forces shows little sign of abating, so it is difficult to see researcher motivation or research funding following these issues in the near future. This is not to say that their time will not resurface; that remains to be seen.

Accounting communications skills have been consistently and thoroughly prosecuted by accounting education researchers. This has been a laudable endeavour, but we cannot remain solely focussed upon the accounting student. The opportunity to marry the research findings and expertise of accounting education and accounting communication researchers to investigate pro-fessional accountants' communication patterns and skills is all too evident. It requires some cross-disciplinary co-operation within the accounting-research discipline that is eminently achievable.

Readability has been a consistently researched concern amongst accounting researchers and shows no signs of abating. It attracts research attention both on a stand-alone basis and as a path-way to allied communication research subjects such as obfuscation, category of reader access, reader-education levels, special-purpose report design and more. This awaits further technical measurement experimentation, development and expansion. This can and should be addressed for assessing narrative text, tabulations, and visual representations.

Visual research offers one of the most exciting research prospects for accounting communication researchers. This is an essential development in an overwhelmingly visual communication age. We have been witnessing an emerging flow of research into visual representations in annual reports, professional advertising, web reporting and more. This stream will hopefully continue to prosper and reveal much more than our narrative and numbers fixation has previously permitted. Beyond this, however, visual research methodologies offer an entirely new horizon of investigative possibilities for the accounting research community. Of the topic areas traversed in this chapter, this could well be the one most deserving of the phrase, 'Watch this space!'

Internet-based research has again demonstrated accounting researchers' remarkable tardiness in responding to the major global societal and business changes occurring around them. The array of issues awaiting attention defies the temptation to lay out a shopping list. However, some of the particularly enticing issues that may justify urgent attention include the opportunities for and manifestations of expanded scope and special interest reporting, as well as the democratization of corporate reporting and stakeholder interaction. Internet and the social-media explosion have already engaged stakeholders, interest groups and individuals around the world in accessing hitherto unavailable government and corporate information, expressing their inquiries and criticisms, and calling for greater and newer forms of disclosure. Counter-accounting, social audit and lobby-group action are all empowered and set for growth in this internet era.

The editors of this book are to be commended for putting together this collection of literature addressing accounting communication; it is long overdue. It is hoped that this preliminary excursion through our research tradition in this field whets the appetite. More importantly, its critique calls for research and practical action. If we fail to heed this call, then much of our profession's travail may end as Logue (2001: 69) has so incisively exampled:

> Last night in London Airport
> I saw a wooden bin
> Labelled UNWANTED LITERATURE
> IS TO BE PLACED HEREIN
> So I wrote a poem
> And popped it in.

References

Abdelsalam, O.H. and Street, D.L. (2007) 'Corporate governance and the timeliness of corporate internet reporting by U.K. listed companies', *Journal of International Accounting, Auditing and Taxation*, 16: 111–130.

Aerts, W. (2005) 'Picking up the pieces: impression management in the retrospective attributional framing of accounting outcomes', *Accounting, Organizations and Society*, 30: 493–517.

Bailey III, K.E., Bylinksi, J.H. and Shields, M.D. (1983) 'Effects of audit report wording changes on the perceived message', *Journal of Accounting Research*, 21: 355–370.

Baker, C.R. (2006) 'Epistemological objectivity in financial reporting: does internet accounting require a new model?', *Accounting, Auditing & Accountability Journal*, 19: 663–680.

Baker, H.K. and Haslem, J.A. (1973) 'Information needs of individual investors', *The Journal of Accountancy*, 136: 64–69.

Baldvinsdottir, G., Burns, J., Nørreklit, H. and Scapens, R.W. (2009) 'The image of accountants: from bean counters to extreme accountants', *Accounting, Auditing & Accountability Journal*, 22: 858–882.

Barrett, M. and Gendron, Y. (2006) 'WebTrust and the "commercialistic auditor": the unrealized vision of developing auditor trustworthiness in cyberspace', *Accounting, Auditing & Accountability Journal*, 19: 631–662.

Bayerlein, L. and Davidson, P. (2012) 'The influence of connotation on readability and obfuscation in Australian chairman addresses', *Managerial Auditing Journal*, 27: 175–198.

Beattie, V. and Jones, M.J. (1992) 'The use and abuse of graphs in annual reports: theoretical framework and empirical study', *Accounting and Business Research*, 22: 291–303.

Beattie, V. and Jones, M.J. (1997) 'A comparative study of the use of financial graphs in the corporate annual reports of major U.S. and U.K. companies', *Journal of International Financial Management and Accounting*, 8: 33–68.

Beattie, V. and Jones, M.J. (1999) 'Australian financial graphs: an empirical study', *ABACUS*, 35: 46–76.

Beattie, V. and Jones, M.J. (2000a) 'Impression management: the case of inter-country financial graphs', *Journal of International Accounting, Auditing and Taxation*, 9: 159–183.

Beattie, V. and Jones, M.J. (2000b) 'Changing graph use in corporate annual reports: a time-series analysis', *Contemporary Accounting Research*, 17: 213–226.

Beattie, V. and Jones, M.J. (2002) 'Measurement distortion of graphs in corporate reports: an experimental study', *Accounting, Auditing & Accountability Journal*, 15: 546–564.

Beattie, V. and Jones, M.J. (2008) 'Corporate reporting using graphs: a review and synthesis', *Journal of Accounting Literature*, 27: 71–110.

Brennan, N.M., Guillamon-Saorin, E. and Pierce, A. (2009) 'Impression management: developing and illustrating a scheme of analysis for narrative disclosures – a methodological note', *Accounting, Auditing and Accountability Journal*, 22: 789–832.

Brown, J. (2010) 'Accounting and visual cultural studies: potentialities, challenges and prospects', *Accounting, Auditing & Accountability Journal*, 23: 482–505.

Campbell, D., McPhail, K. and Slack, R. (2009) 'Face work in annual reports: a study of the management of encounter through annual reports, informed by Levinas and Bauman', *Accounting, Auditing & Accountability Journal*, 22: 907–932.

Chen, J., Silverthorne, C. and Hung, J. (2006) 'Organization communication, job stress, organizational commitment, and job performance of accounting professionals in Taiwan and America', *Leadership & Organization Development Journal*, 27: 242–249.

Chenhall, R. and Juchau, R. (1976) 'Information needs of Australian investors', *Journal of the Securities Institute of Australia*, 2: 8–13.

Chenhall, R.H. and Morris, D. (1995) 'Organic decision and communication processes and management accounting systems in entrepreneurial and conservative business organizations', *Omega*, 23: 485–497.

Cho, C.H., Phillips, J.R., Hageman, A.M. and Patten, D.M. (2009) 'Media richness, user trust, and perceptions of corporate social responsibility: an experimental investigation of visual web site disclosures', *Accounting, Auditing & Accountability Journal*, 22: 933–952.

Clatworthy, M. and Jones, M.J. (2001) 'The effect of thematic structure on the variability of annual report readability', *Accounting, Auditing & Accountability Journal*, 14: 311–326.

Courtis, J.K. (1986) 'An investigation into annual report readability and corporate risk–return relationships', *Accounting and Business Research*, 16: 285–294.

Courtis, J.K. (1995) 'Readability of annual reports: Western versus Asian evidence', *Accounting, Auditing & Accountability Journal*, 8: 4–17.

Courtis, J.K. (2004a) 'Colour as visual rhetoric in financial reporting', *Accounting Forum*, 28: 265–281.

Courtis, J.K. (2004b) 'Corporate report obfuscation: artefact or phenomenon?', *British Accounting Review*, 36: 291–312.

Courtis, J.K. and Hassan, S. (2002) 'Reading ease of bilingual annual reports', *Journal of Business Communication*, 39: 394–413.

Cumpstone, E.A., Dixon, B.R., Foster, M.D. and Jansen, L.T. (1980) 'Company reporting; the needs of shareholders', *The Accountant's Journal*, September: 287–289.

Davidson, R.A. (2005) 'Analysis of the complexity of writing used in accounting textbooks over the past 100 years', *Accounting Education: An International Journal*, 14: 53–74.

Davison, J. (2009) 'Icon, iconography, iconology: visual branding, banking and the case of the bowler hat', *Accounting, Auditing & Accountability Journal*, 22: 883–906.

Davison, J. (2010) '[In]visible [in]tangibles: visual portraits of the business élite', *Accounting, Organizations and Society*, 35: 165–183.

Davison, J. (2011) 'Barthesian perspectives on accounting communication and visual images of professional accountancy', *Accounting, Auditing & Accountability Journal*, 24: 250–283.

Davison, J. and Warren, S. (2009) 'Imag[in]ing accounting and accountability', *Accounting, Auditing & Accountability Journal*, 22: 845–857.

Dirsmith, M.W. and Covaleski, M.A. (1985) 'Informal communications, nonformal communications and mentoring in public accounting firms', *Accounting, Organizations and Society*, 10: 149–169.

Ettredge, M., Richardson, V.J. and Scholz, S. (2001) 'The presentation of financial information at corporate web sites', *International Journal of Accounting Information Systems*, 2: 149–168.

Fisher, R., Oyelere, P. and Lasward, F. (2004) 'Corporate reporting on the internet: audit issues and content analysis of practices', *Managerial Auditing Journal*, 19: 412–439.

Fong, C.C.S. (2011) 'Strategic management accounting of social networking site service company in China', *Journal of Technology Management in China*, 6: 125–139.

Foy, F.C. (1973) 'Annual reports don't have to be dull', *Harvard Business Review*, January–February: 47–50.

Gallhofer, S. and Haslam, J. (2006) 'Online reporting: accounting in cybersociety', *Accounting, Auditing & Accountability Journal*, 19: 625–630.

Gallhofer, S., Haslam, J. and Monk, E. (2006) 'The emancipatory potential of online reporting: the case of counter accounting', *Accounting, Auditing & Accountability Journal*, 19: 681–718.

Golen, S.P., Catanach, A.H., Jr. and Moeckel, C. (1997) 'The frequency and seriousness of communication barriers in the auditor–client relationship', *Business Communication Quarterly*, 60: 23–37.

Gowthorpe, C. (2004) 'Asymmetrical dialogue? Corporate financial reporting via the internet', *Corporate Communications: An International Journal*, 9: 283–293.

Graves, O.F., Flesher, D.L. and Jordan, R.E. (1996) 'Pictures and the bottom line: the television epistemology of U.S. annual reports', *Accounting, Organizations and Society*, 21: 57–88.

Gray, F.E. (2010) 'Specific oral communication skills desired in new accountancy graduates', *Business Communication Quarterly*, 73: 40–67.

Gray, F.E. and Murray, N. (2011) '"A distinguishing factor": oral communication skills in new accountancy graduates', *Accounting Education: An International Journal*, 20: 275–294.

Hanafi, S.R.B.M., Kasim, M.A.B., Ibrahim, M.K.B. and Hancock, D.R. (2009) 'Business reporting on the internet: development of a disclosure quality index', *International Journal of Business and Economics*, 8: 55–79.

Hewaidy, A.M. (2007) 'Readability of financial statement footnotes of Kuwaiti corporations', *European Journal of Economics, Finance and Administrative Sciences*, 8: 18–28.

Hines, R.D. (1981) 'Are annual reports used by shareholders?', *The Chartered Accountant in Australia*, 51: 48–51.

Hooghiemstra, R. (2000) 'Corporate communication and impression management – new perspectives why companies engage in corporate social reporting', *Journal of Business Ethics*, 27: 55–68.

Hussey, R. and Craig, R.J. (1979) 'Employee reports: what employees think', *The Chartered Accountant in Australia*, May: 39–40, 42–44.

Johnson, D.T., Bauerly, R.J. and Waggle, D. (2002) 'Are mutual fund prospectuses written in plain English?', *Managerial Finance*, 45: 221–247.

Jones, C.G. (2011) 'Written and computer-mediated accounting communication skill: an employer perspective', *Business Communication Quarterly*, 74: 247–271.

Jones, M.J. (1997) 'Methodological themes: critical appraisal of the cloze procedure's use in the accounting domain', *Accounting, Auditing & Accountability Journal*, 10: 105–128.

Jones, M.J. and Shoemaker, P.A. (1994) 'Accounting narratives: a review of empirical studies of content and readability', *Journal of Accounting Literature*, 13: 142–184.

Jones, M.J. and Xiao, J.Z. (2004) 'Financial reporting on the internet by 2010: a consensus view', *Accounting Forum*, 28: 237–263.

Justesen, L. and Mouritsen, J. (2009) 'The triple visual: translations between photographs, 3-D visualizations and calculations', *Accounting, Auditing & Accountability Journal*, 22: 973–990.

Kaplan, A.M. and Haenlein, M. (2010) 'Users of the world, unite! The challenges and opportunities of social media', *Business Horizons*, 53: 59–68.

Kermis, G. and Kermis, M. (2010) 'Professional presence and soft skills: a role for accounting education', *Journal of Instructional Pedagogies*, 2: 1–10.

Koski, T.R., Ehlen, C.R. and Saxby, C.L. (2004) 'The impact of communication the accounting firm/client relationship', *Journal of Applied Business Research*, 20: 81–90.

Laksmana, I., Tietz, W. and Yang, W. (2011) 'Compensation discussion and analysis (CD&A): readability and management obfuscation', *Journal of Accounting and Public Policy*, 31: 185–203.

Lee, T.D. and Tweedie, D.P. (1975) 'Accounting information: an investigation of private shareholder usage', *Accounting and Business Research*, 6: 280–291.

Leventis, S. and Weetman, P. (2004) 'Impression management: dual language reporting and voluntary disclosure', *Accounting Forum*, 28: 307–328.

Lewis, N., Parker, L.D. and Sutcliffe, P. (1984a) 'Financial reporting to employees: the pattern of development 1919 to 1979', *Accounting, Organizations and Society*, 9: 275–289.

Lewis, N., Parker, L.D. and Sutcliffe, P. (1984b) 'Financial reporting to employees: towards a research framework', *Accounting and Business Research*, 14: 229–239.

Lewis, N., Parker, L.D., Pound, G.D. and Sutcliffe, P. (1986) 'Accounting report readability: the use of readability techniques', *Accounting and Business Research*, 16: 199–209.

Li, F. (2008) 'Annual report readability, current earnings, and earnings persistence', *Journal of Accounting and Economics*, 45: 221–247.

Linsley, P.M. and Lawrence, M.J. (2007) 'Risk reporting by the largest UK companies: readability and lack of obfuscation', *Accounting, Auditing & Accountability Journal*, 20: 620–627.

Logue, C. (2001) 'London Airport', in G. Benson, J. Cherniak, and C. Herbert (eds), *Poems on the Underground*, 10th edn, London: Cassell.

Lyall, D. (1981) 'Financial reporting for employees', *Management Decision*, 19: 33–38.

Lymer, A. and Debreceny, R. (2003) 'The auditor and corporate reporting on the internet: challenges and institutional responses', *International Journal of Auditing*, 7: 103–120.

Marston, C. (2003) 'Financial reporting on the internet by leading Japanese companies', *Corporate Communications: An International Journal*, 8: 23–34.

Mather, P., Ramsey, A. and Steen, A. (2000) 'The use and representational faithfulness of graphs in Australian IPO prospectuses', *Accounting, Auditing & Accountability Journal*, 13: 65–83.

Matilal, S. and Höpfl, H. (2009) 'Accounting for the Bhopal disaster: footnotes and photographs', *Accounting, Auditing & Accountability Journal*, 22: 953–972.

May, G.S. and May, C.B. (1989) 'Communication instruction: what is being done to develop the communication skills of accounting students?', *Journal of Accounting Education*, 7: 233–244.

McKinstry, S. (1996) 'Designing the annual reports of Burton PLC from 1930 to 1994', *Accounting, Organizations and Society*, 21: 89–111.

Merkl-Davies, D.M. and Brennan, N.M. (2007) 'Discretionary disclosure strategies in corporate narratives: incremental information or impression management?', *Journal of Accounting Literature*, 26: 116–194.

Moriarty, S. (1979) 'Communicating financial information through multi-dimensional graphics', *Journal of Accounting Research*, April: 205–224.

Most, K.S. and Chang, L.S. (1979) 'How useful are annual reports to investors?', *Journal of Accountancy*, 148: 111–113.

Neilson, W.C. and Lind, G.G. (1971) 'Is Aunt Jane worth it?' *Financial Executive*, January: 51.

Ogden, S. and Clarke, J. (2005) 'Customer disclosures, impression management and the construction of legitimacy', *Accounting, Auditing & Accountability Journal*, 18: 313–345.

Paisey, C. and Paisey, N.J. (2006a) 'And they all lived happily ever after? Exploring the possibilities of mobilising the internet to promote a more enabling accounting for occupational pension schemes', *Accounting, Auditing & Accountability Journal*, 19: 719–758.

Paisey, C. and Paisey, N.J. (2006b) 'The internet and possibilities for counter accounts: some reflections: a reply', *Accounting, Auditing & Accountability Journal*, 19: 774–778.

Parker, L.D. (1976) *The Reporting of Company Financial Results to Employees*, London: Institute of Chartered Accountants in England and Wales.

Parker, L.D. (1977) 'The accounting responsibility towards corporate financial reporting to employees', *Accounting Education*, 17: 62–83.

Parker, L.D. (1978) 'Communication in the corporate budgetary system', *Accounting and Business Research*, 31: 191–207.

Parker, L.D. (1981) 'Corporate annual reports: a failure to communicate', *International Journal of Accounting Education and Research*, 16: 35–48.

Parker, L.D. (1982) 'Corporate annual reporting: a mass communication perspective', *Accounting and Business Research*, 12: 279–286.

Parker, L.D. (1986) *Communicating Financial Information through the Annual Report*, London: ICAEW.

Parker, L.D. (1988a) 'Communicative effectiveness' in K.R. Ferris (ed.), *Behavioral Accounting Research: A Critical Analysis*, Columbus, OH: Century VII Publishing Co.

Parker, L.D. (ed.) (1988b) *Financial Reporting to Employees: From Past to Present*, New York: Garland Publishing, Inc.

Parker, L.D. (2009) 'Photo-elicitation: an ethno-historical accounting and management history research prospect', *Accounting, Auditing & Accountability Journal*, 22: 1111–1129.

Parker, L.D., Ferris, K.R. and Otley, D.T. (1989) *Accounting for the Human Factor*, New York: Prentice Hall.

Plucinski, K.J., Olsavsky, J. and Hall, L. (2009) 'Readability of introductory financial and managerial accounting textbooks', *Academy of Educational Leadership Journal*, 13: 119–127.

Preston, A.M., Wright, C. and Young, J.J. (1996) 'Imag[in]ing annual reports', *Accounting, Organizations and Society*, 21: 113–137.

Purdy, D. (1981) 'The provision of financial information to employees: a study of the reporting practices of some large public companies in the United Kingdom', *Accounting, Organizations and Society*, 6: 327–338.

Rutherford, B.A. (2003) 'Obfuscation, textual complexity and the role of regulated narrative accounting disclosure in corporate governance', *Journal of Management and Governance*, 7: 187–210.

Sikka, P. (2006) 'The internet and possibilities for counter accounts: some reflections', *Accounting, Auditing & Accountability Journal*, 19: 759–769.

Simons, K., Higgins, M. and Lowe, D. (1995) 'A profile of communication apprehension in accounting majors: implications for teaching and curriculum revision', *Journal of Accounting Education*, 13: 159–176.

Smith, M. and Taffler, R. (1984) 'Improving the communication function of published accounting statements', *Accounting and Business Research*, 14: 139–146.

Smith, M. and Taffler, R. (1992) 'Readability and understandability: different measure of the textual complexity of accounting narrative', *Accounting, Auditing & Accountability Journal*, 5: 84–98.

Smith, M. and Taffler, R. (1996) 'Improving the communication of accounting information through cartoon graphics', *Accounting, Auditing & Accountability Journal*, 9: 68–85.

Smith, M., Jamil, A., Johari, Y.C. and Ahmad, S.A. (2006) 'The chairman's statement in Malaysian companies: a test of the obfuscation hypothesis, *Asian Review of Accounting*, 14: 49–65.

Sriram, R.S. and Coppage, R.E. (1992) 'A comparison of educators and CPA practitioners views on communication training in the accounting curriculum', *Journal of Applied Business Research*, 8: 1–11.

Stone, G.W. (2011a) 'Readability of accountants' communications with small business – some Australian evidence', *Accounting Forum*, 35: 247–261.

Stone, G.W. (2011b) 'Let's talk: adapting accountants' communications to small business managers' objectives and preferences', *Accounting, Auditing & Accountability Journal*, 24: 781–809.

Stone, G.W. (2012) 'The effectiveness of newsletters in accountants' client relations with small business managers: an Australian qualitative study', *Qualitative Research in Accounting & Management*, 9: 21–43.

Stowers, R.H. and White, G.T. (1999) 'Connecting accounting and communication: a survey of public accounting firms', *Business Communication Quarterly*, 62: 23–40.

Sun, M. (2007) 'An exploratory study of the understandability of listed companies' annual reports', *Frontiers of Business Research in China*, 1: 39–49.

Warren, S. (2005) 'Photography and voice in critical qualitative management research', *Accounting, Auditing & Accountability Journal*, 18: 861–882.

Warren, S. and Parker, L. (2009) 'Bean counters or bright young things? Towards the visual study of identity construction among professional accountants', *Qualitative Research in Accounting and Management*, 6: 205–223.

Wilton, R.L. and Tabb, J.B. (1978) 'An investigation into private shareholder usage of financial statements in New Zealand', *Accounting Education*, 18: 93–101.

Winfield, R.R. (1978) 'Shareholder opinion of published financial statements' in J. Courtis (ed.), *Corporate Annual Report Analysis*, AFM Exploratory Series No. 5, Armidale: University of New England.

Worthington, J. (1979) 'More understanding with simpler footnotes', *CA Magazine*, July: 44–47.

3

An historical perspective from the work of Chambers

Frank Clarke, Graeme Dean and John Richard Edwards

Introduction: illusion and reality

Early ideas on information and communication theory were fostered by those with an interest in mathematical logic. Some have claimed they arose from attempts by governments during World War II to crack security codes. Early developers included Claude Shannon from the Bell Laboratories' experiments in the 1940s (e.g. Shannon 1948, 1949; see also Shannon and Weaver 1949), Wiener's (1949) work on cybernetics, and the Alan Turing and von Neumann forays into artificial intelligence and automata theory (see Aspray 1985; Gleick 2011). Shannon and others led the development of a general theory of communication, including the need (i) to understand that the bigger the surprise, the more informative a message is, and (ii) to recognize, as Shannon did (Gleick, 2011: 281), that information is identified with entropy.

Their work was soon transported into many social-science arenas (see Aspray 1985; Gleick 2011) with accounting theorists drawing on insights provided by (amongst others) Cherry (1957) on communication and Wiener (1949) and Beer (1961) on cybernetics. Prominent amongst the early accounting theorists is Chambers' work on management decision making (1952, 1955a, 1955b, 1957, 1961, 1962, 1966), which reveals that the notion of communication was critical to his understanding of the function of accounting. The key requirements that need to be satisfied for accounting communication to be effective were later reflected upon in correspondence with Abraham ('Abe') Briloff:

> I believe several generations of teachers are to blame (though the fault lies not only there) … man may clothe his utterances in words of his own choice. But communication rests on cognitions shared by the speaker and his audience; *if* he *is* to convey any message, his freedom of choice is thus restricted, disciplined, by what his audience can grasp … when an accountant adds up numbers which auditors make some assuring noises about, we do not expect the result to be, or to be intended to be, an illusion. And yet it is, if the aggregation is logically improper. … Until accountants have established the linkages between specific kinds of information and their specific uses (separately or in combination), it cannot be claimed that their processes are 'disciplined', and the prospect of weeds over-running the garden will persist.
>
> *(Chambers, 22 March 1979, USA P202, #5788)*[1]

Chambers' concerns have current resonance given the development by financial engineers of the instruments that arguably underpinned the recent global financial crisis (GFC) and the related currency crisis. Patterson (2010) shows that Chambers and his fellow travellers drew heavily on their understanding of information theory as it related to accounting and securities market prices. Chambers' observations on the difference between illusion and reality is, therefore, particularly apt. His letter to Briloff notes that when an accountant adds up numbers and auditors make assuring noises regarding their veracity, we do not expect the result to be, or to be intended to be, an illusion. And yet so frequently it is the former and all too often also the latter. Communication is thereby frustrated.

The remainder of this chapter is organized as follows. In the next two sections, ideas about how communication and information were introduced into the accounting literature in the 1950s are explained. The following section considers the issue of 'bad communication', generating entropy, giving some examples of how misstatements (insofar as they are about nonsense in the first place) and failure to communicate (inform, etc.) were evident in the aftermath of the unexpected collapses and financial difficulties of several large corporates during the GFC and related currency crisis. In particular, we consider the brouhaha surrounding the prescribed mark-to-market accounting treatment by the Securities and Exchange Commission (SEC), the Financial Accounting Standards Board (FASB) and the International Accounting Standards Board (IASB). The last two sections of this chapter focus on a possible way forward to better accounting communication with a particular focus on 'telling it as it is'.

Communication in accounting

The idea that business entities should prepare and publish accounting statements showing the state of their financial affairs has prevailed since the public at large began to invest in joint-stock companies and to become shareholders. This is evident in companies legislation worldwide since the creation of the modern company by registration under the UK Joint Stock Companies Act 1844. That theme has been expanded over nearly170 years through extending the composition and form of compulsory published financial statements, the timeliness of their presentation to the public, compulsory audit and the imposition of a compulsory quality criterion – that those financial statements had to provide (according to the current terminology)[2] *a true and fair view of the company's financial position and financial performance*. Hence, accounting data have to satisfy technical and social communication criteria.

While perhaps the role accounting data had in financial communications was obvious, nonetheless, neither communication as a technical domain nor accounting as a means by which it was prosecuted entered the accounting literature until the early 1950s. This occurred through the work of a small coterie of scholars consisting mainly of accounting's *golden age theorists*[3] such as Chambers, Robert Sterling, Richard Mattessich, Maurice Moonitz, Yuji Ijiri and scholars (on accounting) from other disciplines like Kenneth Boulding and Samuel Hayakawa.[4]

Chambers on information and communication

One of the first accountants to draw heavily on the technical aspects of communication was Raymond John Chambers, founder of the *Sydney School*.[5] Accordingly, this account of communication in accounting draws heavily upon his thoughts and enquiries, through his publications, readings and correspondence. In that context, Chambers' own academic work is characterized by very careful and meticulous use of language (his desk was always littered with an array of dictionaries, books of synonyms and antonyms, thesauruses and similar wordsmiths' tools), by tight logic that could be demonstrated graphically, by the use of empirical data that was directly to the point being argued, and conclusions that could clearly and exclusively be drawn from the preceding argument – all of which are demonstrated *par excellence* in *Accounting, Evaluation and Economic Behavior* (Chambers 1966) and *An Accounting Thesaurus: 500 Years of Accounting* (Chambers 1995).[6]

Chambers was keen to use words properly. For him, the lack of terminological rigour was a major reason for the problems plaguing accounting thought and practice. Recently, Sterling (2006), upon being inducted to the Ohio State University Accounting Hall of Fame, lamented that his career had to be described properly as a failure since:

> Accounting is very nearly the same in my end as it was in my beginning [p. 8] … what was being put in accountants' minds … [in the current texts are] the same useless concepts, invalid claims and senseless numerals that I studied in my first accounting class circa 1952 … Strike one [p. 9] … the careless use of language [p. 9] … If avoiding equivocal terms requires jargon, invent it. Jargon is undesirable but it is better than equivocation. In my beginning I identified this error and its solution. In my end I am still identifying it. Strike two. [p. 10]

Chambers' 22 March 1979 response to Abe Briloff's earlier communication (5 March 1979, #5787) noted that, in developing his theory of accounting, communication, measurement and identifying the function of accounting were fundamental issues. Briloff's 1964 doctoral thesis (published as 'Briloff 1967') also examined the issue of communication, though not the aspect canvassed by Chambers, Mattessich and others in the 1960s. Briloff focussed on the nomenclature of the audit opinion rather than the accounting data upon which it was based. Mattessich (1964), Ijiri (1967), Lev (1968, 1969), Feltham and Demski (1970) and Feltham (1972) were consistent with Chambers when drawing on developments in mathematics by Shannon and others but, in other respects, addressed the communication issue in very different ways. Marschak (1955; see also Marschak and Radner 1972) is another who should be mentioned as arguably influencing the thinking of those pursuing another information path, namely information economics (Mattessich 1980: 169, fn. 27).

When Maurice Moonitz of the University of California, Berkeley, enthusiastically endorsed Chambers' (1966) *Accounting, Evaluation and Economic Behavior* in correspondence with the University of Sydney Registrar (Moonitz 1972), he particularly praised the emphasis on communication:

> The book probes more deeply the 'foundations' of accounting than any other similar work. …. explores the contributions of related fields in a manner that if not unique, is certainly not equalled by any other work with which I am familiar. For example, I found his Chapter 7, 'Information and Information Processing', Chapter 8, 'Communication' and Chapter 12, 'Financial Communication Within Organizations', to be lucid summaries of the work done recently in those fields, summaries … superior in many respects to those prepared by scholars in the fields themselves.

To provide a fuller assessment, Moonitz appended material from his 1971 'UCLA Berkeley Spring 1971 Course Notes' that contained references to the accounting system described in Chambers (1966). Points 7 and 8 below are taken from that source (Moonitz 1972):

> 7. This book [Chambers 1966] is more elegant than Mattessich's, more compact, less diffuse. Its scope is narrower since it probes more deeply into the characteristics (including

the limits) of the ideal accounting system. Chambers explicitly acknowledges his debt to recent developments in the theories of organization, communication and regulatory systems. ...

8. Chambers leads a group which agrees with Mattessich (and others) on the need for increased rigor in accounting analysis, but disagrees sharply on the concept of the field (scope of accounting). Chambers holds firmly to the notion that accounting is measurement, and that future events cannot be measured. ... Accounting properly supplies data on the present position, but it does not properly supply estimates of the future (e.g. in budgeting or even in its valuation procedures).

A major theme in Chambers' early works was his criticism of the failure to communicate precise financial information about an entity's financial position and performance – notions he regarded as being well understood by the lay person – because of the loose terminology used in technical accounting discourse. See, for example: 'Blueprint for a theory of accounting' in *Accounting Research* (1955a); 'A scientific pattern of accounting theory' in *The Australian Accountant* (1955b); 'Detail for a blueprint' in *The Accounting Review* (1957); 'Measurement and misrepresentation' in *Management Science* (1960); 'Towards a general theory of accounting', Australian Society of Accountants Annual Research Lecture (1961); and *The Resolution of Some Paradoxes in Accounting* (1962).

Chambers' early literary forays also focussed on precision in the use of accounting terminology. For example, his 1964 NZ *Accountants' Journal* article 'Conventions, doctrines and commonsense' carefully distinguished between postulates, principles, standards, rules and stressed the need for commercial 'commonsense' to underpin usage. Consider also his major works on 'Information Processing and Communication', Chapters 7, 8 and 12 from *Accounting, Evaluation and Economic Behavior* (1966), and extracts focussing on these aspects of communication in *An Accounting Thesaurus* (1995).

Chambers drew on the 1940s and 1950s technical analyses of information processing and communication (Shannon 1948, 1949; Shannon and Weaver 1949; Wiener 1949; Cherry 1957) in his early works on management decision making within organisations (1952, 1955a, 1955b, 1957, 1961, 1962). Thus Lee's (1982) contribution to a festschrift, prepared to mark Chambers' retirement from formal university appointment, describes Chambers' penchant for discussing accounting communication in terms of the 'transmission of messages about economic events and effects' with signs and symbols being the means of transmission. This view of accounting as a language contrasted with the conventional view of accounting as a procedural device. Lee (1982: 155) also observed that Chambers regarded one of the major problems of accounting communication being the faulty information processing by the accountant who acts as an agent for the entrepreneur.

Chambers' *communication* journey therefore drew on his wide readings on management which had provided the foundations for his early teaching. Thus an internal, as much as an external, decision-making focus was to the fore. In the papers cited in the previous paragraph, Chambers suggested that accounting statements were an established means of communication between entrepreneurs (actors) and the several parties on whose participation business organizations depend, namely investors, creditors, workers and consumers. The nature of these communications may influence the confidence and willingness of those interested parties to participate. They affect the economic life of a community, and they enable the evaluation of the influence of conventional accounting and of alternative accounting systems on all who make decisions having economic consequences.[7] Specifically, financial and cost accounting statements are part of the systems of internal communications by which an organization adjusts its activities as internal and external exigencies arise; and it is necessary to consider whether existing accounting techniques or variants of them are equal to this task.

The 1953 edition of Chambers' *Financial Management* summarized well his early thoughts on communication. There, communication is said to rest on cognitions shared by the speaker and his or her audience. The 1986 edition of that book is particularly apt. Chapter 7 'Organisation' discusses communication and feedback matters in some depth, deftly using diagrams and text it summarizes general issues and those especially pertaining to accounting. Consider the following:

> Integrated direction, interaction and co-ordination depend on interpersonal communication. 'An organisation might almost be defined as a structure of roles tied together with lines of communication' (Boulding, 1961, 27). '... without communication there can be no organisation, for there is no possibility then of the group influencing the behaviour of the individual' (Simon, 1949, 154). Communication is the transmission of verbal and other messages or signals, with the object of providing or influencing the premises of judgment and choice.
>
> Messages may be oral or documentary. Oral communication may suffice where prompt or personal action is required by one person of another. But there are few circumstances in which oral communication alone is used. Documented messages are protection against fallible recollection of oral messages on the part of the transmitter or receiver. They are the protection against faulty transmission where lines of communication are long. They may be prepared in sets or copied where knowledge of the authorisation or completion of tasks is required at a number of points in an organisation. And, where, for any reason, the persons assigned particular tasks change over time, documentary messages may serve as organisational memory.
>
> All messages are formally arranged sets of signs or symbols. The signs may be words of the vernacular language, terms of technical languages, numerical and mathematical terms, diagram; a message may be any combination of such signs. All signs and the messages constructed of them are artifacts. Every sign has a referent, an observable or imaginable object, action, event, quality or property, or another sign. But the referent of any sign is not unique. ... Many of the terms used in respect of financial matters may have a variety of referents – value may mean value in use or value in exchange; price may mean buying price or selling price; a number preceded by a money symbol may refer to the outcome of a calculation or the amount of an observable price; the same money quantity may have widely different significance for judgment or action at different dates. Ambiguity and confusion are inevitable unless such general terms are qualified by description or date and unless the duly qualified usage approximates what is commonly understood among the varied persons who may, or may be expected, to respond to message or discourse.
>
> *(Chambers 1986: 93–4)*

Chambers then notes that, in any organization, classes of communications vary. Again using diagrams as well as text, he describes 'factual', 'prescriptive', 'motivational', 'appraisive' and 'advisory' communication classes. Among these, he observes that factual messages are the only class that relate to the organization itself:

> Since the capacity of an organisation to satisfy its participants depends on its factual state and the factual outcome of its operations, and since the facts of a situation are inevitably among the premises of directives, opinions and judgments, the greater the correspondence between

factual messages and the events and states they purport to depict, the greater is the possibility of apt response. Writing of descriptive sentences generally, Russell (1940, 178) observed: 'A sentential sign present to an organism is true when, as a sign, it promotes behaviour which would have been promoted by a situation that exists, if this situation had been present to the organism.' To satisfy these conditions, the matter represented should be an observation made under known or specified conditions; the content of the message should be couched in terms understandable to the recipient; and there should be no cause of interference or distortion in the channel or line of communication. There may seem to be no good reason why the conditions would not be met. However, there are reasons. They stem principally from the synthetic linkages between the individual observers and agents of an organisation, and the dependence of those agents on processed information. The possibility of misdirection is reduced if there are means of judging the quality of processed factual information, and means of rectifying the system that produces it.

(Chambers 1986: 95–6)

He continues, observing that this is the role of feedback within an organization. An organization can be maintained by adaptation that responds to the feedback process. Figure 3.1 (which is Figure 12 from *Accounting, Evaluation and Economic Behavior* (Chambers 1966: 317)) encapsulates those ideas. The debt to Shannon and the early information and communication pioneers who sought to understand information, entropy, feedback and other coordination issues within organizations are evident from the content of Figure 12 and other diagrams in Chambers (1966: Figures 7, 8 and 11) and Chambers (1986: Figures 7.71–7.73). Those diagrams also demonstrate the fact that Chambers' ability to capture succinctly the essence of economics and measurement theory as it relates to accounting was matched by his skill in transporting into accounting the relevant information and communication ideas developed in cognate commercial fields.

Chambers' well-honed views on communication are captured in the following extract[8] from a letter addressed to G. McAuslan, of IBM, who served as an official of the NSW Computer Society. It captures well Chambers' mid-1960s views on communication in general, and on the need for a reformed accounting communication in particular:

The firm is generally regarded as fixing its own goals and norms. [Its] consequential emphasis on communication and control leads to a purely formal approach to information selection and processing and to disregard the functions of information selection in adaptive behaviour. The principles of isomorphism and feedback, basic to physical systems, are equally apposite to the economic aspects of organisations generally. Their adoption entails information and communication systems differing materially from conventional systems.

(8 March 1965, USA P202, #01411)

Chambers' voluminous entries on information and communication in *An Accounting Thesaurus* (Chambers 1995) provide further evidence of his intimate knowledge of these issues. Consider, for example, the implied connections he encourages by the sub-areas examined in Chapter 2 ('The Psychological and social background of accounting'): 'Belief and action', 'Observation and inference', 'Signs, symbols, language', 'Information and communication', 'Measurement and measuring' and 'Measurement in accounting'. The extracts there reveal, indirectly, the strong connections he made between two major elements in his accounting theory development, namely the need to view accounting as both information-cum-communication and as measurement systems.[9] When one examines the *Thesaurus* quotes within the relevant subsection areas, it is evident that Chambers refers to many authors well known for their early

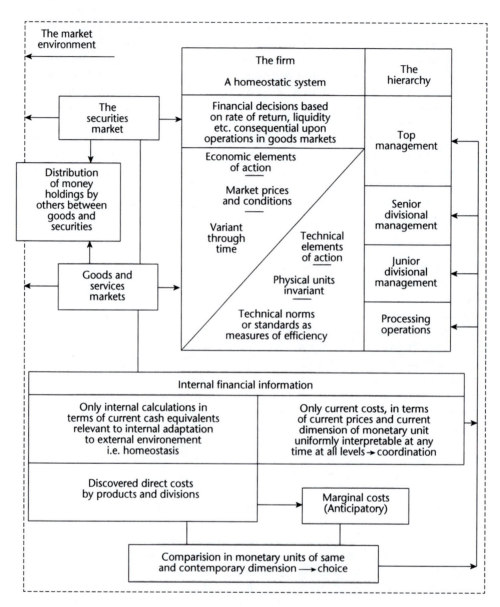

Figure 3.1 Financial communication within organizations
Source: Chambers (1966: 317)

thoughts on signs, symbols, language, information and communication within the 'home' literatures and more generally within the management and organizational literatures.

GFC, currency crisis and accounting: cold comfort from financial delusions

Accounting miscommunications of the kind Chambers wanted to avoid were aptly illustrated
during the 2007–09 GFC and persist during the consequential currency crises. Receiving messages

that tell only what one wants to see and hear, were a feature of that period. From bankers, in particular, communications regarding financial wellbeing portrayed known errors – delighting but deluding their recipients. There, a desire for publishing derivative valuations known to be in excess of the market's indication of current worth overrode the communication principle of 'telling it how it is'. Inbuilt noise in the communication system created the clear potential for entropy and a financial system meltdown.

That episode also provides evidence of the business community's strange penchant for shooting the messenger rather than rooting out the problem. Of course, politicizing things is never far from the surface. Quickly, there were cries of 'told you so' from those who opposed the introduction of the relevant accounting standards – Statements of Financial Accounting Standards (FAS) 157 (Fair Value Measurements) in the US and International Accounting Standard (IAS) 39 (Financial Instruments: Recognition and Measurement) in Europe. Academics soon followed (see Katz 2008; Ryan 2008; Whalen 2008; Magnan 2009). US politicians enthusiastically intoned such a litany with the apparent approbation of the (by then) Presidential candidate John McCain. The refrain was that having to write down assets to their market prices had 'caused' the financial collapses of US corporates Bear Stearns, Lehman Brothers, AIG and the UK's Northern Rock, and the near collapse of numerous others. That causation chain is said to have necessitated the $US700b Troubled Asset Release Programme, 'cash for trash', bailout in the US. It was also suggested that Iceland's near bankruptcy was another 'fair value' casualty. Such sentiments soon resurfaced in the discourse surrounding the sovereign debt problems of Europe's so-called 'PIIGS', namely Portugal, Ireland, Italy, Greece and Spain.

Thus, accounting standards were, for some, the cause of these crises, or at the very least that they made things worse. This line of argument has its historical precedents. The practice of mark-to-market was law in the United States until the late 1930s when President Roosevelt succumbed to pressure from the banks to repeal the rule as part of a measure designed to avoid deepening the Great Depression ('A mark-to-market history lesson' 2011).[10] The problem emerged again in the US during the latter stages of the economic boom presaging the 1980s Savings and Loans crisis when President Regan allowed the write-up of investments as part of his liberalization campaign.

Marking assets to their market prices had long been a permitted accounting practice in the UK and elsewhere when that measurement procedure gained impetus, in 2005, through numerous countries adopting International Accounting Standards. Among these, IAS 39 specified that certain financial instruments (which featured particularly in bank balance sheets) be accounted for at 'fair value through profit and loss' – that is, that they be *marked-to-market*. In 2007 a renewed US push for the application of a current value accounting system came with the FASB's promulgation of FAS 157. And, whereas FAS 157 was voluntary with respect to many assets, other FASs also permitted current values to be used.

In many respects the brouhaha surrounding FAS 157 reflected the tensions between the accounting standards setters in the US and those in the UK and Europe, as well as prudential and securities regulators in various countries.[11] That accounting data are a primary means for the communication of factual financial information seems to have been almost forgotten in this stand-off.

Matters came to a head after Lehman Brothers' collapse in October 2008. Congress rose to the cause. For some commentators accounting's (FAS 157's) mark-to-market prescriptions were said to be *exacerbating* the financial system's procyclicality. For others it was the *cause* of the GFC.[12] In *Alchemists of Loss*, Dowd and Hutchison (2010: 310) opine: 'In the event, FAS 157's timing was terrible' for Goldman Sachs and Bear Stearns. But these commentaries illustrate a misunderstanding of accounting's communicative role of informing financial decisions, 'telling it how it is'. This issue is now considered.

National standards setters were concerned about adopting fair value accounting in markets where items regarded as valuable to those owning them had no buyers other than in a fire-sale-like setting. In an attempt to overcome this inactive markets problem, a five-level hierarchy was proposed. Eventually three levels were agreed upon culminating in the FASB injecting FAS 157 with the following hierarchy of assets for valuation purposes:

level 1 assets – for which a market and prices are available;

level 2 assets – where the existence of a market for like assets allowed some discretion for owners regarding which prices they chose and;

level 3 assets – where markets are inactive, and owners could mark-to-model, or 'mark-to-myth' as Buffett (quoted in Davies 2010: 114) called it.[13]

But the agreed hierarchy did little for some. For those analysts willing to look beyond the reported asset balances (in aggregate), this classification merely exposed the perilous state of many institutions. Goldman Sachs, for example, was shown to have level 3 assets amounting to '3 times its capital', and Bear Stearns $28 billion in level 3s with 'a net equity position of only 11.1 billion' (Dowd and Hutchison 2010: 311).

Complaints from compliant institutions being forced to make considerable write-downs as a result of mark-to-market accounting were common, as evident in the comments made by Standard and Poor's' Mark Zandi in *Financial Shock*. There, he advocated allowing a gradual writing-down process:

> The FAS 157 [mark-to-market] rules put pressure on institutions to quickly adjust the book value of their assets to market prices but I propose that, markdowns … could be tweaked so that changing assets [read also liabilities] values could be phased in over time. . . . Banks would still have to lower their holding as prices fell, but not as rapidly.
>
> *(Zandi 2009: 237–38)*

Such a sugar-coating by Zandi's suggested 'phasing in' completely negates, of course, the purpose of communicating the current financial position.

The introduction of the mark-to-market accounting rules to achieve better communication was also perceived to be a serious problem by Munchau (2011: 211), who argued: 'If accounting rules had not been temporarily relaxed many banks and insurance companies would have had to file for bankruptcy.' As Isaac and Meyer (2010: 10) complained:

> The SEC and FASB did not act immediately to correct its most egregious problems … we really needed a repeal of all vestiges of mark-to-market accounting to restore much of the $500 billion capital in our financial system that mark-to-market accounting had so senselessly destroyed.

But it was far from being a one-sided debate. Many serious observers perceived mark-to-market accounting as providing much needed transparency. Adopting a line put forward by the then Chief Executive of the ICAEW Michael Izza, Davies (2010; see also Ball 2008) saw the drawing of a causal link between mark-to-market accounting and the GFC as a case of 'shooting the messenger', noting with approbation Laux and Leuz's (2009, 2010) finding that there was little evidence that the GFC was the result of mark-to-market accounting. Bonaci et al. (2010)

provided further strong defence of reporting fair values, while Dowd and Hutchison (2010: 310) explained that, in reality, 'FAS 157 was just bringing to the open that Wall Street had taken exorbitant risks based on Modern Finance risk management and valuation models that were pure fantasy'.[14] Contestable analyses of fair value accounting's impact or otherwise on the GFC continue: Cheng et al. (2011); Gebhardt and Novotny-Farkas (2011); Badertscher et al. (2012); Cheng (2012).

Recent commentaries by US standards setters (Linsmeier 2011; Mosso 2011) adopt the stance that current data of the fair value genre are essential for the effective and efficient operation of capital markets. One can reasonably infer that the focus on write-downs, by many observers at the time of crisis, misdirected attention to its symptoms rather than its cause. Whilst the level of transparency invoked by the mark-to-market rule drove prices down, it would only do so if those in the market accepted that the reduced prices better reflected what the securities were worth – to them. That is how markets work. When it is thought that securities are under-priced, buyers will move in and, ordinarily, prices will rise. So, whereas it is possibly true to say that the write-downs were major drivers of the loss in confidence underpinning the collapse of the world's stock markets and the related pessimism, marking-to-market did not 'cause' the initial loss in the worth of the securities, collateralized debt obligations (CDOs) and credit default swaps (CDSs). In principle, marking-to-market simply forced current asset prices to be disclosed by requiring financial institutions to 'tell it as it is'.

But it seems that many of the interested parties, particularly in the US, perceived virtue in ignoring the truth about market prices, found comfort in being deluded, were content, even happy, to 'push the can down the road' by invoking marking-to-model. In early October 2008, Christopher Cox, Chairman of the SEC, declared the relaxation of the mark-to-market valuation. FAS 157 effectively could be ignored. This endorsed 'less transparency' and allowed institutions to report what they thought assets were worth rather than what the market disclosed regarding their worth. It legitimized a return to the 'mark-to-magic' practices of the not-too-distant past, epitomized by Enron's 'mark-to-model' of future energy price returns.

A possible way forward: the pursuit of *serviceability*

To inform, to communicate, to tell it how it is, the data in financial statements must be serviceable, fit for the uses ordinarily made of them. This necessitates data in published financial statements to be indicative of a company's current and past financial progress, and indicative of its financial position – the nature, composition and money's worth of its assets and the nature and the amount of the liabilities enforceable against the company. The data must therefore be serviceable for the purpose of deriving indicators of financial performance, rate of return, liquidity, solvency, debt to equity and similar gearing indicators, asset backing, whether a company satisfies its debt covenants, and the like. That is a rather tight specification. Where no market exists for an item at the accounting date and, therefore, doesn't have a market price, or where a highly specialized item results in a thin or an inactive market, such information needs to be communicated, not ignored. For the owners of the particular item with no market price, the options regarding its use are limited, and owners need to know that is the case. Perhaps the item can be used to produce a revenue stream, it can be retired, allowed to sit idle, given away, but no market price means simply that the item generally cannot be exchanged for cash, cannot be pledged as collateral for borrowing and cannot contribute directly to the fund to extinguish debts.

The above actions draw and rely upon the facts as they are at the date of the financials. It is preferable to be aware of 'what is', and to use that information as the base for speculating 'what might be' in the future, and to act accordingly. There is nothing to stop directors injecting their accompanying statements with anticipatory data, of course, so long as they clearly label them as such. What is reported in the financials does not preclude expectations that the future will be different, that an item currently unsaleable (not having a price now) may later be saleable, or those currently saleable may later be marketable for something different than the current price, or that any obligation of an entity is more or less based on current prices and price levels. Neither does it preclude communication of those expectations as a memorandum in, for instance, the notes to the accounts, nor from being the basis for (say) a directors' statement. Indeed, everybody trading in the equities market might be expected to consider the marketability of their holdings. Consistent with the plea by James Chanos (2009) in the *Wall Street Journal*, financial statements need to be factual, even when the facts offer 'cold comfort', as they do in respect of the so-called 'toxic assets' held by financial institutions since 2007. Those assets are not simply 'poorly performing' in the jargon of earlier days – they represent a bad investment. The financial effect of that bad investment needs to be communicated.

It follows that the prices of items reported in dated financial statements hold only for that precise point in time. Positions thereafter must recognize subsequent deviations. That is why we date positions – financial positions have dated balance sheets to specify the time-spans between which either income has been earned or losses incurred. Without recognizing the dates of measurements, we cannot evaluate performance, assess progress or regress. Indeed, without reference to specified dates, 'progress' and 'regress' are meaningless terms. Specifying dates is inherent in notions of *improvement* and *decline*, *increase* and *decrease*, *expansion* and *contraction*, *increase* and *diminish*, etc. Expectations regarding such matters must *follow* the current position. That is what *expectation* entails; departure from the present is the inherent nature of every anticipatory calculation. Indeed, without knowledge of the present state-of-play, the present market position, predictions of the future market prices are without a market foundation. Resort to an expectational-based model – *marking-to-model* – when a market is thin or no market exists is to produce a reported figure that replaces market truth with make-believe. Bromwich (2007) evocatively observed that this produces 'imaginary prices and in mystical markets'.

The Credit Suisse Equity Research Report (Zion et al. 2009) reveals that the need to communicate the non-existence of markets, and therefore market prices, or the existence of thin markets, for whatever reason, is shared by some practitioners:

> So would changing the current rules, maybe providing a time-out from fair value accounting, save the market from its sins? We don't think so. Just ask yourself a simple question: Which information is more relevant today, what you paid for an asset in the past or what it's worth right now? Ultimately, the job of accounting should be to provide information to creditors, investors, and counterparties to help them in their decision making process. It should reflect economic reality, not a company's preferred view of what the economic reality should be ... For example, contrast the investment banks that got hit by the first wave of 'write-downs' as many of their assets are reported on balance sheet at fair value and marked-to-market through earnings, with many of the banks, insurance companies, and GSEs that have not yet taken other than temporary impairments of investments in debt and equity securities, or the banks where most of their loans are not reported at fair value and instead could get hit slowly and painfully by increasing loan losses over the next few years. We would prefer to see all financial instruments on the balance sheet at fair value with changes in fair value run through earnings. ... To make the information more useful to investors, we would also like to see the mark-to-market changes highlighted separately in earnings, which companies are only required to provide today for Level 3 assets.

Market prices (whatever they may be) should be reported. The GFC and currency crisis episodes witnessed a familiar form of 'special pleading' by some in the press and elsewhere in a different setting: namely, that 'block sales' potentially distort reporting on a market price basis. Elsewhere two of the current writers have contended that:

> Information is never complete. But the market prices of items are as objective an evaluation of their contemporary money's worth, of their current contribution to the wealth of their owners, as can be found. The better the information, the better the evaluation, the better the financial assessments, the better – should be – decisions to invest and disinvest. Properly informed securities markets require accurate information of the current wealth and past financial progress of companies. Share prices might reasonably be expected to capture not only their companies' current financial position and an understanding of how it arose, but also impound all the expectations and fears for the future that the information might evoke.
>
> *(Clarke and Dean 2007: 199)*

Telling it as it is

In sum, whether in respect of prices where block sales occur, or when an asset does not have an observable market price, such as for the GFC's financial institutions' 'toxic' mortgage-based assets and liabilities, the role of a factual accounting is, and indeed can only be, to 'tell it as it is'. Only if this happens can it be described as an 'honest accounting'. As this chapter is being finalised, some analysts and markets continue to claim that declines in the values of toxic assets are 'temporary' and hence do not need to be recognized in financial reports, defying the 'truth' of the situation.[15] The Chambers (*to* Briloff) letter revealed different interpretations of communication. That dichotomy persists. The observations reproduced above from Zion et al. (2009) show an ongoing concern about accounting's lack of serviceability for decision uses, whilst reviews from the UK and EU regarding audit quality (Financial Reporting Council 2008) note auditing's need to improve communication regarding matters contained in the audit report.

Confirming the need to understand accounting's communicative role is the recent announcement that US federal regulators have filed lawsuits against 17 financial institutions alleging that, during the period prior to the GFC, they 'sold mortgage giants Fannie Mae and Freddie Mac nearly US$200 billion in mortgage backed securities that later soured' (Schwarz and Rosse 2011). Amongst other matters, the focus, will be on when that 'souring' took place and the reporting of it. And suggestions will be made that accounting 'did not tell it as it is', that the sub-prime mortgages in their CDO formats should not have been reported *as if* they were AAA assets. Risk assessments are alleged to have been based on that misinformation. Importantly for our story, these are not new problems with, for example, similar allegations made concerning the role of faulty accounting in the aftermath of the 1980s savings and loans crisis.

Chambers' early insights into information and communication were gleaned from developments in cognate business fields. His wide reading, as extracts from *An Accounting Thesaurus* (Chambers 1995) clearly testify, led to him to be very careful with words – a true wordsmith. We have sought here to show some of those literary wordsmith's skills, and especially those associated with his desire to rid accounting of loose terminology and to achieve recognition of accounting as a communication language with the associated need to reduce entropy when one receives financial signals from financial reports.

The accounting discipline has failed to progress in the fifty or so years since communication was a major issue occupying the attention of leading accounting theorists. There is an opportunity to redress this if accounting is properly recognized as a communication device, in the way that Shannon and others perceived information and communication generally. This ideal will be achievable only when accounting *tells it as it is*.

Notes

1   Reference here and below is made to material from the University of Sydney Archives, USA P202. This archive contains the hard copy of thousands of correspondence items involving Chambers from 1947–1999. That material is now digitized under the university's Market Price Accounting Archive – accessible as at the end of 2012 from www.sydney.edu.au/business/mpa.
2   The phrase has changed sequentially from 'full and fair' to 'true and correct' and now 'true and fair' – but the general ethos has endured.
3   It is generally acknowledged (see Gaffikin 1988) that the phrase was coined by Nelson (1973: 4).
4   Other early writers included Avery (1953) and, in the 1960s, Mattessich (1964), Briloff (1967; the published version of his 1964 PhD thesis) and Lev (1968, 1969). In the economics literature, Boulding (1961) and Theil (1967a, 1967b) addressed communication issues. An alternative approach to communication was shepherded by Jacob Marschak and Roy Radner, arguably assisting the development of the information economics view of the world (see Mattessich 1980).
5   Clarke et al. (2010) provides an account of the 'Chambers Years' and the founding of the 'Sydney School of Accounting'.
6   One of the writers, Dean, who was a research assistant for Chambers from 1974 to 1976, recalls often being sent to the University of Sydney library to check the exact meaning of words Chambers was considering using. Chambers wanted to be certain that the usage was precise. Augmenting extracts below from Chambers' *An Accounting Thesaurus* (1995) is Chambers' extensive library of over 2500 books that now form part of the Chambers hard copy collection (see note 1). It contains many publications focusing on language and discourse, including Ayer's *Language, Truth and Logic* (1952), Breal's *Semantics: Studies in the Science of Meaning* (1964), Hayakawa's *Language in Thought and Action* (1965), Campbell's *Grammatical Man* (1984) and Postman's *Amusing Ourselves to Death* (1987).
7   This is explored in depth in the 1986 edition of Chambers' *Financial Management*, and is especially revealed in Figure 6.1 in that book and the related text.
8   It formed the abstract of an address to the NSW Computer Society on 29 July 1965 under the title: 'The firm as an information complex' (Chambers 1965).
9   Measurement matters are discussed in a chapter studying this aspect of Chambers' theory (Dean and Clarke 2010).
10 Walker (1992) provides a contrary explanation for the SEC's contestable 'banning' of asset revaluations.
11 Davies (2010: 111) notes also tensions between US and European politicians regarding accounting and between prudential and the corporate regulators – implying that, whereas the IASB was promoting a set of international standards with a view to a 'convergence' with US GAAP, the SEC merely went along for the ride without any real commitment to achieve such an outcome.
12 Magnan and Markarian (2011: 216) note the following as examples of this group: Katz (2008), Whalen (2008), Gingrich (2008) and Zion et al. (2009). They also note that others (as we do) perceived accounting as 'merely an uninvolved messenger' (e.g. Ball 2008; SEC 2008; Turner – quoted in Johnson 2008; Veron 2008; Bonaci et al. 2010; Badertscher et al. 2012).
13 The recent IASB International Financial Reporting Standard 13 (Fair Value Measurement, 2011) adopted a three-level hierarchy equivalent to FAS 157.
14 Disconcertingly, this 'fantasy' suggestion was not new. Some informed observers, such as Taleb (2004, 2007) and Mandelbrot (1999), had been issuing warnings for over a decade.
15 Gottliebsen (2011) has suggested that the US Federal Reserve appears to be committing the 'unpardonable banking sin' – seeking the truth.

References

A mark-to-market history lesson 2011. Online. Available HTTP: http://ftalphaville.ft.com/blog/2009/03/53587/a-mark-to-market-history-lesson/ (accessed 21 September 2011).
Aspray, W. (1985) 'The scientific conceptualization of information: a survey', *Annals of the History of Computing*, 7(2): 117–40.

Avery, H.G. (1953) 'Accounting as a language', *The Accounting Review*, 28(1): 83–87.

Ayer, A.J. (1952) *Language, Truth and Logic*, New York: Dover Publications.

Ayer, A.J. (1955) *Studies in Communication*, London: Secker & Warburg.

Badertscher, B.A., Burks, J.J. and Easton, P.D. (2012) 'A convenient scapegoat: fair value accounting by commercial banks during the financial crisis', *The Accounting Review*, 87(1): 59–90.

Ball, R. (2008) 'Don't blame the messenger... or ignore the message', working paper. Online. Available HTTP: http://faculty.chicagobooth.edu/brian.barry/igm/ShootingtheMessenger2008-10-12.pdf. (accessed 10 January 2012).

Beer, S. (1961) *Cybernetics and Management*, New York: John Wiley.

Bonaci, C.G., Matis, D. and Strouhal, J. (2010) 'Fair value and crisis: defense welcomed', *Proceedings of the 8th WSEAS International Conference on Recent Advances in Management, Marketing, Finances*, Penang, Malaysia, 23–25 March, pp. 71–75.

Boulding, K.E. (1961) *The Image*, Ann Arbor, MI: University of Michigan.

Breal, M. (1964) *Semantics: Studies in the Science of Meaning*, New York: Dover Publications, Inc.

Briloff, A. (1967) *The Effectiveness of Accounting Communication*, New York: Frederick A. Praeger.

Briloff, A. (1979) 5 March letter to Chambers, Chambers Archive, USA P202 #5787.

Bromwich, M. (2007) 'Fair values: imaginary prices and mystical markets', in P.J. Walton (ed.) *The Routledge Companion to Fair Value and Financial Reporting*, London: Routledge, pp. 46–68.

Campbell, J. (1984) *Grammatical Man: Information, Entropy, Language and Life – the Story of the Modern Revolution of Human Thought*, New York: Pelican.

Chambers, R.J. (1952) 'Accounting and business finance', *The Australian Accountant*, November: 14–23.

Chambers, R.J. (1953) *Financial Management*, 2nd edition, Sydney: The Law Book Company.

Chambers, R.J. (1955a) 'Blueprint for a theory of accounting', *Accounting Research*, 6(1): 17–25.

Chambers, R.J. (1955b) 'A scientific pattern of accounting theory', *The Australian Accountant*, February: 73–80.

Chambers, R.J. (1957) 'Detail for a blueprint', *The Accounting Review*, 32(2): 206–15.

Chambers, R.J. (1960) 'Measurement and misrepresentation', *Management Science*, 6(2): 141–48.

Chambers, R.J. (1961) 'Towards a general theory of accounting', Australian Society of Accountants Annual Research Lecture, University of Adelaide, 2 August.

Chambers, R.J. (1962) 'The resolution of some paradoxes in accounting', Australian Society of Accountants Annual Research Lecture, University of Tasmania, 30 April.

Chambers, R.J. (1964) 'Conventions, doctrines and commonsense', *Accountants' Journal*, February: 182–87.

Chambers, R.J. (1965) 'The firm as an information complex', address to the NSW Computer Society, 29 July; abstract of which appears in Chambers letter to Mr G. McAuslan, 8 March 1965, USA P202, #01411.

Chambers, R.J. (1966) *Accounting, Evaluation and Economic Behavior*, Englewood Cliffs, NJ: Prentice Hall.

Chambers, R.J. (1979) 22 March letter to Briloff, Chambers Archive, USA P202 #5788.

Chambers, R.J. (1986) *Financial Management*, 4th edition, Sydney: The Law Book Company.

Chambers, R.J. (1995) *An Accounting Thesaurus: 500 Years of Accounting*, Oxford: Pergamon.

Chanos, J. (2009) 'We need honest accounting: relax regulatory capital rules if need be, but don't let banks hide the truth', *Wall Street Journal*, 23 March.

Cheng, K. (2012) 'Accounting discretion and fair value reporting: a study of US banks' fair value reporting of mortgage backed securities', *Journal of Business Finance & Accounting*, 39(5/6): 531–66.

Cheng, M., Dhaliwal, D.S. and Neamtiu, M. (2011) 'Asset securitization, securitization recourses and information uncertainty', *The Accounting Review*, 86(2): 541–68.

Cherry, C. (1957) *On Communication: A Review, a Survey and a Criticism*, Cambridge, MA: MIT Press.

Clarke, F.L. and Dean, G.W. (2007) *Indecent Disclosure: Gilding the Corporate Lily*, Cambridge: Cambridge University Press.

Clarke, F.L., Dean, G.W. and Wells, M.C. (2010) *The Chambers Years: The Sydney School of Accounting*, Sydney: Sydney University.

Davies, H. (2010) *Financial Crisis: Who is to Blame?* Malden, MA: Polity Press.

Dean, G.W. and Clarke, F.L. (2010) 'Unresolved methodological questions at the cross-section of accounting and finance', in T. Wise and V. Wise (eds) *A Festschrift for Bob Clift, special issue of International Review of Business Research Papers*, 6(5): 20–32.

Dowd, K. and Hutchinson, M. (2010) *Alchemists of Loss: How Modern Finance and Government Intervention Crashed the Financial System*, New York: John Wiley.

Duncan, H.D. (1968) *Communication and Social Order*, New York: Oxford University Press.

Feltham, G. (1972) *Information Evaluation*, Studies in Accounting Research #5, Sarasota, FL: American Accounting Association.

Feltham, G.A. and Demski, J.S. (1970) 'The use of models of information evaluation', *The Accounting Review*, 45(4): 623–40.

Financial Reporting Council (2008) *The Audit Quality Framework*, London. Online. Available HTTP: www.frc.org.uk/documents/pagemanager/frc/promoting_audit_quality_responses/audit%20 quality%20framework%20for%20web.pdf (accessed 10 January 2012).

Gaffikin, M.J.R. (1988) 'Legacy of the golden age: recent developments in the methodology of accounting', *Abacus*, 24(1): 16–36.

Gebhardt, G. and Novotny-Farkas, Z. (2011) 'Mandatory IFRS adoption and accounting quality of European banks', *Journal of Business Finance & Accounting*, 38(3/4): 289–333.

Gingrich, N. (2008) 'Suspend mark-to-market now!', *Forbes*, 29 September. Online. Available HTTP: www. forbes.com/2008/09/29/mark-to-market-oped-cx_ng_0929gingrich.html (accessed 21 September 2011).

Gleick, J. (2011) *The Information: A History, a Theory, a Flood*, London: Fourth Estate.

Gottliebsen, R. (2011) 'Lurching into a banking crisis?', *Business Spectator*, 19 August.

Hayakawa, S. (1965) *Language in Thought and Action: How Men Use Words and Words Use Men*, London: George Allen & Unwin.

Ijiri, Y. (1967) *The Foundations of Accounting Measurement*, Englewood Cliffs, NJ: Prentice Hall.

Isaac, W.M. and Meyer, P.C. (2010) *Senseless Panic: How Washington Failed America*, Hoboken, NJ: John Wiley.

Johnson, C. (2008) 'Wall Street points to disclosure as issue', *Washington Post*, 23 September.

Katz, I. (2008) 'SEC recommends keeping fair-value rule with changes', *Bloomberg*, 30 December.

Laux, C. and Leuz, C. (2009) 'The crisis of fair-value accounting: making sense of the recent debate', *Accounting, Organizations and Society*, 34(6/7): 826–34.

Laux, C. and Leuz, C. (2010) 'Did fair value contribute to the crisis?', *Journal of Economic Perspectives*, 24(1): 93–118.

Lee, T. (1982) 'Chambers and accounting communication', *Abacus*, 18(2): 152–65.

Lev, B. (1968) 'The aggregation problem in financial statements: an informational approach', *Journal of Accounting Research*, 6(2): 247–61.

Lev, B. (1969) *Accounting and Information Theory*, Studies in Accounting Research #2, Chicago: American Accounting Association.

Linsmeier, T. J. (2011) 'Financial reporting and financial crises: the case for measuring financial instruments at fair value in the financial statements', *Accounting Horizons*, 25(2): 409–17.

Magnan, M. (2009) 'Fair value accounting and the financial crisis: messenger or contributor?', working paper, CIRANO – Scientific Publications Paper No. 2009 s-27.

Magnan, M. and Markarian, G. (2011) 'Accounting, governance, and the crisis: is risk the missing link?', *European Accounting Review*, 20(2): 215–31.

Mandelbrot, B.B. (1999) 'A multifractal walk down Wall Street', *Scientific American*, 280(2): 70–73.

Marschak, J. (1955) 'Elements for a theory of teams', *Management Science*, 1: 127–37.

Marschak, J. and Radner, R. (1972) *Economic Theory of Teams*, New Haven, CT: Yale University Press.

Mattessich, R. (1964) *Accounting and Analytical Methods: Measurement and Projection of Income and Wealth in the Micro- and Macro-Economy*, Homewood, IL: R.D. Irwin.

Mattessich, R. (1980) 'On the evolution of theory construction in accounting: a personal account', *Accounting and Business Research*, 10(37A): 158–73.

Moonitz, M. (1972) 'UCLA Berkeley Spring 1971 Course Notes', appended to letter from Maurice Moonitz, 16 May, to the University of Sydney Registrar in support of Chambers being awarded a DSc of Economics, University of Sydney Archives, USA (P202 #12253).

Mosso, D. (2011) 'Financial analysts need sharper accounting tools', *Accounting Horizons*, 25(2): 419–35.

Munchau, W. (2011) *The Meltdown Years: The Unfolding of the Global Economic Crisis*. New York: McGraw Hill.

Nelson, C. (1973) 'A priori research in accounting', in N. Dopuch and L. Revsine (eds) *Accounting Research 1960–1970: A Critical Evaluation*, Urbana, IL: Center for International Education and Research in Accounting, pp. 3–19.

Patterson, S. (2010) *The Quants: How a Small Band of Maths Wizards Took Over Wall Street and Nearly Destroyed It*, London: Random House Business Books.

Postman, N. (1987) *Amusing Ourselves to Death: Public Discourse in the Age of Show Business*, London: Methuen.

Russell, B. (1940) *An Inquiry into Meaning and Truth*, New York: W.W. Norton.

Ryan, S. (2008) 'Accounting in and for the sub-prime crisis', *The Accounting Review*, 83: 1605–39.

Schwarz, N. and Rosse, K. (2011) 'I want you: Uncle Sam sues banks for billions', *Sydney Morning Herald*, Business Day, 5 September: 1, 4.

Securities and Exchange Commission (SEC) (2008) *Report and Recommendations Pursuant to Section 133 of the Emergency Economic Stabilization Act of 2008: Study on Mark-to-Market Accounting*, SEC. Online. Available HTTP: www.sec.gov/news/studies/2008/marktomarket123008.pdf (accessed 21 September 2011).

Shannon, C.E. (1948) 'A mathematical theory of communication', *Bell System Technical Journal*, 27: 379–423, 623–56.

Shannon, C.E., (1949) 'Communication in the presence of noise', *Proceedings of I.R.E.*, 37(1): 10–21.

Shannon, C.E. and Weaver, W. (1949) *The Mathematical Theory of Communication*, Urbana, IL: University of Illinois.

Simon, H.A. (1949) *Administrative Behavior*, New York: Macmillan.

Sterling, R.R. (2006) *Accounting Hall of Fame Remarks, Citation and Response*, 'Response by Robert R Sterling', AAA Meeting, Ohio State University, Fisher College of Business, 7 August, pp. 7–13.

Taleb, N. (2004) *Fooled by Randomness: The Hidden Role of Chance in Life and in the Markets*, London: Penguin.

Taleb, N. (2007) *The Black Swan: The Impact of the Highly Improbable*, London: Penguin.

Thayer, L.O. (1961) *Administrative Communication*, Homewood, IL: Irwin.

Theil, H. (1967a) *Economics and Information Theory*, Chicago and Amsterdam: Rand McNally and North Holland Publishing.

Theil, H. (1967b) 'On the use of information theory concepts in the analysis of financial statements', Report 6722 of the Centre for Mathematical Studies in Business and Economics, University of Chicago.

Veron, N. (2008) 'Fair value accounting is the wrong scapegoat for this crisis', *Accounting in Europe*, 5(2): 63–69.

Walker, R.G. (1992) 'The SEC's ban on upward asset revaluations and the disclosure of current values', *Abacus*, 28(1): 3–35.

Whalen, R.C. (2008) 'The subprime crisis: cause, effect and consequences', Networks Financial Institute Policy Brief No. 2008-PB-04. Online. Available HTTP: http://ssrn.com/abstarct =1113888 (accessed 12 September 2011).

Wiener, N. (1949) *Cybernetics*, Cambridge, MA: MIT Press.

Zandi, M. (2009) *Financial Shock*, Upper Saddle River, NJ: FT Press.

Zion, D., Varshney, A. and Cornett, C. (2009) 'Focusing on fair value', *Credit Suisse Equity Research Report*, 27 June.

Part 2
A variety of media
Beyond numbers

4

The language of corporate annual reports
A critical discourse analysis

Theo van Leeuwen

Introduction

Corporate annual reports are the key vehicles through which companies account for themselves to their stakeholders and ask them to accept their account of themselves and their predictions of future performance. As Bhatia (2012: 80) has said, they are 'the pulse of corporate realities'.

In this chapter I will analyse the lavishly produced annual report of an Australian company engaging in investment in, and management of, commercial real estate through twelve main portfolios, including the 'Office Fund', with which I will be particularly concerned in this chapter. In the year the report deals with, the company performed poorly. The Office Fund portfolio reported a $37m loss and made no distributions to its shareholders. In contrast to specialist institutional shareholders, small shareholders do not always have the expertise or the time to fully understand the details disclosed in the financial sections of annual reports. But annual reports also contain analysis and discussion. This is easier to understand and often downplays the company's weaknesses, in an attempt to maintain or restore shareholder confidence. The resulting contradictions between disclosure and obfuscation, reporting and reassuring can be brought to light by critical discourse analysis.

In a recent paper, Bhatia (2012) noted that corporate annual reports comprise four different discourses. The 'accounting discourse' is realized by financial statements which are endorsed and certified by a public accountant. The 'discourse of finance' is 'a discussion and analysis of the facts and figures' (ibid.: 83), prepared by the company's financial specialists. The 'public relations' discourse, in the form of the chairman's letter to shareholders, aims at reassuring shareholders that the performance of the company is strong and will, in future, be even stronger, or, if the company has performed badly, that improvement is just round the corner. Bhatia points out that these three discourses mutually influence each other because of the way they are contained in a single document. The factual accounting discourse lends credibility to the interpretations, and the interpretations colour the reader's understanding of the accounting discourse. There is, finally, a fourth discourse, the 'legal disclaimer', which casts a shadow of doubt over the company's predictions, but may be hidden away in an unobtrusive corner of the document – in the case of our investment company on the inside of the front cover, in small print and preceding the table of contents. It reads like this:

> This document contains forward looking statements which are identified by words such as "may", "could", "believes", "estimates", "expects", "intends" and other similar words that imply risks and uncertainties. These forward looking statements are subject to known and unknowns risks, uncertainties and other factors that could cause the actual results, performance or achievements of the Fund or Trust to vary materially from those expressed or implied in such forward looking statements.

The report I will analyse in this paper contains all four of these discourses. In addition it has three pages with photographs and short biographies of the company's senior staff, and an appendix that documents the real estate the company holds, in a format which resembles that of real-estate brochures, with photos, short descriptions and details such as the properties' value, capitalization rate, net lettable area and occupancy rate.

I will take Bhatia's characterization of the discourse of the corporate annual report as my point of departure, but while Bhatia analyses the four discourses as 'genres', in terms of their communicative purpose and overall structure, I will focus on content, on the way they understand and represent the company's practices through selective representation and through uses of language which make it often hard to understand precisely what has been going on, and do so mainly in relation to the 'accounting discourse' and the 'public relations' discourse, as I am not an accounting expert but a linguist, and as these are the discourses which make most use of the kinds of linguistic strategies which my approach to discourse analysis is able to reveal. This approach is known as critical discourse analysis (CDA), a form of discourse analysis which focuses on unpacking and critiquing selective and obfuscating uses of language, especially where selection and obfuscation are used to mask contradictions, or to legitimate discrimination and abuses of power (Van Dijk, 1993; Wodak and Meyer, 2009). In the past CDA has often focused on political discourse, but, ever since Fairclough wrote his seminal paper 'The marketization of discourse' (1993), CDA has also paid increasing attention to the corporate discourses which today play such an important role in society.

Methodology: discourse as the recontextualization of social practice

The approach to critical discourse analysis I will use here is based on Bernstein's (1981) notion of 'recontextualization'. As I have explained in greater detail in Van Leeuwen (2008), and as will hopefully become clear from the examples below, I see discourses as ultimately always grounded in social practices, as ultimately always representing what people *do*. But when actions are changed into words, transformations occur. Discourses select what actions will be represented, transform actions through the way they are worded, and add *motives* to actions – purposes, justifications and value judgments. They do so differently depending on the interests that prevail in the social context in which the representation is embedded – hence the use of the term 'recontextualization' rather than 'representation'.

To explain this more fully I will first need to list the key elements of social practices. A sequence of *actions*, occurring in a specific order, forms the backbone of all practices. The actions will involve two principal actors – the '*agents*' who perform the actions and the '*patients*' to whom the actions are done. For both there will be what might be called '*eligibility criteria*' – not everyone can legitimately be given the role agent or patient in a given practice. This is why the annual report contains biographies that detail the credentials of the company's financial experts.

Practices also take place at certain *times*, which may be strictly or more loosely regulated, and they require specific *locations* or spatial arrangements and specific *resources* (tools and materials), both of which are also subject to 'eligibility criteria'.

The actions that make up a practice may be *communicative actions*. In that case they at once form themselves a practice and recontextualize another practice (which, in turn, may either be communicative or not). An annual report, for instance, is itself a practice of company–shareholder communication, made up of communicative actions such as reporting, explaining, predicting and reassuring. But it also recontextualizes other practices such as buying, selling and managing properties. Traditionally the report would be called a 'text' and the other elements of the practice (for instance the producers and readers of the text, its 'agents' and 'patients') 'context'. In the current approach it is no longer necessary to distinguish between 'text' and 'context' as both come together in the concept of 'practice'. What used to be called a 'text' may then either realize all or most of the actions, as in the case of reading a report, or very few. It may even be a 'resource'. A recipe on the kitchen sink, for instance, is a resource for the practice of cooking, required for occasional actions of recipe-consulting that are interspersed with other, non-communicative actions such as peeling potatoes or stirring the sauce.

Analysing an annual corporate report as the recontextualization of company practices requires three steps: (1) analysing the text in terms of the elements of the social practice I have just listed; (2) constructing a 'scenario' from this analysis by rearranging the actions in chronological order; and (3) relating the scenario to the 'motives' that are expressed in the text.

Analysing a text in terms of the elements of social practices is not always straightforward. First, actions are not necessarily realized by verbs. In the sentence 'The Fund's forbearance strategy minimizes risk', for instance, 'forbearance', 'strategy' and 'risk' all express, not objects, but things people *do* – tolerating, planning, risking – even though they are formulated as nouns or nominalizations. Second, the agents and patients of such actions are not always included. Who, for instance, is taking the risks that the company wishes to minimize? Nor is it made explicit who or what is being tolerated by the forbearance strategy. In such cases we will enter an X. The sentence above could therefore be analysed as containing four actions:

> The Fund forbears X.
> The Fund strategizes.
> The Fund minimizes risk.
> X risks.

I will now apply the first step of the analysis to the excerpt below[1]:

Text 1: Forbearance strategy episode

The Fund's forbearance strategy minimizes risk and best preserves Fund asset value. During FY2011, the Office Fund sold 155.0 million of assets and the Fund will continue to monitor the Office Fund's divestment program. Once a certain level of asset sales is achieved and Office Fund debt is refinanced, the Fund will consult Unitholders and recommend strategies to realize Unitholder value. Based on the current disposal program strategies will be formulated prior to December 2011, and a recommendation to Unitholders made prior to the expiry of the BOSI facility in February 2012.

The analysis is shown in Table 4.1. While times are included for some actions, locations and resources have clearly not been considered relevant in this recontextualization.

Table 4.1 Analysis of the forbearance strategy episode

Agent	Action	Patient	Time
The Fund	forbearance strategy		
"	minimize risk		
"	preserve Fund asset value		
The Office Fund	sold $155m of assets		during FY2012
The Fund	monitor	the Office Fund's divestment program	
The Office Fund	divestment program		
X	achieve a certain level of asset sales		
X	refinance	Office Fund debt	
The Fund	will consult	Unitholders	once a certain level of asset sales is achieved and Office Fund debt is refinanced
"	recommend strategies to		
"	realize value	Unitholders	
X	disposal program		
X	formulate strategies		
X	make recommendation to	Unitholders	prior to December 2011
BOSI	[provide] facility	X	prior to expiry of the BOSI facility
"	expire		in February 2012

Step two involves four elements. First, all instances in which the same action is repeated or reformulated are eliminated. Text 1 contains, for instance, four different formulations of a particular (sequence of) actions of the Office Fund:

> sold $155.0 million of assets;
> divestment program;
> achieve a certain level of asset sales;
> disposal program

We will here retain only those which represent a specific 'stage' in the 'divestment program', rather than the terms which denote the 'program' as a whole. Second, agents and patients which are not mentioned in the text but can be inferred from the context are included in square brackets. Third, the actions are rewritten in the active voice and present tense. Fourth, the actions are arranged in chronological order, insofar as possible (an arrow is used to indicate chronology; a '~' to indicate simultaneity; an 'alt' if there is an alternative action and a question mark where chronological order cannot be ascertained). For text 1, this yields the following underlying 'scenario:

BOSI (Bank of Scotland International) lends money [to the Office Fund]
↓
The Fund forbears the Office Fund (gives it time to get its house in order)
↓
The Office Fund sells 155m of assets during FY2011
~

The Fund monitors the Office Fund's 'divestment activities'
↓

[The Office Fund] achieves a certain level of asset sales
↓

The Fund refinances the Office Fund's debt
↓

The Fund consults Unitholders
↓

The Fund formulates strategies prior to December 2011
↓

The Fund recommends strategies to Unitholders prior to BOSI calling in the loan
↓

BOSI calls in the loan in February 2011

Clearly the practice represented in this scenario involves three different agents in closely inter-related actions – the Bank, the Fund (i.e. the company as a whole) and the Office Fund. What is not included, however, is the revaluation of the properties which must have resulted in establishing negative equity, and then in the Bank calling in the loan, which in turn required the Office Fund to engage in its 'divestment program'. Who was responsible for it? Did the Bank call for a revaluation, or was it the 'Group analyst', a company staff member whose biography indicates responsibility for 'valuations, forecasting and modeling'?

The Fund and the Office Fund are represented as two distinct entities. One is in trouble and must sell assets to survive, the other forbears, monitors, and deals with the shareholders. But elsewhere in the report it states that the company has 15 staff, and in the biographies of these staff members no one is specifically listed as being responsible for the Office Fund, or for any of the other portfolios. Investors, on the other hand, invest in specific portfolios.

Clearly, an analysis of this kind can open up gaps, expose the omission of what for some stakeholders may be crucial information. In some cases these gaps can be filled by information provided elsewhere in the report, but this requires very careful reading, very careful comparing, contrasting and cross-referencing.

In reconstructing the 'scenario' that underlies text 1, I eliminated repetitions and reformulations. But critical discourse analysts know that 'over-lexicalization' (Halliday, 1978: 165) can reveal 'areas of intense preoccupation in the experience and values of the group which generates it, allowing the linguist to identify peculiarities in the ideology of that group' (Fowler et al., 1979: 211–12). In the first sentence of text 1, for instance, the Fund's 'forbearance strategy' is re-formulated as 'minimizing risk' and 'preserving value'. Such terms trigger values and are used to justify the company's actions. Awareness of risk, for instance, has, in the past 20 years or so, pervaded many spheres of society. Avoiding risk has therefore become an unquestioned value. The same applies for the repeated use of terms like 'strategy' and 'program' which underline the rationality and purposefulness of the company's approach.

Accounting discourse

In the previous section I focused on the way recontextualization selects what it includes and excludes, the way it rearranges actions according to the rhetorical needs of the practice into which they are recontextualized, and the way it adds oblique justifications which are grounded in the values that prevail in the given context. In this section I will first focus on the way the wording of actions, actors (agents and patients) and timings transforms them in ways that sometimes make it hard to work out who or what is in fact responsible for the recontextualized actions, and then analyse the way in which what Bhatia calls the 'accounting discourse' contextualizes and represents the company's actions and motives.

As explained in more detail in Van Leeuwen (2008), actions can be formulated as *material actions* ('doings'), *semiotic actions* ('meanings') or *mental actions* (actions such as 'knowing', 'feeling' or 'understanding'). One and the same actual action can be recontextualized in any of these three ways. The action of 'recommending' for instance can be formulated as a material action, without any indication of content ('make recommendations'), as a communicative, semiotic action, including an indication of what is recommended ('recommend strategies'), or as a mental action (e.g. 'prefer strategies'). It is always of interest to ask what kinds of actors are associated with what kinds of actions. In text 1 'the Fund' is recontextualized as the agent of mental and semiotic actions (it 'strategizes', 'monitors', 'consults' and 'recommends') while the Office Fund is recontextualized as the agent of material actions (it 'sells', 'divests', and so on), and also as the patient of the Fund's actions of 'monitoring' and 'refinancing'. In reality the two appear to be one and the same group of people. But they are here represented as distinct entities, with the left hand apparently not knowing (unless they 'monitor') what the right hand does.

Material actions can be *transactive*, involving two parties, so that the action is represented as actually having an effect on people or things, or *non-transactive*, as a kind of behaviour which reveals something about the agent, but not about what he or she does in or to the world. Many of the Fund's actions are of the latter kind: 'minimizing risk', 'preserving value', 'forbearing' – actions that are represented as having value in and of themselves, rather than on the basis of their external impact.

Actions may also be either *activated*, represented dynamically, *as* actions, or *de-activated*, represented in a static way, as though they are objects or qualities. In text 1, the same action is sometimes activated ('sell assets') sometimes de-activated ('disposal program', 'divestment program'). To some degree this is a matter of style. 'Lexical density' (Halliday and Martin, 1993: 76) is typical of formal writing. But de-activation also allows the systematic deletion of the people involved in the de-activated actions, especially of 'patients'. This is perhaps most evident in the way the actions of the Bank ('lending' and 'calling in the loan') are de-activated ('the BOSI facility', 'the expiry of the BOSI facility').

Actions may also be either *agentialized*, represented as being brought about by human agency, or *de-agentialized*, represented as being brought about in ways that are impermeable to human action, for example by natural forces or unconscious processes. The clearest example in text 1 is, again, 'the expiry of the BOSI facility', which gives the impression that the action results from the inexorable progress of time, rather than from a financial decision.

Finally actions may be represented as *generalized actions* or as what I call *distillations*. Generalizations abstract away from the specific actions that make up a practice or some episode that forms part of a practice, and label the practice or episode as a whole, as when the Office Fund's actions are called a 'divestment program' or the Fund's practice a 'forbearance strategy'. In the case of distillation, a quality or aspect of the action, often peripheral, is 'distilled' from the whole and used to name the whole of the action, usually for purposes of justification or critique. In text 1, actions such as 'preserving value' and 'minimizing risks' are distillations. They denote the intended effect and the purpose of the 'forbearance strategy' rather than the whole. The same can be said of action nouns like 'strategy' and 'program'.

When it comes to the recontextualization of actors, two types of transformation are particularly relevant. The first is *impersonalization*, the representation of human agents by means of abstract or concrete nouns that do not include the feature 'human', for instance representing human actions as performed by the institution or organization to which specific agents belong, as is the case throughout text 1 ('BOSI', 'The Fund', 'The Office Fund'). The 'unit holders', on the other hand, are personalized. Of course the staff members of the Fund are also personalized, in the biographies. But in the rest of the document no staff member is ever mentioned by name, so that no one can ever be linked to specific actions, as would be the case, for instance, in news reports.

Timing is a key aspect of many practices, including those of the Fund, and timings, too, can be recontextualized in a number of different ways. A key distinction is that between the *time summons* and *synchronization* (Van Leeuwen, 2008: 76ff.). In the case of the time summons, timings are authoritatively ordained, whether by a school bell or a schedule of deadlines. Synchronization is timing by reference to 'the successive order of events in some other change continuum', as the sociologist Elias has put it (1992: 43), whether those events are natural, as in deciding when to harvest, social (as in the case of text 1, where actions must be synchronized with the sale of assets, or the 'expiry of a facility'), or mechanical, as in the timings of the clock. In text 1 there is a clear difference between the timing of the Bank's actions and the timing of the Fund's actions. The former are authoritative ('expiry'), the latter carefully attuned to auspicious external events.

Analysing annual reports with tools of this kind reveals issues of critical relevance. The difference between actions of the Fund and the Office Fund, the one engaged in mental and semiotic action, the other in material action; the representation of the Bank's actions as inescapable facts of nature; the representation of unit holders as 'patients' who are forever unable to engage in any action other than 'making inquiries regarding your investment such as changing your details' (back cover) – all point to an account in which it appears no one can be held to account for any specific decision or action. The 'Responsible Entities of the Funds' and the 'Directors of Responsible Entities' may be listed on the back page of the document, but there is no way of knowing for which of the reported actions they are actually responsible.

The four pages of the annual report which deal specifically with the Office Fund contain six sections: (1) Market Overview; (2) Fund Overview (including a section headed 'performance' and a section headed 'debt summary'); (3) Property Overview; (4) Strategy and Outlook; (5) Financial Information; and (6) Property Information. The whole opens with a glossy colour photo of a shiny new office building at night, bathed in light, and a text box headed 'highlights' with a positive message, against a luscious green background:

Maintained lender support:

– short-term debt extensions

Repaid $155.0m in debt with sale proceeds from:

– five properties

– Units in [company]

The 'Market Overview' which follows discusses the demand for office space. 'Total vacancy' has decreased and 'CBD markets are absorbing new stock, while non-CBD markets are back-filling existing vacant space': 'As a result, the outlook for the Fund's assets has improved. The Fund is … focused on improving property value in light of ongoing required asset sales.'

But what does 'improving property value' mean when properties are being sold below their value to repay debts at short notice?

The next section, headed 'Fund Overview', opens with a table of factual data such as the date of commencement of the Fund, the Fund Expiry Date, etc., and lists, in its sixth row, annual distribution as 'NA', with a footnote in very fine print: 'Value per Unit from a Unitholder's perspective is nil per Unit.' It is only then, in the paragraph headed 'performance' that the full situation is revealed, and called by its name – 'poor' performance, 'soft' market conditions and, most of all, no prospect of any return for the shareholders:

Text 2: Debt reduction

The Fund's poor financial position required all excess cash to reduce senior lender debt and no FY2011 distribution was possible. Further, it is unlikely that Unitholders will receive any further distributions of income or capital prior to Fund expiry, if at all. The negative net asset position of $34.7 million is due to lower asset valuations reflecting soft market conditions for assets of the quality held by the Fund and the senior lender requirement for asset sales despite these market conditions.

Table 4.2 shows the full analysis of the text.

Table 4.2 Analysis of the debt-reduction text

Agent	Action	Patient	Timing
The (Office) Fund	poor financial position		
The (Office) Fund	required excess cash to reduce debt	senior lender	
X	no distribution	Unitholders	FY2011
	not receive further distributions of income or capital		prior to Fund expiry
The (Office) Fund	expire		
X	lower asset valuations		
?	soft market conditions	?	
The (Office) Fund	hold assets of quality		
senior lender	require asset sales		
X	asset sales		
?	market conditions	?	

Reconstructing the underlying 'scenario' on the basis of this analysis paints a picture that differs from that of the 'forbearance' text in the section that provides a financial review of the company as a whole:

The Office Fund holds assets of quality

~

The market X

↓

X values assets at a low level

↓

Senior lenders require excess cash and asset sales [from the Office Fund]

↓

The Office Fund sells assets

↓

The Office Fund repays debt [to the Bank]

↓

The Office Fund makes no distributions to shareholders prior to Office Fund 'expiry'

↓

X discontinues the Office Fund

First of all, the role of the overarching company is deleted here. In the 'forbearance' text, the company as a whole ('the Fund') refinanced the Office Fund, then consulted with shareholders, then formulated a strategy and then recommended this strategy to Unitholders. Here only the actions of the Office Fund (now, confusingly, referred to as 'the Fund') are included.

The market ('soft market conditions') is blamed, even though the 'Market Overview', earlier in the same section, spoke of increasing demand rather than 'soft conditions'. Two terms, 'position' and 'condition', also deserve comment. They denote the end result of actions which are themselves excluded from the report. Actions are here transformed into 'states of being' for which no one can be held responsible, a form of de-agentialization which, elsewhere, I called 'existentialization' (Van Leeuwen, 2009).

The 'Strategy and Outlook' section that follows is brief:

Text 3: Strategy and outlook of the Office Fund

In order to stabilize the capital structure of the Fund, asset sales continue with funds used to repay a portion of the Westpac and CMBS debt. Fost FY2011 balance date, the following properties are for sale [3 properties are listed]. Reflecting the Fund's debt position, no distributions are forecast for FY2012.

Table 4.3 shows the analysis.

Table 4.3 Analysis of the Office Fund Strategy and Outlook

Agent	Action	Patient	Timing
X	stabilize structure	Fund	
X	asset sales		
X	use funds to replay a portion of the debts	Westpac and CMBS	
X	balance		
X	sell properties		Post-FY2011 balance date
X	forecast distributions		
X	not distribute		FY2012

The underlying scenario resembles that of the performance review section quoted in text 2, although there is at least one instance of an abstract reformulation introducing a justification ('stabilize structure') as well as another instance of 'existentialization' ('debt position'):

The Office Fund sells assets
↓
The Office Fund partially repays Westpac and CMBS
↓
The Office Fund draws up the balance sheets
↓
The Office Fund forecast distributions [to shareholders]
↓
The Office Fund sells further assets post FY2011 balance date
↓
The Office Fund makes no distributions [to shareholders] FY2012
↓
X discontinues The Office Fund

The 'Financial Information' section that follows consists of Balance Sheet and Profit and Loss statements that detail the liabilities and losses of the Fund and fully reveal its precarious position, with debts of over $150 million, against an asset value of just under $140 million, even after the asset sales mentioned in the 'highlights' textbox. Unlike running prose, tables cannot obfuscate or omit figures, and they are certified and endorsed by a public accountant. But when they appear as an appendix to the kind of review sections discussed earlier in this chapter, they also function to lend credibility to interpretations and forecasts which, as we have seen, make a much more selective use of facts and figures and at times appear to obfuscate.

Public-relations discourse

Bhatia (2012: 85) characterizes the 'public relations discourse' of the Chairman's letter in corporate annual reports as follows:

> This discourse, of course, is a further resemiotisation of the earlier discourses, and is meant to reassure stakeholders that the performance of the company is reasonably strong and the future seems even better than the past. There are few references of facts and figures, which form an integral part of the two earlier discourses, and most of the estimations and predictions are based on impressions and hopes of the chairman.

Amernic and Craig (2006), discussing the same genre, call for 'greater accountability for CEO-Speak' (ibid.: 137), and show how Chairman's letters reduce the complex world of companies to 'abstractions articulated in accounting language' (ibid.: 81) and embellish them with metaphors and rhetorical flourishes.

The Chairman's letter of the annual report discussed in this chapter is in fact co-signed by the company's Non-Executive Chairman and Managing Director and comes at the beginning of the 68-page report.

After an introduction, the letter opens with a section titled 'Significant events during FY2011'. All are formulated as positive 'achievements', although, reading between the lines, many are measures needed to placate the Banks: refinancing five funds; reducing borrowings; extending the term to expiry of three funds; sold/contracted to sell $243.6 million in assets. This is followed by a lengthy review of the Australian property market which, like the 'market overview' in the Office Fund section, indicates 'stronger demand' and 'lower than average supply', but in a guarded way, and with an eye for challenges such as the influence of online shopping on the retail property market. The 'Summary and Outlook' section follows:

Text 4: Chairman's summary and outlook

The latter half of FY2011 marks the first stage in the transition of the Portfolio towards stabilized, income producing investments focused on restoring Unitholder value.

The implementation of strategies to stabilise Funds and Trusts via restructuring and refinancing, combined with positive achievements from active asset management, has resulted in the reinstatement or increase in distributions, and forecast distributions, in six Funds and Trusts.

While the financial position of some Funds and Trusts limits the strategic options available, [the company] continues to work diligently to maximize the potential outcomes for Unitholders, and we look forward to communicating our progress over the coming year.

The company's problems are acknowledged in this excerpt, albeit obliquely and euphemistically ('the financial position of some Funds and Trusts limits the strategic options available'), and without fully disclosing how many Funds and Trusts are in this position (six, it would appear). However, the overall tone is bright ('active', 'positive') and the company is 'working diligently to maximize the potential outcomes for Unitholders' and 'looking forward to communicating progress'. An analysis is given in Table 4.4.

Table 4.4 Analysis of Chairman's Summary and Outlook

Agent	Action	Patient	Time
The Portfolio	transits towards stabilized investments		the latter half FY2011 marks the first stage
"	transits towards income producing investments	X	"
Investments	produce income	X	"
Investments	restore value	Unitholder	"
X	implementation of strategies		
X	stabilize	Funds and Trusts	
X	restructure	X	
X	refinance	X	
X	positive achievements from active asset management		
X	reinstate distributions		
Six Funds and Trusts	distribute or increase	X	
"	forecast distributions	X	
X	financial position	some Funds and Trusts	
X	strategic options available		
the Fund	works diligently		
the Fund	maximize outcomes	Unitholders	
we	look forward to communicating progress		over the coming year
we	communicate progress	X	

55

In contrast to the 'financial review' examples I have given above, the focus here is not on the company's actions but on abstract reformulations. When all over-lexicalization is removed, the scenario is brief:

The Fund refinances Trusts and Funds during the latter half of FY2011
$\downarrow$
The Fund reinstates distributions to Unitholders
ALT
The Fund increases distributions to Unitholders
ALT
[The Fund does not increase distributions] ('limited strategic options')
$\downarrow$
The Fund communicates progress over the coming year to X

The abstract reformulations ('distillations') reformulate the two main aspects of the 'strategy', 'selling assets' and 're-instating distributions', in ways that suggest that the company's approach is proactive, strategic and rational. Here are seven reformulations of the action of selling assets to reduce debt.

restructure;
refinance;
active asset management;
stabilize investments;
strategic options;
implement strategies.

The reinstatement of distributions is similarly over-lexicalized:

maximize potential outcomes;
reinstatement or increase of distributions;
income producing investments.

As in the 'forbearance' text, this text ascribes both mental and semiotic actions to the company, and, as well as objectivating agency through references to the company, it also personalizes the message with two 'we's. The opening statement establishes the agency of time ('the latter half of FY2011 marks the first stage in the transition of the Portfolio to ...'), as does the reference to 'progress' towards the end.

In short, the letter uses at least four strategies to downplay the company's problems and reassure the shareholders: (1) start and end with positive messages, and give more space to positive achievements than to weaknesses; (2) formulate concrete actions in abstract ways to highlight the strategic nature of the company's approach; (3) use figures selectively and downplay the extent of the company's problems; (4) never name the Funds and Trusts which have performed badly, least of all the Office Fund, on which I have focused in this paper, and whose investors are not likely to receive positive communication about 'progress'.

Above all, the letter is as much about predicting the future as it is about financial reporting. It must, as Bhatia has said (2012: 86), 'manage the sentiments of the public and the shareholders so as not to make any dramatic share price movement'. The critical analysis of texts of this kind is clearly important in a time when the power of corporations is steadily growing, and in which public media generally do not call companies to account to the same degree as they do with politicians.

Note

1 As 'patients' I include only human 'patients'. This category should therefore not be confused with grammatical objects, even though 'patients' are often realized as grammatical objects.

References

Amernic, J. and Craig, R. (2006) *CEO Speak: The Language of Corporate Leadership.* Montreal: McGill-Queen's University Press.

Bernstein, B. (1981) 'Codes, modalities and the process of cultural reproduction: a model' *Language and Society* 19: 327–363.

Bhatia, V. (2012) 'Creative exploitation of socio-pragmatic space in professional discourse', in R.H. Jones (ed.) *Discourse and Creativity.* Harlow: Pearson, pp. 75–92.

Elias, N. (1992) *Time: An Essay.* Oxford: Blackwell.

Fairclough, N. (1993) 'The marketization of discourse', *Discourse and Society* 4(2): 133–168.

Fowler, R., Hodge, B., Kress, G. and Trew, T. (1979) *Language and Control.* London: Routledge & Kegan Paul.

Halliday, M.A.K. (1978) *Language as Social Semiotic.* London: Arnold.

Halliday, M.A.K. (1996) *An Introduction to Functional Grammar.* 2nd edn. London: Arnold.

Halliday, M.A.K. and Martin, J.R. (1993) *Writing Science: Literacy and Discursive Power,* London: The Falmer Press.

Van Dijk, T.A. (1993) 'Principles of critical discourse analysis', *Discourse and Society* 4(2): 249–284.

Van Leeuwen, T. (2008) *Discourse and Practice: New Tools for Critical Discourse Analysis.* New York: Oxford University Press.

Van Leeuwen, T. (2009) 'Discourse as the recontextualization of social practice: a guide', in R. Wodak and M Meyer (eds) *Methods of Critical Discourse Analysis.* London: Sage, pp. 144–161.

Wodak, R. and Meyer, M. (2009) *Methods of Critical Discourse Analysis.* London: Sage.

5

Visual perspectives

Jane Davison

What is the visual in accounting and why is it important?

What do we understand by the visual in relation to accounting? Why is it important? Accountants and non-accountants are sometimes perplexed as to what is meant by the relationship between accounting and the visual, for surely accounting is all about numbers? The technicalities of accounting numbers and their impact on users have received strong attention from regulators, practitioners and researchers. Yet linguistic and visual media are just as important in communicating issues relevant to accounting. Narratives have come to constitute a significant part of regulatory and voluntary financial reporting, and research on accounting narratives is well established. The visual is similarly significant, but until recently has been neglected in accounting communication research.

Visualization that is relevant to accounting exists in various media, and takes various forms, which may be two-dimensional or three-dimensional, static or moving. In financial reporting and related documents, visualization occurs in the pictures and photographs that form part of corporate disclosures; in the graphs, charts, diagrams that visually represent numerical information; in sketches of intellectual capital; and in the format, typography and colour of numbers and narratives. This visualization actively conveys messages that interact with our reception of the financial statements. Beyond accounting documents, visual images (pictures, photographs, caricatures, cartoons, logos) circulate more generally in the media, in films, and in press releases or advertising, moulding our impressions, for example, of accountants' professional identity or of business leadership, or relevant to visual branding. The visual set-up of web pages directs our thought processes and classifies information. Architecture communicates messages about the professions, including accounting, and frames the business space we occupy.

It is essential that attention be given to the role of the visual in the accounting arena for a number of reasons. First, the visual has become ubiquitous in business and everyday life, in association with the rise in digital technology that has permitted ease of photographic reproduction and electronic dissemination. Second, evidence from psychology points to the power of the visual in memory and in cognition: pictures attract more mental attention than words, and have more power than words in cognitive memory. Third, visualization can provide important framing and impression management to the reception of information and thus influence decision-making. Finally visual media can carry messages beyond the capacity of accounting statements.

There has nonetheless been suspicion of the worth and meaning of the visual since classical times. Critics of the visual might argue that its meaning always remains ambiguous and subjective; yet this is true of aspects of the accounting framework. It might be objected that business visualizations belong to marketing or advertising rather than accounting; yet both professions are involved in varying degrees of representation and construction rather than in scientific objectivity. It might be argued that the visual is illustration, or at best information; yet the visual carries messages, moulds impressions and directs our thought processes. While it might be the case that the visual does not easily lend itself to quantification, this does not give grounds for its dismissal.[1]

This chapter demonstrates the omnipresence, importance and interest of the visual in relation to accounting. It provides a review that should be of use to practitioners, students and researchers, and to those with or without accounting knowledge. It also aims to bring together for the first time the various strands of research work in this area. Visual aspects have been fundamental to the presentation of accounts since medieval times and earlier, but have extended to further dimensions over recent decades, in the creative design attention to corporate reporting and web pages, for example. While for some time the visual remained a surprising 'blind spot' in accounting research, in recent years it has been fast-developing. The breadth and richness of visual studies in accounting is perhaps quite surprising given the general view of accounting as a technical and quantitative discipline with no clear links with the visual.

This chapter therefore aims, in conjunction with relevant research: (1) to outline the forms that the visual may take in accounting contexts; (2) to explore methods and theory that may be useful in examining the visual in accounting; (3) to consider the issues that are communicated through visual forms; and (4) to suggest future paths for the visual in accounting.

Visual forms

A few definitions and indications of visual forms are necessary. It should, however, be remembered that visual media often consist of several elements, that visual media are often mixed with linguistic messages and that the following forms do not constitute an exhaustive list. An appendix lists the main research papers on visual aspects of accounting, classified by the visual form addressed.

A word of definition: graphics, graphic design, graphs

The terms 'graphics', 'graphic design' and 'graphs' cause frequent confusion regarding definitions of the visual in accounting. 'Graphics' and 'graphic design' are generally used to designate the attention given to all visual media in an accounting document such as an annual report, including pictures, photographs, graphs, charts, colour and the visual presentation of numbers and words. 'Graphs', on the other hand, designates the visual representation of quantitative data, such as column graphs (see Beattie and Jones' (2008) illustration of graphical components using a typical five-year column graph), line graphs or pie charts.

Graphs

Some considerable attention has been devoted to the role of financial graphs in financial reporting and their scope for impression management, notably in the work of Beattie and Jones (for example, 1992, 2001, 2002). Financial graphs are voluntary disclosures that fall outside full audit procedures. Graphs (especially column graphs) are commonly prominently displayed in the early pages of annual reports to highlight key financial performance indicators, and are often additionally used to chart many other aspects of a company's operations throughout the pages of annual reports. Financial graphs have communicative power: graphs provide interludes of colour and interest in the pages of annual reports, appeal to spatial intelligence, convey patterns and relationships, and are memorable. Yet graphs can also be used to manipulate impressions of corporate performance: this may take the form of selectivity, or it may be through various forms of graph distortion. Flattering impressions may be conveyed through selective highlighting of favourable years or of favourable key performance variables, or through the distortion of the components of graph construction using devices such as the exaggeration of basic measurements, or the use of non-zero or broken axes. In the UK there has been considerable evidence of material discrepancy in the financial graphs of top companies. Partly as a result of Beattie and Jones' work, UK regulation now specifies that where financial graphs are incorporated into annual reports care should be taken with their objectivity and a set of guidelines should be followed (ASB 2000). Beattie and Jones (2008) provide an excellent review of research on the use of graphs in financial reporting, to which the reader is directed.

Traditional graphs can, however, become over-complicated when presenting multivariate information, such as that of accounting. Less conventionally, accounting information may be presented through cartoon graphics, and in particular schematic faces (see illustrations in Smith and Taffler 1996). It has been shown that schematic faces can be more effective in communicating accounting information than the more traditional methods of financial statements and financial ratios (Smith and Taffler 1996), and that information is processed more quickly when presented in this format. Contemporary communication, particularly through email and text messaging, has seen recent widespread adoption of schematic faces in the form of emoticons, indicating the importance and richness of facial expression and associated emotional and social signals in extending the messages of verbal language (see Malamed (2011) on visual language such as schematic faces in the work of designers), which suggests that this is an area worth exploring further in accounting communication.

Although much research attention has been directed to conventional financial graphs in annual reports, and despite their undeniable power and direct relationship with accounting numbers, on average, in the UK, they occupy a small amount of the space of financial reporting (one page), compared to the much larger amount of space (ten pages) occupied by pictures and photographs (Davison and Skerratt 2007: 57).

Pictures and photographs

As well as occupying more space, pictures and photographs arguably have more impact and power than financial graphs, since they connect directly with organizations and society through abstract forms (Figure 5.1) and through representations of people, objects and places (Figure 5.2), even if they do not (like graphs) connect directly with the accounting numbers. Pictures and photographs frequently carry symbolical or ideological messages as well as abstract design or 'apparent' representation – 'apparent', because all pictures and photographs are constructions however straightforward they might appear. The secondary or symbolic messages are often the more important, but are likely to be ambiguous and open to interpretation. For example, in the images of the 1998 Ernst & Young annual report front cover (Figure 5.1), the viewer might 'see the recognised accounting qualities of balance, measurement and

Figure 5.1 Abstract forms: Ernst & Young Annual Report 1998 front cover (Courtesy of Ernst & Young)

Figure 5.2 Representational forms: Ernst & Young Annual Review 2001 front cover (Courtesy of Ernst & Young)

harmony in their geometry and abstraction'. This is to be contrasted with the 2001 front cover (Figure 5.2) where,

> the image is one of surprise and discovery, perhaps of hidden value in the hidden faces of the canvases. The linguistic text 'expect ...' reinforces this message of anticipation and imagination, further injects the mystery of unspecified things to come, repeated throughout the inner pages [...] that put creative skills to the fore as follows:

Expect to be surprised	Expect originality
Expect imagination	Expect diversity
Expect passion	Expect to be challenged

> *(Davison, 2011b: 264)*

However, these interpretations will not be the only possible 'readings', and other interpretations might be equally valid.

Many and diverse themes may be traced in the pictures and photographs of annual reports. For example, it has been suggested that in the US the influence of television may be discerned in the progressive trivialization of annual reports with photographs, prizes and other material that serve both to entertain and to add credibility to the accounting statements (Graves et al. 1996). The impact of globalization in organizations and society has been shown in an array of striking cartoons, maps, diagrams, pictures and photographs that have appeared in annual reports and that reflect changing global ethnoscapes (migration of people), technoscapes (movement of technology), financescapes (rapid movement of global capital), mediascapes (new communication media) and ideoscapes (fluid ideology) (Preston and Young 2000). In a very different view of the importance of the human face to that of the schematic faces discussed in connection with graphs, an increasing representation of human faces may be traced in the photographs of corporate reporting, and although many of these representations may be interpreted as being dehumanizing, paradoxically the fact of their presence indicates an Other-interestedness by corporations in addition to the expected presence of self-interest (Campbell et al. 2009).

Not all pictures and photographs of interest to accounting are contemporary and business-based. An alternative field of interest is to be found in the art works that provide visual comment on accounting-related matters. Historically, several portraits of merchants and book-keepers from the Dutch art of the fifteenth to eighteenth centuries, for example by Vermeer, incorporate the image of an account-book, which plays more than a merely incidental role (Yamey 1989). Italian Renaissance art includes the well-known 1495 portrait by Jacopo de Barbari of Luca Pacioli (author of the first published account of the double-entry book-keeping system, in the *Summa de arithmetica, geometrica, proportioni et proportionalita* of 1494) with Guidobaldo di Montefeltro, gazing together at a suspended icosahexahedron. The portrait has attracted some attention in the fields of art history and mathematics for its use of perspective and its depiction of mathematics, but rather less attention in accounting.

Sketches/diagrams/maps/colour/typography/logos and other aspects

As well as graphs, pictures and photographs, there are many further forms of the visual in corporate reporting and other accounting functions, although so far these have received scant research attention. Sketches, diagrams and maps may convey messages about products, supply networks and company locations. For example, intellectual capital statements often take the form of diagrammatic representations (see illustrations in Mouritsen et al. 2001), and stories and sketches are arguably as important as digits in transforming intellectual capital from 'invisibility or nothingness into visibility or somethingness' (Mouritsen et al. 2001).

Numbers and words are in themselves visual representations. In the field of statistics Tufte's books, *The visual display of quantitative information* (Tufte 1983, (1990)) and *Envisioning information* are well known, and might be drawn on in accounting. Among many other matters, Tufte discusses colour, little-researched in accounting despite the fact that 'the presence of colour in our environment is basic, integral and pervasive', is important in business and 'has the ability to impress and to affect moods and behaviour' and may therefore not be neutral in financial reporting (Courtis 2004a: 265–66). Colour graphics can improve decision-making (So and Smith 2002), while adding aesthetics, especially colour, to an annual report makes it more likely that investors will place a higher value on the company (Townsend and Shu 2010). Typography and font are also important in mood-setting, and communicating a corporate style that might lean more towards the conventional or the innovative and creative. Thus, accounting texts can be explored for their pictorial form rather than their textual and representational content, and the acknowledged power of the visual to classify, engage and mobilise (Quattrone 2009: 113–14). Indeed, early Italian accounting textbooks of the sixteenth and seventeenth centuries attach great importance to visual presentation, and Luca Pacioli himself included a striking visualization of Bede's counting system in his *Summa de arithmetica, geometrica, proportioni et proportionalita* (Figure 5.3).

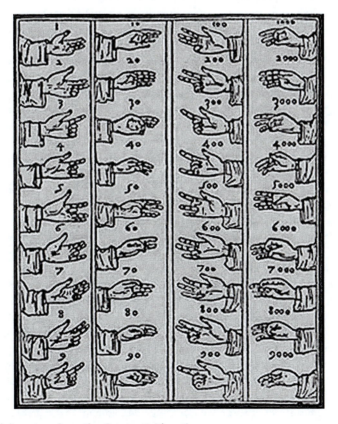

Figure 5.3　Bede's system from the *Summa Arithmetica*

Branding is essentially visual (Schroeder 2005). Companies spend large sums on branding, but accounting for branding, as for other intangibles, is inconsistent, and expenditure on branding is only capitalized when it is purchased rather than internally generated. Elements of branding such as logos allow for instant recognition of an organization, but also carry rich and sometimes contradictory messages. For example, the supposed modernization of the visual branding of the ICAEW based on the figure of Economia (see the ICAEW website) continues to carry old and contradictory messages (Page and Spira 2009). The branding (carried in logos, letterheads, leaflets, annual reports, web pages and television video) of the collapsed Bradford and Bingley Bank began in the 1960s using the well-recognized black bowler-hat as a symbol of quintessential Britishness and good *class*, and old-boy networks that were traditionally associated with London banks and their male 'City gent' who was perhaps dull but yet reliable and trustworthy (Davison 2009). Over the years, with globalization, a changing society and a deregulated and more competitive business environment, and alongside the bank's more innovative lending and funding initiatives, the traditional bowler-hat image metamorphosed by the early twenty-first century into a duo of mixed gender in a more aggressive yet humorous *detective* mould, followed by the more open, colourful and seductive *music-hall* female identity of 'Ms Bradford & Bingley'. Thus, logos may have a rhetorical impact (Amernic and Craig 2000).

Web pages, film, theatre and architecture

Beyond forms of the visual that remain static and two-dimensional, there are dynamic and two-dimensional visual forms that are of interest in an accounting context.

Web pages rely especially heavily on visual layout to structure information and visual clues to navigate between pages and between layers of information. Corporate web pages and web-based financial reporting, in an early stage of development around 2000, are a decade later the primary source of corporate information for all major companies. Corporate web pages attract major investment and creative design, becoming steadily more sophisticated to include moving interactive pages and video in addition to static images. They have been almost totally neglected by research. One notable exception is a study that shows, with regard to CSR communications, that web-page readers have greater trust for messages conveyed by means of the visual media of photographs and video as compared to those conveyed in narrative text (Cho et al. 2009).

Film and theatre are further dynamic visual media, used in the organizational realm – for example the annual general meeting may be construed as a theatrical and highly visual event (Biehl-Missal 2011). Organizations also produce films and presentational videos about themselves, but these internally generated visual media have attracted little research interest. A number of popular films produced externally in the UK and the US have included accountants among their characters; indeed a film called *The Accountant* (2001) won an Academy Award for the Best Live Action Short Film. Sometimes these characters conform to stereotypical views of accountants, as males in poor physical shape, with boring and fastidious work habits, and who are shy, spineless, cold and with no social conscience (Cory 1992), but later films portray accountants in a more positive light and as coming from a more diverse range of backgrounds (Dimnik and Felton 2006).

Architecture is a complex visual form that incorporates both two-dimensional and three-dimensional elements. In the stone inscriptions of ancient Egyptian temples, accounting numbers were frequently combined with linguistic texts and pictorial scenes to produce a monumental discourse that made possible the construction and perpetuation of an established scheme of order as Ezzamel (2009) shows in a reproduced extract. Frequently, architecture is a rhetorical status symbol, and this can often be seen in the grand buildings that organizations construct as their headquarters. This was argued to be the *raison d'être* of the magnificent nineteenth-century

Victorian neo-Baroque Chartered Accountants Hall in the City of London, which was conceived to promote the growing importance of the accountancy profession and to vie with the headquarters of the then better-established English medical and legal professions (McKinstry 1997). Economics and accounting, even architecture, has paid little attention to the striking architecture that accompanied the recent growth in power of the financial sector. Yet

> even in financially sophisticated times, however, symbols matter, and the message communicated by these symbols is one which cannot be communicated in any other way. There is a visceral appeal of an architecturally distinguished building to the senses that speaks to us in a way that the cerebral appeal of pure information cannot.
>
> *(McGoun 2004: 1085)*

Visual research methods and theories[2]

The importance and ubiquity of the visual in contemporary society has been reflected in the 'pictorial turn' (Mitchell 1994) taken by academic arts and social science disciplines as a shift from the earlier 'linguistic turn' (Rorty 1979). There are signs that visual research is now starting to become established in the field of accountancy, but it has been slower to develop. One of the reasons for resistance to the visual in accounting has been the difficulties associated with finding appropriate visual methods and theories. Visual media communicate in different ways from verbal language, and are inherently ambiguous and open to multiple and subjective interpretations. It is therefore hard to conduct 'scientific' empirical research of large samples, since visual media largely elude quantification. While language-based theories can be related to the visual, they need careful adaptation and many would argue that pictorial meaning cannot be expressed in linguistic terms, leading to an acute need for 'picture theory' (Mitchell 1994), which is often interdisciplinary. The following outlines some of the main methods and theories that have been employed in visual accounting research.

Visual content analysis

Visual content analysis is an empirically driven method that has been used by a number of researchers. Typically such analyses count and/or code pictures and photographs, and thus frequently combine quantitative and qualitative techniques. For example, content analyses have been used to examine photographs in annual reports, in the context of gender and diversity studies (Benschop and Meihuizen 2002), or to examine films in the context of studies of accountants' professional identity (Dimnik and Felton 2006). Sometimes content analysis is used in conjunction with questionnaire surveys, and frequently it is used as the basis of statistical analyses. Visual content methods have the benefits of enabling the examination of a large number of images, and permitting quantitative analyses comparing variables. They also need to be used with great care, since there are problems such as: deciding what constitutes a visual image; how to code mixed data that contain several images, a picture together with a photograph, or a picture together with text; how to deal with words presented as a visual image; interpreting the meaning of an image – even description may not be straightforward (Bell and Davison 2012). Further, there are quantification difficulties, and difficulties regarding whether, for example, to measure by occurrence or by space occupied. Studies sometimes give scant detail on the precise method that has been employed. Visual media are complex modes of communication that do not easily lend themselves to quantification, and content analysis is often poorly supported by theory.

Visual elicitation

Visual elicitation methods, originating in social anthropology, are new to accounting research, although they are well-established elsewhere. They too are empirically driven, as the visual data stimulate the research. Images can be pre-existing images discussed in an interview, or they can be generated by the research participants, thereby giving the participants a high degree of control over their choice and selection of images (Warren 2005). Such methods can be usefully employed, for example with archival history or oral history, and with groups as well as individuals (Parker 2009). They can be used as 'auto-photography', where research participants are enjoined to take photographs of objects associated with their professional selves. Subsequently these photographs can be coded, and thus prove useful in research into the professional identity of accountants (Warren and Parker 2009).

Visual experiments

Experiments also feature in visual methods, sometimes supported by theory from psychology, where such experiments are a regular research method. Experiments typically involve presenting groups of students with visual stimuli and asking them to record their responses on Likert scale questionnaires whose results are analysed statistically. Sometimes experiments may be conducted in a 'laboratory' environment where all other stimuli are removed; sometimes real-life environments are simulated. Experiments are invaluable in endeavouring to test reactions, and find evidence regarding the impact on decision-making of different forms of visual presentation, such as schematic faces, colour, aesthetics including colour, photographs, web pages or aspects of graph distortion (see, for example, Beattie and Jones 2002; Courtis 2004a; Cho et al. 2009). Again, great care and precision is required in all aspects of the conduct of the experiment, from the visual materials provided, the research participants (including their level of expertise, and whether or not their response might be biased, for example by receiving financial recompense), to the surroundings in which the experiment is conducted.

Theoretical and interpretive approaches

Thought-provoking theoretical and interpretive approaches are especially rich in visual studies in accounting. They are useful in focusing attention on analytical and interpretive approaches, rather than on data collection (Bell and Davison 2012), and in building interdisciplinary bridges with a wide variety of disciplines whose knowledge may be fruitfully applied in accounting contexts. However, challenges are again present, such as the imagination to make connections, the need for adequate expertise in more than one discipline, with the accompanying risk of amateurism (Pink et al. 2004), together with the resistance, discomfort or bewilderment of those in one discipline unfamiliar with the conventions and skills of another discipline (Quattrone 2000).

Theoretical approaches that are perhaps the most accessible to accountants are those based in sociology. Thus, an argument based in Habermasian communicative rationalization underpins photographic content analysis of gender (Kuasirikun 2011). Goffman's theories of the self have framed work on professional identity in graduate recruitment brochures (Jeacle 2008). Giddens' theories of modernity inform the changing presentation of accountants in magazine advertisements over the past four decades from responsible bean-counter to pleasure-seeker (Baldvinsdottir et al. 2009). Actor–network theory explains diagrammatic intellectual capital statements (Mouritsen et al. 2001). Preston and Young (2000) have employed theory from the socio-cultural anthropologist Appadurai to frame their essay on depictions of globalization in the pictures of annual reports. The representational properties of accounts themselves may be compared to those of maps – neither the cartographical nor the accounting domain is as objective and neutral as many would like to believe, since they both constitute constructions and necessarily involve questions of choice and judgement (Napier 2011).

Yet, in many ways, arts disciplines are the main sources of expertise with regard to the complex manner in which visual media communicate. Rhetoric as a pictorial framing device has been explored in the use of antithesis (Davison 2002), and in the deep-seated ramifications of conscious and unconscious repetition (Davison 2008; Quattrone 2009). Critical semiotics makes no distinction between so-called high art and the everyday, and notions of plurality, multiple interpretations, and the importance of the reader or viewer in constructing meaning also originate in semiotics. Key writers in the area of visual studies, such as Berger, Mitchell and Sontag, have featured in accounting research. The work of Barthes is notably fundamental in semiotic exploration of the visual image: Barthes' 'Rhetoric of the Image' informs work on pictures and photographs as ways of seeing and as impression management, while Barthes' *Camera Lucida* provides the basis for a study of NGO accountability (see, for example, Preston et al. 1996; Davison 2007, 2009, 2011a). Parallels are drawn between debates in critical art theory and the emancipatory project in accounting (Gallhofer and Haslam 1996). Visual portraiture based in art theory frames a study of CEO portraits (Davison 2010). Elsewhere accounting texts are analysed through theoretical history of the book or Genette's construction of the 'paratext' of the book (Quattrone 2009; Davison 2011b).

Visual studies based in ethical philosophy have similarly extended the boundaries of accounting. Levinas' (1993) ethics of the Other is used to interpret a rise in photographic human representation in annual reports from 1989 to 2003 (Campbell et al. 2009). Ancient Egyptian accounting inscriptions are interpreted in the light of Hobbes' (1991) philosophy of order (Ezzamel 2009). Driven by a theoretical framework constructed of Kristeva's (1983) duality of the (paternal) law versus the (maternal) body, Matilal and Höpfl (2009) compare and contrast official reports of the Indian Bhopal disaster with the moving and tragic story of photographs taken at the time. In a similarly theological vein, Davison (2004) explores the cross-cultural notion of salvation through ascension, in the light of Eliade (1980), in an illustrative sample of corporate annual report photographic depictions of ascension, from staircases to escalators and cliff-climbing.

Issues associated with visual communication

Various issues that are apparent in visual forms have already been discussed above. Clusters of research papers have emerged under the following three headings, but these are far from exhaustive. There are numerous further issues to be explored, such as communication in sustainability reporting, reflections of globalization and the communication of intellectual capital, as well as matters of ideology.

Impression management, framing and decision-making

One fundamental issue concerns impression management and the framing of information used for decision-making through the use of a variety of visual media. Visual forms such as graphs and schematic faces may be used to represent financial data, but in a manner that is sympathetic to the company (Beattie and Jones 2008). The colour and other aesthetic devices in which financial data are packaged can favourably impact, albeit less directly, the reception of financial results (Townsend and Shu 2010). Pictures and photographs carry messages that are beyond the capacity of the financial statements, and that are more powerful and memorable than those of narratives, but equally more plural and more ambiguous. Pictures and photographs can be used to convey longstanding corporate reputation, especially in times of risk, and are significant sites for conveying impressions of leadership, of the workforce and corporate projects; they have the capacity to reflect the complexity of non-governmental organizations, their dual engagement in the charitable and corporate sectors, and their greater need to express sentiment, to arouse compassion and instil trust (see, for example, Davison 2002, 2007, 2010). This relationship with trust extends to sustainability reporting (Cho et al. 2009).

Accountancy and accountants' professional identity

Visual rhetorical promotion of accounting as a discipline was present in the Italian accounting textbooks of Renaissance times, and continued in the neo-Baroque Victorian architecture of Chartered Accountants Hall in London (McKinstry 1997). In more recent times, the photographs of professional firms' annual reports have endeavoured to highlight the creative, people-oriented and business-aware sides of professional accountancy, in addition to its traditional role as trustworthy provider of reliable information, while the photographs of graduate recruitment brochures demonstrate a latter-day mythologization of the glamour of a career in professional accountancy (Hancock 2005; Davison 2011). Views from outside the profession (to be found notably in popular film, but also in the business press) vary. Sometimes there is negative stereotyping, such as the accountant in the film *Ghostbusters* who 'talked nonstop, issuing an endless stream of useless information, all of which centred on money, costs, or others' salary or net worth' (Cory 1992: 10), or accountants portrayed as inept, dysfunctional misfits, subordinates, sometimes with criminal tendencies (Beard 1994), frequently lacking in communication skills. Sometimes there are more positive depictions of dedicated, competent and well-educated professionals, but who have a tendency towards unethical behaviour, these unethical tendencies being associated with the smarter accountants (Felton et al. 2008).

Gender and diversity

Pictures and photographs are often the only source of rich and important (and perhaps unconscious) messages regarding organizational gender and diversity. For example, female subordination and stereotyping have been evident in organizational photographs of firms such as General Motors, and the large firms composing the US airline industry. Such gender inequalities can be seen across organizations in the photographs of employees and of board members, where women are under-represented. They can also be seen across the globe, from Europe (Netherlands, UK), to North America (Canada, US) and East Asia. Similar inequalities regarding ethnic minorities are made apparent in the photographs of organizational documents (see, for example, Benschop and Meihuizen (2002) and Bernardi et al. (2005)).

Future paths for accounting and the visual

From little interest a decade ago, visual studies in accounting and related management studies have significantly increased in recent years. As noted by Bell and Davison (2012), since 2000 there have been several initiatives, many of which have incorporated accounting-related visual work. The EIASM (European Institute for Advanced Studies in Management) has supported three workshops on aesthetics, art and management, two workshops on the theme of *Imag[in] ing business*, three on architecture and a forthcoming workshop is planned on fashion. The UK ESRC (Economic and Social Research Council) has supported the Building Capacity in Visual Methods programme and the first international visual methods conference (2009). In conjunction with the foundation of the *in*Visio research network (International Network for Visual Studies in Organisations, www.in-visio.org), the ESRC has also supported a seminar series and a Researcher Development Initiative to advance visual methodologies in business and management. Routledge have recently commissioned several books on the visual in organizations: Schroeder (2002); Styhre (2010); Puyou et al. (2011); Bell et al. (forthcoming). Special issues have also been commissioned of *Accounting, Auditing & Accountability Journal* (2009) and *Qualitative Research in Organizations and Management* (forthcoming 2012) to add to the seminal special issue of *Accounting, Organizations and Society* (1996).

It is generally recognized that annual reports, whether printed or electronic, have become imbued with pictures and photographs that frame, and frequently eclipse, the accounting statements. Yet research attention has only (relatively recently) started to explore the nature and importance of this huge mass of visual material, which is still sometimes regarded as inconsequential packaging bearing little relationship to the financial statements. Indeed, in the UK, regulators continue to overlook the impact of visual images in annual reporting, that have been dismissed as 'promotional material' (ASB 2000) or ignored. This blind spot continues in current UK regulatory work on 'cutting clutter' in annual reports (FRC 2011), which does not mention visual material.

As can be seen from the Appendix, by far the bulk of research has been focused on pictures/ photographs and on graphs, mainly in annual reports, with small clusters of work on (popular) film and architecture. There is much scope for further work on logos, diagrams, sketches and colour, and on aspects so far almost totally neglected, such as web pages, organizational film and video presentations, colour, font and typography. Although pictures/photographs have received more attention than other visual areas, they represent such a wealth of organizational material, communicating such a variety and complexity of messages, that they still remain very much underresearched. The visual methods used in accounting research are fairly evenly divided between content analysis and theoretically framed interpretive analysis. Interpretive analyses are informed by a surprisingly wide range of theory. There is scope for the further development of such approaches, informed by even greater interdisciplinarity. Such development should bring out the complexities of visual media, and highlight that they are far more than decoration or information. The majority of work has been directed towards financial reporting, but there are rich implications for other accounting domains, including auditing, management accounting and CSR reporting.

Working with the visual does, however, present challenges. Before a visual image can be reproduced in a publication, permission may have to be obtained from a prior publisher or organization that holds copyright and from the artist or photographer who created the image; sometimes it can be time-consuming to trace copyright through a series of copyright owners, and there may be fees for reproduction. Additionally, there are ethical considerations such as the rights, privacy and dignity of individuals studied in visual media. These issues become more complex when working across national boundaries, and within laws that vary internationally. Thus, there is a considerable investment in time and costs related simply to the question of reproduction (Bell and Davison, 2012). Further difficulties to be overcome in working with the visual are its plurality and ambiguity of meaning, its resistance to quantification, and the lack of research methods and theory. All these challenges are among the reasons for a degree of resistance to its serious examination among accounting practitioners, regulators and academics.

Yet, the legal and ethical issues associated with visual forms are a sign of the power that is seen to be vested in the visual. Visual forms are important media of communication in accounting. It is imperative that their distinctive *modus operandi* should be better acknowledged and understood by all stakeholders. The visual has become ubiquitous in business and everyday life and is recognized to have a special place in memory and in cognition. Visual media provide important framing and impression management to the reception of information and can influence decisionmaking. Visual media can carry messages beyond the capacity of accounting statements.

Appendix: research papers by visual form and date of publication

Visual form	Research papers
Graphs	Beattie and Jones (2008) Review paper – indicates 25 articles in the area from 1986 to 2008. JAL
Cartoon graphics – schematic faces	Moriarity (1979) JAR Smith and Taffler (1984) ABR Stock and Watson (1984) JAR Smith and Taffler (1996) AAAJ
Visual images – general definition	Hrasky (2012) AF Husin, Hooper and Olesen (2012) JIC
Pictures/ photographs – organizational	Tinker and Neimark (1987) AOS Kuiper (1988) JBC Anderson and Imperia (1992) JBC Cooper, Cooper, Pheby and Puxty (1992) Working paper Graves, Flesher and Jordan (1996) AOS Hopwood (1996) AOS McKinstry (1996) AOS Preston, Wright and Young (1996) AOS Preston and Young (2000) AOS Ewing, Pitt and Murgolo-Poore (2001) PRQ Benschop and Meihuizen (2002) AOS Bernardi, Bean and Wippert (2002) AAAJ Davison (2002) AAAJ Davison (2004) AAAJ Hoffjan (2004) API Stanton, Stanton and Pires (2004) AAAJ Bernardi, Bean and Wippert (2005) CPA Hancock (2005) OWarren (2005) AAAJ Davison (2007) AAAJ McGoun, Bettner and Coyne (2007) CPA Jeacle (2008) CPA Baldvinsdottir (2009) AAAJ Campbell, McPhail and Slack (2009) AAAJ Davison and Warren (2009) AAAJ Kamla and Roberts (2010) AAAJ Matilal and Höpfl (2009) AAAJ Parker (2009) AAAJ Tyson (2009) AAAJ Warren and Parker (2009) QRAM Bujaki and McConomy (2010a) CJAS Bujaki and McConomy (2010b) GIM Davison (2010) AOS Hooks, Steenkamp and Stewart (2010) QRAM Davison (2011) AAAJ Duff (2011) CPA Kuasirikun (2011) CPA Steenkamp and Hooks (2011) PAR Ramo (2011) JBE
Pictures – fine art	Yamey (1989) Book, Yale University Press

Sketches, diagrams	Mouritsen, Larken and Bukh (2001) AOS
	Spira and Page (2011) EIASM
Maps	Napier (2011) Working paper
Colour	So and Smith (2002) AAAJ
	Courtis (2004a) AF
	Townsend and Shu (2010) JCP
Presentation, format, book history	Quattrone (2009) AOS
	Davison (2011b) CPA
Visual branding and logos	Amernic and Craig (2000) CPA
	Davison (2009) AAAJ
	Page and Spira (2009) AAAJ
Postal marks	Courtis (2004b) AF
Web pages	Cho et al. (2009) AAAJ
Film	Cory (1992) JAE
	Beard (1994) AOS
	Holt (1994) NA
	Smith and Briggs (1999) MA
	Dimnik and Felton (2006) AOS
	Felton, Dimnik and Bay (2008) JBE
	Jeacle (2009) AAAJ
Video	Daly and Schuler (1998) AOS
Theatre	Biehl-Missal (2011) JMS
Architecture	McKinstry (1997) AOS
	McGoun (2004) CPA
	McKinstry (2008) CPA
	Justesen and Mouritsen (2009) AAAJ
	Ezzamel (2009) AOS
	Czarniawska (2010) AAAJ
Beauty and cosmetics	Jeacle (2006) CPA
Theory, method, review	Gallhofer and Haslam (1996) AAAJ
	Davison and Warren (2009) AAAJ
	Brown (2010) AAAJ
	Bell and Davison (2012) IJMR

AAAJ	*Journal of Accounting, Auditing and Accountability*	JAE	*Journal of Accounting Education*
		JAL	*Journal of Accounting Literature*
ABR	*Accounting and Business Research*	JAR	*Journal of Accounting Research*
AF	*Accounting Forum*	JBC	*Journal of Business Communication*
AOS	*Accounting, Organizations and Society*	JBE	*Journal of Business Ethics*
API	*Accounting and the Public Interest*	JIC	*Journal of Intellectual Capital*
CPA	*Critical Perspectives on Accounting*	JMS	*Journal of Management Studies*
CJAS	*Canadian Journal of Administrative Sciences*	JCP	*Journal of Consumer Psychology*
EIASM	*European Institute of Advanced Studies in Management*	NA	*New Accountant*
		O	*Organization*
ESRC	*Economic and Social Research Council*	PRQ	*Public Relations Quarterly*
GIM	*Gender in Management: An International Journal*	QRAM	*Qualitative Research in Accounting and Management*
IJMR	*International Journal of Management Reviews*		

Notes

1 For a longer discussion of the points in this paragraph see Davison (2010: 167–169).
2 The reader is directed to the *in*Visio website (in-visio.org) where the UK Economic and Social Research Council Researcher Development Initiative pages give training in visual methods and theories – 'inSpire'.

References

Accounting, Auditing & Accountability Journal Special Issue 2009.
Accounting, Organizations and Society Special Issue 1996.
Accounting Standards Board (2000) 'Year-end Financial Reports: Improving Communication'. Discussion Paper, Milton Keynes: ASB Publications.
Amernic, J. and Craig, R. (2000) 'The rhetoric of teaching financial accounting on the corporate web: a critical review of content and metaphor in IBM's internet webpage guide to understanding financials', *Critical Perspectives on Accounting*, 11(3): 259–287.
Anderson, C. and Imperia, G. (1992) 'The corporate annual report: a photo analysis of male and female portrayals', *Journal of Business Communication*, 22: 113–128.
Baldvinsdottir, G., Burns, J., Nørreklit, H. and Scapens, R. W. (2009) 'The image of accountants: from bean counters to extreme accountants', *Accounting, Auditing & Accountability Journal*, 22: 858–882.
Barthes, R. (1982) 'Rhétorique de l'image', in *L'obvie et l'obtus*, Paris: Le Seuil.
Beard, V. (1994) 'Popular culture and professional identity: accountants in the movies', *Accounting, Organizations and Society*, 19: 303–318.
Beattie, V. A., and Jones, M. J. (1992) 'The use and abuse of graphs in annual reports: theoretical framework and empirical study', *Accounting and Business Research*, 22: 291–303.
Beattie, V. A. and Jones, M. J. (2001) 'A six-country comparison of the use of graphs in annual reports', *International Journal of Accounting*, 36: 195–222.
Beattie, V. A., and Jones, M. J. (2002) 'Measurement distortion of graphs in corporate reports: an experimental study', *Accounting, Auditing & Accountability Journal*, 15: 546–564.
Beattie, V. A., and Jones, M. J. (2008) 'Corporate reporting using graphs: a review and synthesis', *Journal of Accounting Literature*, 27: 71–110.
Bell, E. and Davison, J. (2012) 'Visual management studies: empirical and theoretical approaches', *International Journal of Management Reviews*, online: http://onlinelibrary.wiley.com/doi/10.1111/j.1468-2370.2012.00342.x/abstract.
Bell, A., Schroeder, J. and Warren, S. (eds) (forthcoming) *The Routledge Companion to Visual Organization*, Oxford: Routledge.
Benschop, Y. and Meihuizen, H. E. (2002) 'Keeping up gendered appearances: representations of gender in financial annual reports', *Accounting, Organizations and Society*, 27: 611–636.
Berger, J. (1972) *Ways of Seeing*, London: Penguin.
Bernardi, R. A., Bean, D. F. and Weippert, K. M. (2002) 'Signaling gender diversity through annual report pictures: a research note on image management', *Accounting, Auditing & Accountability Journal*, 15: 609–616.
Bernardi, R. A., Bean, D. F. and Weippert, K. M. (2005) 'Minority membership on boards of directors: the case for requiring pictures of boards in annual reports', *Critical Perspectives on Accounting*, 16: 1019–1033.
Biehl-Missal, B. (2011) 'Business is show-business: management presentations as performance', *Journal of Management Studies*, 48: 619–645.
Brown, J. (2010) 'Accounting and visual cultural studies: potentialities, challenges and prospects', *Accounting, Auditing & Accountability Journal*, 23: 482–505.
Bujaki, M. L. and McConomy, B. J. (2010a) 'The portrayal of women in Canadian corporate annual reports', *Canadian Journal of Administrative Sciences*, 27: 210–223.
Bujaki, M. L. and McConomy, B. J. (2010b) 'Gendered interactions in corporate annual report photographs', *Gender in Management: An International Journal*, 25: 119–136.
Campbell, D. McPhail, K. and Slack, R. (2009) 'Facework in annual reports', *Accounting, Auditing & Accountability Journal*, 22: 907–932.
Cho, C. H. Phillips, J. R. Hageman, A. M. and Patten, D. M. (2009) 'Media richness, user trust and perceptions of corporate social responsibility', *Accounting, Auditing & Accountability Journal*, 22: 933–952.

Cooper, C., Pheby, D., Pheby, K. and Puxty, A. (1992) 'Accounting, truth and beauty', working paper, Glasgow: Strathclyde Business School, University of Strathclyde.

Cory, S. N. (1992) 'Quality and quantity of accounting students and the stereotypical accountant: is there a relationship?', *Journal of Accounting Education*, 10: 1–24.

Courtis, J. (2004a) 'Colour as visual rhetoric in financial reporting', *Accounting Forum*, 28: 265–282.

Courtis, J. (2004b) 'Red and black interpostal accountancy marks', *Accounting Forum*, 28: 385–402.

Czarniawska, B. (2010) 'Translation impossible? Accounting for a city project', *Accounting, Auditing & Accountability Journal*, 23: 420–437.

Daly, B. and Schuler, D. K. (1998) 'Redefining a certified public accounting firm', *Accounting, Organizations and Society*, 23: 549–567.

Davison, J. (2002) 'Communication and antithesis in corporate annual reports: a research note', *Accounting, Auditing & Accountability Journal*, 15: 594–608.

Davison, J. (2004) 'Sacred vestiges in financial reporting: mythical readings guided by Mircea Eliade', *Accounting, Auditing & Accountability Journal*, 17: 476–497.

Davison, J. (2007) 'Photographs and accountability: cracking the codes of an NGO', *Accounting, Auditing & Accountability Journal*, 20: 133–158.

Davison, J. (2008) 'Rhetoric, repetition, reporting and the "dot.com" era: words, pictures, intangibles', *Accounting, Auditing & Accountability Journal*, 21: 791–826.

Davison, J. (2009) 'Icon, iconography, iconology: visual branding, banking and the case of the bowler hat', *Accounting, Auditing & Accountability Journal*, 22: 883–906.

Davison, J. (2010) '(In)visible (in)tangibles: visual portraits of the business élite', *Accounting, Organizations and Society*, 35: 165–183.

Davison, J. (2011a) 'Barthesian perspectives on accounting communication and visual images of accountancy', *Accounting, Auditing & Accountability Journal*, 24: 250–83.

Davison, J. (2011b) 'Paratextual framing of the annual report: liminal literary conventions and visual devices', *Critical Perspectives on Accounting*, 22: 118–134.

Davison, J. and Skerratt, L. (2007) *Words, Pictures and Intangibles in the Corporate Report*, Edinburgh: The Institute of Chartered Accountants of Scotland.

Davison, J. and Warren, S. (2009) 'Imag[in]ing accounting and accountability', *Accounting, Auditing & Accountability Journal*, 22: 845–857.

Dimnik, T. and Felton, S. (2006) 'Accountant stereotypes in movies distributed in North America in the twentieth century', *Accounting Organizations and Society*, 31: 129–155.

Duff, A. (2011) 'Big four accounting firms' annual reviews: a photo analysis of gender and race portrayals', *Critical Perspectives on Accounting*, 22: 20–38.

Eliade, M. (1980) *Images et symboles*, Paris: Gallimard.

Ewing, M. T., Pitt, L. F. and Murgolo-Poore, M. E. (2001) 'Bean couture: using photographs and publicity to re-position the accounting profession', *Public Relations Quarterly*, Winter: 23–30.

'Exploring the visual in organizations and management' (2012) Special issue of *Qualitative Research in Organizations and Management* 7(1).

Ezzamel, M. (2009) 'Order and accounting as a performative ritual: evidence from ancient Egypt', *Accounting, Organizations and Society*, 34: 348–380.

Felton, S., Dimnik, T. and Bay, D. (2008) 'Perceptions of accountants' ethics: evidence from their portrayal in cinema', *Journal of Business Ethics*, 83: 217–232.

Financial Reporting Council (2011) *Cutting Clutter: Combating Clutter in Annual Reports*, London: The Financial Reporting Council Limited.

Gallhofer, S. and Haslam, J. (1996) 'Accounting/art and the emancipatory project: some reflections', *Accounting, Auditing & Accountability Journal*, 9: 23–24.

Graves, O. F., Flesher, D. L. and Jordan R. E. (1996) 'Pictures and the bottom line: the television epistemology of US annual reports', *Accounting, Organizations and Society*, 21: 57–88.

Hancock, P. (2005) 'Uncovering the semiotic in organizational aesthetics', *Organization*, 12: 29–50.

Hobbes, T. (1991) *Leviathan*, ed. R. Tuck, Cambridge: Cambridge University Press.

Hoffjan, J. (2004) 'The image of the accountant in a German context', *Accounting and the Public Interest*, 4: 63–89.

Holt, P. E. (1994) 'Stereotypes of the accounting professional as reflected in popular movies, accounting students and society', *New Accountant*, April: 24–25.

Hooks, J. Steenkamp, N. and Stewart, R. (2010) 'Interpreting pictorial messages of intellectual capital in company media', *Qualitative Research in Accounting & Management*, 7: 353–378.

Hopwood, A. G. (1996) 'Making visible and the construction of visibilities: shifting agendas in the design of the corporate report: introduction', *Accounting, Organizations and Society*, 21: 55–56.

Hrasky, S. (2012) 'Visual disclosure strategies adopted by more and less sustainability-driven companies', *Accounting Forum*, 36: 154–165.

Husen, N. M., Hooper, K. and Olesen, K. (2012) 'Analysis of intellectual capital disclosure – an illustrative example', *Journal of Intellectual Capital*, 13(2): 196–220.

Jeacle, I. (2006) 'Face facts: accounting, feminism and the business of beauty', *Critical Perspectives on Accounting*, 17: 87–108.

Jeacle, I. (2008) 'Beyond the boring grey: the construction of the colourful accountant', *Critical Perspectives on Accounting*, 19: 1296–1320.

Jeacle, I. (2009) '"Going to the movies": accounting and 20th century cinema', *Accounting, Auditing & Accountability Journal*, 22: 667–708.

Justesen, L. and Mouritsen, J. (2009) 'The triple visual: translations between photographs, 3-d visualizations and calculations', *Accounting, Auditing & Accountability Journal*, 22: 973–990.

Kamla, R. and Roberts, C. (2010) 'The local and the global: the use of images in Arab companies' annual reports', *Accounting, Auditing & Accountability Journal*, 23: 449–481.

Kristeva, J. (1983) *Tales of Love*, New York: Columbia University Press.

Kuasirikun, N. (2011) 'The portrayal of gender in corporate annual reports in Thailand', *Critical Perspectives on Accounting*, 22: 53–78.

Kuiper, S. (1998) 'Gender representation in corporate annual reports and perceptions of corporate climate', *Journal of Business Communication*, 25: 87–94.

Lee, T. (1994) 'The changing form of the corporate annual report', *Accounting Historians Journal*, 21: 215–232.

Levinas, E. (1993) *Outside The Subject*, trans. M. B. Smith, London: Athlone Press.

Malamed, C. (2011) *Visual Language for Designers: Principles for Creating Graphics that People Understand*, Beverly, MA: Rockport.

Matilal, S. and Höpfl, H. (2009) 'Accounting for the Bhopal disaster: footnotes and photographs', *Accounting, Auditing & Accountability Journal*, 22: 953–972.

McGoun, E. G. (2004) 'Form, function, and finance: architecture and finance theory', *Critical Perspectives on Accounting*, 15: 1085–1107.

McGoun, E., Bettner, M. and Coyne, M. (2007) 'Pedagogic metaphors and the nature of accounting signification', *Critical Perspectives on Accounting*, 18: 213–230.

McKinstry, S. (1996) 'Designing the annual reports of Burton plc from 1930 to 1994', *Accounting, Organizations and Society*, 21: 89–111.

McKinstry, S. (1997) 'Status building: some reflections on the architectural history of Chartered Accountants' Hall, London, 1889–1893', *Accounting, Organizations and Society*, 22: 779–798.

McKinstry, S. (2008) 'Re-framing a "subfusc" institute: building on the past for the future at Chartered Accountants' Hall, London, 1965–1970', *Critical Perspectives on Accounting*, 19: 1384–1413.

Mitchell, W. J. T. (1994) *Picture Theory*, Chicago: University of Chicago Press.

Moriarity, S. (1979) 'Communicating financial information through multidimensional graphics', *Journal of Accounting Research*, 17: 205–224.

Mouritsen, J., Larsen H. T. and Bukh, P. N. D. (2001) 'Intellectual capital and the "capable firm": narrating, visualising and numbering for managing knowledge', *Accounting, Organizations and Society*, 26: 735–762.

Napier, C. (2011) 'The allegory of the fields: accounting, cartography and representation', paper presented at the Financial Reporting and Business Communication Conference, Bristol.

Page, M. and Spira, L. F. (2009) 'Economia, or a woman in a man's world', *Accounting, Auditing & Accountability Journal*, 22: 146–160.

Parker, L. D. (2009) 'Photo-elicitation: an ethno-historical accounting and management research project', *Accounting, Auditing & Accountability Journal*, 22: 1111–1129.

Pink, S. (2004) 'Visual methods' in C. Seale, G. Gobo, J. F. Gubrium and D. Silverman (eds), *Qualitative Research Practice*, London: Sage.

Preston, A. M., Wright, C. and Young, J. J. (1996) 'Imag[in]ing annual reports', *Accounting, Organizations and Society*, 21: 113–137.

Preston, A. M. and Young, J. J. (2000) 'Constructing the global corporation and corporate constructions of the global: a picture essay', *Accounting, Organizations and Society*, 25: 427–449.

Puyou, F. R., Quattrone, P., McLean, C. and Thrift, N. (eds) (2011) *Imagining Business: Performative Imagery in Business and Beyond*, London: Routledge.

Quattrone, P. (2000) 'Constructivism and accounting research: towards a trans-disciplinary perspective', *Accounting, Auditing & Accountability Journal*, 13: 130–155.

Quattrone, P. (2009) 'Books to be practiced: memory, the power of the visual, and the success of accounting', *Accounting, Organizations and Society*, 34: 85–118.

Ramo, H. (2011) 'Visualising the phronetic organisation: the case of photographs in CSR reports', *Journal of Business Ethics*, 104(3): 371–387.

Rinaldi, L. and Davison, J. (2011) 'Imagining sustainability reporting: *videri quam esse?*', paper presented at the European Institute of Management Workshop on Imagining Business, Segovia.

Rorty, R. (1979) *Philosophy and the Mirror of Nature*, Princeton, NJ: Princeton University Press.

Schroeder, J. E. (2002) *Visual Consumption*, Oxford: Routledge.

Schroeder, J. (2005) 'The artist and the brand', *European Journal of Marketing*, 39: 1291–1305.

Smith, M. and Briggs, S. (1999) 'From bean-counter to action hero: changing the image of the accountant', *Management Accounting*, January: 28–30.

Smith, M. and Taffler, R. J. (1984) 'Improving the communication function of published accounting statements', *Accounting and Business Research*, 54: 139–46.

Smith, M. and Taffler, R. J. (1996) 'Improving the communication of accounting information through cartoon graphics', *Accounting, Auditing & Accountability Journal*, 9: 68–85.

So, S. and Smith, M. (2002) 'Colour graphics and task complexity in multivariate decision-making', *Accounting, Auditing & Accountability Journal*, 15: 565–593.

Sontag, S. (1971) *On Photography*, New York and London: Penguin.

Spira, L. F., and Page, M. (2011) 'Visualising corporate governance and strategy', paper presented at the European Institute of Management Workshop on Imagining Business, Segovia.

Stanton, P., Stanton, J. and Pires, G. (2004) 'Impressions of an annual report: an experimental study', *Corporate Communications: An International Journal*, 9: 57–69.

Steenkamp, N. and Hooks, J. (2011) 'Does including pictorial disclosure of intellectual capital resources make a difference?', *Pacific Accounting Review*, 23: 52–68.

Stock, D. and Watson C. J. (1984) 'Human judgement accuracy, multidimensional graphics and human versus models', *Journal of Accounting Research*, 22: 192–206.

Styhre, A. (2010) *Visual Culture in Organizations: Theory and Cases*, Oxford: Routledge.

The Accountant (2001) www.theaccountantmovie.com (accessed 6 February 2012).

Tinker, T. and Neimark, M. (1987) 'The role of annual reports in gender and class contradictions at General Motors 1917–1976', *Accounting, Organizations and Society*, 12: 71–88.

Townsend, C. and Shu, S. B. (2010) 'When and how aesthetics influences financial decisions', *Journal of Consumer Psychology*, 20: 452–458.

Tufte, E. (1983) *The Visual Display of Quantitative Information*, Cheshire, CT: Graphics Press.

Tufte, E. (1990) *Envisioning Information*, Cheshire, CT: Graphics Press.

Tversky, A. and Kahneman, D. (1986) 'Rational choice and the framing of decisions', *Journal of Business*, 59: 251–278.

Tyson, T. (2009) 'Discussion of photo-elicitation: an ethno-historical accounting and management research project', *Accounting, Auditing & Accountability Journal*, 22: 1130–1141.

Warren, S. (2005) 'Photography and voice in critical qualitative management research', *Accounting, Auditing & Accountability Journal*, 18: 861–882.

Warren, S. and Parker, L. D. (2009) 'Bean counters or bright young things? Towards the visual study of identity construction among professional accountants', *Qualitative Research in Accounting and Management*, 6: 205–223.

Yamey, B. S. (1989) *Art & Accounting*, New Haven, CT, and London: Yale University Press.

6

Perspectives on the role of metaphor

Joel Amernic

[A] The power of accounting lies in its role in shaping the discourse of performance …
(Power 2004: 778)

[B] A metaphor is not an ornament. It is an organ of perception.
(Postman 1996: 174)

[C] Metaphors are at the basis of our thought processes, and they help us to make sense of social reality.
(Spicer and Alvesson 2011: 38)

[D] We do not and perhaps never shall have an explicit understanding of metaphor.
(Isenberg 1963: 612)

[E] IFRS MONOPOLY: THE PIED PIPER OF FINANCIAL REPORTING
(Sunder 2011)

Aims and scope

Is it true, as one of the editors of this volume suggested, that "metaphor is neglected (overtly at least) by accountants and … the discipline (and communication in the discipline) is lesser for this"?[1] I think that at least some (but not many) accounting researchers and educators do not entirely neglect metaphor overtly, and many practitioners (although unavoidably inhabiting a professional world rife with metaphor) probably sense it but avoid it. Such neglect seems (at the very least) injudicious since, as Dirsmith, Covaleski and McAllister write about auditing thought (although their comment relates to accounting communication generally), "what is called for is metaphorical pluralism in order to engender multiple understandings …" (1985: 52).

Everywhere one looks, it seems *metaphor* is to be found: "A person with a sharp eye can find metaphors almost anywhere" (Gibbs and Matlock 2008: 161). Insofar as accounting communication is concerned, if the first three epigraphs ([A], [B], and [C]) at the beginning of this chapter are reasonably accurate, metaphor in accounting communication plausibly has a strong influence in shaping accounting, the discourse of performance, in subtle and also not-so-subtle ways. Talking about and thinking about *something* in terms of *something else* can affect not only how individuals behave, but also affect broad policies. For example, Walters and Young (2008) suggest that when stock options began to be metaphorically viewed as dysfunctional tools rather than as good devices for achieving socially-desirable ends such as aligning manager and shareholder interests, the FASB's imposition of a mandatory expensing standard was facilitated.

With the publication of Lakoff and Johnson's *Metaphors We Live By* (1980b) and the ongoing development of various strands of cognitive metaphor theory,[2] consideration of *metaphor* has infiltrated a wide spectrum of academic and popular literature. Indeed, it has found a place within various niches of accounting as well (see, for example, Morgan 1988; Thornton 1988; Walters-York 1996, Amernic and Craig 2000; Walters and Young 2008), including accounting education and related literature (see, for example, Amernic 1996, 1998; Craig and Amernic 2002; McGoun, Bettner and Coyne 2007; Durkee 2011). However, accounting has been hesitant to pursue metaphor along a broad front. This hesitation may be due at least partly because of Reimer and Camp's caution that "metaphor is itself a vague and elusive phenomenon" (2006: 846), and many accounting scholars seem to shun such equivocality. Indeed, it is because of this vagueness and elusiveness of metaphor that examining it abstractly beyond a certain point seems imprudent: the concrete situation in which a metaphor-candidate appears is crucial. As Bergmann wrote regarding the salience of metaphors: "Salience, then, is context-dependent" (1982: 237; see also Eubanks 1999).

The structure of this chapter is as follows: the second section suggests the richness and importance of metaphor in accounting education and accounting practice; the third section lists and comments briefly on some papers in which metaphor has appeared as an explicit focus in the accounting literature; the fourth section explores a foundational accounting construct, "the reporting entity," for large firms particularly, from a metaphorical perspective, as an illustrative case study; and the final section contains a short summary. Comments on metaphor and accounting communication research are included throughout.

The reader should keep in mind that the metaphor literature in cognitive linguistics and related fields, in psychology, in the humanities, and in applied social-science fields such as law and management is vast. Thus this chapter just skims the surface of *metaphor and accounting communication*. The literature that is cited focuses only on English-language cultures, and also does not consider visual and related metaphor (see Gibbs 2008).

The richness and importance of metaphor in accounting communication

What is metaphor?

Grady (2007) writes: "Within Cognitive Linguistics the term *metaphor* is understood to refer to a pattern of conceptual associations, rather than an individual metaphorical usage or a linguistic convention" (p. 188). Grady then cites Lakoff and Johnson's (1980b: 5) well-known definition: "The essence of metaphor is understanding and experiencing one kind of thing in terms of another." Grady elaborates as follows:

> When Robert Frost refers to the "road less traveled," he uses the words *road* and *traveled* in metaphorical ways; in conventional usage, this phrase is "the metaphor", but for cognitive linguists the more important object of study … is the underlying pattern of thought which allows the phrase to have the meaning it does. Since this pattern involves associations at the conceptual level, it can be expressed by many different lexical means—metaphorical uses of *path*, *fork in the road*, *direction*, and numerous other terms reflecting the same basic set of associations, between traveling and making life choices.
>
> *(2007: 188–189)*

Grady continues by contending, based upon a review of "several types of evidence," that "conceptual metaphor mappings are psychologically real" (2007: 195).

One does not have to accept metaphor as characterized solely by a cognitive linguistics perspective as in, for example, Lakoff (1993), to accept that metaphor is a foundationally-important perspective for accounting communication, from research, practitioner, and teaching perspectives. In their introduction to the 25th edition of *Yearbook of Research in English and American Literature*, devoted to the topic "Metaphors Shaping Culture and Theory," editors Nünning, Grabes and Baumbach (2009) argue that metaphors are "worldmaking devices" (p. xii), which "play an essential and constitutive role in shaping the structure(s) of both cultural phenomena and theories" (p. xvii), and that metaphors work "simultaneously on different cognitive, emotional, ethical, normative, and ideological levels."

But aside from some ostensibly straightforward cases, such as "theories are buildings" (Grady 1997),[3] metaphor is not particularly easy to grasp or talk about. Some definitions of the word "metaphor" are provided in Table 6.1. Like definitions generally, the various definitions in this small sampling are at least partly ideological and arbitrary (Schiappa 2003), and thus emphasize some things but not others. The *Oxford English Dictionary* definitions, [1] in Table 6.1, seem technical and abstract (perhaps definitions are necessarily so in order to be succinct; they are thus almost always at least partly misleading), and say nothing regarding the plausible cognitive character of metaphors, and also avoid any mention of context.[4] Definition [2] describes what seems like the essential skeleton of what is often referred to as the contemporary theory of metaphor, but cries out for much more descriptive richness. In fact, all the definitions included

Table 6.1 Definition of the word "metaphor"

Definition of the word "metaphor"	*Source*
1 1. A figure of speech in which a name or descriptive word or phrase is transferred to an object or action different from, but analogous to, that to which it is literally applicable; an instance of this, a metaphorical expression. 2. Something regarded as representative or suggestive of something else, esp. as a material emblem of an abstract quality, condition, notion, etc.; a symbol, a token. Freq. with for, of.	Oxford English Dictionary Online at: www.oed.com.myaccess.library.utoronto.ca/view/Entry/117328?redirectedFrom=metaphor#eid (last accessed August 12, 2011)
2 A cross-domain mapping in the conceptual system.	Lakoff (1993: 203) writes: "The term 'metaphorical expression' refers to a linguistic expression (a word, phrase, or sentence) that is the surface realization of such a cross-domain mapping..."
3 "Metaphor can be thought of as the currency of the emotional mind ... Metaphor not only *transfers* meaning between different domains, but by means of novel recombinations metaphor can *transform* meaning" (emphasis in original).	(Modell 2009: 6)
4 "At its most basic, a metaphor is created when a term (sometimes referred to as a 'source') is transferred from one system or level of meaning to another (the 'target'), thereby illuminating central aspects of the latter and shadowing others ... A metaphor allows an object to be perceived and understood from the viewpoint of another object. It thus creates a departure from literal meaning ..."	(Spicer and Alvesson 2011: 34)

in Table 6.1 (and indeed all the definitions that a reader may discover) are partial, or too cryptic, and therefore demonstrate some support for epigraph [D]. Perhaps more importantly, this epigraph reinforces the notion that the word *metaphor* refers to a social, psychological, cognitive, ideological, linguistic (and more) *complexity* the meaning of which can scarcely be captured by a succinct definition. Perhaps this is one reason why using computer-assisted, corpus-based approaches to metaphor analysis face challenges.[5]

Identifying metaphors in accounting communication

There is a good and evolving literature focusing on the practical problem of developing defensible protocols for identifying metaphors in text and talk.[6] For example, scholars writing in the metaphor literature have proposed a "metaphor identification procedure," or MIP (Pragglejaz Group 2007), Cameron and colleagues (2009) describe a method of metaphor-led discourse analysis, and Deignan (2008) discusses benefits and challenges of empirical work focusing on metaphor within corpora. Steen (2011a) summarizes his extensive work in metaphor identification. Dunn (2011) addresses the relative degree of metaphoricity of metaphoric expressions. An example of an explicit description of metaphor identification in the accounting literature is Amernic and Craig (2001), in which an appendix is devoted to disclosing the authors' working notes prepared in metaphor identification. Some short examples of tentative metaphor identification in accounting are offered later in this chapter; readers can assess whether they agree with the attempts at identification and analysis therein.

On balance, metaphor analysis ranges from being relatively straightforward to being not straightforward at all. The identification of pervasive or root metaphors may be the most difficult of all; a productive example of root metaphor identification in the accounting literature is Ravenscroft and Williams (2009).

The importance of metaphor in accounting communication

Morgan offers "a list of some of the major metaphors that have exerted an impact on recent accounting theory" (1988: 481; see also Davis, Menon and Morgan 1982): accounting as history; accounting as economics; accounting as information; accounting as a language; accounting as rhetoric; accounting as politics; accounting as mythology, accounting as magic; accounting as disciplined control; accounting as ideology; and, accounting as domination and exploitation. Whilst one might dispute details of this list, if the conceptual theory of metaphor is credible, then researchers' *thinking* in any narrow accounting research paradigm might vividly represent a "prison-house of metaphor" (Walters 2004). That is, if the metaphorical character of any narrow field of accounting research is ignored, then theoretical and empirical research conducted solely within this narrow paradigm may be deficient and partial at best, and misguided at worst. Consequently established broad policies and standards based upon such research may have serious unintended consequences. That is because—as some allege—metaphor is not innocent; Tinker (1986) for example, contends that "Metaphors are never neutral representations of social affairs" (p. 378). Hamington (2009) asserts that:

> Sport and game metaphors are ubiquitous in the culture and language of business. As evocative linguistic devices, such metaphors are morally neutral; however, if they are indicative of a deep structure of understanding that filters experience, then they have the potential to be ethically problematic.
>
> *(p. 473)*

Hamington's concerns have direct implications for accounting, since "the discourse of performance" (Power 2004: 778) thus shaped would inevitably be influenced strongly by such metaphors that induce "a deep structure of understanding that filters experience".

More ominously, Harrington (1995) describes the pervasiveness of broad, cultural, metaphoric-based holistic discourse during the Nazi era, as a form of Gestalt,[7] and Cohn (1987) writes about her own experience of being seduced by the language of nuclear deterrence, a language replete with metaphor.

Does *mere* language have such power? Is it possible that "metaphors may be used to manipulate the social imagination by reifying social relations" (Tinker 1986: 378)? If, as Eagleton (1991) writes, "What persuades men and women to mistake each other from time to time for gods or vermin is ideology" (p. xiii), then is metaphor ideology's handmaiden?

The evidence is persuasive that metaphor is cognitive,[8] manifest largely (but not exclusively) in language, is unavoidably ideological, as well as largely inescapable.[9] Its deployment ranges from the interesting but obvious, as in the title that Sunder (2011) chose for his article in *Accounting and Business Research* (epigraph [E]) to the more subtle (and perhaps often unobtrusive) in virtually all papers in accounting research and virtually all teaching materials in accounting education—and perhaps in virtually all financial statements and management control systems, and International Financial Reporting Standards (IFRS) and other accounting standards. As Thornton (1988), Walters-York (1996), and others nicely show, much of the theoretical and practitioner vocabulary of accounting communication is replete with metaphor.

Morgan (1988) contends that "accountants typically construct reality in limited and one-sided ways" (p. 477), and that accounting is "a metaphorical enterprise" since "accounting is ultimately concerned with the problems of representation and 'accounting for'. Like organization theorists, accountants ultimately have to represent complex multi-dimensional realities through metaphorical constructs that are always limited and incomplete" (p. 480; see also Hines 1988 among others). As an example, some words with metaphoric potential in the following quotation from Kaplan (2006) regarding the balanced scorecard are set out in italics. How might possible metaphors suggested by these words influence the thinking, including reasoning, of accounting students, accounting practitioners, and managers?

> The development of *strategy maps* and *Balanced Scorecards* has *transformed* the *foundations of management control systems*. The leading paradigm of *organizational structure* and control of just a generation ago, based upon cost, profit, investment, revenue and discretionary expense *centers*, has been *replaced* by a *robust, powerful framework* in which every organizational unit—whether line or staff, whether *centralized or decentralized*—can be considered a strategic business unit. The management control system is no longer based on the budget—whether for profits, ROI, costs, revenues, or discretionary expenses. Companies now use the more general and powerful strategy management system, *built upon the framework of strategy maps and Balanced Scorecards*, to motivate, align, and evaluate the performance of diverse organizational units.
>
> *Kaplan (2006; emphasis added)*

Take the first sentence: "*The development of strategy maps and Balanced Scorecards has transformed the foundations of management control systems.*" There is considerable metaphorical potential in this sentence, including:

- MANAGEMENT CONTROL SYSTEMS ARE STRUCTURES (they have foundations, just like most structures, such as buildings).
- THE FOUNDATIONS OF MANAGEMENT CONTROL SYSTEMS' STRUCTURES ARE TRANSFORMABLE FOUNDATIONS.

- STRATEGY MAPS AND BALANCED SCORECARDS ARE OBJECTS THAT CAN BE DEVELOPED.
- STRATEGY MAPS AND BALANCED SCORECARDS ARE (NOW) FOUNDATIONAL FOR MANAGEMENT CONTROL SYSTEMS.

This chain of potential metaphors emphasizes the static features of management control systems rather than the process-dynamic features. It also prioritizes strategy maps and balanced scorecards (creating a hierarchy in which they are "foundational"), thus emphasizing the more formal aspects of management control systems over the more informal. Also, the political, ideological, sociological, and cognitive aspects of management control systems are slighted, and a (non-existent) rigid logic of management control systems development is signaled (i.e., develop strategy maps and balanced scorecards → transform the foundations of management control systems), thereby ignoring the ecology of management control systems change. In other words, if (again) the first three epigrams at the start of this chapter are plausible, there is a lot going on under the textual surface of just this first sentence. Of course, this is just one very tiny piece of accounting textual microdiscourse (Alvesson and Karreman 2000; Craig and Amernic 2004), but the notion that metaphors can traipse at times unnoticed across our writing, perceptions, and thinking as accounting academics, educators, students, practitioners, standard-setters, and corporate leaders, managers, shareholders, analysts, employees, etc., is surely worthy of attention.[10]

Metaphor and accounting education: some implications

Botha (2009: 433) provides the following "provisional list" of some roles for metaphor in university educational settings:

1. Metaphors could be constitutive to the educational policies we devise, e.g. the "market" metaphor or school choice (goods, services, consumers).
2. They can also be constitutive of the teaching process (e.g. teaching as orchestrating, conditioning, guiding or training).
3. They could function heuristically as a tool for discovery (spiral staircase or ladder).
4. The often function didactically as approaches to teaching (dramatization and role playing).
5. They sometimes qualify the teaching actions of the teacher (pottery, gardening, artistry, policeman, entertainer, sermonizer, scholar, a guide, a coach, a researcher, a sculptor, conductor, gardener, midwife, etc.).
6. At times they determine the way the learner or learning process is seen (sponge, filter, funnel, and strainer).
7. They are also characteristic of the content of the subject matter that is being taught and this in turn is often determined by the curricular metaphors (system, mechanism, organism) within which the subject matter is taught.
8. Metaphors can function as tools for communication.
9. Metaphors mediate the understanding of the nature of the school as educational institution (family, factory, etc.).

Each item on Botha's list has implications for accounting education. In the accounting literature, Amernic and Craig (2004) emphasize the following four metaphors:

- metaphors we have about accounting the subject;[11]
- metaphors about the things accounted for;

- metaphors about accounting students;
- metaphors about ourselves as accounting educators.

Amernic and Craig (2004: 357) use Figure 6.1 to suggest that metaphors for these four aspects of accounting education seem to work together to frame the way we, as accounting educators, engage accounting education, for better or worse.

"Metaphors of ourselves as accounting educators," for example, encourage reflection on just what is the process of accounting education in which we are engaged. Four possible metaphoric conceptions of the teaching process are (Fox 1983):

- a "transfer" conception: knowledge is a commodity to be transferred from one vessel to another, and accounting educators perform the transferring;
- a "shaping" conception: teaching is usually directed to "developing" the minds of students;
- a "traveling" conception: the teacher "leads" students into new territory and, in doing so, gains new perspectives too;
- a "growing" conception: the teacher is a "nurturer."

The transfer metaphor of the teaching process might go hand-in-hand with "subject matter as food" and "learning as digestion" metaphors, both inconsistent with normative university aspirations (Whitehead [1929] 1957). Additionally, if accounting educators promote the shaping conception of what we do *as* educators, this suggests that responsibility for learning is to be placed on the teacher rather than the student, with the accounting educator acting perhaps as a sculptor fashioning the pliable minds of students into something (allegedly) more developed and beautiful. But such a metaphor—and its attendant metaphors regarding students—seems surely contestable and thus open to debate, again particularly in a university context.

Thus, the metaphors that are explicit and implicit in the way we think about accounting education, in the curriculum materials that we assign, in the structure and process aspects of our

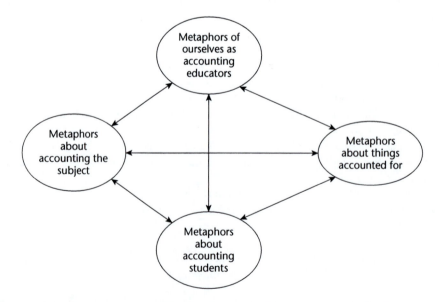

Figure 6.1 Diagram representing the four aspects of accounting education as metaphors
Source: Amernic and Craig (2004: 357)

courses, in the design of our accounting and business programs, and in myriad other ways connected to accounting education, all seem bound to affect both us and our students, for better or worse, and ultimately the lives our students lead after graduation. So it is little wonder why Postman (1993: 124) encouraged metaphor to be uppermost in our minds since understanding metaphor might be useful in revealing an "ideological agenda that is apt to be hidden from view." This encouragement dovetails nicely with Wilkerson's message to accounting educators that

> accounting educators are called to a dual standard, one that is different from, and more complex than, that of university and business school educators generally. We must honor one public trust as members of the academy and another as educators associated with the accounting profession.
>
> *(2010: 3)*

Metaphor and accounting educational materials: some suggestions

- Assisting students to become aware of metaphors for financial statements has good pedagogical benefit. McGoun, Bettner and Coyne (2007) is a useful resource here.
- Having students identify and then speculate about the metaphoric implications of authoritative bodies' definitions of accounting elements such as *assets* encourages a more critical appreciation of the strengths and weaknesses of definitions (see later in this chapter).
- Metaphors in CEO letters published in annual reports and sustainability reports are worthy of analysis, and will almost always reveal interesting perspectives apparently held by the CEO-author of such reports. For example, in his CEO letter in Walmart's 2011 *Global Responsibility Report*, CEO Duke invokes a metaphor originated by Walmart founder Sam Walton, "WALMART IS THE LIGHTHOUSE TO THE WORLD."[12]
- Identifying and discussing metaphors for key terms in accounting textbooks and accounting standards should assist students in becoming more self-confident in reading the literature.
- Press releases and quarterly accounting releases are especially useful for student metaphor analysis. For example, BP's first quarterly interim financial statements released after the Deepwater Horizon tragedy of April 20, 2010, and in following months (and years), introduces students to the narrative and accounting reporting that a company deploys under duress. The metaphors employed in such accountability documents are useful curriculum materials.
- The relatively-new Compensation Discussion and Analysis report is another candidate for identifying and analyzing possible metaphors. Such an analysis has potential for both financial accounting and management control courses.
- It might be enlightening for students to attempt to identify and analyze metaphors in the published cases that they are assigned in their courses. The often unobtrusive ideologies in such teaching materials might then be more apparent.

Metaphor and accounting practice

Aside from educators, why should audit and accounting practitioners generally be concerned with *metaphor*? A short answer flows from a *Harvard Business Review* article published in 1979. The author claimed that managers continuously send "hidden messages" in images, settings, and body language, which have potential to reveal much about themselves and "the ways they see the world" (McCaskey 1979: 135), since the "imagery and metaphors that a person most frequently uses can be clues to understanding the world he or she inhabits" (p. 136).

An auditor's understanding of the way client leaders understand their world seems fundamental in assessing important phenomena such as audit risk.

The metaphors deployed and endorsed by corporate leaders, either explicitly or implicitly, are essential to the language of leadership and to setting the "tone at the top" (Amernic, Craig and Tourish 2010). Thus, a close analysis of metaphors-in-use by a CEO may assist in the auditor's comprehension of CEO-based audit risk. Perhaps a forensic analysis of BP CEOs John Browne's and Tony Hayward's use of metaphors of safety and safety culture in their speeches and CEO letters in the years preceding the Deepwater Horizon Gulf of Mexico tragedy would have provided at least some clues as to the ways they saw their company's safety world, given the high-risk technical and geopolitical environment in which BP operated.

In addition to direct audit-risk implications, practitioners' sensitivity to metaphor seems crucial to accounting communication more generally. For example, in its first quarterly report issued after the Deepwater Horizon tragedy, BP wrote: (p. 33):

The Gulf of Mexico oil spill
Significant uncertainties over the extent and timing of costs and liabilities relating to the incident and the changes in the regulatory and operating environment that may result from the incident have increased the risks to which the group is exposed. These uncertainties are likely to continue for a significant period. These risks have had and are expected to have a material adverse impact on the group's business, competitive position, cash flows, prospects, liquidity, shareholder returns and/or implementation of its strategic agenda. Furthermore, we have taken a charge of $32.2 billion in the second quarter, and these risks may continue to have a material adverse effect on the group's results of operations and financial position. The risks associated with the Gulf of Mexico incident could heighten the consequence of the other risks to which the group is exposed.

This report was dated July 27, 2010, over two months after the April 20 explosion and sinking of the deepwater drilling rig, the deaths of eleven rig workers in the immediate aftermath, and by which time the profound environmental-social-economic crisis was revealing itself. Yet, BP refers to this intense tragedy in two interesting metaphorical ways in this report: as an "oil spill" and as an "incident." Using capital letters to signal conceptual metaphors, and "X" to indicate the great tragedy, the metaphors may be written:

X IS AN OIL SPILL
X IS AN INCIDENT

BP's deployment of both metaphors, perhaps especially "X IS AN INCIDENT," which appears three times in the excerpt from the report above, seems disingenuous at the very least, since both metaphors ignore implications of the existing and prior risk and safety culture at the company and thus may reflect inapt accounting communication. Of course, legal and other impression management implications might drive management's selection of such metaphors, but the tension with transparency in financial reporting, especially narrative reporting, seems evident.

"Metaphor" as an explicit focus in the accounting scholarly literature

Although it is a bit surprising that metaphor, as an explicit theoretical and empirical focus, has not had much influence on accounting scholarly literature, there have been several

Table 6.2 Articles with a focus on metaphor in the accounting and related literature

Papers listed by year of publication	Brief description
Morgan, G. (1988)	Denying unthinking objectivity in accounting, this paper argues that accountants must represent complex realities via necessarily partial metaphors.
Thornton, D.B. (1988)	Urges, among other things, that accounting students—and, by extension, practitioners—be introduced to accounting's metaphorical nature early on, so that "users, preparers, and auditors of accounting data will eventually speak the same language" (p. 9).
Walters-York, L.M. (1996)	A detailed interrogation of metaphor in accounting discourse which builds upon a review of literature successfully challenging the view that metaphor is a sort of deviation.
Young, J.J. (2001)	Assesses FASB's use of metaphors for risk, questioning aspects of risk thus overlooked.
Milne, M.J., K. Kearins, and S. Walton (2006)	Employs a particular metaphor—the journey metaphor—to critically analyze sustainability discourse.
Chatelain-Ponroy, S. (2010)	Employs a metaphor of the iceberg to explore visible, formal versus hidden, informal dimensions of management control.
Patriotta, G., and A.D. Brown (2011)	Drawing upon the sensemaking and performance evaluation literatures, the authors provide empirical support for the notion that "one way people make sense of being evaluated is through metaphor" (p. 34).
Gibbon, J. (in press)	Employs metaphor as an instrument, a research tool, in a personal reflection on social accounting.

contributions that are worthy additions to accounting communications. Some of these are listed chronologically in Table 6.2. (Note that space limitations permit only a very small sampling of papers being included, and examples from several sub-genres in accounting communication were selected. Although the metaphor-focused accounting literature in general is rather sparse, it is also unevenly located. For example, journals such as *The Accounting Review*, *Journal of Accounting Research*, *Journal of Accounting and Economics*, and *Contemporary Accounting Research* generally do not contemplate such work.) Even this small sample shows that the idea and literature of metaphor has been used in a variety of interesting and creative ways in the accounting scholarly literature; however, the surface has just barely been scratched.

The next section presents an introductory discussion about metaphors of "the reporting entity" as a research focus. The reporting entity is a foundational concept in accounting, and in accounting communication, since it is the focal point of the communication process involving accounting reports and accounting discourse at the firm level. Thus, its metaphorical construction has important implications for practice and standard-setting.

Metaphor in accounting communication construction: the case of "the reporting entity"

Naming and metaphors in accounting communication

In their commentary on aspects of the eminent critical thinker Kenneth Burke's social impact, Cheney, Garvin-Doxas, and Torrens (1999) write:

The power of words is further demonstrated in the magic of ostensibly descriptive naming ... Burke notes the great potency of "accurate" naming: our drive to find the best label for something. How objects, feelings and events are named affects orientation, interests, perspectives, and pieties. Whether we ... call a foreign movement "freedom fighters" or "rebels" has profound implication for policy formation with respect to that other group in another country; each term, with its historical and ideological baggage, is highly suggestive of a policy.

(p. 145)

One particularly interesting instance of "ostensibly descriptive" naming which has potential to "affect ... orientation, interests, perspectives, and pieties" in the accounting discipline is "the reporting entity." In this section, the reporting entity is explored as a metaphoric construction, from a financial reporting perspective. Exploring this central accounting construct in this way has considerable potential, since all stakeholders in an organization should be concerned about the metaphors guiding the way the organization itself is viewed. For example, if a CEO views the corporation that the CEO leads as—metaphorically—an extension of his or her self, this may create an added layer of risk in financial reporting and auditing. As another example, if— after examining behavior and rhetoric occurring within and without a company—an informed observer concludes that the corporation has attributes of a (metaphoric) psychotic organization (Sievers 1999), this would seem to have important implications for the (re-)design of incentive rewards and other key aspects of the organization's management control system, and for corporate governance and board of directors' oversight generally.

We focus on the reporting entity from a financial reporting perspective, using as our jumping-off point the Conceptual Framework exposure draft on the reporting entity of the International Accounting Standard Board (IASB).

The development of the IASB's work plan on its joint Conceptual Framework project with the FASB has, apparently, been slowed down due to reaction to the attempt to develop the reporting entity chapter of the framework.[13] It is not surprising that elaboration of this concept is problematic; indeed, in his review of the reporting entity concept, Walker (2007) illustrates some of the practical issues involved.[14] And in their critical discussion of consolidated financial statements, Clarke and Dean (2007: 187–188) make the following comment illustrating the problematic nature of the reporting entity:

From the start, accounting consolidations are counterfactual—the group is not a legal entity. Accordingly, there is no such thing as group performance, group financial position, group insolvency, group gearing, and the like. Such matters relate to the financial characteristics of separate legal entities. Corporate groups are accounting fictions. At best, the group label is a convenient, though sloppy and misleading, shorthand way of referring to a metaphoric bundling of a parent company and its subsidiaries. Consolidated financial statements are the ultimate in misinformation.

Clarke and Dean's engaging phrase "metaphoric bundling" seems apt in connection not only with their specific interest in consolidated reporting entities, but for the phrase "reporting entity" more generally. This phrase is a complex metaphor with strong rhetorical import.

"Reporting entity" may be construed as being metaphorical in several ways. One of these is the metaphor or metaphors deployed by a company's CEO in his or her discourse about the company the CEO leads. Such metaphors may be particularly revealing about the perspective that the CEO has regarding important issues such as the corporation's "tone at the top" and corporate culture, management control and compensation incentives, and financial reporting.[15]

Other perspectives on metaphor and the reporting entity involve other members of the top management team (such as the CFO), employees, customers, communities in which a company physically resides, the company's internet presence, etc. In other words, all the possible near and far stakeholders in the company might plausibly have different conceptions, metaphors, for the reporting entity. An interesting perspective is that of standard-setters: what sort of metaphors inhabit the language (and thus, from the view of cognitive metaphor theory, the mental model) of standard-setters regarding the reporting entity? The standard-setters' perspective is explored in the following subsection.

The reporting entity and the IASB 2010 exposure draft[16]

The reporting entity concept in the exposure draft is defined as shown in Table 6.3 with some illustrative metaphors identified (pp. 1–2 of the exposure draft; see endnote 16).

Let's examine the word "entity" in a bit of detail, briefly. From the *Oxford English Dictionary* online (at http://oed.com.myaccess.library.utoronto.ca/view/Entry/62904, last accessed July 5, 2011), we have the following:

1. Being, existence, as opposed to non-existence; the existence, as distinguished from the qualities or relations, of anything.
2. That which constitutes the being of a thing; essence, essential nature.
3. a. *concr.* Something that has a real existence … as distinguished from a mere function, attribute, relation, etc. †rational entity n. = Latin *ens rationis*, a thing which has an existence only as an object of reason.
   †b. An actual quantity (however small).
4. *indefinitely.* What exists; 'being' generally.

Certainly, OED description/definition 3a seems to fit the use of "entity" in accounting literature, especially the IASB exposure draft (although Clarke and Dean, 2007, would probably dispute this, at least in connection with consolidated reporting entities; see above). And OED description/definition 1 seems appropriate to the use of "entity" in accounting literature's phrase "reporting entity" (again, Clarke and Dean would probably disagree). OED description/definition 2 seems attractive, but does suggest problems, because here we become overtly metaphorical, although with 3a and 1, we are also at least mildly metaphorical; for example, in 3a, how does one show that a reporting entity "has a real existence"? (And for 1?!). Thus, on balance, the dictionary so-called definition(s) of "entity" only seem to inflame the degree to which we are dealing with metaphor in connection with "the reporting entity," and in an engaging philosophical sense at that. That this is so is not surprising, since many words in accounting have metaphorical echoes.[17]

Also, this raises an important attribute of "definitions" as enunciated by accounting standard-setting bodies: they are, more or less, rather arbitrary and often ideological and thus power-laden in their support of certain groups or classes at the expense of others. Schiappa (2003) argues that definitional disputes should be treated less as issues of "is" and more as sociopolitical questions of "ought." Instead of asking "What is X?" he advocates that definitions be considered as proposals for shared knowledge and institutional norms, as in "What should count as X in context Y, given our needs and interests?" (www.siupress.com/catalog/productinfo.aspx?id=457&AspxAu toDetectCookieSupport=1). Thus, the definition of "the reporting entity" from the IASB-FASB exposure draft has, according to all the above, both metaphorical and arbitrary features.

Table 6.3 Definition in the exposure draft

The definition in the exposure draft (not including paragraphs RE5 and RE6, which are additional descriptions)	Some illustrative metaphors
"RE2. A reporting entity is a circumscribed area of economic activities whose financial information has the potential to be useful to existing and potential equity investors, lenders, and other creditors who cannot directly obtain the information they need in making decisions about providing resources to the entity and in assessing whether management and the governing board of that entity have made efficient and effective use of the resources provided."	The words "reporting entity" individually and together are metaphorical (see below). The phrase "a circumscribed area" evokes both spatial and geometric metaphors, suggesting (among other things) an unachievable exactness in the practical definition of a reporting entity for financial reporting purposes, particularly in the era of high-speed finance and the Internet and allied digital technology. The word "whose" suggests an almost human-like agency (the "reporting entity" can *possess* something, implying a naturalness of both such ownership and the things being owned).
"RE3. A reporting entity has three features: a. Economic activities of an entity are being conducted, have been conducted, or will be conducted; b. Those economic activities can be objectively distinguished from those of other entities and from the economic environment in which the entity exists; c. Financial information about the economic activities of that entity has the potential to be useful in making decisions about providing resources to the entity and in assessing whether the management and the governing board have made efficient and effective use of the resources provided. These features are necessary but not always sufficient to identify a reporting entity."	The expression "economic activities" seems metaphorical since such activities may range from completed, simple transactions to intended, complex transactions, and also to non-transactions. By choosing to modify "activities" with the adjective "economic," the IASB and FASB put into play a wide range of possibilities that render the resulting phrase "economic activities" more metaphorical than literal. This might be a useful thing, since it would encourage standard-setters and all other participants in financial reporting to creatively engage with their duties.
"RE4. Identifying a reporting entity in a specific situation requires consideration of the boundary of the economic activities that are being conducted, have been conducted, or will be conducted. The existence of a legal entity is neither necessary nor sufficient to identify a reporting entity. A reporting entity can include more than one entity or it can be a portion of a single entity."	The phrase "the boundary of the economic activities that are being conducted" evokes a spatial/geometric metaphor again and also an entity with agency that is responsible for the economic activities "being conducted, have been conducted, or will be conducted." The futurity here also seems to be metaphorical.

In practice, the implications for research and practice of the metaphoricity of "the reporting entity" might include the following for financial reporting, among many other possibilities:

• Inconsistencies between the metaphors for the reporting entity in different standards might lead to inconsistencies in accounting and reporting, for individual companies over time and issues.

- Inconsistencies in the way that those providing comment letters to the IASB/FASB regard, metaphorically, the reporting entity, might lead to different positions on accounting issues. For example, a potentially interesting research issue involving metaphor is the impact, if any, of different metaphors on the positions adopted by various constituencies regarding proposed accounting standards.
- Differences in financial circumstances might affect how management metaphorically re-defines the reporting entity.

Summary: the importance of metaphor and symbolic activity in accounting communication

In this limited overview, the scope and opportunity for addressing *metaphor* in accounting communication education, research, and practice has been just briefly suggested. Acknowledging accounting as a narrative art, an important means of (metaphorically) "shaping the discourse of performance" (Power 2004: 778), places metaphor at the centre of the symbolic roles of accounting communication. The practical importance of metaphor sensitivity is summarized cogently by a retired American army colonel who at the time of writing served as an associate professor at the U.S. Army Command and General Staff College (Paparone 2008: 64). Although he was writing for a military officer audience and not the accounting community, his comments are pertinent to accounting communication:

> Thought leaders' sense-givings are so prevalent that it is easy to mindlessly treat a metaphor as a certain "truth" rather than as a shadowy image for communicating only dimly per-ceived realities. Unawareness of metaphor can grow and work to anesthetize professionals from feeling and understanding the implications of truth as it is socially constructed into a makeshift correspondence with fact. Unreflective indoctrination can thereby seductively serve to reduce anxiety and confusion while encouraging complacency about knowledge. In uncritical practitioners not tuned to reflection, a leader's over-simplified representations of truths can be crippling.

The act of "mindlessly treat[ing] a metaphor as a certain 'truth'" in accounting demands strong antidote, and continuous challenge of metaphor. Postman's (rhetorical) question—"Do I exaggerate in saying that a student cannot understand what a subject is without some under-standing of the metaphors that are its foundation" (1996: 174)—thus holds for more than "just" students. At its core, this chapter is a "teaser," an introduction to the fundamental roles of metaphor in accounting communication. But more broadly, this chapter (as well as others in this collection) might be regarded as an encouragement to treat most seriously and gingerly language and symbolic activity in accounting communication research, teaching, and practice.

Notes

1 Personal communication from Russell Craig, September 4, 2011.
2 Lakoff and Johnson's book is rightly credited with inspiring a groundswell of scholarly (and other) work on metaphor. But their formalization of cognitive metaphor (see also Lakoff 1993) has strong precursors (for example, see Jäkel 1999). Gibbs (2006: 1) describes the empirical foundation for cognitive linguistic work on metaphor. Steen (2011b) extends and modifies what he calls contemporary metaphor theory by emphasizing a social approach focusing on communication.
3 Grady (1997) illustrates that the case of such a seemingly-straightforward metaphor is rife with complex-ity and nuance.

4 Regarding the context, or social setting, in which metaphor occurs, Eubanks (1999: 195), has argued that

metaphor is rhetorically constituted. No metaphor is spoken or written except in the context of a sociohistorically bound communicative situation. Therefore, all metaphors are inflected by politics, economics, philosophy, social interests, professional commitments, and personal attitudes—in short by the whole of our cultural and conceptual repertoire. Because metaphors are inflected, we cannot explain how they work unless we consider concrete instances of metaphor, taking into account how inflections constrain the way metaphors are uttered and understood.

5 This complexity might also impair the goal of a global set of IFRS. For example, metaphor scholars such as Grady (1997) distinguish between *primary* metaphors that seem universal and relate to physical functions, and *complex* metaphors, which although based upon primary metaphors also have important cultural aspects and thus may differ between cultures.

6 Also, see various contributions in Gibbs (2008) which focus on metaphor identification and analysis in pictures, art, music, and gestures.

7 In the accounting literature, Amernic and Craig (2001) explore a Gestalt-like metaphor in the case of a three-way multinational merger announcement.

8 Thibodeau and Boroditsky (2011) provide some current evidence. See also Gibbs (1994).

9 A U.S. government agency's intent to analyze metaphors employed in various languages as part of anti-terrorist intelligence-gathering prompted Rosen to write a news item entitled "Shakespeare: the metaphorical terrorist" (Rosen 2011).

10 Sackmann (1989: 482) writes that metaphors help to "succinctly transmit a large amount of information simultaneously at a cognitive, behavioural, and emotional level." This suggests that metaphors in authoritative texts, such as papers by accounting and other scholars, accounting standards, financial statements (including their notes and associated texts such as the MD&A and the CD&A) all require close metaphor investigation.

11 Batstone (2000: 251) contends that metaphoric frames "can influence how a problem is perceived, as well as the possibilities that are generated for its solution" (see also Schön 1993). Benoit (2001) contends that a skillful selection of metaphors may serve as an important framing mechanism in discourse. Amernic and Robb (2003) apply this notion to accounting education by illustrating how the metaphor "quality of earnings" may be used to productively frame a course in intermediate financial accounting.

12 Amernic (2012) provides an analysis of this metaphor.

13 In its work plan for the Conceptual Framework project, the IASB announced the following (with particular focus on Phase D, The Reporting Entity; online at: www.ifrs.org/Current+Projects/IASB+Projects/IASB+Work+Plan.htm (last visited August 12, 2011):

Conceptual Framework: The Board completed Phase A by publishing in September 2010 the *Objectives* and *Qualitative characteristics* chapters of the new Conceptual Framework. The IASB and the FASB will amend sections of their conceptual frameworks as they complete individual phases of the project. *The boards have considered the comments they received on the exposure draft for Phase D Reporting Entity. In the light of those comments the boards have decided that they will need more time to finalise this chapter than they initially anticipated. Therefore, the boards do not expect to continue their deliberations until after June 2011.* ... [emphasis added]

14 Walker refers to "the concept of an *accounting entity* ... for which accounting records were compiled" (p. 54).

15 See, for example, Amernic, Craig and Tourish (2007, 2010).

16 The exposure draft was part of a joint IASB–FASB project on the conceptual framework. It was issued March 11, 2010 as Proposed Statement of Financial Accounting Concepts—*Conceptual Framework for Financial Reporting: The Reporting Entity*, and the comment period ended July 16, 2010 (accessed online at www.iasb.org (last visited August 15, 2011)).

17 See, for example, Thornton 1988; Walters-York 1996. Amernic and Craig (2004) describe some of the metaphors inhabiting an official accounting definition of "assets".

References

Alvesson, M., and D. Karreman (2000), "Varieties of Discourse: On the Study of Organizations through Discourse Analysis," *Human Relations*, 53(9), pp. 1125–1149.

Alvesson, M., and A. Spicer (2011), *Metaphors We Lead By: Understanding Leadership in the Real World*, London and New York: Routledge.

Amernic, J.H. (1996), "The Rhetoric versus the Reality, or is the Reality 'Mere' Rhetoric? A Case Study of Public Accounting Firms' Responses to a Company's Invitation for Alternative Opinions on an Accounting Matter," *Critical Perspectives on Accounting*, 7, pp. 57–75.

Amernic, J.H. (1998), "'Close Readings' of Internet Corporate Financial Reporting: Towards a More Critical Pedagogy on the Information Highway," *The Internet and Higher Education*, 1(2), pp. 87–112.

Amernic, J.H. (2012), "The Reporting Entity for Large Public Companies: CEO as Metaphor-Maker-in-Chief," working paper, University of Toronto.

Amernic, J.H., and R.J. Craig (2000), "Accountability and Rhetoric during a Crisis: Walt Disney's 1940 Letter to Stockholders," *Accounting Historians Journal*, 27(2), pp. 49–86.

Amernic, J.H., and R.J. Craig (2001), "Three Tenors in Perfect Harmony: 'Close Readings' of the Joint Letter by the Heads of Aluminium Giants Alcan, Pechiney, and Alusuisse Announcing Their Mega-Merger Plan," *Critical Perspectives on Accounting*, 12, pp. 763–795.

Amernic, J., and R. Craig (2004), "Reform of Accounting Education in the Post-Enron Era: Moving Accounting 'Out of the Shadows'," *Abacus*, 40(3), pp. 342–478.

Amernic, J., and R. Craig (2006), *CEO-speak: The Language of Corporate Leadership*, Montreal and Kingston: McGill Queen's University Press.

Amernic, J., and R. Craig (2009), "Understanding Accounting Through Conceptual Metaphor: ACCOUNTING IS AN INSTRUMENT," *Critical Perspectives on Accounting*, 20, pp. 875–883.

Amernic, J., R. Craig, and D. Tourish (2007), "The Transformational Leader as Pedagogue, Physician, Architect, Commander, and Saint: Five Root Metaphors in Jack Welch's Letters to Stockholders of General Electric," *Human Relations*, 60(12), pp. 1839–1872.

Amernic, J., R. Craig, and D. Tourish (2010), *Measuring and Assessing Tone at the Top Using Annual Report CEO Letters*, Edinburgh: Institute of Chartered Accountants of Scotland.

Amernic, J., and S. Robb (2003), "*Quality of Earnings* as a Framing Device and Unifying Theme in Intermediate Financial Accounting," *Issues in Accounting Education*, 18(1), pp. 1–21.

Batstone, K. (2000), "'One's Terms Defy One's Arguments': The Metaphoric Framing of UNIVERSITY AS COMMUNITY and UNIVERSITY AS BUSINESS in the Second Report of the Task Force on Strategic Planning at the University of Manitoba," *Metaphor and Symbol*, 15(4), pp. 241–251.

Benoit, W.L. (2001), "Framing through Temporal Metaphor: The 'Bridges' of Bob Dole and Bill Clinton in their 1996 Acceptance Speeches," *Communication Studies*, 52(1), pp. 70–84.

Bergmann, M. (1982), "Metaphorical Assertions," *The Philosophical Review*, XCI(2), pp. 229–245.

Botha, E. (2009), "Why Metaphor Matters in Education," *South African Journal of Education*, 29, pp. 431–444.

Cameron, L., R. Maslen, Z. Todd, J. Maule, P. Stratton, and N. Stanley (2009), "The Discourse Dynamics Approach to Metaphor and Metaphor-Led Discourse Analysis," *Metaphor and Symbol*, 24(2), pp. 63–89.

Chatelain-Ponroy, S. (2010), "A New Metaphor for Understanding Management Control Practices," International Federation of Scholarly Associations of Management—"Justice and Sustainability in the Global Economy," France (2010), available at: http://halshs.archives-ouvertes.fr/docs/0050/24/13/PDF/Chatelain-Ponroy_ofsam_2010.pdf (last visited July 2, 2011).

Cheney, G., K. Garvin-Doxas, and K. Torrens (1999), "Kenneth Burk's Implicit Theory of Power," in B.L. Brock (ed.) *Kenneth Burke and the 21st Century*, Albany, N.Y.: State University of New York Press, pp. 133–150.

Clarke, F.L., and G.W. Dean (2007), *Indecent Disclosure: Gilding the Corporate Lily*, Cambridge: Cambridge University Press.

Cohn, C. (1987), "Sex and Death in the Rational World of Defense Intellectuals," *Signs: Journal of Women in Culture and Society*, 12(4), pp. 687–718.

Craig, R., and J. Amernic (2002), "Accountability of Accounting Educators and the Rhythm of the University: Resistance Strategies for Postmodern Blues," *Accounting Education*, 11(2), pp. 121–171.

Craig, R.J., and J.H. Amernic (2004), "Enron Discourse: The Rhetoric of a Resilient Capitalism," *Critical Perspectives on Accounting*, 15, pp. 813–851.

Davis, S.W., K. Menon, and G. Morgan (1982), "The Images that Have Shaped Accounting Theory," *Accounting, Organizations and Society*, 7(4), pp. 307–318.

Deignan, A. (2008), "Corpus Linguistics and Metaphor," in R.W. Gibbs, Jr. (ed.) *The Cambridge Handbook of Metaphor and Thought*, Cambridge: Cambridge University Press, pp. 280–294.

Dirsmith, M.W., M.A. Covaleski, and J.P. McAllister (1985), "Of Paradigms and Metaphors in Auditing Thought," *Contemporary Accounting Research*, 2(1), pp. 46–68.

Dunn, J. (2011), "Gradient Semantic Intuitions of Metaphoric Expressions," *Metaphor and Symbol*, 26, pp. 53–67.

Durkee, D.A. (2011), "Teaching with Metaphor: The Case of Alice in GAAP Land," *Academy of Educational Leadership Journal*, 15(1), pp. 39–56.

Eagleton, T. (1991), *Ideology: An Introduction*, London: Verso.

Eubanks, P. (1999), "Conceptual Metaphor as Rhetorical Response: A Reconsideration of Metaphor," *Written Communication*, 16(2), pp. 171–199.

Fox, D. (1983), "Personal Theories of Teaching," *Studies in Higher Education*, 8(2), pp. 151–163.

Gibbon, J. (in press), "Understandings of Accountability: An Autoethnographic Account Using Metaphor," *Critical Perspectives on Accounting*.

Gibbs, Jr., R.W. (1994), *The Poetics of Mind: Figurative Thought, Language, and Understanding*, Cambridge: Cambridge University Press.

Gibbs, Jr., R.W. (2006), "Cognitive Linguistics and Metaphor Research," *D.E.L.T.A.*, 22, ESPECIAL, pp. 1–20.

Gibbs, Jr. R.W. (ed.) (2008) *The Cambridge Handbook of Metaphor and Thought*, Cambridge, U.K.: Cambridge University Press.

Gibbs, Jr., R.W., and T. Matlock (2008), "Metaphor, Imagination, and Simulation: Psycholinguistic Evidence," in R.W. Gibbs, Jr. (ed.) *The Cambridge Handbook of Metaphor and Thought*, Cambridge, U.K.: Cambridge University Press, pp. 161–176.

Grady, J.E. (1997), "THEORIES ARE BUILDINGS revisited," *Cognitive Linguistics*, 8, pp. 267–290.

Grady, J.E. (2007), "Metaphor," in D. Geeraerts and H. Cuyckens (eds) *The Oxford Handbook of Cognitive Linguistics*, Oxford: Oxford University Press, pp. 188–213.

Hamington, M. (2009), "Business is Not a Game: The Metaphoric Fallacy," *Journal of Business Ethics*, 86, pp. 473–484.

Harrington, A. (1995), "Metaphoric Connections: Holistic Science in the Shadow of the Third Reich," *Social Research*, 62(2), pp. 357–385.

Hines, R.D. (1988), "Financial Accounting: In Communicating Reality, We Construct Reality," *Accounting, Organizations and Society*, 13(3), pp. 251–261.

Isenberg, A. (1963), "On Defining Metaphor," *Journal of Philosophy*, 60(21), pp. 609–622.

Jäkel, O. (1999), "Kant, Blumenberg, Weinrich: Some Forgotten Contributions to the Cognitive Theory of Metaphor," in R.W. Gibbs, and G. Steen (eds) *Metaphor in Cognitive Linguistics*, Amsterdam: John Benjamin, pp. 9–28.

Kaplan, R. (2006), "The Demise of Cost and Profit Centers" (online at: www.hbs.edu/research/pdf/07-030.pdf).

Lakoff, G. (1993), "The Contemporary Theory of Metaphor," in A. Ortony (ed.) *Metaphor and Thought*, 2nd edition, Cambridge: Cambridge University Press, pp. 202–251.

Lakoff, G., and M. Johnson (1980a), "Conceptual Metaphor in Everyday Language," *Journal of Philosophy*, 77(8), pp. 453–486.

Lakoff, G. and Johnson, M. (1980b), *Metaphors We Live By*, Chicago: University of Chicago Press.

McCaskey, M.B. (1979), "The Hidden Messages Managers Send," *Harvard Business Review*, November–December, pp. 135–148.

McGoun, E.G., M.S. Bettner, and M.P. Coyne (2007), "Pedagogical Metaphors and the Nature of Accounting Signification," *Critical Perspectives on Accounting*, 18, pp. 213–230.

Milne, M.J., K. Kearins, and S. Walton (2006), "Creating Adventures in Wonderland: The Journey Metaphor and Environmental Sustainability," *Organization*, 13(6), pp. 801–839.

Modell, A.H. (2009), "Metaphor—The Bridge Between Feelings and Knowledge," *Psychoanalytic Inquiry*, 29, pp. 6–11.

Morgan, G. (1988), "Accounting as Reality Construction: Towards a New Epistemology for Accounting Practice," *Accounting, Organizations and Society*, 13(5), pp. 477–485.

Nünning, A., H. Grabes, and S. Baumbach (2009), "Metaphor as a Way of Worldmaking, or Where Metaphors and Culture Meet," in H. Grabes, A. Nünning, and S. Baumbach (eds) *Yearbook of Research in English and American Literature 25: Metaphors Shaping Culture and Theory*, Tübingen: Gunter Narr Verlag, pp. xi–xxviii.

Ortony, A. (ed.) (1993), *Metaphor and Thought*, 2nd edition, Cambridge: Cambridge University Press.

Paparone, C.R. (2008), "On Metaphors We are Led By," *Military Review: The Professional Journal of the US Army*, November–December, pp. 55–64.

Patriotta, G., and A.D. Brown (2011), "Sensemaking, Metaphors and Performance Evaluation," *Scandinavian Journal of Management*, 27, pp. 34–43.

Postman, N. (1993), *Technopoly: The Surrender of Culture to Technology*, New York: Vintage Books.

Postman, N. (1996), *The End of Education*, New York: Vintage Books.

Power, M. (2004), "Counting, Control and Calculation: Reflections on Measuring and Management," *Human Relations*, 57(6), pp. 765–783.

Pragglejaz Group (2007), "MIP: A Method for Identifying Metaphorically Used Words in Discourse," *Metaphor and Symbol*, 22(1), pp. 1–39.

Ravenscroft, S., and P.F. Williams (2009), "Making Imaginary Worlds Real: The Case of Expensing Employee Stock Options," *Accounting, Organizations and Society*, 34, pp. 770–786.

Reimer, M., and E. Camp (2006), "Metaphor," in E. Lapore and B. Smith (eds) *The Oxford Handbook of Philosophy of Language*, Oxford: Oxford University Press, pp. 845–863.

Rosen, M. (2011), "Shakespeare: The Metaphorical Terrorist," *Guardian*, www.guardian.co.uk (last accessed August 2, 2011).

Sackmann, S. (1989), "The Role of Metaphor in Organizational Transformation," *Human Relations*, 42(6), pp. 463–485.

Schiappa, E. (2003), *Defining Reality: Definitions and the Politics of Meaning*, Carbondale, IL: Southern Illinois University Press.

Schön, D.A. (1993), "Generative Metaphor: A Perspective on Problem-setting in Social Policy," in A. Ortony (ed.) *Metaphor and Thought*, 2nd edition, Cambridge: Cambridge University Press, pp. 137–163.

Sievers, B. (1999), "Psychotic Organization as a Metaphoric Frame for the Socioanalysis of Organizational and Interorganizational Dynamics," *Administration and Society*, 31(5), pp. 588–615.

Spicer, A., and M. Alvesson (2011), "Metaphors for Leadership," in M. Alvesson and A. Spicer (eds) *Metaphors We Lead By*, New York: Routledge, pp. 31–50.

Steen, G.J. (2011a), "The Language of Knowledge Management: A Linguistic Approach to Metaphor Analysis," *Systems Research and Behavioral Science*, 28, pp. 181–188.

Steen, G.J. (2011b), "The Contemporary Theory of Metaphor: Now New and Improved!," *Review of Cognitive Linguistics*, 9(1), pp. 26–64.

Sunder, S. (2011), "IFRS Monopoly: The Pied Piper of Financial Reporting," *Accounting and Business Research*, 41(3), pp. 291–306.

Thibodeau, P.H., and L. Boroditsky (2011), "Metaphors We Think With: The Role of Metaphor in Reasoning," *PLoS ONE*, 6(2): e16782. Doi:10.1371/journal.pone.0016782.

Thornton, D.B. (1988), "Theory and Metaphor in Accounting," *Accounting Horizons*, December, pp. 1–9.

Tinker, T. (1986), "Metaphor or Reification: Are Radical Humanists Really Libertarian Anarchists?," *Journal of Management Studies*, 23(4), pp. 363–384.

Walker, R.G. (2007), "Reporting Entity Concept: A Case Study of the Failure of Principles-Based Regulation," *ABACUS*, 43(1), pp. 49–75.

Walters, M. (2004), "Alternative Accounting Thought and the Prison-House of Metaphor," *Accounting, Organizations and Society*, 29, pp. 157–187.

Walters, M., and Young, J.J. (2008), "Metaphors and Accounting for Stock Options," *Critical Perspectives on Accounting*, 19, pp. 805–833.

Walters-York, L.M. (1996), "Metaphor in Accounting Discourse," *Accounting, Auditing and Accountability Journal*, 9(5), pp. 45–70.

Whitehead, A.N. ([1929]/1957), *The Aims of Education and Other Essays*, New York: Free Press.

Wilkerson, Jr., J.E. (2010), "Accounting Educators as the Accounting Profession's Trustees: Lessons from a Study of Peer Professions," *Issues in Accounting Education*, 25(1), pp. 1–13.

Young, J.J. (2001), "Risk(ing) Metaphors," *Critical Perspectives on Accounting*, 12, pp. 607–625.

7

Rhetoric and the art of memory[1]

Paolo Quattrone

Introduction

Even after the recent financial crisis, lay people think of accounting, finance and other management techniques as having some kind of concrete features that make them functional to the pursuit of precise objectives, typically profit. Often, with respect to the role played by accounting, these objectives are thought to be given, or at least, accounting is seen as a neutral technique aimed at representation. However, this view forgets what Hines (1988: 251) taught us, that is, "in communicating reality, we construct reality".

In this chapter I argue that this link between accounting and communication has a long albeit forgotten history that links it to key features of rhetoric and the art of memory. Bringing these links out to the fore can shed light on how accounting can be viewed not only as a functional tool for representation but also as an instrument for innovation, management of stakeholders and imagining organizations' future.[2]

Drawing on the historical analysis of the genesis and development of accounting in the sixteenth and seventeenth centuries and on case-study material on the implementation of the balanced scorecard (BSC) in contemporary corporations, I theorize accounting as a "rhetorical machine" (Bolzoni 1995; Carruthers 1998) and illustrate four salient features that allow these fashionable business solutions to diffuse and persist in economies and societies, while remaining quite immaterial in their nature. Management practices conceived of as rhetorical machines are:

1. *methods of engagement*, as they offer a method of ordering and innovation without clearly specifying what should be ordered, thus leaving the user free to make such a discovery;
2. *visually appealing inscriptions*, as they always rely on some kind of visualization to represent the organizational world in "its absence" (Latour 1986);
3. *media of communication and translation*, as in communicating business knowledge they permit its continuous translation and appropriation by a multiplicity of users;
4. *performable spaces*, as they are instruments which are designed to elicit users' actions by offering a space where meanings can be constructed via practising the machine.

The combination of these four features makes management practices malleable instruments which succeed in contemporary organizations, economies and society because they help organizational actors to deal with uncertainty, address unexpected problems and imagine pragmatic organizational solutions. In this respect, this success is quite a-teleological as it is meant in the Latin etymological sense of the word, from *succedor*, i.e. to happen: management practices repeat

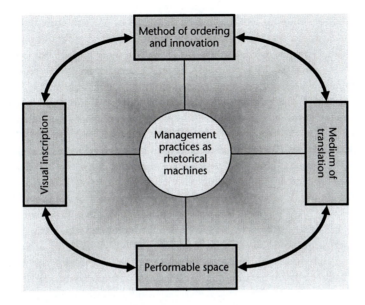

Figure 7.1 Management practices as rhetorical machines

themselves (and thus happen), while always being other than themselves, or rather, they always differ from what people suppose they are or should be and serve purposes that go well beyond those that accounting systems designers had in mind when they draw their contours. This rhetorical nature allows successful management practices to become instruments for the management of diversity. They have indeed become institutions, as they contribute to construct of knowledge and notions of truth, but they have done so not by homogenizing people and organizations' behaviours and views but by allowing the existence, multiplication and incorporation of difference within the very same institution.

This chapter is organized thus. In the following section I briefly recall some of my recent historical work that illustrates the relationships between rhetoric, art of memory and early-modern accounting. This will then be useful to illustrate how contemporary management "best sellers" (e.g. the BSC) show remnants of the rhetorical nature of accounting by illustrating their visual appeal, nature of method, medium of translation and performable space (see Figure 7.1) and how the combination of these four elements makes management solutions and various information technologies immaterial entities. I will then briefly summarize the arguments, illustrate some effects for contemporary organizations, economies and societies, and illustrate possible ways to develop this line of research further.

Accounting, communication and innovation: historical links with the art of memory and rhetoric

Despite the fact that accounting comprises records, the etymology of this word (from the Latin *recordor*, i.e. to remember) has not directed scholarly attention towards the study of the art of memory: a specific set of practices which, like accounting, has a very long history. As M. Carruthers (1990, 1998) noted, the art of memory concerns not only mnemonic techniques aimed at storing and retrieving old reminiscences. It has evolved from antiquity to early modernity through medieval cultures as a complex set of practices for the organization and communication of our thinking. It is composed of a series of precise, albeit varied, procedures which help to identify the ways in which knowledge is defined, classified, organized, and then eventually translated into knowledge artefacts such as manuscripts and books (Bolzoni 1995; Carruthers 1998) – some of the same books of which accounting makes great use. The art of memory comprises a set of techniques (and even "machines": Bolzoni 1995) in which the "imitation of the old is a stage in the production of something new" (ibid., p. xvi): a new understanding, not limited to the simple reproduction of past mental images, but entailing their construction in the present through a web of techniques, practices and artefacts (Bolzoni 2002). Like accounting (see Hines 1988), the art of memory is not a neutral technique which stores and represents facts; it allows the interplay between sameness and diversity (the very problem this chapter addresses), through the performative acts of which it is made (see, for instance, Carruthers 1998, on the relationship between memory, meditation and liturgy). The reference to the art of memory also helps us to focus on other neglected, albeit important issues useful in the understanding of the emergence and spread of accounting and other managerial practices. These issues refer to the role played in the organising of our thinking by analytical methods, images, graphical and visual representations (produced either in the mind or through writing in manuscripts, printed books, economics formula and computer screens). *How* accounting *recording* is intertwined with *remembering* seems to be a fruitful, although not yet charted territory of exploration.

Similarly, while the rhetorical nature of many managerial techniques, including accounting (see Nørreklit 2003), has been highlighted by many researchers, most of this research has focused on the persuasive power of rhetorical techniques in communicating business results but has neglected the links between persuasion, rhetoric's properties in organising knowledge and notions of rationality. As noted by Green: "to be rational is to make persuasive sense. Accordingly, the more persuasive the discursive reasons supporting a managerial practice, the more rational its adoption" (2004, p. 655). Rhetoric is mostly known as a technique of persuasion concerned with the communicative style of language and discourse (the *elocutio*, i.e. the third canon of classic rhetoric; see Carruthers 1998)[3] but less as a classificatory device used for knowledge organization, something that relates more closely to its first two canons: the *inventio*, concerned with figuring out and preparing the arguments to be dealt with; and the *dispositio*, which arranged these arguments in a form coherent with the purposes (*intentiones*) of the exercise. This lack of attention is surprising not only because one of the first and foundational management inventions, the inventory, shares the same etymological root and function with the *inventio*, but also because this tripartite organization of rhetoric informed the structure of both early-modern accounting manuals and accounting systems in practice (see Quattrone 2004, 2009).

As I have argued elsewhere in greater detail (Quattrone 2009), these similarities are more than simple coincidences and direct us to the role that forgotten knowledge and communication practices play in making sense of contemporary organizations economies and societies and on how they engage the adopter, and thus the study of these relationships can help in shedding light on their nature(s), functionalities and historical diffusion. What follows is an attempt at showing how the immaterial nature of management practice allows some substantial organizing work in both historical and contemporary settings.

The visual and imagery appeal of management practices: inscriptions and hope

Studies in the field of medieval and early-modern literature (Yates 1966; Bolzoni 1995; Carruthers 1998) have illustrated how rhetoric made large use of written and mental visual images to aid orators to remember the speech to deliver (Bolzoni 1995, pp. xvi–xvii) or even to organize the structure and format of books (Johns 1998). These images could take the most diverse forms: analytical spaces, hierarchies (or *trees*), logical maps and wheels. Given that contemporary organizing practices make a large use of them (think of accounts, hierarchies, strategy maps and the BSC) and managers widely rely on them in daily life to make sense of their organizational worlds (Craig 2000; Lowy and Hood 2004), to develop fully a rhetorically informed theory of diffusion, it is important to understand better how they worked and diffused.

As argued by Bolzoni (1995, pp. xvi–ii), these rhetorical images presented some common features. They "visualised the logical path to be taken [so that] all of the material [was] presented to the eye reordered and reorganised in a clear, effective fashion that is easy to remember" (Bolzoni 1995, p. xix).[4] They, thus, and in a first instance, represented *visual inscriptions*, i.e. "transformations through which an entity becomes materialised into a sign, an archive, a document, a piece of paper, a trace" (Latour 1999, p. 306).

Wheels, maps and logical cause-and-effect relationships are widely utilized in managers' daily life to make sense of their organisational worlds (Craig 2000; Lowy and Hood 2004) and all of them constitute key elements of BSC's graphical designs and functioning. But they have a long history and most of this happened within religious orders.[5]

Figures 7.2 and 7.3 illustrate some of the tables provided in accounting manuals to facilitate learning of accounting techniques (from Pietra 1589 and Browne 1670), their use in practice and their role in interpreting various forms of economic activities in colleges, monasteries and private families. They are a triumph of dichotomies and analysis in a perfect Ramist[6] fashion, where the appropriation by the reader of accounting principles and techniques such as double entry is made easier by the dichotomical representation in trees and other graphical representations. Thomas Browne's *The Accurate Accomptant* (1670) is such an example. Browne drew upon analytical representations in order to offer an overview of the entire accounting system he exemplified through entries in the cash book, ledger and journal of a merchant. The use of these dichotomized representations was sufficient, in Browne's mind, to become an *Accurate Accomptant*. A text commenting on the images was not even required; the images did it all. They spoke more than one thousand words, if one knew how to listen to them.

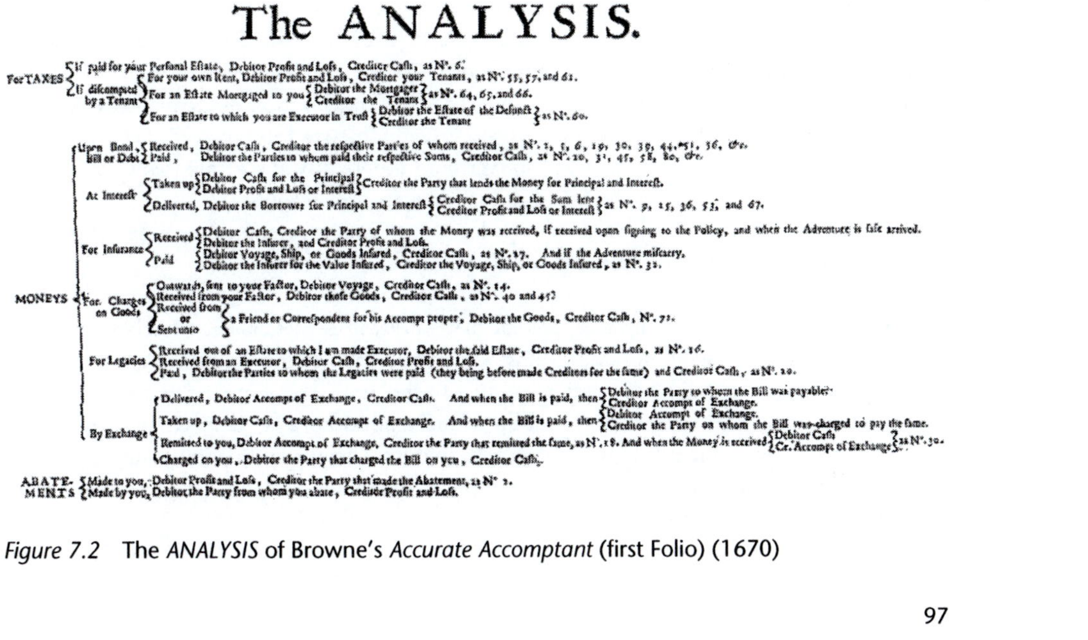

Figure 7.2 The *ANALYSIS* of Browne's *Accurate Accomptant* (first Folio) (1670)

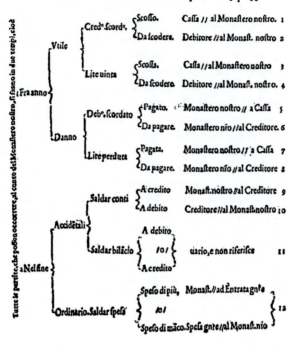

Figure 7.3   Tavola Metodica delle dette dodici partite

This clarity and linearity recalls and expands upon earlier forms of the organization of text in the space of manuscripts and printed books, which allowed easier access to the contents of the book itself, for consultation or mnemonic purposes (see, for instance, Camille 1992; Carruthers 1990). The presence of a table of contents (see those in Pietra's and Flori's texts), marginalia, headings and various *tituli* for sections and chapters (Crick and Walsham 2004, p. 21) merge with the medieval attention paid to images and the visual organization of the manuscript. They made of the book "an object to be used" (Cavallo and Chartier 1999, pp. 18–19) – an object which begs to be utilized and "practiced" for various purposes, from worship (see Camille 1998 on how reading books involves the five senses) to keeping the accounts.

As noted by Grafton and Jardine, the pedagogy of Ramist graphical representations had profound implications for what counted as knowledge in societies:

> What was there about Ramus' approach that so threatened established teachers that they dismissed it as … 'seditiously disturbing'? … the threat was institutional: Ramus deliberately discarded the difficulty and rigorous of scholastic schooling and thereby attracted those who regarded education as a means to social position rather than as a preparation for life of scholarship (the theological debate). In so doing, he explicitly (though not necessarily deliberately) achieved the final secularisation of humanist teaching – the transition from "humanism" to "humanities".

(1986, p. 168)

And they continued: "[Ramism] opened the prospect that the purpose of education was to purvey information and skills, not to be morally improving" (1986, p. 168). Skills that instilled hope in the user that the problems they face could be addressed with the use of some management solution. In other words, the contemporary commodification of (management) knowledge finds its *raison d'être* at the crossroad between late-medieval and early-modern times. We should not be surprised, then, if hierarchies, trees and maps increasingly populate contemporary management books and are preached by management consultants as never before. Figure 7a and 7b, for instance, represents the idea of "strategy map" as devised (and sold as a consulting product) by Robert Kaplan, a Harvard professor, and David Norton, founder and director of a consulting firm.

The strategy map is used as a visual aid to make abstract strategies and visions concrete, as testified by one of the managers interviewed in Busco and Quattrone (2010):

> We developed an interactive presentation based on a Balanced Scorecard tree to offer a simple visual metaphor that associates the four elements of a tree – i.e., its roots, trunk, crown and fruits – with the four dimensions of our Balanced Scorecard … During the internal training sessions we strongly emphasized the inter-dependence of the four Balanced Scorecard dimensions, we warned participants that if the roots are weak, the trunk will be unstable, the crown small and the fruits poor … significantly, we stimulated the participants to interact with the Balanced Scorecard tree, and to monitor the consequences of their actions and performances for the health of the tree.

In this sense, the tree illustrated in early accounting treatises, the map and visualization of the company's strategy on a computer screen or on a piece of paper do more than simply representing business visions. They offer a *re*-presentation, that is, they make absent things present *again* through the active engagement of the user. However, for this engagement to happen, it requires a method for these trees, maps and other visualization and some visual conventions and methods of appropriation.

Management practices as methods of knowledge ordering: filling spaces while leaving them empty

Amongst these various images, also called "machines" (Bolzoni 1995), one has a particular relevance for connecting the past and present of management practices and for grasping their immateriality: the wheel (see Bolzoni 1995, pp. 65–73). The rhetorical wheel is a circular pictorial representation that helps orators organize and deliver their speech. The orator is set to define the topic to be discussed (e.g. love), and then to prepare an inventory of cards, that is, a number of pieces of paper upon which s/he can define various subtopics that in his/her views defines the concept of love (e.g. passion, affect). Then s/he places the main topic at the centre of the wheel and surrounds it with, say, four cards taken from the inventory previously made in an order that makes the engagement of the audience possible. The wheel is an interesting pictorial device as it can play two functions. The first is to provide the orator with a structure for the speech to be given by placing the cards around the topic to be discussed in a given order. Displaying the cards around the centre is, in a first instance, a way of semiotically and relationally defining the nature (and ontology) of such a topic. The second function this machine may play is displayed during the speech when the orator is asked questions that s/he could not answer with the four cards displayed around the centre. Then what the orator can do is to go back to the inventory of cards made and substitute one with another. This apparently mundane action has profound

(a)

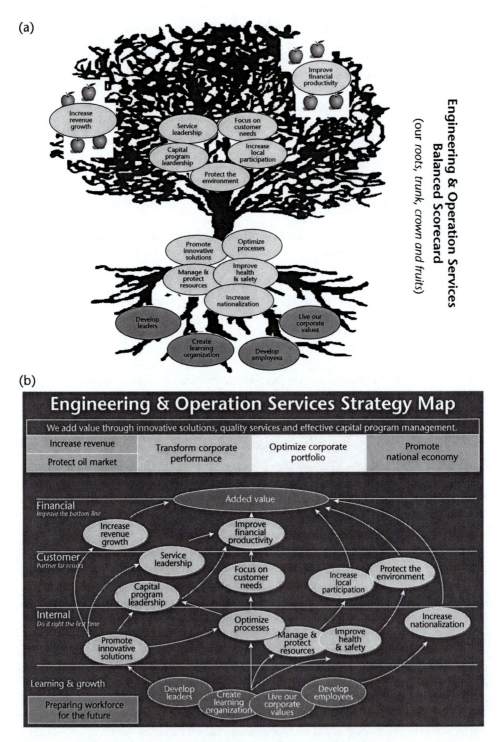

Figure 7.4 a. The Balanced Scorecard as rhetorical tree. b. Strategy map

ontological effects as now the central topic is re-defined in terms of the new four cards, and this process, of course, can be repeated in a theoretically infinite number of combinations.

In other words, "machines" such as the wheel (but the tree would function equally well by adding and recombining branches) did more than creating an inventory of arguments to be dealt with in a speech. It is not by chance that the Latin word *inventio* originated two different words in many contemporary languages: "inventory" (where [i]nventoried materials are counted and placed in locations within an overall structure which allows any item to be retrieved easily and at once", Carruthers 1998, p. 11); and "invention". And in fact:

> the goal of rhetorical mnemotechnical craft was not to give students a prodigious memory ..., but to give an orator the means of wherewithal to invent his material, both beforehand and – crucially – on the spot. *Memoria* is most usefully thought of as a compositional art. The arts of memory are amongst the arts of thinking, especially involved with fostering the qualities we now revere as "imagination" and "creativity".
>
> *(Carruthers 1998, p. 9)*

The *inventio* is therefore the precondition for inventing new knowledge and developing innovative arguments. Rhetorical machines can be seen as visually oriented *methods of ordering and innovation* which helped to give an order but also to invent new arguments and knowledge. This method made the theme positioned at the centre of the rhetorical machine (e.g. love) always fluid, as its meaning depended on what (and how many) cards surrounded the middle of the wheel. The definition of content always happened in the context of the oratorical practice, when a speech was delivered, and could take different routes from those originally planned and designed. If while delivering the speech, the audience raised an unexpected question, the orator could go back (physically or mentally) to the inventory of cards prepared earlier and choose an appropriate topic on a card that could replace, or be added to, the existing ones. This process then favoured the construction of an argument to be used in the answer, and if there were no card which could help, a new one could be created.

If one looks at the BSC, one of the most diffused performance measurement tools, it resembles both in its pictorial representation and, most importantly, in its use as practice, a rhetorical wheel as illustrated by Orazio Toscanella in 1560 (see Bolzoni 1995). In the BSC the strategic imperatives posited at the centre of the pictorial representation are meaningless until they acquire sense through the four dimensions that define what these imperatives mean. What is more interesting is that these cards (and the key performance measures that accompany them) vary in number and content not only when the BSC is implemented in different organizations and social contexts but even within the same organization. And by changing the cards and the performance indicators managers in fact change the nature of the strategic vision, which is nothing than an empty space that acquires meaning only in the process of referring to it (see Figure 7.5). What the BSC does, seemingly to what happens with information technologies (see Quattrone and Hopper 2006), is to prompt a process of reference where inscriptions refer to strategy in its absence.

The same applies to other popular management concepts such as "efficiency" and the like which mean very little until they are made concrete in processes of negotiation and mediation which are never stable and completely closed.[7] This is the case, for example, of ERP systems that make slogans such as "global, common and simple" concrete in different ways depending on how the system is implemented, on how it establishes semiotic relationships with other techniques, such as accounting, and technologies, such as Excel (see Quattrone and Hopper 2006 for an extensive discussion of this point and the effects on the spatial organization of the firm).

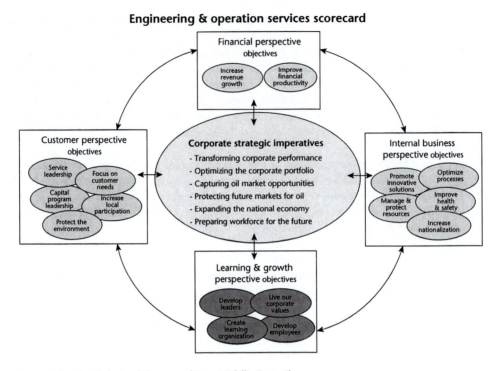

Engineering & operation services scorecard

Figure 7.5 The Balanced Scorecard in a Middle-East oil company

The ontology of management practices is therefore political in nature (Mol 1999) where the mediation and the nature of actor–network make the nature of the practice fluid and unstable.

Management practices as media and mediators: translation and spatial rationalities

Being a pragmatic art, more than a science aiming at the acquisition of transcendental truths, memory practices were not intended to convey objective and immutable messages.[8] They were instead meant to mobilize action, allowing the user to develop an associative ability which ultimately ordered and created by rearranging relations between texts and images.

Because of the malleability that they produce, rhetorical machines are *media of communication* which create the conditions for a *translation* of the knowledge that they are supposed to communicate. They prompt a "displacement, drift, invention, mediation, the creation of a link that did not exist before and that to a degree modifies the original [meaning]" (Latour 1999, p. 179).

Crucial to this translation ability was the capacity to create, order, and make logical relationships between various *loci* (i.e. spaces such as the cards of the wheel or in the BSC or the account as a space organized in a T format), where information could be stored to be then retrieved and recomposed at will, depending on always changing purposes (i.e. the late-medieval and early-modern *intentions*).

Rhetorical machines as knowledge ordering devices which helped deploy logical, persuasive and therefore rational arguments (Green 2004) had thus a crucial spatial connotation. And, indeed, the etymology of words such as "rationality", "ratiocinations" and "reason" reveals their spatial connotation (from Latin *ratio*, "reason" but more importantly, at least at that time, "calculation", and "account", that is, a graphical space where records can be accumulated for inventories of all kinds). It is useful to remember that *Ratio* did not mean only "reason" as much as the *Libro della ragione* ("the book of reason") did not mean "'Book of Logic' but 'Ledger'" (Murray 1978, p. 205). In the Augustinian art of memory, for example, the word *ratio* acquired a broader and more practical meaning, for the *rationes* "are not reasons of the sort that engage a philosopher but 'schemes' or 'ordering devices'.... Latin *ratio* means 'computation' or 'calculation' not reason in exactly our sense of the word" (Carruthers 1998, p. 33). Dealing with *rationes*, with rationalities, thus implied, dealing with schematic images, with the development of a calculative ability that involves the reorganization of spaces as much as calculations with numbers. Rhetorical wheels allowed "*re*-presentations" designed for being open to interpretation, appropriation and translation, beyond any stable and ultimate form of objective and univocal truth. How the spatial dimension of management thinking affects the nature of the practice, its diffusion into managers' thinking is what needs to be explored further if one wants to understand the construction of management representations, beliefs, visions and strategies.

Management practices as performable spaces: performativity as managing difference

After this detour on rhetoric, art of memory, and early-modern accounting, we are back to the core of the link between persuasion and rationality that Green (2004) and others have established in interpreting rationales for management practices' adoption and diffusion.

The analysis of the rhetorical wheel has highlighted that in the definition of what persuades and thus counts as rational, visual inscriptions play an active, albeit often forgotten, role. This introduces us to the fourth feature that management practices as rhetorical machines have: they are *performable spaces*, that is, they are instruments which are designed to elicit users' action by offering a space where meanings can be constructed via the use of the machine. A meaning that is shaped by a shared visually informed and schematic rationality but unstable as it is always subject to re-definition via various forms of rearrangements (such as the displacement of cards around the wheel). The rhetorical wheel, for example, does not provide any stable content and value-based form of knowledge and rationality (it does not state what is "good" and what is "bad"). It rather provides a general method for "figuring out" what count as "rational", "good" and "bad", remaining at a superficial and abstract level that makes the practice suitable to travel across various organizational and specific contexts (Shalin-Anderson and Djelic 2004; Czarniawska-Georges and Sevón 2005). As argued by Lawrence et al. (2002), rhetoric provides an instrument of interaction which makes collaborative efforts to solve complex problems possible.

If we translate the arguments above into the context of managerial practices, the study of rhetorical machines suggests that successful practices diffuse because they provide devices through which the rationale for their adoption can always be re-invented and adapted to changing organizational conditions, also within the same adoption process, the same organization and, more in general, within the same spatio-temporal framework (Carruthers 1998). What remains constant in this process of diffusion is the nature of *visual inscription*, of *method of knowledge ordering*, of *medium of communication and translation* and of *performable space* that allows various local agendas to coexist within the same diffusion process. And it is this form of rationality, meant as schematic ordering (and not as objective and functional ability), that is shared amongst participants and constitutes the legitimating discourse in which organizing processes can take place, beyond any functional and stable rationale for adoption (be this technical efficiency or institutional legitimacy).

As much as the early-modern intellectual had to be versed in rhetoric and the art of memory to be recognized as a legitimated citizen of that virtual community that was the Republic of Letters (Grafton 2009), the contemporary manager deciding on the validity and adoptability of a given managerial practice, needs to share with the community to which s/he belongs a schematic understanding of the world, and a schematic way of doing things. The rationale for adoption is then not in the practice itself. It is not the inscription and the message that it conveys that makes adopters believe that they are making a rational choice, but in the practice mobilized by this inscription, i.e. in the performance that it calls for (the "orthopraxis", Carruthers 1998). Reasons for adoption of management practices therefore are not in a supposedly stable "text" which functionally satisfies certain organizational or social demands, but in the variety of performances that the practice allows through its nature of visual inscription, method of ordering and innovation and medium of communication and translation.

In the context of accounting manuals (Quattrone 2009), it is the book's ability of making others believe that the content of the text can be easily grasped which makes the text and the book an object. It becomes an object that people can refer to, describe and criticize. And this despite the fact that its content may be absolutely evanescent, while the form appears to be clear (the reader may think of a contemporary accounting technique such as activity-based costing or balanced scorecard, to which many refer but few can agree on what they are). Paradoxically, accounting is performable not only because it forces the user along certain directives, as a disciplinary gaze would imply, but also because it leaves the user free to enact that space which is provided by the topology of the ordered method (think of the balanced scorecard in which the core image is constant, while the content of the four boxes and of the central circle always differ, for they relate to the eventual enactment of this abstract method of performance measurement). As De Certeau noticed (1984, pp. 29ff.), the user seems always to have local tactics to react to dominating ordering strategies, which are supposed to force human beings into patterns of behaviour. What seems interesting in accounting terms is that this possibility for resistance and appropriation is *built into* the practice itself.

As I have noted elsewhere, hierarchies and accounting systems appear, at a superficial level, as the result of homogeneous rationales and uses, and thus seem homogeneous prescriptions easily operationable. They seem to be well-ordered traces left on white sheets of paper (Quattrone 2004). However, this apparent homogeneity is, in fact, empty (for these traces are representative of an absence, of nothing), and thus ready to attract a process of (always partially) filling this emptiness.

Some concluding reflections

In this chapter I have sought to illustrate some of the existing, albeit forgotten, links between accounting and rhetoric. This places accounting firmly into the realm of communication practices but, more importantly, it also calls for a greater understanding of how accounting visualizations do more than simply representing financial transactions and prompts complex processes of mediation and meaning construction. In this sense accounting is not simply a medium of communication but a space where mediation and imagination can be prompted and fostered. By referring to some of my earlier work (e.g. Quattrone 2009; Busco and Quattrone 2010), I have argued that a view of accounting that places it within communication studies can be explored by conceiving it as a combination of four related features that have contributed to its success and evolution across centuries, namely (see Figure 7.1): its nature of method, which provides process but not content knowledge; its visual appeal, thanks to the simplicity of its graphical representations; its nature of medium of communication but also of mediation and translation; and its ability to offer a space where performances around abstract management notions and principles can happen. Almost as on a stage, accounting and performance measurement technique offers an opportunity for a performance around concepts such as "efficiency" or abstract notions of "strategy", which become concrete in the process of populating that space with business perspectives and related key performance indicators.

If the above holds, then it is clear that there is very much still to be done to view accounting as a form of generating visions, of "imagining organizations" (Puyou et al. 2012) and of composing rhetorical figures that can contribute to mobilizing organizational action.

Still a lot of work needs to be done to explore this compositional nature of accounting performances. What I intend to say is that rhetoric is full of practices and techniques that help us to make sense of the past, present and, above all, future. Rhetoric intersects a key human ability that is one of composing images about what we are and what we aim to become. This compositional activity, I have tried to argue, is not simply a mental feature of ours. It relates to material artefacts of all kinds. Accounting and other management reports, with their material design, with their links to other kinds of technologies of representation have an important and still unexplored role in making us understand our identities and how we relate ourselves to organizing activities, economies and societies.

This chapter is part of a project that aims at reconstructing the relationships between accounting and some other shared practices in the sphere of communication techniques, in order for knowledge to exist and acquire meaning. As I argued elsewhere in greater detail, most of the practices that are supposed to produce (or aspire to produce in the minds of regulators and policy makers) objective "accounting" knowledge are deeply rooted in the humanities rather than in modern sciences. For Bruno Latour (1991), accounting has "never been modern" and shares with monastic liturgies and the rhetorical techniques that these utilized much more than one would nowadays be willing to accept and able to see.

Notes

1 The chapter draws extensively upon, and expands, the arguments in Quattrone and Hopper, 2006; Quattrone, 2009; Busco and Quattrone, 2010.

2 Critical accounting research has challenged a functional view of accounting and moved away from economic-driven explanations that view it as a tool for administering resources efficiently (see Chandler and Daems 1979) and an aid to rational decision making (see Boyns and Edwards 1997). The literature has also highlighted the rhetorical and persuasive power of accounting (see Nahapiet 1988; Arrington and Schweiker 1992) and how this has a major role in the success and diffusion of contemporary accounting practices (e.g. Nørreklit 2003; Young 2003). The range of available interpretations is now so vast and variegated that as early as 1993, Miller and Napier (1993: 631) rightly affirmed: "there is no essence to accounting, and no invariant object to which the name 'accounting' can be attached". Accounting is characterized by the multiple natures and purposes which it fulfills, along with a sameness which makes one perceive it as having a specific nature and specific purposes (see Quattrone 2004, with regard to the nature of accounting and accountability practices in the Society of Jesus).

3 This is why, for example, some studies have considered the ethos, pathos, and logos as the concepts in rhetorical theory that can help accounting scholars to understand how managers persuade various kinds of audiences (see Carruthers and Espenland 1995; Zbaraki 1998; see also Hartelious and Browing 2008; Nørreklit 2003).

4 These images made of analysis the key principle for the organisation of knowledge. Analysis always implies a division, a word that also hides a visual character as it derives from the Latin *dividere* "to force apart, cleave, distribute" (from *dis-* "apart"; but also *duo* "two" + *-videre* "to separate", but also "to view"). It was therefore intrinsically a visually oriented ordering method, for one breaks things down in order to *see* (and remember) them better, either in the virtual space of the mind or in the concrete space of a piece of paper (be this a medieval ledger or a contemporary performance measurement technique such as the BSC).

5 It is not by chance, for economic and cultural reasons, that authors of the first management and accounting manuals were often members of religious Orders (e.g. Pacioli 1494 – Franciscan; Pietra 1589 – Benedictine; Flori 1636 – Jesuit), what is less clear is the influence of their training as members of the clergy on the development of management. The very idea of hierarchy reveals a religious connotation "'hierarchy': *hiereus*, priest, and *hieros*, what is holy, and *arkhe*, rule (hence sacred or priestly rule)" (Höpfl 2000).

6 Ramism is a movement conventionally identified with the work of Peter Ramus who in the sixteenth century devised analytical methods of representation in the form of dichotomies that could be used initially for pedagogical purposes (the teaching of Aristotelian logics) and then diffused across Western societies to provide forms of organising knowledge and acquire skills in the most disparate realms from cookery to accounting (see Ong 1958).

7 In interviewing the Chancellor of a major British university I found this statement paradigmatically representative of the nature of management principles, fads and fashions: "if by efficiency you mean achieving some saving that help us maintain the tutorial system this is a notion that I like. If instead you mean cutting it, I do not like it any longer".

8 As suggested by Latour, representations, images and inscriptions "are not the world: they only represent it in its absence" (1987, p. 247)

References

Arrington, C. E. and Schweiker, W. (1992). "The Rhetoric and Rationality of Accounting Research", *Accounting, Organizations and Society*, 17(6): 511–534.

Bolzoni, L. (1995). *La stanza della memoria. Modelli letterari e iconografici nell'età della stampa*. Turin: Einaudi (Eng. trans. by Jeremy Parzen, *The Gallery of Memory: Literary and Iconographic Models in the Age of the Printing Press*. Toronto: University of Toronto Press).

Boyns, T. and Edwards, J. R. (1997). "Cost and Management Accounting in Early-Victorian Britain: A Chandleresque Analysis", *Management Accounting Research*, 8(1): 19–46.

Busco, C. and Quattrone, P. (2010). *How Management Practices Diffuse: The Balanced Scorecard as a Rhetorical Machine*, the EIASM Workshop on New Directions in Management Accounting, Brussels.

Camille, M. (1985). "Seeing and Reading: Some Visual Implications of Medieval Literacy and Illiteracy", *Art History*, 8(1): 26–49.

Camille, M. (1992). *Image on the Edge: The Margins of Medieval Art*. London: Reaktion Books.

Camille, M. (1998). "Sensations on the Page: Imagining Technologies and Medieval Illuminated Manuscripts", in G. Bornstein and T. Tinkle (eds), *The Iconic Page in Manuscript Print and Digital Culture* (pp. 33–54). Ann Arbor, MI: University of Michigan Press.

Carmona, S., Ezzamel, M. and Gutiérrez, F. (1997). "Control and Cost Accounting Practices in the Spanish Royal Tobacco Factory", *Accounting, Organizations and Society*, 22(5): 411–446.

Carruthers, B. G. and Espeland, W. N. (1991). "Accounting for Rationality: Double-Entry Bookkeeping and the Rethoric of Economic Rationality", *American Journal of Sociology*, 97(1): 31–69.

Carruthers, M. (1990). *The Book of Memory: A Study of Memory in Medieval Culture*. New York: Cambridge University Press.

Carruthers, M. (1998). *The Craft of Thought: Meditation, Rhetoric, and the Making of Images. 400–1200*. Cambridge: Cambridge University Press.

Cavallo, G. and Chartier, R. (eds) (1999). *A History of Reading in the West*. London: Polity Press.

Chandler, A. D. and Daems, H. (1979). "Administrative Coordination, Allocation and Monitoring: A Comparative Analysis of the Emergence of Accounting and Organization in the USA and Europe", *Accounting, Organizations and Society*, 4(1/2): 3–20.

Craig, M. (2000). *Thinking Visually: Business Applications of 14 Core Diagrams*. New York: South-West Cencage Learning.

Crick, J. and Walsham, A. (eds). (2004). *The Uses of Script and Print, 1300–1700*. Cambridge: Cambridge University Press.

Czarniawska-Joerges, B. and Sevón, G. (2005). *Global Ideas: How Ideas, Objects and Practices Travel in a Global Economy*. Malmö: Liber and Copenhagen Business School Press.

De Certeau, M. (1984). *The Practice of Everyday Life*. Berkeley and Los Angeles: University of California Press.

de Laet, M. and Mol, A. (2002). "The Zimbabwe Bush Pump: Mechanics of a Fluid Technology", *Social Studies of Science*, 30(2): 225–263.

Djelic, M.-L. and Sahlin-Andersen, K. (2006). *Transnational Governance: Institutional Dynamics of Regulation*. Cambridge: Cambridge University Press.

Dugdale, A. (1999). "Materiality: Juggling Sameness and Difference", in J. Law and J. Hassard (eds), *Actor Network Theories and After* (pp. 113–135). London: Sage.

Flori, L. (1636). *Trattato del modo di tenere il libro doppio domestico con suo essemplare composto dal P. Lodovico Flori della Compagnia di Gesù per uso delle case e dei collegi della medesima Compagnia nel Regno di Sicilia*, in Palermo, per Decio Cirillo.

Grafton, A. (2009). *Worlds made by Words: Scholarship and Community in the Modern West*. Cambridge, MA: Harvard University Press.

Grafton, A. and Jardine, L. (1986). *From Humanism to the Humanities: Education and the Liberal Arts in Fifteenth and Sixteenth-century Europe*. London: Duckworth.

Green Jr., S. E. (2004). "A Rhetorical Theory of Diffusion", *Academy of Management Review*, 29(4): 653–669.

Hartelious, E. J. and Browning, L. D. (2008). "The Application of Rhetorical Theory in Managerial Research. A Literature Review", *Management Communication Quarterly*, 20(10): 1–27.

Hines, R. (1988). "Financial Accounting: In Communicating Reality, We Construct Reality", *Accounting, Organisations and Society*, 13(3): 251–262.

Höpfl, H. M. (2000). "Ordered Passions: Commitment and Hierarchy in the Organizational Ideas of the Jesuit Founders", *Management Learning*, 31(3): 313–350.

Johns, A. (1998). *The Nature of the Book: Print and Knowledge in the Making*. Chicago: University of Chicago Press.

Jones, C. and Dugdale, D. (2002). "The ABC Bandwagon and the Juggernaut of Modernity", *Accounting, Organizations and Society*, 27(1–2): 121–164.

Kaplan, R. S. and Norton, D. P. (1996). *Translating Strategy into Action: The Balanced Scorecard*. Boston, MA: Harvard Business School Press.

Latour, B. (1986). "Visualization and Cognition: Thinking with Eyes and Hands", in H. Kuklick and E. Long (eds), *Knowledge and Society: Studies in the Sociology of Culture. Past and Present* (pp. 1–40). London: Jai Press.

Latour, B. (1987). *Science in Action: How to Follow Scientists and Engineers through Society*. Cambridge, MA: Harvard University Press.

Latour, B. (1991). *We Have Never Been Modern*. London: Sage.

Latour, B. (1999). *Pandora's Hope: Essays on the Reality of Science Studies*. Cambridge, MA: Harvard University Press.

Long, P. (2001). *Openness, Secrecy, Authorship: Technical Arts and the Culture of Knowledge from Antiquity to the Renaissance*. Baltimore, MD: Johns Hopkins University Press.

Lowy, A. and Hood, P. (2004). *The Power of the 2x2 Matrix: Using the 2x2 Thinking to Solve Business Problems and Make Better Decisions*. San Francisco: Jossey-Bass.

Miller, P. and Napier, C. (1993). "Genealogies of Calculations", *Accounting, Organizations and Society*, 18(7/8): 631–647.

Miller, P. and O'Leary, T. (1987). "Accounting and the Construction of a Governable Person", *Accounting, Organizations and Society*, 12(3): 235–265.

Mol, A. (1999). "Ontological Politics: A Word and Some Questions", in J. Law and J. Hassard (eds), *Actor Network Theories and After*. London: Sage.

Murray, A. (1978). *Reason and Society in the Middle Ages*. Oxford: Clarendon Press.

Nahapiet, J. (1988). "The Rhetoric and Reality of an Accounting Change: A Study of Resource Allocation", *Accounting, Organizations and Society*, 13(4): 333–358.

Nørreklit, H. (2003). "The Balanced Scorecard: What Is the Score? A Rhetorical Analysis of the Balanced Scorecard", *Accounting, Organizations and Society*, 28(6): 591–619.

Ong, W. (1958). *Ramus: Method, and the Decay of Dialogue: From the Art of Discourse to the Art of Reason*. Cambridge, MA: Harvard University Press.

Pietra, A. (1586). *Indirizzo degli economi o sia ordinatissima istruttione da regolamente formare qualunque scrittura in un libro doppio. Aggiuntovi l'essemplare di un Libro nobile co 'l suo Giornale ad uso della Congregatione Cassinese dell'Ordine in San Benedetto*. Mantova: Francesco Osanna.

Power, M. (1997). *The Audit Society: Rituals of Verification*. Oxford: Oxford University Press.

Puyou, F.-R., Quattrone, P., McLean, C., Thrift, N. (2012). *Imagining Organizations: Performative Imagery in Business and Beyond*. London: Routledge.

Quattrone, P. (2004). "Accounting for God: Accounting and Accountability Practices in the Society of Jesus (Italy, 16th—17th centuries)", *Accounting, Organizations and Society*, 29(7): 647–683.

Quattrone, P. (2009). "Books to be Practiced: Memory, the Power of the Visual and the Success of Accounting", *Accounting, Organizations and Society*, 34: 85–118.

Quattrone, P. and Hopper, T. (2006). "What Is IT? SAP, Accounting, and Visibility in a Multinational Organisation", *Information and Organization*, 16(3): 212–250.

Shalin-Anderson, K. and Djelic, M. L. (2004). *Transnational Governance: Institutional Dynamics of Regulation*. Cambridge: Cambridge University Press.

Star, S. L. and Griesemer, J. R. (1989). "Institutional Ecology, 'Translations' and Boundary Objects: Amateurs and Professionals in Berkeley's Museum of Vertebrate Zoology", *Social Studies of Science*, 19: 387–420.

Suzuki, T. (2003). "The Espistemology of Macroeconomic Reality: The Keynesian Revolution from an Accounting Point of View", *Accounting, Organizations and Society*, 28(5): 451–517.

Wedlin, L. and Hedmo, T. (2008). *New Modes of Governance: The Re-Regulation of European Higher Education and Research*, in C. Mazza, A. Riccaboni and P. Quattrone (eds), *European Universities in Transition: Issues, Models and Cases*. Cheltenham: Edward Elgar.

Yates, F. A. (1966). *The Art of Memory*. Chicago: University of Chicago Press.

Young, J. (2003). "Constructing, Persuading and Silencing: The Rhetoric of Accounting Standards", *Accounting, Organizations and Society*, 23(6): 621–638.

Zbaracki, M. J. (1998). "The Rhetoric and Reality of Total Quality Management", *Administrative Science Quarterly*, 43: 602–636.

8

Accounting narratives and impression management

Niamh M. Brennan and Doris M. Merkl-Davies

People like [Berni Madoff] become sort of like chameleons. They are very good at impression management ... They manage the impression you receive of them. They know what people want, and they give it to them.

(Cresswell and Thomas, 2009)

Introduction

Arthur Levitt (2000), former chairman of the US Securities and Exchange Commission, has pointed to the gradual, but perceptible, erosion in the quality of financial reporting. Arguably one means by which this is achieved is impression management, as the quote above illustrates. Berni Madoff was an establishment figure, a former non-executive chairman of NASDAQ, and perpetrator of the biggest Ponzi fraud in history. Understanding impression management communication choices is important in assisting readers of corporate reports in detecting the potential deception inherent in such practices.

Financial information is frequently communicated through written narratives which are largely qualitative in nature and which are sometimes referred to as 'soft' or unquantified information. Accounting narratives can be found in annual reports, including financial statements, accounting textbooks, official pronouncements by accounting bodies and legal judgments concerning accounting issues (Jones and Shoemaker, 1994). For example, Young (2003) analyses the rhetorical devices in accounting standards used to persuade readers of their worth or to silence alternative opinions and criticism. The function of accounting narratives in corporate reports is to amplify quantified accounting information. Most accounting narratives in corporate reports are not subject to external audit, which makes it easier for managers to manipulate the information disclosed therein. For example, the scope of auditors' reports in company annual reports is limited to the financial statements and the notes therein. At best, other narrative accounting disclosures are merely monitored by external auditors for consistency with the financial statements. The scope of this chapter is restricted to accounting narratives in corporate reports, excluding those in audited financial statements, such as the notes to the financial statements. Although audited financial statements contain accounting narratives, much prior research focuses on accounting narratives outside the audited accounts. In this chapter these are referred to as discretionary accounting narratives in order to distinguish them from accounting narratives supporting numerical information in audited financial statements.

This chapter discusses prior research by reference to four perspectives on impression management: economic, psychological, sociological and critical. Seven communication choices in discretionary accounting narratives in corporate reports are also examined. These constitute the categories of analysis in research adopting the economic and psychological perspective on impression management. As the sociological and the critical perspectives adopt a more interpretive approach to text analysis, the analytical categories emerge inductively from the data (Merkl-Davies et al., 2013). The effect of impression management on investors and other users of corporate reports is not addressed, other than in passing. The chapter concludes with some suggestions for future research and some implications for the practice of corporate reporting.

The concept of impression management originates in social psychology and is concerned with 'studying how individuals present themselves to others to be perceived favourably by others' (Hooghiemstra, 2000: 60). Using a dramaturgical metaphor, Goffman (1959) explains impression management as the performance of self vis-à-vis an audience. Impression management entails shaping an audience's impression of a person, an object, an event or an idea (Schlenker, 1980), usually with the intention to appeal to audiences (Gioia et al., 2000). The impression conveyed may correspond to an ostensible reality. Alternatively, it may entail enhancing desirable aspects of the organization or obfuscating less desirable aspects, thus attempting to manipulate organizational audiences' perceptions (Gioia et al., 2000).

Impression management in a corporate reporting context

The concept of impression management is applied in a corporate reporting context to analyse attempts to influence audiences' perceptions of organizations, particularly financial performance (e.g. Clatworthy and Jones, 2001, 2003, 2006; Courtis, 2004a; Rutherford, 2003) and social environmental performance (e.g. Hooghiemstra, 2000). This entails 'vertical borrowing' (Highhouse et al., 2009: 1483) in that social psychology research on individuals is applied to organizations. Depending on the theoretical position adopted, organizational audiences are defined either narrowly as consisting of shareholders and financial intermediaries, or more broadly as including stakeholders and society at large. The definition adopted affects the focus of analysis. A narrow agency theory based approach results in impression management conceptualized as managerial manipulation of shareholders' perceptions of financial performance (e.g. Clatworthy and Jones, 2001, 2003, 2006; Courtis, 2004a; Rutherford, 2003). By contrast, a wider systems-oriented theory based approach shifts the focus of analysis to managerial manipulation of stakeholders' impressions of social and environmental performance, organizational legitimacy (e.g. Hooghiemstra, 2000; Breton and Côté, 2006; Linsley and Kajüter, 2008) and organizational changes such as restructuring and reorganization, privatisation, demutualization, mergers or acquisitions (Arndt and Bigelow, 2000; Odgen and Clarke, 2005).

If discretionary accounting narratives are used for impression management purposes, then financial reporting quality will be undermined and capital misallocations may result (if users are susceptible to impression management). Wider social and political consequences of impression management include unwarranted support of organizations and their activities by non-financial stakeholders or by society at large. Thus, impression management constitutes an important area of accounting research. To illustrate the persuasive power of impression management, Illustration 8.1 includes extracts from the annual report of Enron immediately prior to its collapse. Phrases presented in italics are consistent with a positive bias introduced by Enron. We believe this is a reflection of opportunistic managerial behaviour aimed at manipulating readers' perceptions of corporate achievements, rather than an attempt to provide investors with useful incremental information. Notwithstanding the hyperbolic claims, few quantitative amounts are included in

> **Illustration 8.1: Extracts from Enron's letter to shareholders, Annual Report 2000 (emphasis added)**
>
> Enron's performance in 2000 was a *success by any measure*, as we continued to *outdistance the competition* and *solidify our leadership* in each of our major businesses. In our largest business, wholesale services, we experienced an *enormous increase* of 59 percent in physical energy deliveries. Our retail energy business achieved its *highest level ever* of total contract value. Our newest business, broadband services, *significantly accelerated* transaction activity, and our oldest business, the interstate pipelines, registered *increased earnings*. The company's net income reached a *record* $1.3 billion in 2000. (p. 4)
>
> Enron hardly resembles the company we were in the early days. During our 15-year history, we have *stretched ourselves beyond our own expectations*. We have metamorphosed from an asset-based pipeline and power generating company to a marketing and logistics company whose *biggest assets* are its well-established business approach and its innovative people. (pp. 6–7)
>
> Our performance and capabilities cannot be compared to a traditional energy peer group. Our results put us in the *top tier of the world's corporations*. We have a proven business concept that is eminently scalable in our existing businesses and adaptable enough to extend to new markets. (p. 7)
>
> Our talented people, global presence, financial strength and *massive market knowledge* have created our sustainable and unique businesses. EnronOnline will *accelerate their growth*. We plan to leverage all of these *competitive advantages to create significant value* for our shareholders. (p. 7)

the extracts. An exception is the reference to 'record' net income of $1.3 billion. This amount does not appear in Enron's 2000 audited income statement. Rather, it relates to an unaudited amount of $1,266 million 'net income before items impacting comparability'. Enron appears to have managed impressions with words, when the underlying audited numbers told another story.

Impression management and disclosure media

Discretionary accounting narratives generally appear in the unregulated sections of corporate documents to support and expand upon the regulated accounting disclosures in the audited financial statements. We use the term 'corporate reports'/'corporate documents' in a broad sense to include a wide variety of disclosure vehicles or media containing accounting narratives, including:

- annual reports, particularly chairmen's statements (Smith and Taffler, 1992a, 2000);
- CEO letters to shareholders (Amernic et al., 2007; Craig and Amernic, 2008; Hooghiemstra, 2010);
- operating and financial reviews (Rutherford, 2003; Sydserff and Weetman, 1999, 2002)/ management discussion and analyses (Feldman et al., 2010);
- initial public offering prospectuses (Aerts and Cheng, 2011; Lang and Lundholm, 2000);
- takeover documents (Brennan et al., 2010);
- press releases (Bowen et al., 2005; Henry, 2006, 2008; Davis et al., 2012);
- websites (Campbell and Beck, 2004);
- conference calls (Matsumoto et al., 2011).

Davis and Tama-Sweet (2012) find the news content/tone varies depending on the disclosure vehicle. Disclosures in earnings press releases are less pessimistic than in management discussion and analysis documents.

Organizational reputation, image and legitimacy

Impression management can play a role in restoring reputation, image or legitimacy in times of crisis or change, such as during adverse financial performance (e.g. Abrahamson and Park, 1994; Courtis, 2004a), corporate scandals (e.g. Linsley and Kajüter, 2008), environmental disasters (e.g. Hooghiemstra, 2000) and major reorganization (e.g. Arndt and Bigelow, 2000; Odgen and Clarke, 2005). Impression management is used to persuade organizational audiences of the exceptional nature of the circumstances resulting in negative financial performance, to portray the financial scandal as an isolated incident, or to convince them of the validity, legitimacy or necessity of reorganization (Merkl-Davies and Koller, 2012). Impression management may be used reactively as a means of restoring reputation, image or legitimacy after a crisis or incident (e.g. Odgen and Clarke, 2005; Craig and Amernic, 2008; Linsley and Kajüter, 2008) or prospectively to shape perceptions of a controversial issue, such as a reorganization, demutualization or merger (Arndt and Bigelow, 2000; Craig and Amernic, 2004a, 2008).

Impression management is used to establish, maintain and restore image, reputation and legitimacy. These concepts denote organizational audiences' perceptions and assessments of organizations (Deephouse and Carter, 2005: 329). Reputation refers to a temporally stable evaluative judgement of the desirability of organizations as a whole (Highhouse et al., 2009), often with respect to their peer group (Deephouse and Carter, 2005: 331). By contrast, image involves the dynamic perception of a specific area of distinction, such as market image, investment image, or corporate social responsibility image (Highhouse et al., 2009: 1489). Finally, legitimacy refers to a shared judgement about the normative appropriateness of organizations (Highhouse et al., 2009: 1487). Reputation and image are concerned with the evaluation of organizations, whereas legitimacy focuses on their acceptability with respect to social norms and rules (Deephouse and Suchman, 2008). Impression management thus entails constructing an impression of the quality or normative appropriateness of organizational structures, processes, practices or outcomes. Table 8.1 provides an overview of the three concepts.

Table 8.1 Organizational reputation, image and legitimacy

Concepts	Key aspects	Time dimension	Definition
Organizational reputation	• Whole organization • Quality • Evaluation	• Short-term • Stable	A general, temporally stable, shared evaluative judgment about a firm
Organizational image	• Aspect of the organization (e.g. investment image) • Quality • Evaluation	• Short-term • Dynamic	A dynamic perception of a specific area of organizational distinction
Organizational legitimacy	• Whole organization or industry • Social norms and rules • Appropriateness	• Long-term • Stable	A shared general judgment about normative appropriateness

Source: adapted from Highhouse et al. (2009: 1487, Table 1)

Adverse financial performance, pollution or product recalls can have a negative impact on the organizational image affected (i.e. investment image, environmental image, corporate social responsibility image or product image). These may affect organizational reputation. By contrast, corporate scandals involving a breach of law (e.g. tax evasion, corporate fraud) or a violation of social norms and rules (e.g. environmental disasters or human-rights violations in Third World countries) can be regarded as damaging organizational legitimacy. Such legitimacy is particularly important for firms operating in socially contested industries, such as the nuclear industry, the oil and gas industry or the tobacco industry (e.g. Prasad and Mir, 2002). In these cases, an incident in a particular firm (e.g. BP's oil spill in the Mexican Gulf or the nuclear accident in Fukushima) not only threatens the legitimacy of the affected company, but of the whole industry (e.g. Beelitz and Merkl-Davies, 2012).

Four perspectives on impression management

In accounting research, four broad perspectives on impression management can be differentiated: (1) economic, (2) psychological, (3) sociological and (4) critical. Table 8.2 outlines differences between the four perspectives along five dimensions, namely underlying theories, assumptions about the managerial motivation to engage in impression management, the underlying concept of impression management, the focus of analysis and consequences of impression management. The economic and social psychology perspectives are primarily concerned with investment image and focus on managerial attempts to manage shareholders' and financial stakeholders' perceptions of financial performance. If successful, this results in short-term capital misallocations (Merkl-Davies and Brennan, 2007). By contrast, the sociological perspective is concerned with the corporate social and environmental responsibility image and legitimacy. This perspective focuses on impression management influencing organizational audiences' perceptions of social and environmental performance and on organizational compliance with social norms and rules. If organizational audiences are convinced by impression management attempts, it results in unwarranted support by stakeholders and the general public. Finally, the critical perspective is concerned with power and focuses on managerial attempts to influence organizational audiences' perceptions of corporate influence and control. If impression management is successful, it results in hegemony. In the context of corporate reporting, hegemony refers to the process of influencing the minds of organizational audiences in such a way that they are persuaded to support organizations out of their own free will.

The perspective adopted affects the explanation for the motives underlying impression management, the manifestations of impression management in discretionary accounting narratives and the way impression management is conceptualized (i.e. reporting bias, self-serving bias, symbolic management/decoupling, ideological bias). The economic and psychological perspectives predominate. Impression management is viewed as falling into the broad category of voluntary disclosure research and is conceptualized as biased discretionary disclosures. A wide variety of impression management communication choices in discretionary accounting narratives have been studied, including the seven identified in Figure 8.1.

Economic perspective

Regarded as part of the discretionary choice literature, most impression management studies are based on agency theory assumptions. Managers are assumed to exercise judgement in order to 'alter financial reports to ... mislead some stakeholders about the underlying economic

Table 8.2 Differences between the four perspectives across five dimensions

Perspectives	Underlying theories	Motivation to engage in impression management	Concept of impression management	Focus of analysis	Consequences of impression management
(1) Economic	• Agency theory	• Maximize compensation	• Reporting bias	• Obfuscation of negative organizational outcomes • Emphasis of positive organizational outcomes	• Capital misallocations
(2) Psychological	• Attribution theory	• Win social and material rewards and avoid sanctions	• Self-serving bias	• Performance attributions	• Capital misallocations
(3) Sociological	• Stakeholder theory • Legitimacy theory • Institutional theory	• Attract social and material resources and support	• Symbolic management • Decoupling	• Normalizing accounts • Strategic restructuring	• Unwarranted support from stakeholders & society
(4) Critical	• Political economy • Critical theories	• Gain and maintain power	• Ideological bias	• Strategic use of rhetorical, semantic and grammatical features	• Hegemony

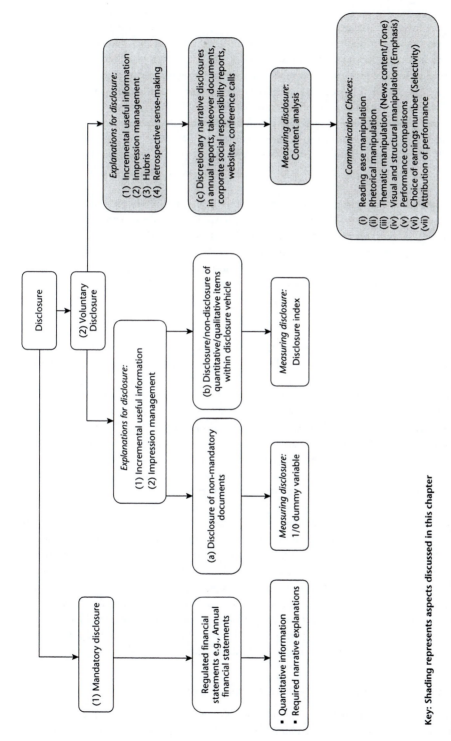

Key: Shading represents aspects discussed in this chapter

Figure 8.1 Locating impression management research in the voluntary disclosure literature

performance of the company' (Healy and Wahlen, 1999: 368). Thus, impression management constitutes opportunistic managerial behaviour arising from information asymmetries between managers and investors. Focusing on the valence (i.e. favourable or unfavourable) and tone (i.e. optimistic or pessimistic) of disclosures, impression management involves emphasizing positive organizational outcomes or obfuscating negative organizational outcomes. Negative organizational outcomes give rise to conflicts of interest between managers and shareholders. Managers are prompted to manipulate outsiders' perceptions of financial performance and prospects in order to 'divert attention from financial distress' (Tennyson et al., 1990: 395–396). Corporate narrative documents are impression management vehicles used to present a self-interested view of corporate performance (Staw et al., 1983: 584; Abrahamson and Park, 1994: 1302; Clatworthy and Jones, 2006: 493). Managers introduce reporting bias to benefit from increased compensation, particularly via managerial stock options (Rutherford, 2003; Courtis, 2004a).

Reporting bias entails 'selecting the information to display and presenting that information in a manner that is intended to distort readers' perceptions of corporate achievements' (Godfrey et al., 2003: 96). This involves manipulating the presentation and disclosure of both verbal (e.g. reading ease manipulation, rhetorical manipulation, thematic manipulation, visual and structural manipulation, attribution of performance) and numerical information (e.g. visual and structural manipulation, performance comparisons, choice of earnings number).

Psychological perspective

Studies based on the social psychology perspective replace the economic view of managers, who make corporate reporting decisions solely on the basis of cost–benefit calculations, with a psychological view which takes the social relations inherent in the decision context into consideration. Managerial behaviour is regarded as embedded in and dependent on managers' relationships with organizational audiences and is thus inherently social in character. Impression management arises from 'the actual, imagined and implied presence' (Allport, 1985: 5) of organizational audiences to whom managers are accountable. Corporate reports, particularly annual reports, serve as an accountability mechanism to address the concerns of external parties. Under conditions of accountability, managers engage in impression management in anticipation of an evaluation of their actions and decisions by (primarily) shareholders.

In the psychological perspective, managers use self-serving bias in anticipation of an evaluation of performance by shareholders and stakeholders with the aim of winning rewards and avoiding sanctions (Frink and Ferris, 1998). Self-serving bias is explained by reference to attribution theory which is concerned with people's explanations of events. People's attribution of actions and events is biased in that they take credit for success and deny responsibility for failure (Knee and Zuckerman, 1996). In a corporate reporting context, self-serving bias entails attributing positive organizational outcomes to internal factors (taking credit for good performance) and negative organizational outcomes to external circumstances (assigning blame for bad performance), to influence investors' perceptions of financial performance (Aerts, 1994, 2001; Clatworthy and Jones, 2003; Hooghiemstra, 2008; Aerts and Cheng, 2011).

Seven impression management communication choices

As accounting standards generally do not prescribe the choice of wording in the accounting policies and explanatory notes to the audited financial statements, impression management may take place in required narrative disclosures. However, we treat these required disclosures as mandatory for the purpose of Figure 8.1. The majority of research conceptualises impression management in the form of discretionary disclosure strategies or communication choices. Merkl-Davies and Brennan (2007) identify seven categories of communication choices as shown in Figure 8.1: (i) Reading ease manipulation, (ii) Rhetorical manipulation, (iii) Thematic manipulation (News content/Tone), (iv) Visual and structural manipulation (Emphasis), (v) Performance comparisons, (vi) Choice of earnings number (Selectivity) and (vii) Attribution of performance.

(i) Reading ease manipulation studies use readability scores to examine whether managers make accounting narratives more difficult to read with the objective of obfuscating bad news (e.g. Smith and Taffler, 1992b; Li, 2008). Readability is measured using readability formulae such as Flesch, Fog, Lix, Fry Graph, Dale-Chall and Kwolek, which compare a calculated score with 'predetermined standards of written materials graded according to difficulty' (Courtis, 1995: 5), ranging from children's comics to scientific articles. One of the commonest, the Flesch Reading Ease score, is based on word and sentence length. It rates text on a 100-point scale. The higher the score, the easier it is to understand the text. A score of 60 to 70 is considered optimal for text comprehension. In Illustration 8.2, the first example contains short words and sentences, leading to a Flesch Reading Ease score of 69.16, while the second example contains long words and sentences, with a much lower Flesch Reading Ease score of 18.39.

Studies focusing on (ii) rhetorical manipulation argue that companies may frame their results using rhetorical devices. In examining the rhetorical effects of discourse, Hyland (1998) includes 41 examples in her paper, of which a number are reproduced in Illustration 8.3. She argues that creating an ethos of the CEO as a competent, trustworthy, authoritative and honest person are essential elements in credible communication.

Illustration 8.2: Measuring readability using Flesch Reading Ease scores

Illustration 2.1: The year to 30th June 2002 was the Barratt Group's most successful year to date. We delivered record profits of £220m, almost double our profits of 3 years ago, and ended the year with record forward sales. (Barratt Developments Chairman's Statement 2002 – 2 sentences; 37 words; 52 syllables)

Flesch score:
206.835 – (1.015 x no. words 37 /no. sentences 2) – (84.6 x no. syllables 52 / no. words 37) = 69.16

Illustration 2.1: The Group continued to invest in the expansion of its Precision components operations where prospects for further growth remain encouraging. The disappointing profit performance of the Copal gravity diecasting unit, while unconnected to the investment programme in high-pressure technology, led nevertheless to a moderate level of spend in the year. (Alumasc Group Chairman's Statement 2002 – 2 sentences; 51 words; 98 syllables)

Flesch score:
206.835 – (1.015 x no. words 51 /no. sentences 2) – (84.6 x no. syllables 98 / no. words 51) = 18.39

(Source: Merkl-Davies et al., 2011b, Table 3)

Illustration 8.3: Rhetorical analysis – establishing credibility in corporate reporting

---

Illustration 3.1: Use of emphatics

As our H.K. $31,400 million worth of aircraft and equipment orders clearly show, we remain very confident about the future of Hong Kong

Illustration 3.2: Use of personal pronouns

I know from my year as chairman of the Administration Board that budgeting has been a very delicate operation over the last two years.

Illustration 3.3: Use of hedges to portray modest, trustworthy cautious steward

It is possible to envisage a future when many banking services will be delivered direct to the home or business place via television screens.

(Source: Hyland 1998: 236–237, Examples 13, 16, 20)

(iii) Thematic manipulation studies mainly examine whether corporate narratives overstate good news and understate bad news, for example by means of coding sentences in the chairman's statement/president's letter, (e.g. Staw et al., 1983; Clatworthy and Jones, 2001, 2003; Smith and Taffler, 1995, 2000). Brennan et al. (2010) adapt this stream of research to defensive and attacking themes and rhetorical devices used in hostile takeover defence documents. Thematic manipulation has also been studied in the context of social and environmental reporting and intellectual capital reporting. In Illustration 8.4, keywords are used to analyse good news and bad news themes in discretionary accounting narratives. The illustration indicates the presence of two positive keywords and one negative keyword. In examining the readability of sections of chairman's statements, Clatworthy and Jones (2003) coded the text into 11 major themes, as shown in Illustration 8.5.

(iv) Visual emphasis and structural manipulation may be used to overemphasize good news, including positioning good news first in documents (Bowen et al., 2005), burying bad news in middle passages of text within documents (Courtis, 1998), highlighting text (Brennan et al., 2009), use of colour (Courtis, 2004b) and repetition (Courtis, 1996; Davison, 2008). In Illustration 8.6, text in target-company defence documents was categorized into three levels of visual emphasis – most-emphasized, next-most-emphasized and least-emphasized. Target-company managers, battling against an unwelcome bidder, use every means to get their point of view across to target-company shareholders, including visual emphasis. There is also some evidence of rhetorical manipulation in the form of repetition in Illustration 8.6 ('don't let', 'Do not let').

Illustration 8.4: Thematic analysis – measuring good news/bad news themes

---

Profit before tax up [Keyword+1] 7.4% to £43.5m; investment profit down [Keyword−1] 2.2% to £39.6m; total dividend 10.3p per share, an increase [Keyword+2] of 3.0%.

(Source: Example 1, Brennan et al., 2009: 806)

Illustration 8.5: Thematic analysis – key themes in chairmen's statements

---

Future and/or outlook

Results

Employees

Acquisitions and disposals

Outline of major events

Discussion of major events

Overview of the year

Board changes

Operations

Business segments

Finance/investment

(Source: Clatworthy and Jones, 2001: 317)

(v) Performance comparison involves choosing benchmarks (prior year and others) as comparators to portray firm performance in the best possible light (Lewellen et al., 1996; Schrand and Walther, 2000; Short and Palmer, 2003).

(vi) Earnings choice or selectivity has been studied by Johnson and Schwartz (2005). This involves the judicious choice or selection of a favourable earnings number to disclose in accounting narratives, such as *pro forma* earnings. Illustration 8.7 exemplifies both performance comparison and choice of earnings number/selectivity. In a study of discretionary accounting narratives in annual results press releases, the profit figure of £373.2 million selected by this company for inclusion in its press release is the second largest amount (in absolute terms) of the ten profit figures available in the audited profit and loss account. Illustration 8.7 also includes a

---

Illustration 8.6: Visual emphasis

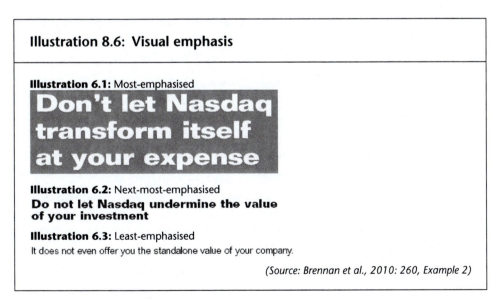

Illustration 6.1: Most-emphasised

Don't let Nasdaq transform itself at your expense

Illustration 6.2: Next-most-emphasised

Do not let Nasdaq undermine the value of your investment

Illustration 6.3: Least-emphasised

It does not even offer you the standalone value of your company.

(Source: Brennan et al., 2010: 260, Example 2)

Illustration 8.7: Performance comparison *and* earnings choice/ selectivity

---

Profit figures

Group trading profit up £60 million (19.2%) to £373.2 million

(Source: Brennan et al., 2009: 808, Example 6)

---

performance comparison in the form of percentage increase in profit over the prior year. The selected profit number shows an increase of 19.2 per cent over the prior-year performance comparison. Had the largest absolute profit amount been selected, this would only have shown an increase of 16.8 per cent over the prior-year performance comparison. The performance comparison possibly accounts for the selection of the second highest rather than the highest profit amount.

(vii) Attribution analysis examines, for example, whether a company takes credit for positive outcomes and blames external factors for negative outcomes. Baginski et al. (2000) classify causal attributions in management earnings forecasts, as shown in Illustration 8.8.

Alternative explanations for communication choices in discretionary accounting narratives

As shown in Figure 8.1, three explanations other than impression management have been suggested for the seven communication choices in discretionary accounting narratives outlined

---

Illustration 8.8: Attribution

External causes

General economic/environmental issues: recession/inflation, dollar weakness/strength, foreign currency fluctuation, input cost changes – increasing/decreasing costs, change in market for product, general loss/gain of customers, weather/catastrophe, order backlogs

Government/third party issues: tax law/other law changes, SEC actions/regulatory actions, expropriation by foreign governments, lawsuits/legal actions, competition action/issues, involuntary accounting changes

Internal causes

Product/services issues/actions: changes in product prices, changes in product mix, advertising/ marketing, new products/processes/production

Organizational issues/actions: management techniques/strategies/plans/repositioning, changes in management personnel, cost cutting/savings, asset write downs, going public, selling/buying stocks, merger/acquisition/disposal of a business segment, investment in plant assets, voluntary accounting changes

(Source: Baginski et al., 2000: 377, Table 2)

---

above: (1) incremental useful information, (2) hubris and (3) retrospective sense-making (Merkl-Davies and Brennan, 2011). The impression management explanation assumes that managers opportunistically exploit information asymmetries between them and organizational audiences by means of biased reporting. By contrast, the incremental information explanation assumes that managers provide discretionary accounting narratives to facilitate better decision making by investors and other corporate report users. A number of studies reviewed in Merkl-Davies and Brennan (2007) test both the incremental information and the impression management hypotheses. These favour an impression management explanation for discretionary accounting narratives.

However, biased reporting can also be due to managerial hubris. Whereas impression management constitutes opportunistic managerial behaviour, hubris constitutes self-deception or egocentric bias. Egocentric bias results in managers being biased towards their own performance. Finally, in an accountability context, particularly in annual reports, biased reporting, particularly in the form of performance attributions, may also be the result of managerial retrospective sense-making. This entails managers providing an account of organizational actions and events by retrospectively assigning causes to them (Aerts, 2005).

The predominant economic and psychological perspectives are based on a narrow view of impression management, as they are primarily concerned with the relationship between managers and financial stakeholders (e.g. investors, lenders and financial intermediaries). They focus on reporting bias or self-serving bias with respect to the financial performance of the firm. The role of corporate reporting in mediating the relationship between organizations and their non-financial stakeholders, and biased reporting of social and environmental performance, are ignored. The relationship between organizations and their audiences is regarded solely in terms of market exchange (Mouck, 1995). By contrast, the sociological and the critical perspectives take into account the wider socio-political context in which corporate reporting takes place. This shifts the focus of analysis to the managerial manipulation of organizational audiences' perceptions of social and environmental performance, organizational (non)compliance with social rules and norms and power relations between organizations and their constituents. The focus of analysis is not on narrow predetermined communication choices, but on wider strategies, including symbolic management or decoupling and the strategic use of rhetorical, grammatical and semantic features used in order to appear to comply with social norms and rules or to gain and maintain power. For example, Davison (2002) examines the rhetorical device of antithesis used not only to embellish, but also to induce patterns of reading and thinking in users of annual reports. Walters-York (1996) and Walters (2004) advocate analysis of the use of metaphor in accounting discourse to open up new ways of 'seeing' impression management in a corporate reporting context resulting in new modes of investigation and raising new issues and concerns (Walters, 2004: 171). Rhetorical devices may be used such as silence (Young, 2003), antithesis (Davison, 2002), metaphor (Walters-York, 1996) or repetition (Davison, 2008). Milne et al. (2006) examine the use of journey metaphor in sustainability reporting. Portraying sustainability as a journey evokes images of organizational adaptation, learning, progress and a movement away from business-as-usual practices as exemplified in Illustration 8.9.

Repetition is exemplified in Illustration 8.10, where repeating short key phrases at the beginning of successive sentences (anaphora) is used to emphasize business intangibles and future growth.

Sociological perspective

Studies adopting the sociological perspective regard impression management as resulting from structural constraints exerted either by different stakeholder groups or by society at large.

Illustration 8.9: Sociological perspective – analysis of metaphor in sustainability reporting

Illustration 9.1: It is my belief that radical targets are also required if we are to stimulate the innovation and thinking "out of the square" necessary to make significant progress along the road towards sustainable development. (Landcare Research New Zealand annual report 2000 (p. 4)

Illustration 9.2: Creating a sustainable world will be a daunting challenge – a tough journey of continual learning (Shell *There Is No Alternative*)

(Source: Milne et al., 2006: 816)

Illustration 8.10: Sociological perspective – analysis of rhetoric in the form of repetition

It's about the liberation
It's about the creation [. . .] [note also the repetitive rhyme of "ion"]
And it's about growth [. . .]

The first phrase continues thus:
It's about the liberation of our people and our assets – these new businesses will be free to innovate and free to operate at speed.

(Source: Davison, 2008: 803)

Impression management is seen either as a response to concerns of various stakeholder groups or as a response to public pressure and media attention relating to a controversial issue or event (stakeholder theory) or as arising from inconsistencies between organizational and societal norms and values (legitimacy theory). In the latter case, it constitutes an attempt on the part of managers to gain or restore organizational legitimacy by seemingly aligning firms' norms and values with those of society, particularly in situations where firms face legitimacy threats, such as corporate scandals, product-safety issues or environmental disasters.

Although it is not always explicitly stated, legitimacy is a social construct in the sense that it refers to 'a generalized perception or assumption that the actions of an entity are desirable, proper, or appropriate within some socially constructed system of norms, values, beliefs, and definitions' (Suchman, 1995: 574). Legitimacy is conceptualized from either a strategic or an institutional perspective. Adopting an agency focus, the strategic perspective regards legitimacy as an operational resource to be employed in the pursuit of organizational goals (Suchman, 1995). Adopting a structure focus, the institutional perspective views legitimacy as the collective awareness and recognition of an organization's practices as acceptable, appropriate and desirable (Suchman, 1995). From the institutional perspective, legitimacy 'resides in people's minds' (Breton and Côté, 2006: 512) and is granted by organizational audiences when they perceive organizational practices to be congruent with social rules, norms and values. The strategic perspective is predominant, as it provides a better fit with the agency-based concept of impression management put forward by social psychology.

Prior research has identified a variety of impression management communication choices used by managers to (re)establish legitimacy. These can be classified according to the underlying concept of legitimacy, i.e. either strategic or institutional. From a strategic perspective, impression management is conceptualized as symbolic management (Ashforth and Gibbs, 1990). Symbolic management entails adopting communication choices which make organizations *appear* to respond to stakeholder concerns or *appear* to be congruent with society's norms and expectations. Firms facing a major legitimacy threat engage in symbolic management by separating negative events (e.g. fraud, scandal, product safety issue) from organizations as a whole (1) by providing normalizing accounts (e.g. by means of excuses, apologies, or justifications) and (2) engaging in strategic restructuring (e.g. executive replacement, establishment of monitors or watchdogs). The purpose of normalizing accounts and strategic restructuring is to construct a 'firewall' between audience assessments of legitimacy-threatening events and organizations as a whole. Normalizing accounts entail the use of verbal remedial strategies to repair organizational legitimacy. This involves the use of a wide variety of mainly defensive tactics identified by social psychology research. Defensive tactics, such as justifications and excuses, are deployed in situations where organizations expect to be met by disapproval, for example during events threatening organizational image, reputation or legitimacy. Alternatively, acquisitive tactics, such as self-promotion, exemplification, ingratiation, enhancements and entitlements, are used in situations when organizations expect to be met by approval (Benoit, 1995; Ogden and Clarke, 2005; Aerts and Cormier, 2009).

Strategic restructuring entails 'selectively confess[ing] that limited aspects of its operations were flawed' (Suchman, 1995: 598) and then decisively and visibly remedying them by introducing small and narrowly tailored changes. Two types of strategic restructuring have been identified: (1) creating monitors and watchdogs and (2) disassociation. Disassociation entails symbolically distancing organizations from negative influences. For example, executive replacement allows organizations to dissociate themselves from legitimacy-threatening events by blaming individuals. Organizations can also dissociate themselves from de-legitimated procedures and structures (Ogden and Clarke, 2005). From an institutional perspective, impression management is conceptualized as decoupling (DiMaggio and Powell, 1983).

Decoupling entails rendering organizational structures and processes so that they *appear* to conform to social and institutional norms and rules. Decoupling manifests itself in espousing socially acceptable goals, redefining means as ends and ceremonial conformity (Linsley and Kajüter, 2008). Espousing socially acceptable goals, for example, involves claiming customer-focus or equal opportunities employer status when, in effect, the opposite is the case. Redefining means as ends, for example, involves justifying closure of employee pension schemes on the basis of the introduction of a new accounting standard. Finally, ceremonial conformity entails adopting specific practices considered consistent with rational behaviour, even though they do not improve organizational practices, for example public-sector organizations introducing private-sector management accounting practices or performance evaluation schemes (see Merkl-Davies and Brennan, 2011).

Critical perspective

The critical perspective is characterized by a critical realist view of organizational reality combined with a critical stance. The aim of critical research is emancipation and commitment to changing oppressive realities. The aim of critical impression management research is to expose hidden interests in corporate reporting (Chua, 1986). This entails analysing the linguistic means by which dominant constructions of reality are achieved. For example, Prasad and Mir's (2002: 96) analysis of CEO letters to shareholders of US oil companies in the 1970s and 1980s aims to expose the 'hidden meanings [in corporate narrative documents] that serve the interests of the socially and politically powerful'. Studies adopting a critical perspective predominantly focus on the use of impression management during controversial issues and legitimacy threatening events, such as privatisation (Craig and Amernic, 2004a, 2008), difficult financial circumstances (Amernic and Craig, 2000), financial scandals (Craig and Amernic, 2004b) and transformational changes (Amernic et al., 2007). The focus of analysis is on the way language is used by managers to convince organizational audiences of the validity, legitimacy or necessity of organizational changes, to portray financial scandals as isolated incidents, or to persuade organizational audiences of the exceptional nature of the circumstances resulting in the negative financial performance. However, language use in corporate documents is never 'innocent', because it is used to achieve a variety of economic, social and political goals and is thus 'as ideologically saturated as ... text[s] which wear [their] ideological constitution overtly' (Kress, 1993: 174). Thus, impression management can be regarded as part of 'routine' corporate communication used by management to 'control the way in which the corporate story is interpreted' (Crowther et al., 2006: 199).

Impression management is regarded as resulting from the desire of powerful managers to impose their perspective of (1) organizational activities and outcomes (White and Hanson, 2002; Amernic and Craig, 2004), (2) specific stakeholders with whom they are in conflict (Driscoll and Crombie, 2001; Prasad and Mir, 2002), or (3) socio-economic and socio-political issues affecting their activities or reputation such as climate change, minimum pay or human rights (Livesey, 2002). Corporate narrative documents are assumed to have ideological effects in the sense that 'they can help produce and reproduce unequal power relations ... through the ways in which they represent things and position people' (Fairclough and Wodak, 1997: 258). Language is regarded as a medium in which prevailing power relations are articulated. Impression management in the form of ideological bias focuses on rhetorical (e.g. repetition, hyperbole), semantic (e.g. metaphor, differentiation) and grammatical (e.g. passivization) features employed by managers to impose their view of organizations and firm performance and of social, political or environmental issues affecting organizations (e.g. Craig and Amernic, 2004a, 2004b; Crowther et al., 2006). Metaphors entail 'understanding and experiencing one kind of thing in terms of another' (Lakoff and Johnson, 1980: 5) as a means of knowledge construction and perception engineering (Walters, 2004). In their analysis of Enron's Letter to Shareholders after the bankruptcy, Craig and Amernic (2004b) show how metaphors of war, sport and extremism and hyperbole are used to portray the firm's competitive advantage, despite mounting evidence to the contrary. Illustration 8.11 exemplifies the use of metaphors and hyperboles as a means of imposing management's monological interpretation of the organization and organizational activities and outcomes.

Differentiation refers to people understanding the world in terms of significant pairings, contrasts, or dualities, such as up–down, mind–body and public–private, which are often seen 'in contradiction to each other, frequently with one term assuming dominance' (Llewellyn, 2003: 670). Differentiation is a characteristic feature of discourse which is used to set up specific value systems and thus indicates the stance adopted (Fairclough, 2003). In their analysis of managerial discourse ('CEO-speak') during a six-month period following an incident in a German nuclear power plant, Beelitz and Merkl-Davies (2012) find that CEOs strategically use the discourse of stakeholder engagement as a means of signalling change, yet maintain the *status quo*. It suggests that CEOs strategically use discourse to manufacture organizational audiences' consent regarding the continued operation of the nuclear power plant affected by the incident.

Illustration 8.11: Critical perspective – analysis of metaphors and hyperboles

---

Illustration 11.1: Metaphors (of sport and extremism)

Enron's performance in 2000 was a <u>success</u> by any measure, as we continued to <u>outdistance the competition</u> and solidify <u>our leadership</u> in each of our major businesses.

Illustration 11.2: Hyperboles

Enron has built <u>unique</u> and <u>strong</u> businesses that have <u>tremendous opportunities for growth</u>. These businesses ... can be <u>significantly expanded</u> within their <u>very large</u> existing markets and extended to new markets with <u>enormous growth potential</u>.

(Source: Craig and Amernic, 2004b: 821 and 824)

Illustration 8.12 shows the role differentiation plays in identifying stances in a particular discourse. The examples juxtapose the organization's initial technocratic discourse and subsequent discourse of stakeholder engagement.

Future research directions

Most prior research is archival, inducing interpretations from accounting narratives in published corporate reports. Relatively little is understood about the processes underlying their construction (Gibbins et al., 1990 is an exception). Who writes the accounting narratives? In this respect, Goffman's (1981) differentiation between (1) the principal, whose position the text reflects, (2) the author, who performs the writing task, and (3) the animator, who articulates the text, may be useful. Even less is understood about the effect of accounting narratives on organizational audiences. Prior research is generally based (1) on share price reaction studies, which make inferences about the interpretation of accounting narratives by shareholders depending on the behaviour of share prices, and (2) on experiments, often conducted on students. There is relatively little direct research on shareholders and stakeholders.

Illustration 8.12: Critical perspective – analysis of differentiation

---

(1) Organizational purpose

Regulatory body (obligation)
'Clearly, immediate and extensive information was submitted to the <u>authorities</u>.' (Document 4)

Stakeholders (Trust)
'Ensuring that the general public feel safe and <u>trust</u> our ability to provide power.' (Document 9)

(2) Stakeholder identification and salience

'<u>Employees</u> at nuclear power plants often don't understand other people, while outsiders don't understand nuclear energy.' (Document 3)

'Employees at nuclear power plants often don't understand <u>other people</u>, while <u>outsiders</u> don't understand nuclear energy.' (Document 3)

(Source: Beelitz and Merkl-Davies, 2012: 116–117)

Potential and pitfalls of impression management research

The characteristics of managers in relation to their communication choices, and the reactions of audiences to managerial impression management, are under-researched opportunities. There is lack of consensus on whether impression management in a corporate-reporting context has an impact on organizational audiences. Are they taken in by impression management or do they see through it, thus treating it as executive hyperbole ('cheap talk')? If they are susceptible to impression management, why is this the case? Prior research attributes the predisposition of organizational audiences towards impression management to cognitive limitations and affective factors. There is little understanding of the short-term as well as long-term effects of the impact of impression management (if any). Further, most prior research focuses on accounting narratives in corporate reports, particularly in annual reports. Less attention is given to other disclosure vehicles (e.g. press releases, prospectuses and statements and speeches by senior management) and to other reporting contexts outside the annual reporting accountability cycle (e.g. *ad hoc* corporate reporting, such as during initial public offerings, bankruptcy, takeovers, redundancies, fatalities, other crisis events). Four explanations were put forward for discretionary accounting narratives. Two of these, hubris and retrospective sense-making, have attracted little attention, thus providing opportunities for researchers. Of the four perspectives discussed in the chapter, the sociological and critical are under-researched. On the downside, impression-management research does not lend itself to large sample sizes. Much corporate reporting impression management research is conducted manually. Where computer-software packages are applied, there are concerns at the validity of using such methods. By contrast, with manual techniques, there are concerns around reliability and replicability issues, due to the subjective nature of the coding involved.

Relationship between organizational reputation, image, legitimacy and impression management

Prior impression management research does not differentiate between situations affecting an organization's desirability (reputation and image) and situations affecting its appropriateness (legitimacy). However, due to differences in the characteristics of reputation, image and legitimacy (see Table 8.1), organizations may use different communication choices, depending on whether organizational reputation, image or legitimacy is affected. Impression management (in the form of symbolic management) might be more effective when organizational image is affected, as it is dynamic and thus more susceptible to change than reputation or legitimacy. By contrast, substantive management by changing organizational practices and the adoption of violated values might be more effective when organizational reputation and legitimacy is under threat, as they are more stable than image. Short-term communication choices, such as symbolic management and substantive management, might be more effective in situations affecting reputation and image than legitimacy. Long-term communication choices, such as isomorphism and decoupling, might be more effective in situations affecting legitimacy.

Organizational audiences' actual beliefs about organizational desirability or acceptability are difficult to establish by archival research. Aerts and Cormier (2009) measure external legitimacy concerning organizational environmental responsibility by analysing the press-media coverage of environmental issues relating to the firms in their sample. These press articles are classified as good news, bad news or neutral news coverage. Legitimacy is equated with good news coverage. However, it could be argued that they measure environmental reputation or image, as legitimacy is associated with appropriateness, whereas reputation and image are associated with evaluation.

Interaction between management and organizational audiences

A social constructivist view of organizational reality implies that organizational reputation, image and legitimacy are discursively constructed in interactions between organizations and their audiences over time. Impression management thus needs to be conceptualized as an inter-active process between organizations and their audiences, i.e. a process of negotiation between management and organizational audiences (Ginzel et al., 2004). This process consists of at least three phases:

1. the account-generation process during which managers provide interpretations of issues or events;
2. the reaction of organizational audiences to managers' interpretations of issues or events;
3. a subsequent account-generation process during which managers attempt to negotiate a reso-lution between its initial account and the interpretation thereof by organizational audiences.

The negotiation process constitutes a struggle over meaning with both parties aiming to have their definition of reality accepted (Suchman, 1995: 597). Driscoll and Crombie (2001), Beelitz and Merkl-Davies (2012), and Brennan et al. (2014) are rare examples of studies of impression management as an interactive process between two parties. Driscoll and Crombie (2001) analyse a conflict between a large timber firm and a small monastery situated in a forest where the firm is operating. They find that the timber firm uses language and symbolic activity to increase its own legitimacy and decrease the legitimacy of the monastery. Beelitz and Merkl-Davies (2012) analyse the discursive negotiation of legitimacy between an energy company and organizational audiences following an incident in a German nuclear-power plant. They find that managers use discourse to manufacture organizational audiences' consent. Brennan et al. (2014) develop a methodology based on the concept of dialogism to analyse the interactions between Greenpeace and six textile firms during a conflict over environmental performance.

Insights for preparers and users of corporate reports

This chapter has provided evidence that preparers use the flexibility inherent in corporate narrative reporting to mislead users. Organizations such as the Global Reporting Initiative advo-cate a balanced reporting framework which reflects firm economic, environmental and social impact – the so-called triple bottom line. If managers continue to adopt questionable reporting practices, they risk bringing upon themselves increasing regulation in this domain. Users of corporate reports need to be aware of these practices, as a means of detecting the potential underlying deception involved. Research in psychology finds the texts of individuals who engage in deception to show distinct linguistic characteristics. Merkl-Davies et al. (2011b) adapt a content analysis approach based on the linguistic style associated with self-presentational dissimulation developed by Newman et al. (2003).

Concluding comment

In this chapter, we consider how accounting narratives may be used for impression management purposes. After some discussion of the corporate-reporting context, impression management is considered by reference to four perspectives on impression management (economic, psycho-logical, sociological and critical). Seven communication choices in discretionary accounting narratives in corporate reports are examined in some detail (see illustrations 8.1–8.12).

The chapter concludes with some suggestions for future research and some insights for preparers and users of corporate reports.

Impression management is a rich and complex phenomenon. Depending on the disciplinary perspective adopted (economic, psychological, sociological, critical), impression management can be conceptualized as reporting bias, self-serving bias, symbolic management/decoupling or ideological bias. If accounting narratives are used for impression management purposes, this can have a negative impact on shareholders, stakeholders and society at large. Impression management constitutes an important area of research, as it not only has the potential to undermine financial reporting quality (resulting in adverse capital allocations), but may also contribute to social and political inequality. However, due to its subtle, more qualitative nature and the consequent difficulties in data collection and coding (often manual), it may not attract as many researchers as other forms of managerial opportunistic behaviour, such as earnings management. Still, so many questions remain unanswered that it represents a fertile opportunity for researchers looking for an under-researched field with rich potential.

References

Abrahamson, E. and Park, C. (1994) 'Concealment of negative organizational outcomes: An agency theory perspective', *Academy of Management Journal*, 37(5): 1302–1334.

Aerts, W. (1994) 'On the use of accounting logic as an explanatory category in narrative accounting disclosures', *Accounting, Organizations and Society*, 19(4/5): 337–353.

Aerts, W. (2001) 'Inertia in the attributional content of annual accounting narratives', *European Accounting Review*, 10(1): 3–32.

Aerts, W. (2005) 'Picking up the pieces: impression management in the retrospective attributional framing of accounting outcomes', *Accounting, Organizations and Society*, 30(6): 493–517.

Aerts, W. and Cheng, P. (2011) 'Causal disclosures on earnings and earnings management in an IPO setting', *Journal of Accounting and Public Policy*, 30(5): 431–459.

Aerts, W. and Cormier, D. (2009) 'Media legitimacy and corporate environmental communication', *Accounting, Organizations and Society*, 34(1): 1–27.

Allport, G.W. (1985) 'The historical background of social psychology', in G. Lindzey and E. Aronson (eds), *Handbook of Social Psychology*, Vol. 1, New York: Random House, pp. 1–46.

Amernic, J.H. and Craig, R.J. (2000) 'Accountability and rhetoric during a crisis: Walt Disney's 1940 letter to stockholders', *Accounting Historians Journal*, 27(2): 49–86.

Amernic, J.H. and Craig, R.J. (2004) '9/11 in the service of corporate rhetoric: Southwest Airlines' 2001 letter to shareholders', *Journal of Communication Inquiry*, 28(4): 325–341.

Amernic, J., Craig, R. and Tourish, D. (2007) 'The transformational leader as pedagogue, physical, architect, commander and saint: five root metaphors in Jack Welch's letters to stockholders of General Electric', *Human Relations*, 60(12): 1839–1872.

Arndt, M. and Bigelow, B. (2000) 'Presenting structural innovation in an institutional environment: hospital's use of impression management', *Administrative Science Quarterly*, 45(3): 494–522.

Ashforth, B. and Gibbs, B. (1990) 'The double-edged sword of organizational legitimation', *Organization Science*, 1(2): 177–194.

Baginski, S.P., Hassell, J.M. and Hillison, W.A. (2000) 'Voluntary causal disclosures: tendencies and capital market reaction', *Review of Quantitative Accounting and Finance*, 15(4): 371–389.

Beelitz, A. and Merkl-Davies, D.M. (2012) 'Using discourse to restore organizational legitimacy: "CEO-speak" after an incident in a German nuclear power plant', *Journal of Business Ethics*, 108(1): 101–120.

Benoit, W. (1995) *Accounts, Excuses and Apologies: A Theory of Image Restoration*, Albany, NY: State University of New York Press.

Bowen, R.M., Davis, A.K. and Matsumoto, D.A. (2005) 'Emphasis on pro forma versus GAAP earnings in quarterly press releases: determinants, SEC intervention and market reactions', *The Accounting Review*, 80(4): 1011–1038.

Brennan, N.M., Daly, C.A. and Harrington, C.S. (2010) 'Rhetoric, argument and impression management in hostile takeover defence documents', *British Accounting Review*, 42(4): 253–268.

Brennan, N.M., Guillamon-Saorin, E. and Pierce, A. (2009) 'Impression management: developing and illustrating a scheme of analysis for narrative disclosures – a methodological note', *Accounting, Auditing & Accountability Journal*, 22(5): 789–832.

Brennan, N.M., Merkl-Davies, D.M., and Beelitz, A. (2014) 'Dialogism in corporate social responsibility communications: conceptualising verbal interaction between organisations and their audiences', *Journal of Business Ethics*, in press.

Breton, G. and Côté, L. (2006) 'Profit and the legitimacy of the Canadian banking industry', *Accounting, Auditing & Accountability Journal*, 19(2): 512–539.

Campbell, D.J. and Beck, A.-C. (2004) 'Answering allegations: the use of the corporate website for issue-specific reputation management', *Business Ethics: A European Review* 13(2/3): 100–116.

Chua, W.F. (1986) 'Radical developments in accounting thought', *The Accounting Review*, LXI(4): 601–632.

Clatworthy, M. and Jones, M.J. (2001) 'The effect of thematic structure on the variability of annual report readability', *Accounting, Auditing & Accountability Journal*, 14(3): 311–326.

Clatworthy, M. and Jones, M.J. (2003) 'Financial reporting of good news and bad news: evidence from accounting narratives', *Accounting and Business Research*, 33(3): 171–185.

Clatworthy, M.A. and Jones, M.J. (2006) 'Differential reporting patterns of textual characteristics and company performance in the chairman's statement', *Accounting, Auditing & Accountability Journal*, 19(4): 493–511.

Courtis, J.K. (1995) 'Readability of annual reports: Western versus Asian evidence', *Accounting, Auditing & Accountability Journal*, 8(2): 4–17.

Courtis, J.K. (1996) 'Information redundancy in annual reports', *Accountability and Performance*, 12(3): 1–16.

Courtis, J.K. (1998) 'Annual report readability variability: tests of the obfuscation hypothesis', *Accounting, Auditing & Accountability Journal*, 11(4): 459–471.

Courtis, J.K. (2004a) 'Corporate report obfuscation: artefact or phenomenon?', *British Accounting Review*, 36(3): 291–312.

Courtis, J.K. (2004b) 'Colour as visual rhetoric in financial reporting', *Accounting Forum*, 28(3): 265–281.

Craig, R.J. and Amernic, J.H. (2004a) 'The deployment of accounting-related rhetoric in the prelude to privatization', *Accounting, Auditing & Accountability Journal*, 17(1): 41–58.

Craig, R.J. and Amernic, J.H. (2004b) 'Enron discourse: the rhetoric of a resilient capitalism', *Critical Perspectives on Accounting*, 15(6/7): 813–851.

Craig, R.J. and Amernic, J.H. (2008) 'A privatization success story: accounting and narrative expression over time', *Accounting, Auditing & Accountability Journal*, 21(8): 1085–1115.

Cresswell, J. and Thomas, L. (2009) 'The talented Mr Madoff', *New York Times*, 24 January.

Crowther, D., Carter, C. and Cooper, S. (2006) 'The poetics of corporate reporting: evidence from the UK water industry', *Critical Perspectives on Accounting*, 17(1/2): 175–201.

Davis, A.K., Piger, J.M. and Sedor, L.M. (2012) 'Beyond the numbers: measuring the information content of earnings press release language', *Contemporary Accounting Research*, 29(3): 845–868.

Davis, A. and Tama-Sweet, I. (2012) 'Managers' use of language across alternative disclosure outlets: earnings press releases versus MD&A', *Contemporary Accounting Research*, 29(3): 804–837.

Davison, J. (2002) 'Communication and antithesis in corporate annual reports: a research note', *Accounting, Auditing & Accountability Journal*, 15(4): 594–608.

Davison, J. (2008) 'Rhetoric, repetition, reporting and the "dot.com" era: words, pictures, intangibles', *Accounting, Auditing & Accountability Journal*, 21(6): 791–826.

Deephouse, D.L. and Carter, S.M. (2005) 'An examination of differences between organizational legitimacy and organizational reputation', *Journal of Management Studies*, 42(2): 329–360.

Deephouse, D.L. and Suchman, M.C. (2008) 'Legitimacy in organizational institutionalism', in R. Greenwood, C. Oliver, K. Sahlin and R. Suddaby (eds), *The SAGE Handbook of Organizational Institutionalism*, Thousand Oaks CA: Sage, pp. 49–77.

DiMaggio, P. J. and Powell, W. (1983) 'The iron cage revisited: institutional isomorphism and collective rationality in organizational fields', *American Sociological Review*, 48: 147–160.

Driscoll, C. and Crombie, A. (2001) 'Stakeholder legitimacy management and the qualified good neighbor', *Business & Society*, 40(4): 442–471.

Fairclough, N. (2003) *Analysing Discourse: Text Analysis for Social Research*, London: Routledge.

Fairclough, N. and Wodak, R. (1997) 'Critical discourse analysis', in T. Van Dijk (ed.) *Discourse as Social Interaction*, London: Sage, pp. 258–284.

Feldman, R., Govindaraj, S., Livnat, J. and Segal, B. (2010) 'Management's tone change, post earnings announcement drift and accruals', *Review of Accounting Studies*, 15: 915–953.

Frink, D.D. and Ferris, G.R. (1998) 'Accountability, impression management, and goal setting in the performance evaluation process', *Human Relations*, 51(10): 1259–1283.

Gibbins, M., Richardson, A. and Waterhouse, J. (1990) 'The management of corporate financial disclosure: opportunism, ritualism, policies and processes', *Journal of Accounting Research*, 28(1): 121–143.

Ginzel, L.E., Kramer, R.M. and Sutton, R.I. (2004) 'Organizational impression management as a reciprocal influence process: the neglected role of the organizational audience', in M.J. Hatch and M. Schultx (eds), *Organizational Identity*, Oxford: Oxford University Press, pp. 223–261.

Gioia, D.A., Schultz, M. and Corley, K.G. (2000) 'Organizational identity, image, and adaptive instability', *Academy of Management Review*, 25(1): 63–81.

Godfrey, J., Maher, P. and Ramsey, A. (2003) 'Earnings and impression management in financial reports: the case of CEO changes', *Abacus*, 39(1): 95–123.

Goffman, E. (1959) *The Presentation of Self in Everyday Life*, New York: Doubleday Anchor Books.

Goffman, E. (1981) *Forms of Talk*. Philadelphia, PA: University of Pennsylvania Press.

Healy, P.M. and Wahlen, J.M. (1999) 'A review of the earnings management literature and its implications for standard setting', *Accounting Horizons* 13(4): 365–383.

Henry, E. (2006) 'Market reaction to verbal components of earnings press releases: event study using a predictive algorithm', *Journal of Emerging Technologies in Accounting*, 3: 1–19.

Henry, E. (2008) 'Are investors influenced by how earnings press releases are written?' *Journal of Business Communications*, 45(4): 363–407.

Highhouse, S., Brooks, M.E. and Gregarus, G. (2009) 'An organizational impression management perspective on the formation of corporate reputations', *Journal of Management*, 35(6): 1481–1493.

Hooghiemstra, R. (2000) 'Corporate communication and impression management – new perspectives why companies engage in corporate social reporting', *Journal of Business Ethics*, 27: 55–68.

Hooghiemstra, R. (2008) 'East-West differences in attributions for company performance: a content analysis of Japanese and US corporate annual reports', *Journal of Cross-Cultural Psychology*, 39: 618–629.

Hooghiemstra, R. (2010) 'Letters to the shareholders: a content analysis comparison of letters written by CEOs in the US and Japan', *International Journal of Accounting*, 45: 275–300.

Hyland, K. (1998) 'Exploring corporate rhetoric: metadiscourse in the CEO's letters', *Journal of Business Communication*, 35(2): 224–245.

Johnson, W.B. and Schwartz, W.C. (2005) 'Are investors misled by "pro forma" earnings?', *Contemporary Accounting Research*, 22(4): 915–963.

Jones, M.J. and Shoemaker, P.A. (1994) 'Accounting narratives: a review of empirical studies of content and readability', *Journal of Accounting Literature*, 13: 142–184.

Knee, C.R. and Zuckerman, M. (1996) 'Causality orientations and the disappearance of the self-serving bias', *Journal of Research in Personality*, 30: 76–87.

Kress, G. (1993) 'Against arbitrariness: the social production of the sign as a foundational issue in Critical Discourse Analysis', *Discourse and Society*, 4(2): 169–193.

Lakoff, G. and Johnson. M. (1980) *Metaphors We Live By*, Chicago: University of Chicago Press.

Lang, M. and Lundholm, R. (2000) 'Voluntary disclosure and equity offerings: reducing information asymmetry or hyping the stock?', *Contemporary Accounting Research*, 17(4): 623–662.

Levitt, A. (2000) 'Remarks before the conference on the rise and effectiveness of new corporate governance standards', 12 December. Available at www.sec.gov/news/speech/spch449.htm (accessed 17 October 2011).

Lewellen, W.G., Park, T. and Ro, B.T. (1996) 'Self-serving behavior in managers' discretionary information disclosure decisions', *Journal of Accounting and Economics*, 21(2): 227–251.

Li, F. (2008) 'Annual report readability, current earnings, and earnings persistence', *Journal of Accounting and Economics*, 45(2–3): 221–247.

Linsley, P. and Kajüter, P.M. (2008) 'Restoring reputation and repairing legitimacy: a case study of impression management in response to a major risk event at Allied Irish Banks plc', *International Journal of Financial Services Management*, 3(1): 65–82.

Livesey, S.M. (2002) 'Global warming wars: rhetorical and discourse analytic approaches to Exxonmobil's corporate public discourse', *Journal of Business Communication*, 39(1): 117–146.

Llewellyn, S. (2003) 'What counts as "theory" in qualitative management and accounting research? Introducing five levels of theorizing', *Accounting, Auditing & Accountability Journal*, 16(4): 662–705.

Matsumoto, D., Pronk, M. and Roelofsen, E. (2011) 'What makes conference calls useful? The information content of managers' presentations and analysts' discussion sessions', *The Accounting Review*, 86(4): 1383–1414.

Merkl-Davies, D.M. and Brennan, N.M. (2007) 'Discretionary disclosure strategies in corporate narratives: incremental information or impression management?', *Journal of Accounting Literature*, 26: 116–196.

Merkl-Davies, D.M. and Brennan, N.M. (2011) 'A conceptual framework of impression management: new insights from psychology, sociology and critical perspectives', *Accounting and Business Research*, 41(5): 415–437.

Merkl-Davies, D.M., Brennan, N.M. and McLeay, S.J. (2011a) 'Impression management and retrospective sense-making in corporate narratives: a social psychology perspective', *Accounting, Auditing & Accountability Journal*, 24(3): 315–344.

Merkl-Davies, D.M., Brennan, N.M. and McLeay, S.J. (2011b) 'Traditional and cohesion-based approaches to analysing readability in corporate narratives using Coh-Metrix', working paper, Centre for Impression Management in Accounting Communication, Bangor Business School, UK.

Merkl-Davies, D.M., Brennan, N.M. and Vourvachis, P. (2013) 'A taxonomy of text analysis approaches in corporate narrative reporting research', working paper, Centre for Impression Management in Accounting Communication, Bangor Business School, UK.

Merkl-Davies, D.M. and Koller, V. (2012) '"Metaphoring" people out of this world: a critical discourse analysis of a chairman's statement of a UK defence firms', *Accounting Forum*, 36(3): 178–193.

Milne, M.J., Kearns, K. and Walton, S. (2006) 'Creating adventures in wonderland the journey metaphor and environmental sustainability', *Organization*, 13(6): 801–839.

Mouck, T. (1995) 'Financial reporting, democracy and environmentalism: a critique of the commodification of information', *Critical Perspectives on Accounting*, 6(6): 535–553.

Newman, M.L., Pennebaker, J.W., Berry, D.S. and Richards, J.M. (2003) 'Lying words: predicting deception from linguistic styles', *Personality and Social Psychology Bulletin*, 29(5): 665–675.

Ogden, S. and Clarke, J. (2005) 'Customer disclosures, impression management and the construction of legitimacy: corporate reports in the UK privatised water industry', *Accounting, Auditing & Accountability Journal*, 18(3): 313–345.

Prasad, A. and Mir, R. (2002) 'Digging deep for meaning: a critical hermeneutic analysis of CEO letters to shareholders in the oil industry', *Journal of Business Communication*, 39(1): 92–116.

Rutherford, B.A. (2003) 'Obfuscation, textual complexity and the role of regulated narrative accounting disclosure in corporate governance', *Journal of Management and Governance*, 7: 187–210.

Schlenker, B.R. (1980) *Impression Management: The Self Concept, Social Identity and Interpersonal Relations*, Monterey, CA: Brooks-Cole.

Schrand, C. and Walther, B.R. (2000) 'Strategic benchmarks in earnings announcements: the selective disclosure of prior-period earnings components', *The Accounting Review*, 75(2): 151–177.

Short, J.C. and Palmer, T.B. (2003) 'Organizational performance referents: an empirical examination of their content and influences', *Organizational Behavior and Human Decision Processes*, 90(2): 209–224.

Smith, M. and Taffler, R.J. (1992a) 'The chairman's statement and corporate financial performance', *Accounting and Finance*, 32(2): 75–90.

Smith, M. and Taffler, R.J. (1992b) 'Readability and understandability: different measures of the textual complexity of accounting narrative', *Accounting, Auditing & Accountability Journal*, 5(4): 84–98.

Smith, M. and Taffler, R.J. (1995) 'The incremental effect of narrative accounting information in corporate annual reports', *Journal of Business Finance and Accounting*, 22(8): 1195–1210.

Smith, M. and Taffler, R.J. (2000) 'The chairman's statement: a content analysis of discretionary narrative disclosures', *Accounting, Auditing & Accountability Journal*, 13(5): 624–646.

Staw, B., McKechnie, P. and Puffer, S. (1983) 'The justification of organizational performance', *Administrative Science Quarterly*, 28: 582–600.

Suchman, M.C. (1995) 'Managing legitimacy: strategic and institutional approaches', *Academy of Management Review*, 20(3): 571–610.

Sydserff, R. and Weetman, P. (1999) 'A texture index for evaluating accounting narratives: an alternative to readability formulae', *Accounting, Auditing & Accountability Journal*, 12(4): 459–488.

Sydserff, R. and Weetman, P. (2002) 'Developments in content analysis: a transitivity index and DICTION scores', *Accounting, Auditing & Accountability Journal*, 15(4): 523–545.

Tennyson, B., Ingram, R.W. and Dugan, M.T. (1990) 'Assessing the information content of narrative disclosures in explaining bankruptcy', *Journal of Business Finance and Accounting*, 17(3): 391–410.

Walters L.M. (2004) 'Alternative accounting thought and the prison-house of metaphor', *Accounting, Organizations and Society*, 29(2): 157–187.

Walters-York, L.M. (1996) 'Metaphor in accounting discourse', *Accounting, Auditing & Accountability Journal*, 9(5): 45–70.

White, R. and Hanson, D. (2002) 'Corporate self, corporate reputation and corporate annual reports: re-enrolling Goffman', *Scandinavian Journal of Management*, 18: 285–301.

Young, J.J. (2003) 'Constructing, persuading and silencing: the rhetoric of accounting standards', *Accounting, Organizations and Society*, 28(6): 621–638.

Part 3

Contemporary and professional issues

9

Phantasmagoria, sustain-a-babbling in social and environmental reporting

Markus J. Milne

Introduction

Thirty years ago corporate social reporting, as it was known then, was largely an erudite concept – it was something academics argued about but few business and other organizations did. There was academic dissatisfaction over the dearth of organizational practice as well as significant debate about the possibilities for such practice. Academics argued about whether organizations *should* produce social and environmental accounts and reports, and whether organizations *could* do so. In the last thirty years, and particularly so over the last two decades, social and environmental reporting practice (and more recently triple bottom line reporting, sustainability reporting and soon-to-be integrated reporting) has increased significantly and is now something many (large) organizations proclaim they can do and are doing. Despite burgeoning practice, however, many proponents of social and environmental reporting remain dissatisfied and critical of such developments. Time and again I have been asked, somewhat quizzically, surely as a social and environmental accountant you would be in favour of sustainability reporting, so why are you so critical of such organizational reporting and communication practices?

As with many issues, the devil is in the detail. The short answer is that the communication practices that have emerged over the past two decades, as well as the rationales for them, do not live up to the ideals of the proponents of thirty years ago. Central to this mismatch and disappointment (as some academics suspected) has been the dashing of the (perhaps forlorn) hope that such communication practices would lead to greater levels of organizational transparency and accountability about the non-economic impacts they have on society and the physical environment. Such practices it was then anticipated would ultimately drive deep-seated behavioural reform, and assist in moving away from unsustainability. That is, away from increasing levels of environmental harm and social injustice, which are believed unable to be continued without drastic levels of overshoot and irrevocable damage. In contrast, what is now seen as the outcome by some is the embedding and entrenchment of *existing* values, beliefs and practices. The fear some commentators hold is that rather than being a catalyst and facilitating change, such communication practices excuse and shelter existing practices and stifle change. Despite a new coat of green paint some believe organizations remain capitalist juggernauts – crushing, exploiting and exacerbating an unsustainable existence for humans and other species. A good question to ask is: 'if all organizations were to practise as so-called leading sustainability reporters do, would we be any closer to living on a planet that could sustain us (humans) and other species?' To label and dismiss such reporting practices as merely 'greenwash' or public relations puffery, however, is to underestimate the power of communication, discourse and ideology. This is particularly so when the communication is systematically organized and developed by and for particular interests. To act on something is to know it, and to know it involves thinking, writing and reading, and talking about it. Ultimately, practice is caught up in discourse, constraining as well as enabling action. Organizational reporting constitutes a powerful part of that discourse.

The purpose of this chapter is to provide the long answer: to provide the detail and to make clear the gaps that exist between (a) what are organizational social and environmental communication practices; (b) what they claim and appear to be, but are not, and can never be; and (c) what they could be, but are not. The next section sketches some of the history of the developments in social and environmental accounting and reporting, turning attention to what is actually reported and how. As we shall see, such reporting remains voluntary, little regulated, non-standardized and largely unaudited. In fact, a large majority of companies do not report at all, including many very large organizations. So far, companies have been rather effective at lobbying against mandatory social and environmental reporting, but guidance for those who care to report has emerged from the Global Reporting Initiative, other reporting organizations, and reporting awards schemes.

Given the relatively recent and important attention focused on sustainability, the next section then turns to 'sustain-a-babbling' – a term coined to describe how organizations simply write nonsense when it comes to understanding and articulating sustainability. Key questions for any organization wishing to claim it is reporting on 'sustainability' performance are: (1) what does sustainability *mean*? (2) What is to be sustained? (3) For how long? (4) In whose interests? Most so-called 'sustainability' reports simply ignore such questions, and for most organizations it will become clear that what they mean by 'sustainability' reporting is reporting on their social, environmental and economic/financial *impacts*. Such *impact* accounting, however, tells us nothing about the pressure on, the state of, or the future capacity of, the social and environmental systems on which organizations rely. Indeed, 'sustainability reporting' has grown to mean reporting on (self-selected) elements of each of an organization's impacts on society, economy and environment. 'Social reporting', on the other hand, typically limits such reporting to an organization's impacts on society. Despite the babbling, however, it also becomes clear how organizations, through rhetorical communication, have moved from aspiring towards sustainability to actually claiming to be sustainable, leaving one to wonder what actually is meant by such claims.

The final section returns to several shortcomings of existing reporting and communication practices that have been identified for 20 years or more and yet continue to persist. Adjudicators' reports from social and environmental reporting awards since 1991 consistently identify such shortfalls as verification practice, stakeholder engagement and other means by which organizations can seriously discharge their accountability. To make their reporting more meaningful, more transparent and useful to stakeholders and, in the process, discharge an appropriate level of accountability for their social and environmental impacts, a template of best-practice reporting is offered by which this can be achieved. What is also made clear, however, is that organizations need to give up their pitiful claims to be doing anything meaningful under the name of sustainability.

Organizations have only ever reported their social and/or environmental impacts

Despite a rapidly evolving nomenclature surrounding non-financial organizational reporting (e.g. triple bottom line, sustainability, integrated), evidence suggests that organizations do little more than report on their social, environmental and/or economic/financial impacts, either singularly, or in some combination. In other words, the content of such reports is organization-centric and limited to organization impacts. It remains largely without social and environmental context. Such reporting initially tended to focus singularly on environmental impacts. Corporate *environmental* reporting emerged in Europe, Canada and the USA during the late 1980s and early 1990s, and while corporate *social* (and employee and human resource) reporting and *social auditing* have a history dating back into the 1970s (see, e.g., Flamholtz, 1985; Gray et al., 1987), they also re-emerged during the 1990s when organizations like The Body Shop began issuing 'values' or 'social' reports. Particularly influential in promoting the recent widespread development of these practices in Europe have been the London-based consultancies of SustainAbility (www.sustainability.com) and AccountAbility (www.accountability.org). The emergence of such reporting practices also spawned a host of other developments including new reporting awards schemes (see, for example, www.accaglobal.com), the first of which appeared in the UK in 1991. Attempts to 'standardize' such practices followed, with the multi-agency and international Global Reporting Initiative (GRI) being the prime mover in developing a series of guidelines and revised guidelines for report content since 1999 (www.globalreporting.org). The most recent development in this trend is the promotion of 'integrated reporting' by the International Integrated Reporting Committee (IIRC) which seeks to connect corporate governance and strategy with corporate social and environmental performance (www.theiirc.org). Arguably, in this instance, all three reporting dimensions are 'integrated' into some kind of comprehensive performance report, but most likely organizations will continue to report self-selected elements of each of their social, environmental and economic impacts.

Specific, separate, stand-alone social/environmental reporting typically followed the practice of supplementary annual report disclosure, in which some organizations added narrative and non-financial information about the organization's environmental and/or social impacts to the traditional annual report. Reporting developments over time vary by organization. Some organizations have 'progressed' from supplementary annual report disclosures to fuller stand-alone reports. Typically, in the early/mid-1990s these focused solely on environmental disclosures, reflecting to a large extent some of the earliest exponents of stand-alone reporting: namely, in mining, chemicals, oil and gas, utilities and forestry and pulp and paper (KPMG, 1993, 1996). An important catalyst in UK environmental reporting was Rob Gray's (1990) *The Greening of Accountancy: The Profession after Pearce*. This monograph, which explored the UK accountancy profession in light of David Pearce's government report on a future greening economy, helped galvanize the Association of Certified Chartered Accountants (ACCA). A year later, the ACCA followed with their inaugural environmental reporting awards scheme to help encourage green reporting. Since then, other organizations have entered for the first time with a stand-alone report, and many continue to do so. In the mid-/late 1990s, especially in Europe and the USA, social- *and* environment-related information was often released together in 'health, safety and environment' (HSE) reports. HSE typically reflects the organizational function jointly responsible for environmental and health and safety regulation and compliance. It narrowly confined 'social' issues to matters concerning employees and regulatory compliance. Other less typical developments during the mid-1990s included a group of 'values-based' companies issuing wider ranging social reports including, for example, The Body Shop, the Co-op Bank, Ben and Jerry's Ice Cream, and Traidcraft Inc.

Perhaps the most significant development in the history of reporting practice was the 1997 book by John Elkington (founder of SustainAbility): *Cannibals with Forks: The Triple Bottom Line of 21st Century Business*. By coining the metaphor 'the triple bottom line', Elkington seems to have set alight reporting developments in which organizations' social, environmental and economic impact information might be combined in a single report. Oddly enough, the idea of organizations accounting for their social, environmental and economic impacts was not new. Robert Jensen's 1976 American Accounting Association monograph *Phantasmagoric Accounting: Research and Analysis of Economic, Social and Environmental Impact of Corporate Business* was an early exploration of the issues. Unlike Jensen, however, Elkington's book was not an academic treatise, and became popular progressive business practice. This was helped by Elkington's charismatic leadership and influence as head of his consultancy, SustainAbility. Wheeler and Elkington (2001) single out several influential developments in triple bottom line reporting: a set of case studies in social accounting, auditing and reporting by Zadek et al. (1997); SustainAbility's (1999) *Social Reporting Report*; and *Issues and Trends in Corporate Social Reporting* (PIRC, 1999). Wheeler and Elkington suggest: '… in just five years, social reporting had moved from a fringe activity pioneered by socially conscious but non-mainstream companies into a credible and serious practice embraced by a number of corporations' (Wheeler and Elkington, 2001: 4).

The concept of triple bottom line reporting was further promoted through several of a series of seven UNEP/SustainAbility benchmarking reports which analysed best international reporting practice between 1994 and 2006 (UNEP/SustainAbility, 1994 et seq.). Such a series implicitly provided templates for best-practice reporting, and especially so by making public the reporting assessment methodologies. Table 9.1 illustrates 29 key reporting ingredients in the 2006 Global Reporters' assessment methodology, by which each report was actively scored.

In parallel to Elkington's efforts, the UK-based ACCA has been a long-term facilitator and promoter of reporting developments. Its UK environmental reporting awards scheme dates from 1991, but it has progressed to develop reporting awards schemes around the world. Consequently, among its judging criteria one can also find key reporting ingredients. A current list of 41 criteria for 'excellent' reporting is available. These concentrate on reporting completeness, credibility and communication. Critical dimensions are matters of materiality, stakeholder inclusion, strategy, organizational context, management process, governance, performance, assurance and presentation (see, for example, ACCA, 2011).

Critical in the recent history of stand-alone non-financial reporting developments is the rise of the Global Reporting Initiative (GRI) and its sustainability reporting guidelines. Roger Adams from the ACCA and John Elkington have played influential formative roles in the GRI. Founded in 1997 (for details on the history of the institution, see Brown et al., 2009; and Etzion and Ferraro, 2010), the GRI is currently revising and updating a fourth iteration of its guidelines (G4). A draft is due for release for comment in 2012 and final guidelines are to be made public in early 2014 (GRI, 2011). The current G3 guidelines (GRI, 2006) provide for the following:

- 42 strategy and profile reporting ingredients (e.g. CEO statement, profile, reporting parameters and governance, commitments and engagement);
- 79 performance indicators across three categories: environment (30), social (40) and economic (9);
- 49 of the 79 indicators are identified as 'core' indicators;
- 40 social indicators disaggregated into labour practices (14), human rights (9), society (8) and product responsibility (9).

Not all the GRI indicators, however, need to be reported. The framework provides for three levels of 'compliance'; namely, A, B and C (the lowest).

- An 'A-level' reporter needs to disclose, at a minimum, all 42 strategy and profile indicators and all the 49 core indicators.

Table 9.1 SustainAbility's 2006 global reporters' assessment methodology

---

Governance and Strategy
  1.1 Company and Industry Profile
  1.2 Top Management Statement
  1.3 Issue Identification and Prioritisation (i.e. social, economic and environmental impacts)
  1.4 Values, Principles and Policies
  1.5 Business Strategy and Sustainable Development Vision
  1.6 The Business Case (link social and environmental performance with financial)
  1.7 Sustainable Development Implementation Challenges
  1.8 Governance Responsibilities and Structure
  1.9 Risk Management
  1.10 Meeting Tomorrow's Needs
  1.11 Customer Influence and Market Shaping

Management
  2.1 Management Procedures
  2.2 Value Chain Management
  2.3 Stakeholder Engagement
  2.4 Personnel Performance Management, Training and Development
  2.5 Learning and Knowledge Management
  2.6 Public Policy and Regulatory Affairs (lobbying, association memberships, etc.)
  2.7 Industry Influence
  2.8 Philanthropy and Social Investment
  2.9 Investor Relations

Performance
  3.1 Performance and Strategy Alignment
  3.2 Measuring Sustainable Development Performance (i.e. social, environmental and economic)
  3.3 Context and Interpretation of Performance Measures
  3.4 Target Setting
  3.5 Performance Against Standards (i.e. internal targets, regulatory and benchmarking)

Accessibility and Assurance
  4.1 Assurance (means to enhance credibility of reported information)
  4.2 Reporting Commitment, Policy and Strategy
  4.3 Reporting Standards (reference to use of GRI or other guidelines)
  4.4 Accessibility of Information

Source: adapted from *Global Reporters Methodology* (SustainAbility, 2006)

- A 'B-level' reporter needs to disclose the 42 strategy indicators and at least 20 of the 79 performance indicators, with at least one indicator from each of the main three categories and the four social sub-categories.
- A 'C-level' reporter needs to disclose 28 of the strategy and profile indicators, but only 10 of the 79 performance indicators, with at least one indicator from each of the environmental, social and economic categories.

Clearly, the GRI framework provides for considerable flexibility in reporting. This flexibility has both strengths and weaknesses. There is no shortage of available and detailed frameworks for guiding the production of an excellent organizational report that demonstrates an organization's accountability to a wide range of stakeholders with respect to its economic, environmental and social performance.

The term 'sustainability' features heavily in the language of the GRI and its iterations of guidelines (GRI, 2000, 2002, 2006). This is also the case for pronouncements from ACCA and SustainAbility. Yet what resides at the core of these reporting frameworks, and indeed much so-called sustainability reporting, is a triple bottom line focus on organizations' economic, social and environmental performance. The conflation of sustainability with economic, social and environmental performance indicators may in part be due to Elkington's own references to the relationship between the three aspects of the triple bottom line and sustainability:

> During the 1990s, perhaps five years behind the practice of environmental auditing and reporting, the art of social auditing and reporting began to gather advocates and practitioners ... with the advent of sustainable development as a meaningful concept for both governments and businesses ... and triple-bottom line thinking becoming a convenient metaphor for strategists in the field, the way was clear for the 'third dimension' of sustainability to be tracked and reported on.
>
> *(Wheeler and Elkington, 2001: 4)*

That is, sustainability reporting emerged when social reporting joined the ranks of traditional financial reporting and environmental reporting. The international triennial KPMG surveys of non-financial reporting from 1993 to 2011 also documents this trend and increasing references to a wide range of reporting nomenclature:

> corporate environmental reporting [has become] the 'icebreaker' for a much wider form of corporate responsibility (CR) reporting in the form of sustainability, triple bottom line or corporate social responsibility (CSR) reports. Reporting is aimed at communicating with stakeholders, not only on environmental performance, but also in an integrated manner on environmental, social and economic performance, to be transparent and accountable.
>
> *(KPMG, 2005: 3)*

Despite KPMG's proclamation, it is less clear that these trends represent anything substantive in terms of progressive and improved reporting, increased transparency or greater levels of accountability. Below we specifically examine claims by organizations to be engaging in 'sustainability reporting'. However, it is also worth mentioning several other matters in regard to these trends. First, such reporting largely remains voluntary and unregulated and unstandardized. With these forms of non-financial reporting, there are no equivalents to Companies Acts, Financial Reporting Acts, accounting standards, or GAAP (generally accepted accounting principles) that have to be followed in producing such information. Neither is there any requirement for such information to be independently verified or audited, and similarly there is no mandatory assurance guidance or standards. Indeed, typically organizations have resisted notions of mandatory reporting and assurance of social and environmental impact information. Essentially, organizations are free to report what they like, as and when they like or, as in the great majority of cases, simply not report at all.

The voluntary and unregulated nature of reporting contributes to a second issue: there is no standardized terminology that can be used unambiguously to interpret report content or reporting developments. While environmental reports largely constitute (aspects of) organizations' environmental performance, and social reports of their employee and community performance, the triple bottom line loosely adds an economic dimension to performance. Conceptually, the GRI's 'sustainability' reporting guidelines, for all intents and purposes, simply re-labels the triple bottom line (Gray and Milne, 2002). And the recent integrated reporting (IR) developments seem to drop the economic dimension and pick up environment, social and governance (ESG). ESG has become the latest acronym to emerge with IR. Organizations often re-label their reports without changing content, while others use different titles for similar content. Indeed, noting the difficulties of nomenclature, the 2006 UNEP/SustainAbility benchmark report asked, 'What do you call your report?' Reference was often made to triple bottom line reports, but the notion itself is largely metaphorical – there are no equivalent social or environmental bottom lines in such reports (Norman and MacDonald, 2004). Overall, organizations do not produce systemized social and environmental accounts and statements like they produce financial statements that reduce to a single figure equivalent of net profit.

There are some exceptions to this general statement. In early reporting developments, particularly in Europe and especially Germany, a few pioneering reporters experimented with producing eco-balance or mass-balance statements that sought to track energy and material flows into and out of organizations (White and Wagner, 1996; Owen, 2003). While such reports are undoubtedly complete and relatively systematic they suffered from interpretation problems by non-expert readers. Similarly, during the 1970s some organizations produced employee statements, with one going so far as to attempt to produce human-resource accounts in monetized form (see Flamholtz, 1985). Others experimented with value-added statements that sought to indicate the distribution of organizational revenue to a variety of different stakeholder groups. A somewhat more recent development is greenhouse gas (GHG) accounting and attempts to produce GHG inventories or statements of GHG emissions. These, too, are purportedly systematic attempts to produce 'carbon accounts' (in quantities of carbon dioxide, or carbon dioxide equivalent) which may also be subject to audit or verification (Milne and Grubnic, 2011). Nonetheless, and despite a GHG protocol being developed to guide practice (e.g. WBCSD/WRI, 2004; Kolk et al., 2008; Simnett et al., 2009), there still remains considerable latitude in regard to following the protocol, and producing GHG emissions estimates (see Milne and Grubnic, 2011). Finally, it is noteworthy that at least one organization (Solid Energy, a New Zealand coal-mining organization) attempts to reduce its environmental impacts to a single 'cumulative net environmental effect' figure (see Solid Energy, 2010). However, the figure is largely un-interpretable and seems to represent a meaningless aggregation of multiple data and dimensions.

In summary, the field of non-financial reporting is a mess. The report reader is likely to be confronted with a cocktail of narrative, non-financial physical quantities, as well as perhaps some monetized values – typically expenditure data, on a raft of social and environmental issues.

This, in turn, contributes to a third and further difficulty – that of inter-firm and inter-temporal comparisons. The fact that organizations are free to pick and mix what they report, and when they do so, leaves external audiences unclear or even ignorant about trends in any underlying physical performance to which it might relate. It also makes assessment of reporting trends difficult to assess across organizations and over time. Despite the availability of several frameworks, organizations do not necessarily follow these consistently from one period to another. Reporting develops (i.e. more indicators are added) and also deteriorates (indicators are dropped), often without explanation. The most unambiguous conclusions that can be drawn based on the KPMG triennial surveys are that the numbers of organizations reporting has increased (and this is the case for most countries surveyed); that reporters come from a greater spread of sectors/industries; and that overall at least (but this varies by country), more reporters have their reports verified (ACCA/Corporateregister.com, 2004; Milne and Gray, 2007). Stand-alone reporting is being adopted by a considerably more eclectic and diverse range of organizations than in the mid-1990s (see, for example, Chapman and Milne, 2004; Bebbington et al., 2009; Reverte, 2009; Vormedal, 2009).

Less clear is evidence that over the last two decades report content is improving in terms of its completeness, consistency, veracity, transparency or any other criteria one might want to use to assess reporting practice. Many stand-alone reports are more informative than the cursory discretionary disclosures that used to appear in conventional annual reports. Also clear is that latter-day reports are more comprehensive and credible than the early public-relations-oriented 'green glossies' that appeared from some organizations in the early 1990s. Beyond this, however, any systematic analysis of stand-alone reporting content is patchy. Reviewing the UNEP/SustainAbility report benchmarking series 1994–2004, Milne and Gray (2007) observe that until 2004 the content of reports against the benchmark criteria by leading reporters largely remained static at 45–60 per cent; and that even up to 2002, only seven reporters achieved greater than 50 per cent of the score. The recent advent of the GRI guidelines, however, seems to have stimulated some improvements in reporting – at least among the leading reporters. The 2004 benchmark report noted 20 reporters exceeded the 50 per cent threshold: the Co-op Bank was the clear leader with 71 per cent. In the last of the series in 2006 (UNEP/SustainAbility, 2006), 40 organizations exceeded 50 per cent, five exceeded 70 per cent, and the clear leader was BT (British Telecom) on 80 per cent.[1]

These benchmark reports claim to assess the very best of international practice and typically work with the largest of multinational organizations. Single-country academic studies of samples of smaller organizations tend to reveal much poorer reporting performance when assessed against criteria such as UNEP/SustainAbility's benchmark or the GRI guidelines (see, for example, Milne et al., 2003; Chapman and Milne, 2004; Morhardt et al., 2002; Morhardt, 2009, 2010). Anecdotal evidence of the revisions that produced the G3 guidelines and introduced the A, B and C level categories suggest they may simply have lowered the reporting compliance floor rather than produced a ratchet or development path to higher-quality and more comprehensive reporting. Seasoned reporters issuing their tenth report or so, for example, may yet still post a minimum self-declaration of C level GRI compliance. One wonders what the additional benefits might be to a reporting organization striving to provide an A level report versus one at C level. And one can also wonder about the motives of the GRI in introducing the varying levels of compliance in the first place. Were the previous and much stricter reporting 'in accordance with the GRI' rules (under G1 and G2) too stifling of reporting development, and thereby, at the same time, diminishing the success and legitimacy of the GRI itself? Have the lower thresholds simply allowed the GRI to swell its reporting ranks with low-place getters, thereby diluting its effectiveness and producing increased volumes of GRI compliant reporters at the expense of lower-quality reports? In part, these are moot points anyway, since reporting against the GRI guidelines is often a voluntary self-declared activity by the reporting organization that goes unmonitored and unchallenged. Interestingly, in the preparation of its latest G4 guidelines, the GRI is asking whether there should be a minimum of ten obligatory indicators for all companies reporting against its guidelines. Again, without regulatory backing and/or some kind of public enforcement, this too seems a moot point.

Generally, despite the ever-changing reporting terminology (environmental, social, HSE, TBL, sustainability, integrated), reporting formats (annual reports, web-based, stand-alone, integrated) and reporting criteria/guidelines (ACCA, UNEP/SustainAbility, GRI), most organizations have only ever reported about themselves and (a selection of) their social and environmental intentions, policies and impacts. Such reports address a wider range of stakeholders than shareholders, but hitherto they have not empowered those stakeholders (Gray et al., 1997; Cooper and Owen, 2007; Dingwerth and Eichinger, 2010; Fonseca, 2011). Indeed, some argue that under the typical Western financial regulatory frameworks in which directors are legally bound to privilege shareholders, they never will consider other stakeholders in anything other than an insincere fashion (Bakan, 2004). Consequently, sceptics doubt the extent of the development of social and environmental reporting practice over the past 20 years. Invariably, the organization remains at the controlling hub of this stakeholder reporting model, and stakeholders are arguably accorded lip service in the interests of management and the shareholders. As with financial reporting, the dominant accounting entity concept remains (see Milne, 1996). Consequently, the organization retains control of what is reported, when it is reported and to whom it is reported. More organizations are reporting, but many doubts remain about whether they are any more accountable for their social and environmental impacts than they were 20 years ago. In many ways the ideal of the UK's Accounting Standards Steering Committee's *Corporate Report* of 1975 contemplated a more democratic form of corporate reporting. But it remains just that, an ideal.

'Sustain-a-babbling' or how organizations report nonsense about sustainability

At the heart of assessing corporate 'sustainability' reporting are fundamental differences about what corporate reporting for sustainability *means* and, implicitly within these differences, what purposes it serves (or might serve), and whose interests are (or might be) served by it. 'What is to be sustained?' is a fundamental question Dobson (1998, but also see Sutton, 1999) asks in trying to define concepts of environmental sustainability. With respect to concepts like 'sustainable development', one might argue that what is to be sustained is the option of future generations of humans to sustain themselves and ultimately, for the human species to sustain its existence. However, many point out that to do that one needs to sustain the life-supporting ecology on which humans rely for sustenance (IUCN, 1980; Global Footprint Network, 2010; WWF, 2010). The Brundtland Report's (WCED, 1987) conception of sustainable development is unashamedly anthropocentric, but the basis of this is concern for equity and unequal international development outcomes and opportunities. So what do corporate organizations have in mind in respect to this question? What is it they seek to sustain?

For many organizations, associations and commentators, corporate sustainability reporting is an extension and progression from earlier forms of corporate reporting to include matters of an organization's *environmental policies* and *impacts* (e.g. resource and energy use, waste flows), and its *social policies and impacts* (e.g. health and safety of employees, impacts on local communities and charitable giving). In many ways, the reporting frameworks just outlined have simply consolidated and entrenched these developments. Indeed, the precise purpose of the GRI was to extend the financial accounting framework to include non-financial reporting to a wider range of stakeholders (Brown et al., 2009; Etzion and Ferraro, 2010). Unfortunately, in the process, and along with Elkington and the ACCA, it has coupled these developments with the concept of sustainability through the triple bottom line (Milne et al., 2008). If one were to try and fit an answer to Dobson's question on the basis of what one reads in so-called corporate 'sustainability' reports, it would have to be 'the business or 'economic growth' and likely little or nothing to do with ecology or with society. It is far from clear an organization would put itself out of business if it discovered it was doing irreparable damage to the environment. This should come as no surprise, for that is what the capitalist system demands, and that is what directors and managers are paid for (Bakan, 2004). Yet, what it illustrates amply is that acting alone, voluntarily and on the basis of economic motives, most businesses seem incapable of addressing the fundamental issues of sustainability. If they were being truly honest and transparent, they would refrain from saying they are.

Paul Hawken, social entrepreneur, founder of the Natural Capital Institute and author of *The Ecology of Commerce* and *Natural Capitalism*, gets to the crux of this issue when he savagely critiqued McDonalds Corporation's first corporate social responsibility report as a Ronald McDonald fantasy (Hawken, 2002):

> The question we have to ask is what is enough? Is it enough that one in five meals in the US is a fast food meal? Does that satisfy McDonald's? Or do they want that figure to be one in three, or how about one in two? How about the developing world? ... They won't answer those questions because that is exactly their corporate mission ... A valid report on sustainability and social responsibility must ask the question: What if everybody did it? What would be the ecological footprint of such a company? What is McDonald's footprint now? The report carefully avoids the corporation's real environmental impacts. It talked about water use at the outlets, but failed to note that every quarter-pounder requires 600 gallons of water. It talked about recycled paper, but not the pfisteria-laden waters caused by large-scale pork producers in the southeast. It talked about energy use in the restaurants, but not in the unsustainable food system McDonald's relies upon that uses 10 calories of energy for every calorie of good produced. "Sustaining" McDonald's requires a simple unsustainable formula: cheap food plus cheap non-unionized labor plus deceptive advertising = high profits. An honest report would tell stakeholders how much it truly costs society to support a corporation like McDonald's. It would detail the externalities borne by other people, places, and generations.

Hawken (2002) went on to caution that:

> At this juncture in our history, as corporations and governments turn their attention to sustainability, it is crucial that the meaning of sustainability not get lost in the trappings of corporate speak ... I am concerned that good housekeeping practices such as recycled hamburger shells will be confused with creating a just and sustainable world.

Arguably, this is precisely what has happened. Organizations now routinely conflate strategies that pursue eco-efficiency and stakeholder consultation with efforts to contribute to sustainability. That is, they adopt strategies that could, but do not, produce meaningful reductions in the burden placed on natural systems (Milne et al., 2009). Organizations providing sustainability reports and declaring their intentions to minimise environmental impacts, as Hawken so acutely observes, often ignore the increasing scale of their developments (Gray, 2006). As Milne et al. (2009) illustrate, a fisheries company can eagerly highlight and proclaim success at reducing levels of energy and materials used to produce *each tonne* of processed fish, yet ignore its greater increases in the total tonnage of fish caught and processed. It thereby remains silent and distracts from its greater impact on the oceans, and its greater *overall* impact on energy and materials. At first, organizations were eager to proclaim their good intentions and undertake the 'sustainability journey' and work 'towards sustainability' (Milne et al., 2006). More recently, and considerably more arrogantly, many seem eager to claim results and success (see Gray, 2010 for a review). As Milne (2007) illustrates, a leading provider of scientific knowledge and a pioneer of environmental reporting in New Zealand has boldly proclaimed its carbon-neutral performance, yet at the same time increased its carbon footprint by 20 per cent. Likewise, a leading New Zealand airline proclaimed it is minimizing its environmental impact, and making efficiency savings, yet at the same time increased its carbon footprint by 25 per cent (Milne and Grubnic, 2011). Indeed, as Milne and Grubnic (2011) illustrate, New Zealand's national carbon footprint has increased by 20 per cent since 1990, yet it is physically and economically calculated as infeasible to offset it, or even one tenth of it. Consequently, what sense does it make for organizations to proclaim their sustainability credentials when at more aggregated regional and national (and international) levels the burden on ecological systems is moving in an opposite and unsustainable direction?

For Hawken (1993) along with Gray (1992), Milne (1996) and Birkin (2000) from within accounting, sustainability only really makes sense at a systems level, and perhaps more pertinently at a planetary systems level. This has become rather more obvious with increasing reference to climate change threats, global-level GHG emissions and carbon accounting. It helps little if one organization is reducing its carbon emissions, while another is increasing by yet more. It helps little if one country is reducing its emissions, but another is increasing by yet more. But it is not just the atmospheric commons to which this applies - it concerns all common property 'resources' (e.g. fisheries, water, biodiversity and habitat). The picture is one of an all too familiar 'tragedy of the commons' (Hardin, 1968). Like medieval sheep farmers, and modern fishers, self-styled corporate 'sustainability' reporters singularly fail to address the sustainability requirements of linking micro indicators of performance with systems-level indicators of impacts, and the tolerance limits of the systems in which they operate (Milne, 1996; Gray, 2006). Evidence from analyses of reporting practice suggests companies are preoccupied with their own (selected) performance indicators (see, for example, Livesey, 2002; Livesey and Kearins, 2002; Gray, 2006; Tregidga and Milne, 2006; Milne et al., 2009). In the absence of references to the context of planetary, ecological and social crises (see, for example, Worldwatch, 2003; Meadows et al., 2004; Millennium Ecosystem Assessment, 2005; UNEP, 2007; WWF, 2010), corporate sustainability reports must remain little more than self-deluding babble (Gray and Milne, 2002, 2004; Milne and Gray, 2007). But this babble is far from innocuous. Its danger lies in precisely the fact that it remains separate from (and in the absence of) the wider contradictory evidence of systems failure. Organizations present themselves as efficient, effective, leaders, providers, protectors and, perhaps most dangerously, as sustainable – and thus, as legitimate and beyond reproach (Tregidga et al., 2008; Milne et al., 2009).

Jensen (1976) rejected the idea that it was possible to capture the externalities of single business organizations in a complete monetized account. Milne (1996) doubts sustainability accounting at the level of a single firm is (at all) meaningful. For him, sustainability suggests broader ecosystem-based approaches to accounting that require an understanding of cumulative environmental change and assessments of the cumulative effects of economic activity. As Gray and Milne (2002: 69) articulate, sustainability accounting requires:

> a complete and transparent statement about the extent to which the organization had contributed to—or, more likely, diminished— the sustainability of the planet. For that to occur, however, as we have seen, we need to have a detailed and complex analysis of the organization's interactions with ecological systems, resources, habitats, and societies, and interpret this in the light of all other organizations' past and present impacts on those same systems.

For any single firm, they argue this is impossible, technically and because no business organization would want to take responsibility for the impacts of other organizations. Yet, that is the point of a tragedy of the commons. Milne (2007: 53) explains the intractability of the wider problem. Organizational and national accounts of economic activity fail to capture the social and environmental effects of that activity because financial and economic indicators dominate traditional forms of accounting, whereas bio-physical and social non-financial indicators dominate knowledge of social and ecological impacts. Added to this is the difficulty of boundary problems over where entities finish and end in terms of measurement and responsibilities.

Simply drawing some additional non-financial social and environmental impact indicators into organizational-level reports does not overcome these difficulties, no matter how comprehensive and complete they become. Collective and co-ordinated action for the common good is not improved by superior information sets about individual micro-level behaviours. Moreover, as many others have noted, such an approach continues to reinforce existing institutions (i.e. business) as centres of power and decision making, whereas new and alternative decision-making arrangements and institutions are sought at larger scales and more collective levels of resolution (Bennett and van der Lugt, 2004; Richardson, 2004).

Making organizational social and environmental reporting meaningful

Corporate social and environmental reports might be incapable of delivering sustainability, but they are not necessarily incapable of delivering accountability. Many do not deliver accountability, or not to the degree some would like. It should be obvious from the previous section that there is no shortage of frameworks available to guide comprehensive, credible and informative accounts of an organization's triple bottom line impacts. Neither is there any shortage of leading role models able to do this. In other words, the frameworks can and are being put into practice by some, but there are simply not enough. The trouble is that the vast majority of organizations fail to report at all, even very large organizations with significant social and environmental impacts (Milne and Gray, 2007). Many other organizations fail to take the exercise seriously. Indeed, the revisions to the GRI – namely G3 – seem to have legitimized poor-quality reporting by allowing organizations to report a few indicators in the hope they are at least encouraged to begin reporting.

The central tension in making reporting meaningful is in deciding 'meaningful for whom?' For the organization producing the report? For the stakeholders receiving the report? The professional and business perspective (e.g. Elkington, 1997; WBCSD, 2000, 2002) has tended to argue and promote a 'business case' for such reporting based on claimed reputational and competitive advantages to the reporting organization. The implied logic is that such reporting meets the needs of the organization and the stakeholders in a 'win–win' outcome. In the face of voluntary and un-standardized practices, however, critics often doubt the veracity of the information released, and complain of partial, incomplete and self-serving public-relations exercises that seek organizational legitimacy through appearance rather than changed behaviours. For others, stakeholders are the primary concern. They see there is a need, based on a duty or moral obligation under a 'social contract', for organizations to report their social and environmental impacts (Gray et al., 1987, 1988). In exchange for privileged access to society's commons, organizations have a duty to produce an account, and citizens have a right to know. It is from this latter 'accountability' perspective that many concerns for the practices of corporate social and environmental reporting arise, including (1) the lack of a regulatory framework and requirements for mandatory reporting and its assurance; (2) the standards of corporate reporting and assurance practice; and (3) stakeholder inclusiveness and empowerment.

Despite detailed guidelines and reporting frameworks, business has largely and effectively lobbied against any mandatory requirements for either reporting or assurance. Minor amendments to companies' laws and other regulations have provided for some types of disclosures in some jurisdictions, but on the whole there is nothing comparable to IFRS, GAAP or GAAS. Based on progress to date, the prospect of the GRI reporting guidelines receiving legal backing seems a long way off. Consequently, any pressure and encouragement for reporting falls on a variety of other mechanisms, including peer pressure from competitors and the advantages corporate reporters perceive from it. Similarly, service and assurance consultancies help promote reporting. Reporting awards schemes, too, have played a part. Finally, reporting might be improved by the pressure external stakeholders can muster, including that brought to bear by social and ethical investors and consumers. While these pressures have certainly grown over the last 20 years one wonders about their effectiveness in improving corporate accountability.

Frequently the reports of the judges to the ACCA reporting awards schemes draw attention to the deficiencies of reporting practice. Commonly these reflect concerns for increased transparency and accountability to stakeholders. Fairly consistent observations concern assurance, completeness and stakeholder inclusion.

Often disappointing is the complete absence of an external assurance statement, at best replaced by some kind of stakeholder review panel's observations, or perhaps nothing at all. Also of concern are significant limitations to the scope of the assurance engagement, and/or a complete absence of explanation of the engagement scope (see O'Dwyer and Owen, 2005; Mock et al., 2007; CorporateRegister, 2008). Over the years many academics have raised concerns about the variable nature of auditing processes (Beets and Souther, 1999; Wallage, 2000; Deegan et al., 2006a, 2006b; Mock et al., 2007), and their independence, and whether they primarily serve stakeholders' or management needs (Ball et al., 2000; Gray, 2000; Owen et al., 2000). From an accountability perspective, Gray (2000) has stressed that assurance (or attestation) must remain genuinely third-party if it is to avoid fooling the reader (stakeholder) into believing that social and environmental reports can be relied on as true and fair, when in fact the attestation process provides no such guarantee. If organizations want stakeholders to take their claims about honesty and transparency seriously, then the practices and standards of external verification need to improve dramatically. A set of rules and regulations akin to those used to assure the external reporting of financial information would help. Yet, stakeholders will also require auditors who are willing to act on their behalf or in the public interest than predominantly those of their organizational clients. And that begs the further question about the whole regulatory set up of third-party non-financial assurance.

Patchy, incomplete and cherry-picked reporting remains a problem. Once we get beyond the headline acts of the UNEP/SustainAbility benchmark entrants, studies of smaller reporting organizations tend to reveal long tails of poor-quality reporting. Whether the GRI 'C-level' requirements are helping consolidate and legitimize poor-quality reporting, or whether they are encouraging new entrants and helping others step up, remains far from clear. Anecdotal evidence suggests the former, but a more detailed examination is needed. In addition to narrow reporting, however, judges' reports often reveal disappointment in the narrow categories of stakeholder groups identified in reports – typically employees, groups who receive philanthropic donations, and local community groups. Lacking, too, are references to the processes that are used to identify stakeholders, how the organization engages with them and identifies their concerns, and how the organization prioritizes and deals with those concerns. In short, any demonstration of the materiality of what's reported to stakeholders is often woefully inadequate.

The remedy for producing a best-practice corporate social and environmental report that delivers accountability to stakeholders is not tough. Ample guidelines exist on how to report and what to report. Most organizations will also find good examples of existing reporters in their respective industrial sectors. Leading reporting would place the organization's stakeholders' concerns centre stage (Gray et al., 1997). It would genuinely seek to empower stakeholders and provide a voice in the organization's affairs, in the same way that shareholders arguably have

(Cooper and Owen, 2007; Dingwerth and Eichinger, 2010). To deliver a meaningful account to stakeholders, organizations will produce a report that:[2]

1. is clear and easy to read;
2. identifies the organization's key social and environmental issues and links these to its core business activities and strategy;
3. details clear objectives and targets and shows performance against these;
4. defines stakeholder engagement issues clearly, including how stakeholders are identified, how their issues are identified, what dialogue occurred along with the process of engagement and feedback;
5. reports on all issues material to stakeholders or explains why not;
6. benchmarks the organization's performance against its sector;
7. clearly identifies how social and environmental KPIs are utilized within the organization's remuneration planning;
8. is transparent about the key social and environmental issues and challenges faced;
9. makes appropriate use of reporting frameworks like the GRI;
10. is independently assured using recognized assurance frameworks;
11. concentrates on the organization's social, environmental and economic impacts, policies, and commitments and refrains from sustain-a-babbling – making spurious nonsensical commentary about sustainability.

Conclusion

This chapter has briefly overviewed corporate non-financial reporting practice developments over the past two decades or so. It traces recent reporting to the initial phase of stand-alone reporting of corporate environmental impacts in the early 1990s. Stand-alone social reporting followed and, very soon, in conjunction with efforts from John Elkington and others, morphed into triple bottom line reporting and subsequently corporate sustainability reporting. During this same period, UNEP/SustainAbility benchmark surveys, ACCA reporting awards schemes, and reporting guidelines by the Global Reporting Initiative have emerged to encourage and support such reporting. Stand-alone reporting practice has increased, but doubts remain about its nature and whose interests it serves.

Early academic proponents stressed stand-alone reporting as the means for corporations to deliver accountability to a wider range of stakeholders under a social contract – for the privileged use of common property resources, and for demonstrating fair and just treatment of workers, local communities and others. In many cases, they doubt whether corporate accountability is genuinely being served by current reporting practices. Such fears are based on evidence of poor and incomplete reporting and assurance practices, and any clear demonstration of stakeholder engagement, inclusion and empowerment. These are factors which the ACCA reporting judges draw attention to repeatedly. Added to these concerns are the manner in which businesses, and particularly their associations, have actively resisted reporting regulation and instead promoted the business case for corporate voluntarism. For many, stakeholder reporting is a matter of doing the right thing. It rests on a moral duty to discharge an account, regardless of the economic calculus. In the absence of significant regulatory backing, stakeholders' rights-to-know become the fickle properties of corporate largesse – a proposition rejected as the basis for genuine corporate accountability.

The failure of reporting to deliver corporate accountability can be remedied through regulation and improved reporting and disclosure practices. Such is not the case for corporate claims to be delivering sustainability. Unlike accountability, sustainability is simply beyond the reach of any single business organization. A lot more can be done to understand, measure and articulate the organization's social and environmental *context* and the extent to which it is impacted by the organization, as Hawken so vividly illustrates. However, to make any claims or even imply any claims about the state of such environmental and social systems and their capacity to continue to function (i.e. to be sustained) seems a step too far. To do otherwise involves either extreme ignorance or extreme arrogance. When it comes to 'sustainability' reporting, Jensen's (1976) reference to 'phantasmagoric accounting' seems apt. Unlike others who rejected social responsibility and social reporting on ideological grounds (e.g. Friedman, 1970; Benston, 1982), Jensen was not hopeful a fully monetized, triple bottom line account could be meaningfully produced by business organizations, and he rejected the idea as phantasmagoric. Phantasmagoria appears to be a blend of French and Greek – *fantasme* (illusion) and *allégorie* or *allegory* (symbolic or metaphorical representation), or *agora* (an assembly). It is wonderfully defined as 'a fantastic sequence of haphazardly associative imagery, as in dreams or fever', 'having a fantastic or deceptive appearance', a 'scene that constantly changes' and 'a bizarre or fantastic combination, collection, or assemblage'. For coming to grips with the unsustainable basis of the human enterprise, could the ever-changing, haphazard and deceptive nature of corporate sustainability reporting be anything other than a bizarre or fantastic assemblage or delusional fantasy? Business organizations and researchers keen on non-financial communication would do well to forget about sustainability, a likely chimera, and keep their efforts trained on providing full and complete social and environmental accounts that deliver genuine accountability.

Notes

1 Some care is needed in interpreting these benchmarking trends. First, the sample of reporters over time is not consistent. The series works with the world's leading 50 organizations/reporters it identifies each time. These change (and often considerably so) in some years. In 2006, for example, 25 of the 50 reporters were 'new entrants'. While this illustrates high-quality entry-level reporting for some organizations, it also illustrates how inter-temporal comparisons are difficult. A second complicating factor is that the UNEP/SustainAbility benchmark criteria themselves have evolved and have been revised over time, further limiting inter-temporal comparisons.
2 Based on recommendations contained in the 2011 ACCA Australian Sustainability Reporting Awards Judges Comments.

References

ACCA (2011) *Report of the Judges: ACCA New Zealand Sustainability Reporting Awards 2011.* www.ausnz. accaglobal.com/pubs/australia/general/sustainability_nz/report/NZ2011.pdf.
ACCA/CorporateRegister (2004) *Towards transparency: progress on global sustainability reporting 2004,* London: Certified Accountants Educational Trust.
Accounting Standards Steering Committee (ASSC) (1975) *The Corporate Report: A Discussion Paper Published for Comment,* London: ASSC.
Bakan, J. (2004) *The Corporation: The Pathological Pursuit of Profit and Power,* London: Constable & Robinson.
Ball, A., Owen, D. L. and Gray, R. (2000) 'External transparency or internal capture? The role of third party statements in adding value to corporate environmental reports', *Business Strategy and the Environment,* 9(1): 1–23.
Bebbington, J., Higgins, C., and Frame, B. (2009) 'Initiating sustainable development reporting: Evidence from New Zealand', *Accounting, Auditing & Accountability Journal,* 22(4): 588–625.
Beets, S. D. and Souther, C. C. (1999) 'Corporate environmental reports: the need for standards and an environmental assurance service', *Accounting Horizons,* 13(2): 129–145.
Bennett, N. and van der Lugt, C. (2004) 'Tracking Global governance and sustainability: is the system working?', in A. Henriques and Richardson, J. (eds), *The Triple Bottom Line: Does it All Add Up?* London: Earthscan.

Benston, G. (1982) 'Accounting and corporate accountability', *Accounting, Organizations and Society*, 7(2): 87–105.

Birkin, F. (2000) 'The art of accounting for science: a prerequisite for sustainable development?', *Critical Perspectives on Accounting*, 11(3): 289–309.

Brown, H. S., de Jong, M. and Levy, D. L. (2009) 'Building institutions based on information disclosure: lessons from GRI's sustainability', *Journal of Cleaner Production*, 17(6): 571–580.

Chapman, R. and Milne, M. (2004) 'The triple bottom line: how New Zealand companies measure up', *International Journal for Sustainable Business*, 11(2): 37–50.

Cooper, S. M. and Owen, D. L. (2007) 'Corporate social reporting and stakeholder accountability: the missing link', *Accounting, Organizations and Society*, 32: 649–667.

CorporateRegister.com (2008) *Assure View: The CSR Assurance Statement Report*. London: Park Communications.

Deegan, C., Cooper, B. J. and Shelly, M. (2006a) 'An investigation of TBL report assurance statements: UK and European evidence', *Managerial Auditing Journal*, 21(4): 329–371.

Deegan, C., Cooper, B. J. and Shelly, M. (2006b) 'An investigation of TBL report assurance statements: Australian evidence', *Australian Accounting Review*, 16(2): 2–18.

Dingwerth, K. and Eichinger, M. (2010) 'Tamed transparency: how information disclosure under the Global Reporting Initiative fails to empower', *Global Environmental Politics*, 10(3): 74–96.

Dobson, A. (1998) *Justice and the Environment: Conceptions of Environmental Sustainability and Dimensions of Social Justice*, Oxford: Oxford University Press.

Elkington, J. (ed.). (1997) *Cannibals with forks: The triple bottom line of 21st Century business*, London: Earthscan.

Etzion, D. and Ferraro, F. (2010) 'The role of analogy in the institutionalization of sustainability reporting', *Organization Science*, 21(5): 1092–1107.

Flamholtz, E. (1985) *Human Resource Accounting*, San Francisco: Jossey-Bass Inc.

Fonseca, A. (2011) 'Barriers to strengthening the Global Reporting Initiative framework: exploring the perceptions of consultants, practitioners, and researchers', working paper, University of Waterloo, Canada, available at: www.csin-rcid.ca/downloads/csin_conf_alberto_fonseca.pdf.

Friedman, M. (1970) 'The social responsibility of business is to increase its profits', *New York Times Magazine*, September 13. Also available at: www.umich.edu/~thecore/doc/Friedman.pdf.

Global Footprint Network (2010) *The Ecological Wealth of Nations*, available at: www.footprintnetwork. org/images/uploads/Ecological_Wealth_of_Nations.pdf.

Global Reporting Initiative (GRI) (2000) *Sustainability Reporting Guidelines on Economic, Environmental and Social Performance, Global Reporting Initiative*, Amsterdam: GRI.

Global Reporting Initiative (GRI) (2002) *Sustainability Reporting Guidelines*, Amsterdam: GRI.

Global Reporting Initiative (GRI) (2006) *G3 Sustainability Reporting Guidelines*, Amsterdam: GRI.

Global Reporting Initiative (GRI) (2011) Update on G4 developments at: www.globalreporting.org/CurrentPriorities/G4Developments/.

Gray, R. H. (1990) *The Greening of Accountancy: The Profession after Pearce*, London: Chartered Association of Certified Accountants.

Gray, R. (1992) 'Accounting and environmentalism: an exploration of the challenge of gently accounting for accountability, transparency and sustainability', *Accounting, Organizations and Society*, 17(5): 399–426.

Gray, R. (2000) 'Current developments and trends in social and environmental auditing, reporting and attestation: a review and comment', *International Journal of Auditing*, 4: 247–268.

Gray, R. (2006) 'Social, environmental, and sustainability reporting and organizational value creation? Whose value? Whose Creation?', *Accounting, Auditing & Accountability Journal*, 19(3): 319–348.

Gray, R. (2010) 'Is accounting for sustainability actually accounting for sustainability... and how would we know? An exploration of narratives of organizations and the planet', *Accounting, Organizations and Society*, 35(1): 47–62.

Gray, R. H. and Milne, M. J. (2002) 'Sustainability reporting: who's kidding whom?', *Chartered Accountants Journal of New Zealand*, July: 66–70.

Gray, R. and Milne, M. J. (2004) 'Towards reporting on the triple bottom line: mirages, methods and myths', in A Henriques and J. Richardson (eds), *The Triple Bottom Line: Does it All Add Up?* London: Earthscan.

Gray, R., Owen, D. and Maunders, K. (1987) *Corporate Social Reporting: Accounting and Accountability*, London: Prentice-Hall.

Gray, R., Owen, D. and Maunders, K. (1988) 'Corporate social reporting: emerging trends in accountability and the social contract', *Accounting, Auditing, & Accountability Journal*, 1(1): 6–20.

Gray, R., Dey, C., Owen, D., Evans, R. and Zadek, S. (1997) 'Struggling with the praxis of social accounting: stakeholders, accountability, audits and procedures', *Accounting, Auditing & Accountability Journal*, 10(3): 325–364.

Hardin, G. (1968) 'The tragedy of the commons', *Science*, 162 (3859): 1243–1248.

Hawken, P. (1993) *The Ecology of Commerce: a Declaration of Sustainability*, New York: HarperCollins.

Hawken, P. (2002) 'On corporate responsibility: a Ronald McDonald fantasy', *San Francisco Chronicle*, June 2, also available at Food First/Institute for Food and Development Policy, www.foodfirst.org/media/.

International Union for the Conservation of Nature (IUCN) (1980) *World Conservation Strategy*, Gland, Switzerland: IUCN.

Jensen, R. E. (1976) 'Phantasmagoric accounting: research and analysis of economic, social and environmental impact of corporate business', *Studies in Accounting Research # 14*, Sarasota, FL: American Accounting Association.

Kolk, A., Levy, D. and Pinkse, J. (2008) 'Corporate responses in an emerging climate regime: the institutionalization and commensuration of carbon disclosure', *European Accounting Review*, 17(4): 719–745.

KPMG (1993) *KPMG International survey of environmental reporting 1993*. Amsterdam: KPMG Environmental Consulting.

KPMG (1996) *KPMG International survey of environmental reporting 1996*. Amsterdam: KPMG Environmental Consulting.

KPMG (2005) *International survey of corporate social responsibility reporting 2005*, Amsterdam: KPMG International.

Livesey, S. (2002) 'The discourse of the middle ground: citizen Shell commits to sustainable development', *Management Communication Quarterly*, 15(3): 313–349.

Livesey, S. M. and Kearins, K. (2002) 'Transparent and caring corporations? A study of sustainability reports by The Body Shop and Royal Dutch/Shell', *Organization & Environment*, 15(3): 233–258.

Meadows D. H., Randers, J. and D. L. Meadows (2004) *The Limits to Growth: The 30-Year Update*, London: Earthscan.

Millennium Ecosystem Assessment (2005*) Living Beyond Our Means: Natural Assets and Human Well-Being: Statement from the board* (available at: www.millenniumassessment.org/en/Products.BoardStatement).

Milne, M. J. (1996) 'On sustainability, the environment and management accounting', *Management Accounting Research*, 7(1): 135–161.

Milne, M. J. (2007), 'Downsizing Reg (me and you)! Addressing the 'real' sustainability agenda at work and home', in R.H. Gray and J. Guthrie (eds), *Social Accounting, Mega Accounting and Beyond: Festschrift in Honour of Martin (Reg) Mathews*, St Andrews: CSEAR.

Milne, M. and Gray, R. (2007) 'Future prospects for sustainability reporting', in J. Unerman, B. O'Dwyer and J. Bebbington (eds), *Sustainability Accounting and Accountability* (pp. 184–207), London: Routledge.

Milne, M. J. and Grubnic, S. (2011) 'Climate change accounting research: keeping it interesting and different', *Accounting, Auditing & Accountability Journal*, 24(8): 948–977.

Milne, M. J., Ball, A. and Gray, R. H. (2008) 'W(h)ither ecology? The triple bottom line, the global reporting initiative and corporate sustainability reporting', *American Accounting Association Annual Meetings*, Anaheim, CA, August.

Milne, M. J., Kearins, K. and Walton, S. (2006) 'Creating adventures in wonderland? The journey metaphor and environmental sustainability', *Organization*, 13(6): 801–839.

Milne, M. J., Tregidga, H. and Walton, S. (2003) 'The triple bottom line: benchmarking New Zealand's early reporters', *University of Auckland Business Review*, 5(2): 36–50.

Milne M. J., Tregidga, H. M. and S. Walton (2009) 'Words not actions! The ideological role of sustainable development reporting', *Accounting Auditing & Accountability Journal*, 22(8): 1211–1257.

Mock, T. J., Strohm, C., Swartz, K. M. (2007) 'An examination of worldwide assured sustainability reporting', *Australian Accounting Review*, 17(1): 67–77.

Morhardt, J. (2009) 'General disregard for details of GRI human rights reporting by large corporations', *Global Business Review*, 10(2): 141–158.

Morhardt, J. (2010) 'Corporate social responsibility and sustainability reporting on the Internet', *Business, Strategy & the Environment*, 19(7): 436–452.

Morhardt, J., Baird, S. and Freeman, K. (2002) 'Scoring corporate environmental and sustainability reports using GRI2000, ISO14031 and other criteria', *Corporate Social Responsibility and Environmental Management*, 9: 215–233.

Norman, W. and MacDonald, C. (2004) 'Getting to the bottom of the 'Triple Bottom Line'?', *Business Ethics Quarterly*, 14(2): 243–262.

O'Dwyer, B. and Owen, D. (2005) 'Assurance statement practice in environmental, social and sustainability reporting: a critical evaluation', *British Accounting Review*, 37: 205–229.

Owen, D. L., Swift, T. A., Humphrey, C. and Bowerman, M. (2000) 'The new social audits: accountability, managerial capture or the agenda of social champions?', *European Accounting Review*, 9(1): 81–98.

Owen, D. L. (2003) 'Recent developments in European social and environmental reporting and auditing practice – a critical evaluation and tentative prognosis', No. 03-2003 ICCSR Research Paper Series, International Centre for Corporate Social Responsibility, Nottingham University Business School.

Pensions Investment Research Consultants (PIRC) (1999) *Issues and Trends in Corporate Social Reporting*, London: PIRC.

Reverte, C. (2009) 'Determinants of corporate social responsibility disclosure ratings by Spanish listed firms', *Journal of Business Ethics*, 88(2): 351–366.

Richardson, J. (2004) 'Accounting for sustainability: measuring quantities or enhancing qualities?', in A. Henriques and J. Richardson (eds), *The Triple Bottom Line: Does it All Add Up?* London: Earthscan.

Simnett, R., Nugent, M. and Huggins, A. L. (2009) 'Developing an international assurance standard on carbon emissions disclosures', *Accounting Horizons*, 23(4): 347–63.

Solid Energy (2010) Environmental Performance, www.coalnz.com/index.cfm/1,463,0,0,html (accessed October 2011).

SustainAbility (1999) *The Social Reporting Report*, London: UNEP/SustainAbility.

SustainAbility (2006) *Global Reporters Methodology*. www.sustainability.com/library/global-reporters-methodology.

Sutton, P. (1999) 'The sustainability-promoting firm', *Greener Management International*, 23: 127–152.

Tregidga H. M. and M. J. Milne (2006) 'From sustainable management to sustainable development: a longitudinal analysis of a leading New Zealand Environmental reporter', *Business Strategy and the Environment*, 15(4): 219–241.

Tregidga, H. M., Milne, M. J. and Kearins, K. N. (2008) '(Re) presenting sustainable organizations: a new discursive identity', *Academy of Management Annual Meetings*, Anaheim, CA, August.

UNEP/SustainAbility (1994) *Company Environmental Reporting: A Measure of the Progress Business & Industry Towards Sustainable Development*, London: UNEP/SustainAbility.

UNEP/SustainAbility (1996) *Engaging Stakeholders: The Benchmark Survey*, London: UNEP/SustainAbility.

UNEP/SustainAbility (1997) *The 1997 Benchmark Survey: The Third International Progress Report on Company Environmental Reporting*, London: UNEP/SustainAbility.

UNEP/SustainAbility (2000) *The Global Reporters: the 2000 Benchmark Survey*, London: UNEP/SustainAbility.

UNEP/SustainAbility (2002) *Trust Us: The Global Reporters 2002 Survey of Corporate Sustainability*, London: UNEP/SustainAbility.

UNEP/SustainAbility and Standard & Poor's (2004) *Risk & Opportunity: Best Practice in Non-Financial Reporting*, London: UNEP/SustainAbility.

UNEP/SustainAbility and Standard & Poor's (2006) *Tomorrow's Value: The Global Reporters 2006 Survey of Corporate Sustainability Reporting*, Nairobi: United Nations Environment Programme.

United Nations Environment Programme (UNEP) (2007) Global Environment Outlook #4 (GEO-4). Available at: www.unep.org/geo/geo4/media/GEO4%20SDM_launch.pdf (last accessed 16 August 2011).

Vormedal, I. (2009) 'Sustainability reporting in Norway – an assessment of performance in the context of legal demands and socio-political drivers', *Business, Strategy & the Environment*, 18(4): 207–222.

Wallage, P. (2000) 'Assurance on sustainability reporting: an auditor's view', *Auditing: A Journal of Practice and Theory*, 19: 53–65.

WBCSD/WRI (2004), *The Greenhouse Gas Protocol: A Corporate Accounting and Reporting Standard*, revised edition. Washington, DC: World Business Council for Sustainable Development; Geneva, Switzerland; World Resources Institute.

Wheeler, D. and Elkington, J. (2001) 'The end of the corporate environmental report? Or the advent of cybernetic sustainability reporting and communication?', *Business, Strategy and the Environment*, 10(1): 1–14.

White, M. A. and Wagner, B. (1996) 'Lessons from Germany: the 'ecobalance' as a tool for pollution prevention', *Social and Environmental Accountability Journal*, 16 (1): 3–6.

World Business Council for Sustainable Development (WBCSD) (2000) *Corporate Social Responsibility: Making Good Business Sense.* Available at: www.wbcsd.org/DocRoot/IunSPdIKvmYH5HjbN4XC/csr2000.pdf.

World Business Council for Sustainable Development (WBCSD) (2002) *Sustainability Reporting Guidelines.* Available at: www.wbcsd.org/web/projects/cement/tf6/GRI_guidelines_print.pdf.

World Commission on Environment and Development (WCED) (1987) *Our Common Future*, Oxford: Oxford University Press.

World Wide Fund International (WWF) (2010) *Living Planet Report 2010*, Gland, Switzerland: WWF International. http://wwf.panda.org/about_our_earth/all_publications/living_planet_report/2010_lpr/.

World Wide Fund International (WWF) (2010) *Living Planet Report 2010*, Gland, Switzerland: WWF International.

Worldwatch Institute (2003) *Vital Signs 2002–2003: The Trends are That Shaping Our Future*, London: Earthscan.

Zadek, S., Prusan, P. and R. Evans (1997) Building Corporate Accountability: Emerging Practice in Social and Ethical Accounting and Auditing, London: Earthscan.

10

Accounting communication inside organizations

Lisa Jack

Introduction

Accounting communication in the context of management accounting and control is nebulous in nature. Unlike those of financial reporting, artefacts in management accounting and control are non-public and ephemeral. Communications are verbal as well as written, *ad hoc* as well as bound to meetings on set days and times, and informal as well as formal. 'Good' communication by management accountants and controllers is a matter of perception: the sort of thing where people say that 'they know it when they see or hear it' but are less able to describe what it ought to be in any detail.

The art of communication in management accounting and control is driven by a need (or desire or maybe demand) to craft simple presentations of accounting information from a mass (or mess) of data from myriad sources. Therefore, a fundamental question in management accounting and control is whether computer systems make communications simpler or more complex? Computerized systems can allow for detailed analyses of very busy datasets but there is a danger that the more visually attractive information generated by modern information technology (IT) could lead to simplistic decision-making characterized by binary thinking.

Existing studies in management accounting explore aspects of communication, such as communication skills and the so-called expectations gap between accountants and managers; the rhetorical nature of devices such as the balanced scorecard; verbal exchanges between accountants/controllers and managers; the change processes in implementing large scale information technology (such as ERP); and the pernicious effects of performance measurement systems. Very few studies capture positively the essence of communication as practised by management accountants and controllers, and in particular, their relationship with computers. The underlying issue is that 'accounting research largely ignores and is indeed ignorant of accounting information systems (AIS) and IT in general' (Granlund, 2011).

There are many different facets of management accounting communication that are yet to be explored fully. One area for research could be communication practices, including the timing and formatting of reports, and the increasing use or otherwise of verbal communication. A pertinent question is the extent to which technology facilitates the communications management accountants would like to make and the extent to which technology makes these communications more or less effective. A second area of research could be the content and presentation of management information in a computerized environment, questioning the extent to which accountants design information for users that create more effective communications. In other words, how is accounting information represented best in a computerized environment, what is it that is being represented, and does simplification have implications for the way in which information is used for decision making? These two areas are presented here with the aim of indicating to early career researchers, in particular, the complexity of the environment in which management accounting operates and the underlying questions with which they might become usefully engaged. It is not an exhaustive review of the field but the following are covered: (1) accounting communication practices inside organizations – known problems, issues related to the conflict of providing internal and external information, verbal communications and technology; and (2) content and design.

Accounting communication practices inside organizations

The introduction of Business Intelligence (BI) software within the last decade is seen by management accountants in larger organizations as an opportunity to move away from a cycle of producing management information reports using spreadsheets (CIMA, 2009) and towards a more fluid role of designing, validating and reconciling information for management decision making purposes (ibid.). Granlund (2011: 5) observes that for management accountants now 'more than half of their working time may be devoted to system design and implementation, negotiations with software vendors, teaching other people to use new systems, and integration of the different systems into a working platform'.

BI is becoming a generic term for Online Analytical Processing (OLAP). These are analytic and search tools, including those that can search unstructured data, that provide greater levels of flexibility in the design of information. The underlying information systems in larger organizations are typically Enterprise Resource Planning (ERP) systems, or similar. However, information technology is moving away from structured computing systems based on distributed client-servers and towards those based on service oriented architectures (SOA). The adoption of BI is being driven by the requirement by senior managers for information relating to performance management. Whilst ERP systems produce operational reports and relieve management accountants from the toil of generating monthly budget variance reports, for example, they are less good at generating higher-level information (Scapens and Jazayeri, 2003).

There are two common patterns of communicating financial information for internal decision-making. A typical pattern (the one that BI is seen to be a replacement for) is that management accountants export transactional and costing data from a mainframe system into spreadsheets and create reports for managers that are essentially extracts or structured pages from a spreadsheet workbook. The documents presented to a board or to senior management are in the form of spreadsheets and Powerpoint presentations, supplemented by a verbal or written narrative. Colour is often used to highlight and to segregate information. Information remains under the control of the accounting office which disseminates it to nominated managers.

The second model is one in which the IT system is programmed to provide an onscreen dashboard of the key indicators, ratios, trends and figures relating to a manager's role. Applications embedded in the visual images enable managers to access underlying data or analytical information by clicking the onscreen image. The management accountant/controller – or more properly in this context, nominated business partner – then acts variously as interpreter, quality controller and system alerter rather than as a document provider. Ideally, managers are presented with near real-time onscreen information, subject to amendment, and managers can create their own outputs alongside or separately from accountants.

The metaphor 'dashboard' has rapidly become the accepted name for this particular medium of communication (Few, 2006). The metaphor has been unfortunate, in the view of Few (2006), as much of the poor design of dashboards derives from the image of driving. Many use dials, gauges and meters similar to those found in cars but these can rapidly become irritating and fall into disuse. He offers a more comprehensive definition of a dashboard that moves away from metaphor – a dashboard is 'a visual display of the most important information needed to achieve one or more objectives which fit entirely on a single computer screen so it can be monitored at a glance' (p. 34). Those that Few (2006) favours are in muted colours and present blocks of information in restrained but clear fashion. A problem here is that in general very little attention is given to visual design and representation of onscreen accounting information. Other problems in internal information production are those of management expectation; proliferation of reports; reconciliation with external information, and verbal communication. These matters are discussed next.

Problems in accounting communication inside organizations

A basic issue that emerges from management surveys is 'that most managers are not satisfied with the information made available to them for performance management or decision making' (Simons, 2011). Researchers identify a preparer–user perception or expectation gap concerning what constitutes useable internal reports (Pierce and O'Dea, 2003).

Expectation gap studies show consistently that management accountants attach a high priority to technical validity and see accounting systems primarily in terms of technical innovations, as opposed to administrative innovations (Shields, 1995). Pierce and O'Dea (2003) report that managers in turn give examples to show that although management accounting information may have technical validity it can lack user relevance or organizational validity. Other common complaints are that management accounting information lacks timeliness, is inflexible, uses an excessively narrow information set, and that there is a persistent use of 'an accountant's format' (i.e. tables of figures) rather than more user-friendly formats such as graphs and piecharts. However, these observations are hardly new. Pierce and O'Dea (2003) cite Schultz and Slevin (1975) to the same effect, that technical validity is not well aligned to user needs. This is even though Schultz and Slevin (1975) are observing the move from a 'book-keeping' to 'service-aid' role for management accountants and Pierce and O'Dea (2003) are seeking signs of moves from 'information provider' to 'business partner' facilitated by the emergence of BI (CIMA, 2009).

These problems are exacerbated in business environments that are complicated by global supply chains, emerging technologies, unpredictable consumer behaviour, and acquisitions and mergers. Responses to each of these, however well intentioned, 'have left us with companies that are increasingly ungovernable, unwieldy, and underperforming' (Ashkensas, 2007: 101). A pharmaceutical company executive voices an ever-present problem when he says:

> Sure, I know [my industry] is going through massive changes. So what? What troubles me is that nobody at [my company] has interconnected those changes with how we change. Our intranet content isn't linked to our quarterly projects, which aren't connected to our performance management system, which doesn't jive with compensation design, which doesn't match our departmental goals, which aren't supported by training, which ... you get the idea.
>
> *(Jensen, 1997: 36)*

In their 2010 annual report Royal Dutch Shell say that, following reorganization in 2009, they are seeking 'a simpler, leaner organizational structure with clearer accountabilities, enabling more customer focus and faster decision making'. Shell have not discussed their specific plans for IT and restructuring publicly but it has been reported that IT functions 'could be better planned and organised and this is about changing that. Shell wants simplicity and better decisions' (CIO Insider, King, 2009, June).

In another example, Ashkensas (2007) explains how in 2005, when a new CEO was appointed at ConAgra, they were a US$14bn company with more than 100 brands, a food service company and a commodity trading operation that, as a result of their successful growth strategy, had no common method for tracking, reporting or analysing results. Customers complained that there was no simple way of contacting the company. There were reports of poor communications, unpleasant competition between business units, duplication of activities and fragmentation of systems. Ashkensas (2007) identifies the causes as structural mitosis, product proliferation, process evolution, and managerial bad habits – such as demanding ad hoc reports at random times. ConAgra adopted a strategy of simplification and overcame many of the issues of poor communication processes.

Within a traditional monthly reporting cycle proliferation of reports is commonplace. Whilst the original information system may have been streamlined and designed to provide logical sets of information at particular times, managers' dissatisfaction with the information (Shields, 1997; Pierce and O'Dea, 2003) led to requests for customized reports. Over time, these special requests for reports became embedded in the system (Ashkensas, 2007; CIMA, 2009) and the ad hoc reports get added to the list of information to be produced on a monthly basis. In addition, managers prepare their own spreadsheets and duplicate effort throughout the organization.

Furthermore, spreadsheets can contain often petty but crucial errors. People forget to protect cells, mis-type formulae and add rows and columns which do not automatically get included in casts and cross-casts. The proliferation of reports reflects the complexity of modern organizations: multi-site, multi-divisional and producing diverse ranges of products and services. Information for decision making can be conflicting, error-ridden and non-transparent. In IS terms, a significant amount of noise in management information feedback and control systems distorts messages.

The answer to problems of incoherent organizational practices is often seen as a strategy of simplicity based around communications. Following writers such as Tofler (1991) and Wheatley (1996), whose searches for a simpler approach to life are popular reading, Jensen (1997: 38) states that 'the way complex systems create order is by focusing on information exchanges – not artificial controls or management structures'. What accounting communications research lacks is empirical studies that examine deeply the role of accounting in achieving or not achieving coherence within organizations.

The relationship between internal and external reporting[1]

Accountants and former accountants point to one issue of timeliness that is untouched in the research literature. This is the practice of 'reconciling to GAAP' before the periodic management reports are released. The reconciliation exists because of disparities between financial accounting and management accounting reporting systems. If the exercise is not carried out there is a significant risk that the internal non-GAAP figures used to manage the business during the year will bear no resemblance to the GAAP numbers produced at year-end. Most management teams prefer their own measures of performance. These are usually better for this purpose than the fixed measures contained with financial reporting standards. However, it is these fixed GAAP measures that many boards need to present to shareholders at the year-end, thus reconciliation is essential albeit often only at a divisional or corporate level. International Financial Reporting Standards have a requirement that internal measures used are disclosed through segmental reports. In effect, these reports in effect show how the measures used internally to manage the business differ from and are reconciled to IFRS. IFRS 8 requires that the companies report the metrics used by the chief decision maker when managing the business at segmental and corporate levels and then reconcile these metrics to the IFRS numbers in the Income Statement.

However, the process of reconciling to GAAP is time consuming. It is one of the main reasons for complaints from managers about the lack of timeliness of reports – in some cases, the next month may be about to start before the previous months figures are available. Most companies prefer to reconcile on a monthly basis to relieve undue workload at the year end and to highlight problems earlier. To avoid delays, a number of large organizations use flash reports, which are essentially the unreconciled figures and measures issued at month end to provide, with caveats, results for managers to work on. Even with the use of flash reporting as a stopgap, issues can still arise (Quattrone and Hopper, 2006), in particular the proliferation of reports as discussed above. The effect of amendments made as a result of reconciliation to GAAP on real-time, onscreen information has not been investigated. Another issue is the use of XBRL (see Chapter 13) for financial reporting and the impact this has on internal reporting and the need for reconciliation.

One solution that many commentators would like to see is greater alignment between internal and external reports irrespective of whether they contain GAAP or non-GAAP metrics. CIMA believes that external narrative reports should represent the 'top slice' of information regularly given to boards for internal decision-making purposes. As such, the two are inextricably linked (or at least should be) in well-managed organizations. CIMA, for example, in a report compiled with PwC and the Centre for Tomorrow's Company, demonstrate a lack of coherence in corporate reporting contributes to the problems of generating meaningful internal information. Complexity arises from standards and regulations as well as business environment and lack of knowledge and skills within organizations of how best to design information (Tomorrow's Company, 2011). Reporting on economic, environmental and social performance in a truly integrated way could have profound implications for the way in which internal management accounting systems deal with non-financial data and analysis.

Verbal communication

Management accountants have always had to engage in verbal communication but changes in IT that may decrease the need for formal printed reports increase the need for verbal and more informal communications. Nonetheless, Grabski et al. (2008: 5) found that although ERP systems result in a significant centralization of data and formalization of communication structures, 'existing organisational structure and culture seems to have a greater impact on the communication structure than does the ERP system' (see also Quattrone and Hopper, 2006). Innovation in accounting information systems also requires careful and thoughtful communication by business partners (Baldvinsdottir et al., 2010). Unless management accountants and controllers communicate well and participate in IS change projects from the start, systems-based innovations to improve communication structures are likely to fail.

Baldvinsdottir et al. (2010: 5) find that 'The language test needs to be passed. It needs simple language – which 400,000 workers can connect to – more than brilliant ideas.' An example is the use of a simple cardboard breakeven analysis chart – learned in an 'accounting for non-accountants' evening class – on the shop floor of a power station. By making the fixed cost, sales and total cost lines moveable, the manager explained how by reducing costs through the measures proposed, profits would increase. The manager reported that the ideas were accepted at once, whereas more complex presentations had failed.

The ability to communicate well appears in most job descriptions for accountants. Nevertheless, Pierce and O'Dea (2003) find that managers claim to turn to IT professionals to provide information because they are perceived to have better communication and interpersonal skills than management accountants. Similar comments are made by Granlund (2011) and CIMA (2009). Good communicators do exist though. Järvenpää (2007: 125) found that accountants and IT professionals had 'made several successful attempts to streamline information handling by applying very novel information systems' but they were forever chasing a very elusive goal of perfect communication 'that was continuously escaping them, somewhere beyond the development work horizon'.

There are very few studies like Järvenpää's (2007) that capture the verbal communications (and visual aids) of management accountants and controllers.

This is unsurprising, given that it is not easy to negotiate access for longitudinal ethnographic or anthropological studies in organisations. However, Jönsson (2009: 235) argued that researchers should aim to capture 'rich (face-to-face) communications' and says (ibid.: 237)

> We want to catch data on how competent managers (including the controller) go about doing their job. Managers work with words and words are used in meetings where problems are solved and decisions made. Words bind subordinates and managers alike to tasks and commitments. Communication has organizing effects.
>
> *(Cooren, 2000)*

In small owner-managed businesses, where management accounting advice is often obtained as a value-enhancing addition to financial statements for taxation and other reporting purposes, Stone (2011: 800) finds that despite 'interviewed practitioners' attempts to increase the appeal and utility of the documents that they produce, owner managers prefer verbal communication'. They received 'instantaneous feedback to validate understanding and correct their misconceptions in a timely manner' and reinforced their perception of empathy from their accountant. A preference for 'rich verbal communication' is also found in studies of relations in larger organizations between accountants and their internal clients (Järvenpää, 2007; Jönssen, 2009).

Faÿ et al. (2010), suggest that BI is problematic unless face-to-face communication also occurs. Other studies also find that business partners sharing offices with the managers they work with are perceived to produce more useful information (Byrne and Pierce, 2007). The job of management can become managing the information presented on the screen, sitting at a desk 'drilling down' through data and analytical information and sending emails in search of explanations. Puyou (forthcoming 2013) examines a sales promotion video for an ERP system extolling the working world where members of an organization communicate but never meet, an example of 'abstract management' directed at control of things rather than building knowledge (Townley, 2002). Certain personalities find this an attractive way to work (Faÿ et al., 2010; Puyou, forthcoming 2013):

> Many users are attracted by the security offered by the software to drive a budget, an activity or a project and prefer 'clicking' on resources that are neatly defined and easily at hand rather than confront interlocutors face to face and tackle messy situations.
>
> *(Puyou, forthcoming 2013)*

But as with Byrne and Pierce (2007), Puyou (forthcoming 2013) and Faÿ et al. (2010) also find that those controllers who also go out and meet managers in person produce information that is perceived as more realistic and more useful. Those who act as interlocutors (controllers who meet managers and vice versa) 'are genuinely concerned with maintaining the links between figures from SAP and actual practices … The representations sensitize them, for example, to the financial issues and expectations' (Puyou, forthcoming 2013).

Does technology facilitate more effective communication?

Management accountants and controllers should be understood therefore as working in complex and messy environments in which information technology has the potential to simplify and streamline the continual demands for information made by management. In the three issues examined briefly above – proliferation, integration of external and internal information and verbal interactions – there is some sense that accountants and controllers are communicating accounting in a continually shifting technological environment.

Yet Granlund (2011) suggests that technological change does not always change underlying behaviours in communication – only its means and presentation. In the nineteenth century, personal letters were circulated among friends in much the same way as emails are now. The cost of telegrams meant that abbreviated words were used as they are in today's electronic messages. Whether BI will generate genuine changes in how accounting information is communicated is an open question. BI is only a 'technology enabler' (CIMA, 2009: 42). Management need to implement BI in such a way that decisions are made effectively and so that the potential for meaningful communications is exploited. Moving towards using BI as normal practice is not universal. Many management accountants are 'still too occupied in the reporting cycle of producing more traditional management information to progress to these new roles' (ibid.)

Outside work the same employees become habituated to social networking and personalized web interfaces for shopping (Tam and Ho, 2006). So, one danger is that personalized spreadsheets become replaced by personalization of screens. Furthermore, Faÿ et al. (2010) find that the work habits of managers change, rather than the fundamentals of the information provided. They find managers and accountants work actively to manage the data that appears on screens, making arbitrary changes to forecasts and other data. Many controllers feel that they are simply feeding the machine for a daily reporting cycle, at the demand of senior management. The monthly/yearly cycles of traditional reporting are simply speeded up. Rather than being simplified, there is a real potential for complexity to re-emerge as managers and accountants reproduce the performance indicators and figures they are familiar with but as real time, on screen icons, graphs and lists.

The content and design of information for decision making

There is a balance to be struck in management-accounting communications between visual appeal, clarity and timeliness. Whilst words, graphs, icons and other images can be combined to make powerful and sophisticated communications sometimes, as one financial director says, 'good enough may be good enough' (CIMA, 2009: 13). There is also an underlying appreciation that there is beauty in simplicity (Karvonen, 2000) but also danger in simplification. It seems always that in the end our 'complex knowledge society is suddenly a handful of numerical representations and a narrative' (Mouritsen, 2011: 233).

Chambers (1999) sees accounting as necessarily made up of such acts of simplification. Analysing paper documentation used in management processes, Lowe and Koh (2007: 956) comment that:

> abbreviation simplifies the complex, provides the instantaneous picture and makes the big into the small. The 'real thing' is reduced or 'condensed' into the model or representation: as much

as is needed is condensed into as little as is needed so as to enable ease of perception and 'appropriate' action.

This is partly a question of aesthetics as much as persuasiveness or marginalization (as Lowe and Koh interpret their case). This again is an under-researched area. Karvonen (2000: 1) states that 'there are only few studies reporting on the influence of aesthetic judgement on the evaluation of a user interface'. She refers not only to meaningful visual aspects (such as graphs) but to 'technical aesthetics' relating to usability and 'trustworthy design'.

On a similar theme, Acton et al. (2008: 10), from an accounting information systems perspective, identify that there is still 'a need for research into the relative advantages and appropriateness of graphical versus tabulated presentation for decision-making' and a 'dearth of research examining the kinds of decision support tools that map to presentation formats'. They point out that it is not just content and form that influence representation of accounting data as 'data that is inherently graphical (such as drawings, icons and other symbols) have implicit spatial relationships with other objects that may pose limitations on their representation'. This may be affected by matters such as screen size, even given 'non-distortion oriented techniques' (ibid.: 3). Few (2006) makes similar points in his work on the design of dashboards.

Mouritsen (2011: 228) argues for a 'constructive account of representation where it is understood not as correspondence but as likeness which only operates because it is linked with the social world in which it is invented'. In other words, we could see management accounting in terms of producing a likeness of the situation about which a decision needs to be made. The representations (whether on paper or on screen) may not be necessarily absolute in terms of truth (whatever might be conceived as truth) nor complete in every detail. Yet they are likely to be perceived as performative to some degree by those designing and those using the information.

In what sense though, is information provided by management accountants for decision-making 'performative'? Management-accounting communications are geared toward the diagnostic/problem solving mode of management. Horngren (1995: 281) comments that 'the search for cost accounting systems that better link causes and effects is unending. Cost–benefit trade-offs between desires for simplicity and elaborate systems are dominant considerations.' Yet the accountant/controller is 'presenting the unpresentable' (Acton et al., 2008) and so a design mentality that is concerned with 'finding the best answer possible, given the skills, time and resources of the team, and takes for granted that it will require the invention of new alternatives' (Boland and Collopy, 2004: 6) would seem desirable. It would avoid the position that they see inherent in a decision-making mode of management, in which there is 'the unrealistic position of assuming that good design work has already taken place, even though it is not usually the case. It is, therefore, doomed to mediocrity in its organizational outcomes' (ibid.)

A fundamental problem is that humans are drawn towards binary thinking (Wood and Petriglieri, 2005). As a cognitive process, our instincts for efficient decision making appear to be to reduce any decision to a binary process: Yes or no? Go or stay? Buy or sell? A recent trend in psychological research examines cognitive fluency. The popular explanation of the theory is that 'Easy = true': 'Cognitive fluency is simply a measure of how easy it is to think about something, and it turns out that people prefer things that are easy to think about to those that are hard' (Bennett, 2010). Prevailing cognitive paradigms of reductive reasoning and, in particular, the fact that education often pre-conditions us to look for cause and effect are found to be barriers 'to visual literacy and the ability to deal effectively with complicated management issues' (Perino, 2001: 27).

Other researchers have recorded managerial preferences for analogies and heuristics. They provide empirical data to demonstrate that decision-making is rarely rational nor exhibits the bounded rationality put forward by Simons (for example Chambers, 1999; Gavetti et al., 2005). Decision-support systems (DSS) contain architectures that facilitate reductive thinking (Courtney, 2001), including Analytical Hierarchy Processes (AHP) which rationalize decisions into a small number of choices from structured data (Bertoloni et al., 2006).

What is unclear from accounting research is the extent to which tendencies towards reductive thinking influence communication, or, conversely, the extent to which accounting communications successfully steer decision-makers towards more complex, abstract reasoning based on fully contextual information. The problems lie even deeper however, and involve reliance by organizations on computers. The relationship between accounting and information systems 'appears to be the most complex, penetrating and unpredictable in the field' of information systems (in Granlund, 2011: 1). Why is this, when intuitively it seems that information systems have developed with the purpose of facilitating accounting practices? Subsumed by relationships between managers, accounting and information systems lies another problematic relationship – the relationship between society and computers.

Documentary film-maker Adam Curtis, interviewed by a reporter from the *Guardian* newspaper in the UK, explained his theory behind his 2011 release:

> *All Watched Over by Machines of Loving Grace* is about how we have been colonised by the machines we have built. Although we don't realise it, the way we see everything in the world today is through the eyes of computers. My underlying argument is that we have given up a dynamic political model of the world, the dream of changing things for the better for a static machine ideology that says we are all components in systems.
>
> *(Pettie, 2011)*

Accountants and controllers are drawn into this thinking as much as anyone: understanding the impact of our reliance on computers in communications will help us unravel the implications for the profession and society. Inside organizations, where people, accounting and computers are enmeshed, would be a good place to begin these investigations. It would take management accounting communications research beyond the problems of process and presentation into areas of more critical cognitive and cultural change.

Further research

Accounting is not a neat and tidy subject. One of the few novelists to capture the essential nature of accounting was Charles Dickens. In *Little Dorrit*, he observed Mr Rugg (General Agent, Accountant, Debts Recovered) at work, saying:

> Mr Rugg's enjoyment of embarrassed affairs was like a housekeeper's enjoyment in pickling and preserving, or a washerwoman's enjoyment of a heavy wash, or a dustman's enjoyment of an overflowing dust-bin, or *any other professional enjoyment of a mess in the way of business.*
>
> *(p. 516; my emphasis)*

Mr Rugg even finds himself trying fruitlessly to persuade his client to hold out for a better class of debtors' prison (anything else would be a slight on his professionalism) – an interesting example of the client–accountant debate and typical of the frustrations accountants have in communicating the optimal course of action only to have it overturned for other considerations.

What would it take to establish accounting communication for management accounting and control as a rigorous sub-discipline? My opinion is that it has to be inter-disciplinary research – in the sense of individuals from different disciplines working together rather than individual polymaths. Information systems, accounting, management behaviour, operational research, psychology and communications theory are the obvious disciplines to call on (but maybe not all at once). There are, of course, many systemic obstacles to interdisciplinary work, in terms of getting funding, publications and promotion. However, it is difficult to see how researchers can carry out scholarship that aims to engage a community of practitioners who are themselves forced to be interdisciplinary as business partners, without themselves working in interdisciplinary environments. At the very least, researchers should be conversant in accounting information systems, and be curious about the craft of accounting and how accountants communicate (Hopwood, 2007).

There is significant expertise within organizations about how and why particular modes of communication are used and what makes them successful. If companies are prepared to share artefacts and conversations (that are by their nature rarely complete or polished), as well as expertise, then communications research in management accounting could be carried out fruit-fully in joint projects between practitioners and researchers. Projects could involve a balance of methodology from various disciplines: accounting researchers' knowledge about the use, abuse and misuse of financial information, and the expertise of those in the field who know how, or who are learning, to create order out of mess – and enjoy the challenge.

Note

1   I would like to thank Nick Topazio of the Institute of Chartered Management Accountants (CIMA) for his contributions to this section. Further information about CIMA's position on this topic can be found in Tomorrow's Company (2011).

References

Acton, T., Golden, W. and van der Heijden, H. (2008) 'Presenting the un-presentable: how to display data for decision making', in Proceedings of the 1st Irish Social Science Platform Conference, Dublin City University, Dublin, September.

Ashkensas, R. (2007) 'Simplicity-minded management: a practical guide to stripping complexity out of your organization', Harvard Business Review, December: 101–109.

Baldvinsdottir, G., Burns, J., Nørreklit, H. and Scapens, R. (2010) 'Risk manager or risqué manager? The new platform for the management accountant', Research Executive Summary Series, 6(2), London: CIMA.

Bennett, D. (2010) 'Easy = true: how "cognitive fluency" shapes what we believe, how we invest, and who will become a supermodel', Boston Globe, 31 January.

Bertolini, M., Braglia, M. and Carmignani, G. (2006) 'Application of the AHP methodology in making a proposal for a public work contract', International Journal of Project Management, 24: 422–430.

Boland, R.J. and Collopy, F. (2004) Managing as Designing, Palo Alto, CA: Stanford University Press.

Bourguignon, A. (2005) 'Management accounting and value creation: the profit and loss of reification', Critical Perspectives on Accounting, 16: 353–389.

Byrne, S. and Pierce, B. (2007) 'Towards a more comprehensive understanding of the roles of management accountants', European Accounting Review, 16: 469–498.

Chambers, R.J. (1999) 'The case for simplicity in accounting', Abacus, 35: 121–137.

CIMA (2009) Improving Decision-making in Organisations: Unlocking Business Intelligence, London: CIMA.

Cooren, F. (2000) The Organizing Property of Communication. Amsterdam/Philadelphia: John Benjamins.

Courtney, J.F. (2001) 'Decision making and knowledge management in inquiring organizations: toward a new decision-making paradigm for DSS', *Decision Support Systems*, 31(1): 17–38.

Dickens, C. (1987, first published 1857) *Little Dorrit*, London: Penguin Books.

Faÿ, E., Introna, L. and Puyou, F.-R. (2010) 'Living with numbers: accounting for subjectivity in/with management accounting systems', *Information and Organization*, 20: 21–43.

Few, S. (2006) *Information Dashboard Design: the Effective Visual Communication of Data*, Sebastopol, CA: O'Reilly Media.

Gavetti, G., Levinthal, D.A. and Rivkin, J.W. (2005) 'Strategy making in novel and complex worlds: the power of analogy', *Strategic Management Journal*, 26(8): 691–712.

Grabski, S., Leech, S. and Sangster, A. (2008) 'Management accountants: a profession dramatically changed by ERP systems', *Research Executive Summary Series*, 4(5), London: CIMA.

Granlund, M. (2011) 'Extending AIS research to management accounting and control issues: a research note', *International Journal of Accounting Information Systems*, 12: 3–19.

Hopwood, A.G. (2007) 'Whither accounting research?', *Accounting Review*, 82: 1365–1374.

Horngren, C. (1995) 'Management accounting: this century and beyond', *Management Accounting Research*, 6: 281–286.

Jäärvenpää, M. (2007) 'Making business partners: a case study on how management accounting culture was changed', *European Accounting Review*, 16: 99–142.

Jensen, B. (1997) 'Make it simple: how simplicity could become your ultimate strategy', *Strategy and Leadership*, March/April: 35–39.

Jönssen, S. (2009) 'The study of controller agency' in C.S. Chapman, D.J. Cooper and P.B. Miller (eds) *Accounting, organizations and institutions: essays in honour of Anthony Hopwood*, pp. 233–258, Oxford: Oxford University Press.

Karvonen, K. (2000) 'The beauty of simplicity', ACM CUU, available at URL: http://dl.acm.org/citation.cfm?id=355478 (last accessed 15 April 2012).

Kelly, K.T. (2006) 'A new solution to the puzzle of simplicity', *Philosophy of Science*, 74: 561–573.

King, L. (2009) 'Shell reorganizes management and IT functions', CIO Insider, June, available at: http://cio.com/article/493872/Shell_Reorganizes_Management_and_IT_Functions (last accessed March 9, 2013).

Lowe, A. and Koh, B. (2007) 'Inscribing the organization: representations in dispute between accounting and production', *Critical Perspectives on Accounting*, 18: 952–974.

Manochin, M., Brignall, S., Lowe, A. and Howell, C. (2011) 'Visual modes of governmentality: traffic lights in a housing association', *Management Accounting Research*, 22: 26–35.

Manochin, M., Jack, L. and Howell, C. (2008) 'The boundaries of reporting sustainable development in social housing', *Public Money and Management*, 28: 345–352.

Mouritsen, J. (2011) 'The operation of representation in accounting: a small addition to Dr. Macintosh's theory of accounting truths', *Critical Perspectives on Accounting*, 22: 228–235.

Perino, G.H. (2001) 'Reductive reasoning: a cognitive barrier to visual literacy', *Journal of Visual Literacy*, 21: 15–30.

Pettie, A. (2011) 'Adam Curtis: the perils of binary thinking', *Guardian*, 20 May.

Pierce, B. and O'Dea, T. (2003) 'Management accounting information and the needs of managers: perception of managers and accountants compared', *British Accounting Review*, 35: 257–290.

Puyou, F.-R. (forthcoming 2013) 'Learning from screens: does ideology prevail over lived experience? The example of ERP Systems', in P. Meusburger, A. Berthoin-Antal and L. Suarsana (eds) *Learning Organisations: the Importance of Place for Organisational Learning*, Series Knowledge and Space, Vol. 6, Dordrecht: Springer Verlag.

Quattrone, P. and Hopper, T. (2006) 'What is IT? SAP, accounting and visibility in a multi-national organisation', *Information and Organisations*, 16: 212–230.

Scapens, R.W and Jazayeri, M. (2003) 'ERPS and management accounting change: opportunities or impact', *European Accounting Review*, 12: 201–233.

Schultz, R.L. and Slevin, D.P. (1975) 'Implementation and management innovation', *Implementing Operations Research/Management Science*, New York: Elsevier.

Shields, M.D. (1995) 'An empirical analysis of firms' implementation experiences with activity-based costing', *Journal of Management Accounting Research*, 7: 148–166.

Simons, P. (2011) 'Surviving and thriving with business intelligence', *CIMA Insight*, March, online: www.cimaglobal.com/en-gb/Thought-leadership/Newsletters/Insight-e-magazine/Insight-2011/Insight-March-2011/Surviving-and-thriving-with-business-intelligence/.

Stone, G. (2011) 'Let's talk: adapting accountants' communications to small business managers' objectives and preferences, *Accounting, Auditing & Accountability Journal*, 24: 781–809.

Tam, K.Y. and Ho, S.Y. (2006) 'Understanding the impact of web personalization on User Information Processing and Decision Outcomes', *MIS Quarterly*, 30: 865–890.

Tofler, A. (1991) *Powershift: knowledge, wealth and violence at the edge of the 21st century*, New York: Bantam.

Tomic, D. (2006) 'Business Intelligence in managerial accounting', *SEEE Journal*, September: 80–89.

Tomorrow's Company (2011) *Tomorrow's Corporate Reporting: a Critical System at Risk*, London: Centre for Tomorrow's Company.

Townley, B. (2002) 'Managing with modernity', *Organization*, 9: 549–573.

Tsai, C.I. and Thomas, M. (2011) 'When does feeling of fluency matter? How abstract and concrete thinking influence fluency effects', *Psychological Science*, 22: 348–354.

Unkelbach, C. (2006) 'The learned interpretation of cognitive fluency', *Psychological Science*, 17: 339–345.

Wheatley, M.J. (1996) *A Simple Way*, San Francisco: Berrett-Koehler Inc.

Wood, J.D. and Petriglieri, G. (2005) 'Transcending polarization: beyond binary thinking', *Transactional Analysis Journal*, 35: 31–39.

Communication apprehension and accounting education

Trevor Hassall, José L. Arquero, John Joyce and José M. González

Introduction

Communication apprehension (CA) is the fear or anxiety associated with communicating. It has been shown to be a potential problem for the accounting profession. Many accounting students exhibit high levels of CA. Consequently the accountants of the future may be deficient in a key skill, communicating, that has been identified as necessary for them to be successful in their chosen careers. This has major implications for students and the accounting profession.

The changing business environment has created problems for the accounting profession. The stereotypical view of the accountant is disappearing and the emerging derived demand is for the accountant to be a business advisor and an important member of the management team. Accountants now play vital roles in strategy formulation and decision making. They no longer work in 'splendid isolation' and consequently there is a need for accountants to possess good communication skills.

Accounting has undergone a process of change. Two of the major developments in the business environment that have driven this change were identified by Albrecht and Sack (2000) as technology and globalization. These developments have resulted in accountants meeting a constantly changing complex and demanding environment (Parker, 2001) and consequently this has brought about changes in the way accountants carry out their work (Walker, 2004). In order to meet these new challenges there is substantial evidence that the development of communication skills will be vital. IFAC (2002) expressed the opinion that finance managers of the future will need to possess strong communication skills, the ability to interpret complex financial data and a broad knowledge of global economic markets and cultural issues.

The call for accountants to possess good communication skills is not new. There is a chronicled history of concern: employers and professional bodies have continually expressed their concerns that the accounting education process is not producing accountants with the skills, including communication skills, which the changing workplace demands. Despite the early and clear recognition of the need for skills development and efforts to rectify the deficit, the concerns are still prevalent today. There is not a simple remedy. Research has indicated that a barrier to the development of communication skills is 'communication apprehension' and that the apprehension is on a personal level.

Communication apprehension

Anxiety can in many instances prevent successful performance and over time form a barrier to future performance and development. Important insights into accounting education are given by Stanga and Ladd (1990) and Ruchala and Hill (1994), who note that, despite the importance of communication skills, relatively little is known about the obstacles that accounting students face when attempting to develop their communication abilities. The early research on barriers that constrained the effectiveness of attempts to develop communication skills focused on 'stage fright' (as typically experienced in a public-speaking context). At that time there was a growing view that an understanding of the emotions experienced when feeling fright was fundamental to overcoming the reluctance to communicate. The research was widening to include a range of contexts in which individuals exhibited a predisposition to avoid communication. A major breakthrough occurred when a connection was made to the concept of CA. McCroskey (1984: 78) defines CA as 'an individual's level of fear and anxiety associated with either real or anticipated communication with another person'. This suggests that individuals who are apprehensive about participating in communicative situations are less able to communicate effectively. The causes and the consequences of CA are emotional, educational and social. Shyness and reticence affect the social skills necessary for children to make friends. Shy students tend to confine their career aspirations to vocations that require little oral communication. They seem to have a higher need to avoid failure, and they have less achievement or success motivation than other students (McCroskey and Anderson, 1976).

Research has focused on the consequence for the individual and organizations of this communication phenomenon. McCroskey et al. (1976) and McCroskey and Richmond (1976) identified that the failure to communicate by an apprehensive individual has a major effect on the perceptions about that individual held by others. This effect has several implications for the apprehensive communicator in individual and group situations. The level of an individual's CA may shape the overall nature of their interpersonal relationships. McCroskey et al. (1976) indicated that individuals with high levels of CA tend to be less interpersonally attractive and attracted to others. This may lead to individuals being less likely to be welcomed as a member of a task-orientated group. The volume and quality of contribution is important in terms of membership acceptance (Borgatta and Bales, 1956; Riecken, 1958). Sorenson and McCroskey (1977) found that CA was a significant indicator of small group interaction.

As indicated above there is evidence to suggest that the effect that CA has on interpersonal relationships may influence education, recruitment and professional development. In the traditional educational system based on a lecture/seminar approach, CA may not create a significant problem. However, where voluntary student participation, such as group work, is required McCroskey and Anderson (1976) reported that CA is a factor that influences the attitude of individuals. McCroskey et al. (1976), using a wide range of personality and intelligence measures, found no evidence of a relationship between intelligence and CA. However, they reported that high levels of CA may lead to avoidance behaviours such as sitting at the back of classrooms, choosing modules that do not require participation/interaction and not seeking tutor assistance. These behaviours will restrict the relationship between student and tutor, hinder the recognition of the student's progress and needs, and may impair educational performance (McCroskey, 1976, 1977; Fordham and Gabbin, 1996).

Perhaps the significance of CA, in broader terms, is indicated by Harris (1980), who indicated that at least 11 per cent of elementary students in the USA had recorded high levels of CA, and that a further 20 per cent were exhibiting levels that were high enough to warrant some sort of intervention.

The effect of CA on communication development

A split between CA and communication development has been indicated. There are clear conceptual differences between the two: individuals may overcome their CA and then go on to develop their communication skills but for others CA may form a barrier that stops the development of their communication skills. Spitzberg and Cupach (1984) and Allen and Bourhis (1996) reported that techniques aimed at the development of communication skills will not resolve CA and that if an individual has a high level of CA the techniques may be ineffective and improved communication performance will not occur. Boorom et al. (1998) argue that a low level of CA is considered to be a necessary, but not sufficient condition, for achieving communication competence.

The extensive research undertaken by communication scholars (see Payne and Richmond, 1984) led to the broad concept being accepted within the discipline area. The initial research on CA focused on the consequences of this phenomenon for individuals and their employers. Research revealed that there were likely to be adverse perceptions of an uncommunicative person in individual and group situations and this could influence their interpersonal relationships (McCroskey and Richmond, 1976; McCroskey et al., 1976; Sorenson and McCroskey, 1977). Allen and Bourhis (1996) found a consistently negative relationship between the level of CA and communication skills. Individuals who register higher levels of CA tend to avoid encounters, display poor cognitive processing during interaction, are perceived to be less confident and are characterized as inattentive and unable to recall important information. In the context of education, McCroskey and Anderson (1976) suggest that CA will not have a major effect in terms of participation in lectures but may be a factor where voluntary student participation, such as group work, is required.

Communication apprehension and accounting students

Early studies indicated that CA (as a barrier to communication skills development) was a potential concern for the accounting profession. The first study by Stanga and Ladd (1990) concluded that accounting majors in the USA appear to have above average levels of oral CA. Research by Simons et al. (1995), also on accounting students in the USA, confirmed this finding for oral CA, and that they also had above average levels of written CA. A study by Fordham and Gabbin (1996) emphasized the need for accounting educators to pay special attention to CA separate from, and in addition to, communication skills. These studies were initially criticized for being focused on American accounting students. However subsequent studies in the UK and Spain (Hassall et al., 2000, Arquero et al., 2007), Ireland (Byrne et al., 2009), New Zealand (Gardner et al., 2005) and Canada (Aly and Islam, 2003) were consistent with the USA studies: they all reported higher than average levels of oral CA in accounting students.

It is disappointing to report that accounting courses appear to have only a minimal impact on reducing the levels of CA. Studies by Hassall et al. (2000), Aly and Islam (2003) and Gardner et al. (2005) identified that there was little or no change in the levels of CA as students progressed through accounting courses.

Measurement of communication apprehension

Reliable measures of CA have been developed for both oral and written contexts. Extensive research studies have reported scores for these measures for many vocations and in many countries. These were measured using the Personal Report of Communication Apprehension

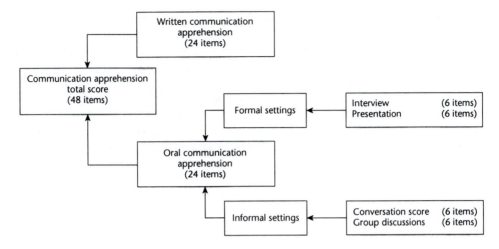

Figure 11.1 Types of communication apprehension

(PRCA-24) developed by McCroskey (1984) to measure oral communication apprehension (OCA) and the written communication apprehension (WCA) instrument was developed by Daly and Miller (1975).

The questionnaires are composed of statements about communicating with others. The respondents must indicate the degree to which each statement is applicable to them on a five-point Likert scale that ranges from strong agreement to strong disagreement. The instrument allows two main measures to be calculated: one for WCA and one for OCA. As shown in Figure 11.1, the OCA score consists of four basic constructs, each having six items on the questionnaire. This enables a deeper analysis to be carried out. For example two individuals may record equal total scores but have differing sub-scores. It is the specific subset of scores that defines the profile of the individual. Two of the constructs are about formal settings (interviews and presentations) and the other two are for informal settings (group discussions and conversations). In order to avoid any confusion or misunderstanding of these contexts a definition of each relevant term was stated on the questionnaire.

A population mean score published from the results of 25,000 respondents in McCroskey (1984) was 65.60 with a standard deviation of 15.3. McCroskey believes that a CA score beyond one standard deviation above or below the mean score of the population can be identified as high or low in oral CA. The overall means for the studies on accountancy students regardless of level and country mostly lie between 63.0 and 70.0. Similar levels of CA have been noted between accounting and other professions such as engineering (Hassall et al., 2005).

Causes and consequences of communication apprehension

Individual or situational

When McCroskey (1984) first advanced the construct of CA in relation to all individuals he did not explore whether it is a trait of an individual or if it is a response to the situational elements of a specific communication transaction (a state). Richmond and McCroskey (1989) developed the categorization of CA as being 'trait' or 'state'. They explained this in terms of an individual's general unease in communication situations being a personal 'trait', whereas the fear of communicating in specific situations being 'state'. Whilst the trait typology refers to individual characteristics (which are habitual patterns of behaviour thought and emotion) there appears to be no correlation between apprehension levels and intelligence. These behaviours will restrict the relationship between student and tutor, hinder the recognition of the student's progress and needs, and may impair educational performance (Fordham and Gabbin, 1996).

The state typology is not personality based but is seen as being situational and is related to the perceived context of the communication situation (McCroskey, 1984). Beatty et al. (1998) reconceptualized CA by identifying it as a communbiological phenomenon. They argued that trait CA had been thought of as being the result of a social learning process despite the fact that there was little evidence to support the view. Their new approach saw CA primarily as a result of biological functioning: the initial cause of CA being biologically rooted and a consequence of having a neurotic, introverted personality or temperament. This could then be reinforced by experiences which consequently result in anxiety, avoidance or behavioural inhibition being exhibited.

Gender and culture

Various studies have indicated that female accounting students were, in general, more apprehensive than male accounting students. This follows the initial observation of Daly and Miller (1975) that women have significantly higher OCA but lower WCA than male counterparts. The results of studies by Simons et al. (1995) and Arquero et al. (2007) indicate that while the WCA of females was lower, it was not significantly so. Female students did, however, have significantly higher overall OCA scores and higher scores associated with formal speaking contexts.

Reeder (1996) is critical of the approach taken to the research on gender in the area of communication studies. She points out that the majority of studies undertaken are from a viewpoint of identifying similarities and differences in communication styles and habits of men and women. She states that even if differences or similarities are found the significance of these is unclear and that the research rarely provides any interpretation of these differences in terms of theoretical frameworks. This is the case both in overall CA research and specifically in the accounting context.

Whilst in the empirical studies similarities and differences have been found the results are confused. Dwyer (1998) investigated the relationship between CA and learning styles. No relationship was identified for men but women with high levels of CA prefer the Hands-on Experimenter and the Analytical Evaluator learning styles, whilst women with low levels of CA prefer the Innovative Explorer learning style.

Many studies have identified comparative geographical differences in levels of CA. However in the research conducted to date, whilst these differences have been measured and noted, there appears to be no existing substantial theoretical framework that has been identified in order to analyse and explain these differences.

Educational background and academic self-confidence

Arquero et al. (2007) have noted that in terms of overall levels of CA, accounting students from a numeric/scientific backgrounds have statistically significant higher levels of apprehension than those from a humanities/arts or mixed backgrounds. However the level varied between countries. In their study UK accounting students from a numerate/scientific background had a higher level of writing apprehension than those from a literate/arts background. This is not replicated in the case of Spanish accounting students where no significant difference was found for written CA. Educational background can be seen to have an impact on OCA for Spanish students. Spanish accounting students from a numerate/scientific background have a higher level of OCA than those from a literate/arts background particularly in a formal context. In order to understand the factors that may give rise to these differences it is again important to fully understand the specific cultural contexts in which they are initiated. Studies have shown that accounting students exhibit relatively high levels of CA wherever studies have been undertaken. However, the constituent areas of overall communication do appear to vary between countries and cultures.

Another explanation for the cause of CA was suggested by Glaser (1981). The Negative Cognitive Appraisal Model suggests that individuals, especially children, will form a reaction to criticism of their communication performance, resulting in an expectation of negative appraisal of feedback and in avoiding behaviors forming low self-confidence and the basis of CA. Hassall et al. (2005, 2006) identified a correlation between academic self-confidence and CA in accounting students; students with high levels of CA also had low levels of academic self-confidence. This is supported by McCroskey et al. (1976) and Allen and Bourhis (1996) who found relationships between high levels of CA and low academic performance.

Vocational choice

Importantly, Daly and McCroskey (1975) found evidence that there was a significant relationship between CA and the perceived desirability of certain professions. Individuals with higher than average levels of CA will be attracted towards vocations and professions that they perceive as needing relatively low levels of communication skills. Consequently major problems will arise if students with high levels of CA perceive the role of the accountant to be one that does not need communications skills. Hassall et al. (2006) and Ameen et al. (2010) provide evidence that students joining accounting courses have above average levels of CA and this suggests that their perception is that the accounting profession does not require communication skills. These studies point to a clear gap between the needs of the profession and the perceptions of those wanting to join it. This expectations gap is created by the difference in image of the accounting profession of those wishing to join the profession and the reality known to those currently practising accounting. The former see accounting as primarily numerate and requiring a skills set of precision, concentration and attention to detail which may conflict with the increased need for communication competences involving a skills set of creativity and gregariousness.

Communication channels

Accountants could be required to communicate in differing contexts to differing audiences through different mediums. The rapid developments in information and communication technology have resulted in the mediums changing and increasing. The major distinction in communication is whether it is oral or written. Oral communication is often face to face but as noted above this is changing. Written communication is rarely face to face but again the medium in which this form of communication is undertaken is changing. There are also minor differences if the individual is required to communicate independently or as a member of a group.

The contexts can be formal or informal. Formal oral communication would normally be with clients or in specific management situations. An accountant may need to make a formal communication to a large audience, such as at an annual general meeting or in a one-to-one situation with a client. Informal communication in the workplace usually occurs between colleagues. Informal conversations occur frequently in a working environment and again may have differing numbers of participants. Meetings may be either formal or informal and a key to success is deciding which type of meeting is happening and adopting the appropriate form style of communication. The participants may be in the same location or not, telephone conversations and conferences, and video-conferencing are being increasingly used. Anxiety appears to grow as oral communication becomes more formal and is often influenced by an increasing audience size.

Written communication can also be formal or informal. Most accountants will be expected to prepare a formal report for circulation to shareholders, senior managers or to a specific client. The formality of the communication appears to increase anxiety. Informal written communication is now increasingly done by electronic means (e-mail, text or social networking). However, the increased informality created by electronic mail is also causing a new series of concerns. It has been accused of the corruption of the English language, lack of punctuation and leading to misinterpretation of the writer's intended tone.

Accountants are expected to communicate accurately, professionally and in a timely manner. The accuracy of their communications will be dependent on their preparation and their ability to transfer the preparation into the relevant form. This can be a problem for both oral and written communication. Spizberg and Cupach (1989) define professional communication as a successful balance between effectiveness and appropriateness. Effectiveness is the extent to which the communication goals are met. Appropriateness refers to fulfilling social expectations in a particular situation. Lack of timeliness may well be caused by prevarication created by the two previous factors. As previously indicated, meeting these expectations is a potential source of anxiety.

With regards to new forms of communication technology, Scott and Rockwell (1997) indicate that where the new medium of communication is written, for example e-mail, then writing apprehension was not strongly related to the new technologies. This suggests that writing-apprehensive individuals may not have much difficulty in using these new technologies. For new oral mediums of communication, such as mobile phones, a relationship was identified between OCA and their use. Their most powerful finding was that experience was a significant predictor of future use. Unfortunately anxious or apprehensive individuals are unlikely to gain that necessary experience. Scott and Timmerman (2005) state that whilst the apprehension levels of individuals remain stable in long-term encounters with new technology, the usage frequency changed for several of the technologies they examined resulting in stronger relationships between apprehensions and those technologies for which use has changed the most in the past five years. In this context they suggest the use of a new measure of CA which generally predicts communication technology use, such as text-based and conferencing tools, more strongly than do more traditional apprehension questionnaire types.

Reducing communication apprehension

There are two approaches to reducing CA: behavioural and pedagogic. Behavioural approaches include techniques such as systematic desensitisation (Friedrich and Goss, 1984), cognitive restructuring (Fremouw, 1984), assertiveness training (Adler, 1977; Zuker, 1983) and visualization techniques. There is evidence (Berger and McCroskey, 1982; Berger et al., 1982) that these techniques can reduce CA. The application of these techniques is normally on an individual basis by qualified practitioners. This is time consuming and resource intensive and is therefore inappropriate for 'mass' education. Pedagogic approaches to reduce CA focus on the use of pedagogical strategies such as restructuring programmes (Daly and Miller, 1975). This calls for actively involving students in communication development exercises, but to do so it will be necessary to overcome the previously reported 'avoiding behaviours' (particularly those associated with oral presentations). If not handled effectively this approach may fail: instead of removing the barrier it could reinforce it. In writing skills there is some evidence of success (Craig and Mckinney, 2010).

The link between anxiety and self-confidence should be explored by further research. Several studies have noted the apparent connection between CA and self-efficacy. Self-efficacy is an individual's self-belief in their ability to achieve a specific outcome. This is again both individual and context specific. This self-belief is independent of the skill requirement to actually achieve the specific outcome. If the individual self-efficacy is substantially below the skill required then this will become a major barrier to development in that contextual area.

Bandura (1986) identified sources of self-efficacy beliefs in individuals and proposed that the most influential source is enactive mastery whereby individuals measure and interpret their own performance. The experiences they have interpreted as 'successes' will raise their self-efficacy whereas those interpreted as 'failures' will erode it. A weaker but still important source of self-efficacy belief is vicarious experience. This is where an individual notices that a peer has successfully completed a task and this success then strengthens the individual's belief in their own abilities. Schunk (1987) has demonstrated the importance of role models in this context. Credible feedback can be an important source of verbal persuasion. Although this is a weaker source of self-efficacy belief than those above, persuaders can play an important part in building self-efficacy belief but it must be noted that negative persuasions can have an erosive effect. An individual's emotional state can also influence self-efficacy beliefs. A positive approach can be beneficial whilst anxiety is a strong undermining factor. Research needs to be carried out on these sources of self-efficacy beliefs in terms of pedagogic approaches that can be used in accounting courses and specifically in communication situations.

Discussion and areas for future research

The changing business environment, principally advances in information technology and globalization, is necessitating change in accounting practice. The most fundamental change is the move from transaction processor to business advisor. To effect this required change there is a need to establish the necessary cognitive and vocational skills. Professional pronouncements and research have indicated that the principal vocational requirement will be competent communication skills. Unfortunately, there is an established body of literature identifying the gap between expectations and actual performance of accountants in this area. The current education process is not developing the necessary communication skills to fulfil the future requirements in this area.

Many research studies have established the existence of CA as a barrier to the development of communication skills that seems prevalent in the accounting context. CA, if present in individuals, will severely inhibit the development of communication skills. There is a heated debate among communication scientists and researchers on the causes of CA. The foundation of this debate is to whether the causal factor is the 'trait' of an individual or a 'state' that is a response to the situational elements of a specific communication transaction. The potential treatments (behavioural and pedagogic) suggested to alleviate CA are in most instances not economically feasible in the context in which accounting education and development exists. This appears to have led to increasing frustration on the part of the employers of accounting students and the profession generally and the development of an expectations gap between the professions need for entrants with good communication skills and their perceptions of the communication skills of students graduating from accounting courses. There is, however, some evidence (Hassall et al., 2003) to show that when students enter the profession and their training and development becomes the responsibility of their employers, the employers remain dissatisfied with their progress when it is measured several years later.

When students choose courses and careers their thoughts are influenced by their desire to avoid certain requirements. Students who think that they have low levels of specific skills will choose to avoid vocations that they perceive as requiring high levels of competence in those skills. There is research evidence that suggests that accounting courses are being chosen by some students because accounting is perceived as being predominantly mathematical and necessitating low levels of communication skills. This perception is inconsistent with the current vocational reality of the ever-increasing demands for the accountant to be a communicator. It is clear that there is a difference between the demands being made on accountants and the perceptions of the role of accountants held by those who influence, and those who subsequently make, career choices.

This needs to be addressed by revising the images of the accountant and the accounting profession, particularly in terms of communication requirements, that are held by the public in general but more importantly with would-be accounting students and the people influencing vocational choices (parents, teachers and career counsellors). This is clearly an area for future research which should be directed at the reasons for choosing accounting as a career, identifying those individuals that are important in the vocational choice process and their knowledge of the skills requirements for entry into the accounting profession. It will take several years to change the image of the accounting profession and possibly even longer before the new skills requirements are fully understood by students and those influencing their vocational choices. In the longer term this may reduce the expectations gap by changing the recruitment patterns of the accounting profession.

The balance of evidence shows that current accounting courses have little effect on students' levels of CA and therefore their communication skills development. The attempts to rectify the expectations gap may have been aimed at improving communication development rather than removing CA. Where successes have been achieved these should form the basis of further research in order to establish good practice.

Until it is known what causes the reactions that erect the barriers it is impossible to prescribe effective mediating interventions. It is a possibility that apprehension could occur at any stage of an individual's career and from that point onwards hinder their ability to communicate. This is another potential area for further research. Establishing the causes of these latent barriers, possibly by qualitative research methodology, could allow remedial actions to be taken. Research methods such as critical incident analysis may be appropriate here.

In the long term the accounting profession and accounting educators need to implement actions to effect a change of image and to communicate this to vocational decision makers and the individuals who influence their vocational decision making. This will mean that vocational decision makers will understand the importance to future accountants of having and maintaining a high level of communication competence. In the short and medium term, accounting educators and researchers need to focus on increasing their understanding of CA and its causes, and undertake further research to identify pedagogic methods that will help to remove any barriers to communication skills development that exist or develop in students and professionals.

References

Adler, R.B. (1977) *Confidence in Communication: A Guide to Assertive and Social Skills*, New York: Holt, Rinehart & Wilson.

Albrecht, W.S. and Sack, R.J. (2000) *Accounting Education: Charting the Course through a Perilous Future*, Accounting Education Series Vol. 16, Sarasota, FL: American Accounting Association.

Allen, M. and Bourhis, J. (1996) 'The relationship of communication apprehension to communication behaviour: a meta-analysis', *Communication Quarterly*, 44, 2: 214–26.

Aly, I.M. and Islam, M. (2003) 'Audit of accounting program on oral communications apprehension: a comparative study among accounting students', *Managerial Auditing Journal*, 18, 9: 751–60.

Ameen, E., Bruns, S.M. and Jackson, C. (2010) 'Communication skills and accounting, do perceptions match reality?', *CPA Journal*, July: 63–6.

Arquero, J.L., Donoso, J.A., Hassall, T. and Joyce, J. (2007) 'Accounting students and accounting apprehension: a study of Spanish and UK students', *European Accounting Review*, 16, 2: 299–322.

Bandura, A. (1986) *Social Foundations of Thought and Action: A Social Cognitive Theory*, Englewood Cliffs, NJ: Prentice Hall.

Beatty, M.J., McCroskey, J.C. and Heisel, A.D. (1998) 'Communication apprehension as temperamental expression: a communiobiological paradigm', *Communication Monographs*, 65: 197–219.

Berger, B.A., Baldwin, H.J., McCroskey, J.C. and Richmond, V.P. (1982) 'Implementation of a systematic desensitization program and classroom instruction to reduce communication apprehension in pharmacy students', *American Journal of Pharmaceutical Education*, Fall: 227–34.

Berger, B.A. and McCroskey, J.C. (1982) 'Reducing communication apprehension in pharmacy students', *American Journal of Pharmaceutical Education*, Summer: 132–36.

Boorom, M.L., Goolsby, J.R. and Ramsey, R.P. (1998) 'Relational communication traits and their effect on adaptiveness and sales performance', *Academy of Marketing Science Journal*, 26, 1: 16–30.

Borgatta, E.F. and Bales, R.F. (1956) 'Sociometric status patterns and characteristics of interaction', *Journal of Social Psychology*, 43, 2: 289–297.

Byrne, M., Flood, B. and Shanahan, D. (2009) 'Communication apprehension among business and accounting students in Ireland', *Irish Accounting Review*, 16, 2: 1–19.

Craig, R. and Mckinney, C.N. (2010) 'A successful competency-based writing skills development programme: results of an experiment', *Accounting Education: An International Journal*, 19, 3: 257–78.

Daly, J.A., McCroskey, J.C. (1975) 'Occupational desirability and choice as a function of communication apprenhension', *Journal of Counseling Psychology*, 22, 4: 309–13.

Daly, J.A. and Millar, M.D. (1975) 'Further studies on writing apprehension: SAT scores, success expectations, willingness to take advanced courses and sex differences', *Research in the Teaching of English*, 9: 249–53.

Dwyer, K.K. (1998) 'Communication apprehension and learning style preference: correlations and implications for teaching', *Communication Education*, 47, 2: 137–50.

Fordham, D.R. and Gabbin, A.L. (1996) 'Skills versus apprehension: empirical evidence on oral communication', *Business Communication Quarterly*, 59, 3: 88–98.

Fremouw, M.J. (1984) 'Cognitive-behavioural therapies for modification of communication apprehension', in J.A. Daly and J.C. McCroskey (eds) *Avoiding Communication: Shyness, Reticence, and Communication Apprehension*, Beverly Hills, CA: Sage Publications.

Friedrich, G. and Goss, B. (1984) 'Systematic desensitization', in J.A. Daly and J.C. McCroskey (eds) *Avoiding Communication: Shyness, Reticence, and Communication Apprehension*, Beverly Hills, CA: Sage Publications.

Gardner, C.T., Milne, M.J., Stringer, C.P. and Whiting, R.H. (2005) 'Oral and written communication apprehension in accounting students: curriculum impacts on academic performance', *Accounting Education: An International Journal*, 14, 3: 313–36.

Glaser, S.R. (1981) 'Oral communication apprehension and avoidance: the current status of treatment research', *Communication Education*, 30: 321–41.

Harris, K.R. (1980) 'The sustained effects of cognitive modification and informed teachers on children's communication apprehension', *Communication Quarterly*, 28: 47–56.

Hassall, T., Joyce, J., Arquero, J.L. and Donoso, J.A (2003) 'The vocational skills gap for management accountants: the stakeholders perspectives', *Innovations in Education and Teaching International*, 40, 1: 78–88.

Hassall, T., Joyce, J., Arquero, J.L. and Donoso, J.A. (2006) 'Communication apprehension and maths anxiety as barriers to communication and numeracy skills development in accounting and business education', *Education and Training*, 48, 6: 454–64.

Hassall, T., Joyce, J., Bramhall, M.D., Robinson, I.M. and Arquero, J.L. (2005) 'The sound of silence? A comparative study of the barriers to communication skills development in accounting and engineering students', *Industry and Higher Education*, 19, 5: 392–98.

Hassall, T., Joyce, J., Ottewill, R., Arquero, J.L. and Donoso, J.A. (2000) 'Communication apprehension in UK and Spanish business and accounting students', *Education and Training*, 42, 2: 93–100.

International Federation of Accountants. Financial and Management Accounting Committee (2002) *The Role of the Chief Financial Officer in 2010*, New York: IFAC.

McCroskey, J.C. (1984) 'The communication apprehension perspective', in J.A. Daly and J.C. McCroskey (eds) *Avoiding Communication: Shyness, Reticence, and Communication Apprehension*, Beverly Hills, CA: Sage Publications.

McCroskey, J.C. and Anderson, J.F. (1976) 'The relationship between communication apprehension and academic achievement among college students', *Human Communication Research*, 3: 73–81.

McCroskey, J.C., Daly, J.A., Richmond, V.P. and Cox, B. (1976) 'The effects of communication apprehension on interpersonal attraction', *Human Communication Research*, 2: 51–65.

McCroskey, J.C. and Richmond, V.P. (1976) 'The effects of communication apprehension on the perceptions of peers', *Western Speech Communication*, 40: 14–21.

Parker, D.L. (2001) 'Back to the future: the broadening accounting trajectory', *British Accounting Review*, 33, 4: 421–53.

Payne, S.K. and Richmond, V.P. (1984) 'A bibliography of related research and theory', in J.A. Day and J.C. McCroskey (eds) *Avoiding Communication: Shyness, Reticence, and Communication Apprehension*, Beverly Hills, CA: Sage Publications.

Reeder, Heidi M. (1996) 'A critical look at gender difference in communication research', *Communication Studies*, Winter, 47, 4: 318.

Richmond, V.P. and McCroskey, J.C. (1989) *Communication Apprehension: Avoidance and Effectiveness*, Scottsdale, AZ: Gorusch.

Riecken, H.W. (1958) 'The effect of talkativeness on ability to influence group solutions of problems', *Sociometry*, 21, 4: 309–321.

Ruchala, L.V. and Hill, J.W. (1994) 'Reducing accounting students' oral communication apprehension: empirical evidence', *Journal of Accounting Education*, 12, 4: 283–303.

Schunk, D.H. (1987) 'Peer models and children's behavioural change', *Review of Educational Research*, 57: 149–74.

Scott, C.R. and Rockwell, S.C. (1997) 'The effect of communication, writing, and technology apprehension on likelihood to use new communication technologies' *Communication Education*, 46, 1: 44–62.

Scott, C.R. and Timmerman, C.E. (2005) 'Relating computer, communication, and computer-mediated communication apprehensions to new communication technology use in the workplace', *Communication Research*, 32, 6, December: 683–725.

Sharifi, M., McCombs, G.B., Fraser, L.L. and McCabe, R.K. (2009) 'Structuring a competency-based accounting communication course at the graduate level', *Business Communication Quarterly*, 72, 2: 177–99.

Simons, K., Higgins, M. and Lowe, D. (1995) 'A profile of communication apprehension in accounting majors: implications for teaching and curriculum revision', *Journal of Accounting Education*, 13, 3: 299–318.

Sorenson, G. and McCroskey, J.C. (1977) 'The prediction of interaction behaviour in small groups', *Communication Monographs*, 44: 73–80.

Spitzberg, B.H. and Cupach, W.R. (1984) *Interpersonal Communication Competence*, Beverly Hills, CA: Sage Publications.

Spitzberg, B.H. and Cupach, W.R. (1989) *Handbook of Interpersonal Competence Research*, New York: Springer Verlag.

Stanga. K.G. and Ladd, R.T. (1990) 'Oral communication apprehension in beginning accounting majors: an exploratory study', *Issues in Accounting Education*, 5, 2: 180–94.

Walker, M. (2004) 'Recovering accounting: an economic perspective', *Critical Perspectives on Accounting*, 15: 519–27.

Zuker, E. (1983) *Mastering Assertiveness Skills*, New York: AMACOM.

12

Review of US pedagogic research and debates on writing in accounting

Sue Ravenscroft and Abhi Rao

Writing and accounting are integrally related. Archeological evidence suggests writing emerged millennia ago from efforts to enact the accountability of citizens to their religious/civic communities (Ezzamel and Hoskin 2002). Records were created and maintained to allow figures of authority to determine whether citizens had met their civic obligations. As a result, accounting emerged from a tradition of inscribed record-keeping rather than an oral tradition. Writing as inscription is valuable for making sense of complex qualitative data. Because accounting began as, and remains, an inherently written practice, powerful motivation exists for academics to understand the role of writing within accounting practice. Thus, one might reasonably conclude that writing plays a central role in university accounting curricula. That conclusion—at least in the US—would be incorrect.

While US accounting academics and accountants historically have a somewhat contentious, or at least uneasy relationship, they agree on both the importance of communication in accounting, and on the low quality of students' and newly-hired recruits' writing (Bloom, Heymann, Fuglister, and Collins 1994; Van Wyhe 2007). Though most accounting students learn to write journal entries adequately and correctly, the practice of accounting requires writing beyond ledgers and cash journals. However, as early as 1920, a time preceding university degree requirements for entry into the profession, complaints were made about new accountants' inability "to write a clear and concise business letter" or to think clearly (Van Wyhe 2007: 173). A participant at a 1948 conference of academics and practitioners observed.

> On one thing the accountants all seem to agree: that is, that nowhere along the educational line do our graduates pick up a really adequate command of written and spoken English. ... Maybe, on the other hand, some college faculty, somewhere, will one of these days really figure out what to do about it, and earn the very real gratitude of the profession.
>
> *(Schmidt 1948: 292)*

In this chapter, we discuss possible reasons for the lack of success accounting academics have had in meeting the long-standing challenge of helping students learn to write well. In the course of that exercise, we look first at "Definitional and Theoretical Challenges" under two headings: (i) why professionals are dissatisfied with new graduates' writing; and (ii) what we learn from

English research on the objectives of writing pedagogy. We look next at "Challenges in Application" under four headings: (i) the difficulty of defining good business writing; (ii) entrenched habits of classroom pedagogy; (iii) the support universities provide faculty; and (iv) accounting firms' inconsistent support for writing excellence. In the concluding section we provide a brief review of representative research on writing in accounting, and offer possible future directions for teaching and research.

Definitional and theoretical challenges

Why are professionals dissatisfied?

Professional pronouncements and survey research reinforce the profession's expressed need for recruits who can communicate better, particularly in writing. The belief that communication skills are essential for success in accounting has a long history (Roy and MacNeill 1967). Though accountants are estimated to spend approximately 25 percent of their time writing,[1] we read repeatedly that students entering the profession are unable to communicate effectively (Corman 1986; Rader and Wunsch 1980; Novin, Pearson, and Seng, 1990; Stowers and White 1999). The (then) eight international accounting firms issued a White Paper in 1989 stressing the importance of adding interpersonal and communication skills to the accounting curriculum. In its first position statement, the resulting Accounting Education Change Commission (AECC) reiterated the importance of these so-called "soft" or "generic" skills (1990).

However, despite expressing dissatisfaction, the major accounting firms fail to provide clear, well-delineated expectations. Almost a decade after the AECC was formed, Stowers and White observe that "little guidance has emerged as to the specific educational outcomes related to communication skills needed by accounting students that both the accounting and communication fields should be addressing" (1999: 23). Albrecht and Sack (2000) find that while accounting practitioners say they want to hire graduates who can communicate effectively, and who think clearly and critically, they fail to define communication skills. Jones concludes: "What is not clear from the literature is what the profession means by 'effective writing' or what should be included in the accountant's written communication skill set" (2011: 248). Confusion arises in part because of the frequent linking and pairing of thinking and writing. Firms often treat clear thinking and strong writing as synonyms or substitutes for each other. Professionals surveyed rated the following four skills as the most important: a) effectively organizing sentences and paragraphs; b) writing clearly and precisely; c) spelling correctly; d) preparing concise, accurate, and supportive documents (Jones 2011). Two challenges for faculty become immediately apparent.

First, the term "communication skill" is overly broad, and excludes almost nothing. That items b and c in the list above are included as alternative choices is quite revealing. Would accounting professors consider, for instance, writing numbers legibly or doing addition correctly comparable to understanding the articulation of the income statement and balance sheet? Would they be considered commensurate items under an umbrella term of "accounting skills"? Accounting professionals fail to appreciate the profound differences between recognizing routine grammatical errors versus expressing complex ideas clearly and gracefully (Williams 1990).

The second challenge is entailed by the first. If one wants to teach "clear writing," particularly writing within a specific discipline, one must understand the relationship of writing and clear thinking generally and within that discipline specifically. We find accounting professionals inconsistently define and differentiate critical thinking and good writing. Similarly, academics do not successfully parse out the distinctions. Therefore, we look next to research in English and Communication to understand better the relationship between writing and learning.

What do we learn from research on writing and learning?

According to Hermsen and Franklin (2008: 411) the practice of teaching "basic composition" began in the early twentieth century. Prior to that time, neither instruction nor faculty research in basic composition occurred. Instead, the training "gentlemen" students received was primarily in the art of rhetorical disputation. Composition studies began in the 1960s; at that time, faculty also began exploring the implications of that research to develop writing pedagogy. This relative recency helps to explain the existence of multiple, conflicting theories and the scarcity of definitive recommendations buttressed by consistent, generalizable results.

In the late 1960s, an English pedagogy called Writing Across the Curriculum (WAC) began. It was based on the underlying assumption that writing is a critical form of learning and provides benefits that other modes of communication can not. This key belief was used to rationalize the dissemination of writing instruction into classrooms across the university, on the grounds that underlying cognitive processes differ across disciplines. WAC supporters believe that writing should be taught across the university to socialize students effectively into their specific discipline and its discourse.

Writing across the curriculum (WAC) has spawned many variations, including Writing in the Disciplines (WID). The latter approach supports the centrality of writing as a form of learning, but relies more heavily on genre analysis, an understanding of the vocabulary, arguments, evidence and other rhetorical devices used to create various writing products in specific fields. WID differs from WAC in placing greater emphasis on rhetorical awareness, i.e. "on the efficacy of writing—or learning to write—as an aid in the acquisition of disciplinary rhetoric" (Oechsner and Fowler 2004: 127).

How we learn to write and to think more clearly are closely interrelated skills that have generated many writing/learning theories. As an illustration of the variety, we look at Klein's review article of four of those theories (1999). The first theory is that writers generate knowledge at the "point of utterance." This approach is appealing intuitively, and is reinforced by writers such as Kurt Vonnegut who say they do not know what is going to emerge from their pen/typewriter/keyboard as they create. Evidence that new knowledge is generated during spontaneous writing is, however, unconvincing and not obtained consistently from one study to the next. This approach does justify assignments such as "freewrites"[2] and ungraded journals, but criticisms include the possibility that students are simply rehearsing existing beliefs and, worse, that those beliefs could be erroneous.

The most complex of the four theories Klein reviews is called "Backward Search." According to this description of the writing/learning connection, writers set high-level rhetorical goals, work on sub-goals, revise and elaborate, retrieve additional information, and in the process generate ideas they did not have initially. Klein recognizes that this describes sophisticated approaches to writing, and that rhetorical effectiveness may not correlate with the creation of *new* knowledge or understanding. Rather, it may reflect a pre-existing sophisticated understanding of both content and communication techniques.

Unfortunately, evidence on the effectiveness of writing pedagogy is inconsistent. Langer notes: "Few studies have been undertaken to learn what people learn from writing, what different kinds of learning result from different kinds of writing experiences, or how writing can be used to help students understand and remember the material they read" (1986: 400). Newell and Winograd state there is a slim hope for empirical evidence that could prove "the writing process and what writers take from writing are interrelated" (1989: 196). Oechsner and Fowler's 2004 review article validates the earlier pessimism about attaining clarity on the writing/learning connection (also see Schumacher and Nash 1991; Ackerman 1993).

In a recent study on the assessment of writing and learning, Deane focuses on the importance of a socially embedded rhetoric, and claims the goal of teaching writing is "socialization into literate communities ... how to participate in a specific set of concrete and socially valued practices" (2011: 2). He finds common themes emerging from previous research. For instance, expert writing involves: fluent text production; the ability to interpret what one reads and revise what one writes; and the ability to be strategic and reflective regarding problems, audience, and goal-setting. Deane offers the following insight on the connections and the distance between clear thinking and strong writing.

> reading, writing and critical thinking are distinct activity systems founded upon common underlying skills. One can have critical thinking without reading or writing (for there is no requirement that reflective thought be expressed in written form). Writing can take place without deep reflection, for there is no guarantee that the thoughts expressed in a written text will be significant, relevant, fair, clear, precise, complex, accurate, or logical. Yet the whole point of skilled writing is to mobilize all of the resources available to the writer to achieve meaningful goals.
>
> *(2011: 16)*

Thus research indicates that to teach writing, faculty must help students develop and coordinate a variety of skills, which differ depending on the discipline within which a student is writing. In the next section we describe some of the classroom and institutional challenges facing accounting faculty who teach writing.

Challenges in application

Improvement in writing depends on a "dizzying array of factors ... the student's readiness, openness, and willingness; the teacher's careful planning, theoretical and pedagogical knowledge, good timing and even showmanship; and careful design of and timing in the curriculum" (Condon 2001: 29). In this section, we discuss various aspects of the accounting classroom, curriculum, and institutional setting that challenge faculty who teach writing.

Difficulty defining good business writing

In literature on teaching writing, genre is a recurring theme (e.g., Klein 1999; Oechsner and Fowler 2004; Deane 2011). To be effective, writing must be done with an audience and a purpose and follow the attendant genre conventions, i.e., the "kind of discourse that a text exemplifies" (Klein 1999: 230). The term "genre" is used by some writers to denote rhetorical categories such as argumentation, persuasion, explanation, analysis, or personal writing. It is also used to denote types of written output, such as report, policy recommendation, literature review, or essay. Genre in both senses differs across disciplines. A major goal of teaching writing is to help students understand the form and rhetorical conventions of various genres; and to be aware of their audience and the expectations related to the type of writing they are engaged in.

Writing is highly formalized. Understanding of specific genres is shared to different degrees across disciplines. We believe that accounting does not have a highly formalized communal understanding of the sorts of writing we should teach students. We offer two extreme examples demonstrating a contrast in the degree of consensual understanding—a highly conventionalized genre compared to a genre that is relatively unformalized.

Within a highly conventionalized genre, Hermsen and Franklin (2008) report on an extensive writing-to-learn study. Hermsen and Franklin create a five-category classification of the sentences that appear in lab reports: all propositions are categorized as either Motivation, Procedure, Observation, Inference, or Speculation. Effective lab reports follow conventions whereby observation or procedure statements generally precede inference or speculation statements. The researchers classify every sentence of the 600 subjects' initial lab reports, and graph the sequence in which the five sentence types occur for each student. They work with the students on their reasoning and then require the students to revise their lab reports by cutting the number of words in half. This study reflects the detailed and very careful planning needed to begin to disentangle and understand the writing/learning relationship within a widely-used, highly formal disciplinary genre. This study could be conducted because scientists have relatively consensual understandings of the genre of lab reports, both in terms of what the output should contain and the process of creating that output.

At the other extreme—a situation without consensus about the form of the genre—we look outside academia. In a US Supreme Court case, former Justice Potter Stewart said that "hard-core pornography" was hard to define, but "I know it when I see it."[3] Accounting faculty are likely to rely—at least to some extent—on an intuitive sense of good writing within genres. We do not have a classification scheme such as the one described in Hermsen and Franklin (2008) that would enable us to work with students on their business memos, or reports, or other written assignments.

To teach good writing, faculty must have more than an intuitive recognition or gut feeling. Faculty know well that many consequences flow from having a poorly defined pedagogical objective. As we noted earlier, we cannot look to the profession, for they have failed to evince a strong awareness of genre or to lay out their expectations unambiguously. Some writers believe that we learn most about writing by reading (Krashen 2003), but what readings do we provide to students as exemplars reflecting our highest expectations? We are not aware of a book of readings in accounting which serves as a repository of excellent writing that exemplifies clarity, coherence, elegance, and readability.

The core of much business writing is an argument, that is rhetoric, intended to persuade. Examples include recommending imposition of an accounting standard, recommending a specific accounting approach to a complicated transaction, or taking a more aggressive position on a tax return. Accounting standards written by the Financial Accounting Standards Board and the International Accounting Standards Board are arguments, statements buttressed with reasons and examples, emanating from the highest accounting authority and defining future practice. However, they are sometimes the result of a highly political process of regulatory capture, with major assumptions that are left implicit and not always defensible. They usually require considerable explanation and interpretation before they can be applied, and often include implicit, but faulty, assumptions. Young (2006) shows that the idealized users presumed in the standards do not reflect real users of financial information. Furthermore, as universal rules, accounting standards are intentionally written without a specific audience or a particular set of circumstances in mind. Yet, rhetorical awareness, in the form of sensitivity to audience and attention to specific situations, is the underlying premise of Writing Across the Curriculum and programs that bring writing into the accounting classroom. Thus, accounting standards are not a genre faculty would find beneficial for students to emulate in their writing.

Students probably spend more time reading textbooks than any other type of accounting material. Again, regardless of the quality of writing, textbooks are not a genre most students will be writing within during their careers. If effective teaching involves modeling well-done work (Gallagher 2011), we need examples within accounting as we help students become more skillful writers. Faculty who teach intermediate financial accounting and other standard subjects have a wide array of ancillary pedagogical infrastructure beyond textbooks, such as computerized homework that is graded immediately. Some publishers offer individual study problems generated for students on demand and videotaped demonstrations, for instance. Yet faculty teaching writing face a lack of clear models to provide students and a lack of consensus on what good writing is. We do not have templates that enable students, through practice (and faced with progressively greater challenges), to become literate members of the professional accounting community.

Entrenched habits of classroom pedagogy

Faculty and student expectations often implicitly minimize the importance of writing, especially relative to speaking, as a way of learning. Classroom pedagogy typically does not involve writing as a learning process. Instead, faculty rely on written assignments or exams for summative evaluation, as a way for students to demonstrate what they have learned. By contrast, classrooms are more frequently arenas for learning through oral discourse. As instructors, we are far more inclined to encourage speech as a mode of discovery and learning than we are to use writing in the same way, and for the same purposes. As Britton notes:

> It is more difficult to convince teachers that writing is a learning process than it is to convince them that talk is, because so often teachers use writing as a way of testing. They use it to find out what students already know, rather than as a way of encouraging them to find out.
>
> *(1970: 86)*

Students occasionally see faculty who wrestle through an unrehearsed argument or an ambiguous accounting situation. For example, accounting faculty routinely demonstrate the process of creating a balance sheet or working out a complex set of journal entries or calculations. But how frequently do faculty demonstrate the writing process for students? Do we show students how we construct a memo, how we revise and edit, cut passages out, reframe an argument? Despite the complexity of the writing process, we provide almost no modeling of that process. This lack only exacerbates the lack of strong writing examples we noted in the previous section. Faculty fail to provide model written products and we infrequently—if ever—model the writing process.

As a final note on the culture of higher education, we observe from a national study that college students average 27 hours per week on academic activities, which includes class attendance and outside studying. This is less time than high-school or secondary students spend in class (Arum and Roksa 2011). Furthermore, business students scored lowest among all majors on the Collegiate Learning Assessment tool, which was used to measure learning growth in college. Arum and Roksa find that few college students read more than 40 pages week, and many never have to write an extended paper of 20 pages or more (2011). Thus, faculty hoping to instill the discipline of writing face significant challenges.

How are universities supporting writing pedagogy?

Many accounting faculty do not see writing as their responsibility and feel pressured to attend instead to an ever-expanding portfolio of essential content. Carnegie and West (2011: 502) refer to this phenomenon as "syllabus overcrowding." Giving up classroom time for a "generic" or "soft" skill such as writing strikes many faculty as unnecessary, because writing should be taught by the English faculty. As a result, writing instruction in accounting courses is usually carried out by particularly dedicated or interested faculty and is not a coordinated departmental effort to provide multi-course pedagogical scaffolding so that students move through a coherent and progressive set of exercises and training. Thus, the careful design and good timing of the curriculum that Condon (2001) notes as necessary are unlikely to occur.

In response to the frustration of faculty, colleges of business are increasingly creating communication centers. Because business communication centers are a relatively recent phenomenon, there is little published scholarship about them and their activities. Our enquiries have revealed there are over 30 centers in the 105 business colleges that offer accounting doctorates in the US. We spoke informally with several of the directors of these business communication centers. Generally, they believe centers have the potential to function as intermediary spaces to engage accounting students deeply in the writing process and to explore how learning relates to writing. However, they also believe that centers are not currently always being used well.

Our college has a recently-formed communication center. Students told us they feel more motivated to complete audience-based writing tasks such as memos or letters, because they perceive immediate benefits to writing in styles they would most likely use in the workplace. Thus, students take a utilitarian approach: reflections, "freewrites," and essays strike them as "busy work." On the other hand, while students express a desire for writing tasks focused on the use of workplace genres and rhetorical approaches, they act inconsistently with this desire. Students tend to see the writing process as two steps—initial write-up and proofreading. For them the communication center functions as a substitute for that second step of proofreading; the consultants will help students avoid run-ons and comma splices.

While accounting faculty often realize that writing centers can help students develop more self-awareness and deeper understanding of the writing process, they tend, like students, to expect to see immediate improvements in written assignments reflected through stronger mechanical and grammar skills. The business communication center allows faculty to off-load consideration of the deeper writing/learning connection and focus instead on written products. Faculty assess student writing with prescriptive, rules-based formulas and a strong focus on correct content. The resulting pedagogy relies on the hope that eventually students might in their own idiosyncratic writing processes make cognitive leaps and develop an awareness of good writing.

Students tend to reinforce the faculty's focus on mechanically correct writing when assigning grades. Often students do not believe writing plays a major role in their future professional tasks; they are skeptical about using accounting class time to learn about writing. Students may accurately intuit what awaits them in their careers, a possibility we examine next.

Do accounting firms reinforce good writing?

As we note earlier, accounting firms have a long history of complaining about students' writing and critical thinking ability but we find their actions do not consistently reinforce their words. Do accounting firms allow new hires to write freely and to write to learn, or do they ask new hires to write in fairly rigidly prescribed formats and to follow last year's work papers? Is there a real benefit after graduating for a student to write as a way to explore a topic, to clarify her thoughts, to recognize patterns or relationships? We argue that those young professionals who use writing in these ways are likely to benefit greatly from such analysis in terms of understanding, but that the actual process of doing that sort of preparatory work is not recognized or rewarded by firms. Firms want memos and other writing generated quickly and carefully by people who are operating on strict time budgets. Potentially contentious writing will be vetted by lawyers when needed. The above observations all beg the following question: do the firms want truly independent and creative thinkers?

Roslender raises this issue:

> there is the question of how creative do those who employ accountants really want them to be ... Few if any prospective employers would deny that they are seeking adaptable, dynamic, inventive, open-minded, lateral thinking, etc., staff. But ... these qualities, if widely distributed, might prove problematic ... One of the dangers of encouraging students to think about accountancy is that they might be tempted to think about other things as well.

(1992: 208)

Thus, students may exhibit great practicality in taking a minimal approach to writing assignments and asking for help only with what appears to be valued most by future employers.

If we look at the actions of the accounting profession (particularly as manifest in the Big Four international firms) we do not see strong reinforcement of the value of writing. The CPA exam does not have a consistent record of including writing as a major requirement. Currently, writing consumes about 75 minutes of a two-day exam, and only two-thirds of the output will be graded for inclusion in an applicant's final score. More significantly, accounting firms do not typically require applicants to demonstrate their ability to write during the recruiting process. Colleagues whose children are recent graduates in other fields tell us it is not uncommon to be asked to provide a writing sample as part of the interview process. Law firms require applicants to provide a writing sample. One young woman applying for a health-care policy position was given 24 hours to write a proposal as part of her application. If accounting firms value writing so highly, one must ask why they fail to include any measure of it while interviewing and selecting potential new hires. If accounting firms routinely asked job applicants to write a one-hour essay, we feel confident that students would take writing instruction much more seriously.

Closing comments

Where is writing pedagogy now?

In the Appendix we provide a partial but representative view of research on writing pedagogy in US accounting education journals. The authors included define, clarify, and operationalize writing pedagogy with varying degrees of attention to writing's effect on learning accounting content. This collection reveals little in the way of acrimonious debate or direct disagreements among the researchers. Instead, we see a range of approaches. Some researchers are more focused on grammar and mechanics and some attempt to measure the effect of learning on content. Others focus on business genres, such as memos or reports, with an emphasis on crisp, clear writing that avoids circumlocution or jargon. However, arguments linking pedagogy to particular learning goals and writing/learning models are brief and not well-developed.

We do not see an extended exposition of which aspects of learning or cognition are fostered by various writing assignments, and even less explicit justification of the assessment used to test improved conceptual learning and more sophisticated understanding of professional accounting. We characterize the research as composed of well-meaning and competently conducted studies that together constitute a rather anemic program which avoids the most profound and interesting questions about writing's relationship to learning. The research does not probe the discipline-specific aspects of accounting communication.

Placing the research stream within a broader context, we observe that researchers do not offer a critique of the social role of professional accounting education or the many ways accounting shapes our world. There is no discussion of the role of the university in an increasingly corporatized world and of the pressures exerted by accounting firms to focus education outcomes narrowly on their needs. Critical discussions of forces acting on higher education and possible responses tend to originate outside of the US (e.g., McPhail 2001; Tinker and Gray 2003), or outside of accounting education journals.[4]

Possible future directions

We observe on an introspective note that writing is essential, challenging, and highly rewarding to us as academics. Writing is a harsh and honest disciplinarian. Revelatory ideas that bear great import and flow seamlessly through one's mind while driving to work or walking the dog show their true nature as vacuous drivel when written down. Thus, we have personal experience with the strongly felt need to write in order to clarify, organize, or understand and to write in order to evaluate the merit of our thoughts.

We have, for example, diagrammed sentences, simplified complex arguments using propositional calculus, and outlined papers after a draft to see where the logical leaps are too broad to follow. These writing exercises create the transformations in our knowledge, referred to earlier as Backward Search (Klein 1999). But this type of writing —which is obviously carried out to learn, clarify, or reformulate—is highly idiosyncratic. The writing that helps one person may take an entirely different format from the writing that helps another person. The very individualistic nature of writing to improve understanding probably contributes to the unpromising and inconsistent experimental results we described earlier (which tend to be based on assignments that are uniformly given).

We also need to analyze what we mean by good reasoning or critical thinking. Those terms are used far more often than they are defined. When students reason well, we recognize that excellence, but we have not created a clear taxonomy of the steps, or the skills that could be progressively improved and expanded upon. Given the extent to which accounting is based on various forms of arguments, and discontent with student writing is co-mingled inextricably with discontent with students' critical reasoning, we see a need for teaching informal logic, i.e., the formulation of well-formed arguments. If we were to adopt that subject we would still face the research question of whether training in argumentation illuminates the relationship of writing and learning.

We must recognize that as faculty of professional studies, our task is related to and shares much with the sciences and humanities, but also differs from them. Subotnik (1987) urges us to consider teaching accounting more in the way that law is taught, not as rules that yield right answers, but with an emphasis on understanding basic principles and the ability to deal with ambiguity. The focus should not be on knowledge but on method. Sullivan and Rosin say that practical reasoning, the type professionals must engage in, occurs when people "think and act through a back-and-forth dialogue between analytical thought and the ongoing constitution of meaning" (2008: 104). Writing within this pedagogy should not be used to demonstrate what one already knows, but should emphasize "learning to confront and ask puzzling questions, and to open oneself to problematic situations and discovery" (Sullivan and Rosin 2008: 119).

Colomb urges those who seeking to create a writing program in accounting to first consider what students need to learn, i.e., the meta-ability to "give specific, principled, intelligible reasons for adopting one communication strategy rather than another" (1992: 116). Second, we must avoid the trap of thinking of writing as a "basic skill,"[5] learned once and easily transferred to new situations and vocabularies. Transferring skills learned in one domain or genre is challenging, yet we do not help students traverse those disciplinary differences. Third, we need to create a body of "good writing vocabulary" learned in English classes and reiterated and reinforced in other disciplines. Fourth, the program must be comprehensive and extend over the students' entire college career. Students need to practice different types of writing at different stages of their college education; we cannot effectively teach writing in a single writing-intensive accounting course. Finally, a writing program should be carried out not by individual faculty, but should be instead supported by entire departments and colleges. Only then can the appropriate scaffolding of progressive assignments be given to students in an integrated fashion. Only then can faculty assume this responsibility without sacrificing their own time and research efforts or depriving students of time spent on accounting content.

We see challenges and rewards for researchers interested in the pedagogy of writing. They need to create valid means of probing and augmenting the learning that occurs through the writing process, and do so within a context of integrated professional education, rather than the inculcation of a narrowly-described skill. If writing can help students' cognition, what type of writing is most likely to result in improving students learning and reasoning? What evidence could be adduced by researchers? Future research in both writing and learning, i.e., the process of becoming a literate, responsible member of the accounting profession and society, could inform accounting instruction and help us to guide students to think and communicate more responsibly, analytically, and creatively.

Appendix

Author(s) and Year	Journal	Thumbnail
Gingras (1987)	*Journal of Accounting Education*	Survey 1500 practitioners—more writing needed.
Borthick and Clark (1987)	*Issues in Accounting Education*	Use a computerized language analysis tool to direct students' attention to syntax. Improvement was found.
Wygal and Stout (1989)	*Journal of Accounting Education*	Use "freewrites," provide anecdotal support of increased student interest.
Mohrweis (1991)	*Journal of Accounting Education*	Writing results in a slight improvement in students' "higher order analytic thinking."
Scofield and Combes (1993)	*Issues in Accounting Education*	Use an audience-based approach to teach writing to promote learning.

Author(s) and Year	Journal	Thumbnail
Scofield (1994)	*Issues in Accounting Education*	Use nongraded writing. Provide anecdotal support student interest improved.
Hirsch and Gabriel (1995)	*Journal of Accounting Education*	Define communication as involving "two inseparable elements: critical thinking and technical skills."
McIsaac and Sepe (1996)	*Journal of Accounting Education*	Writing should be taught as a professional activity.
Gelinas (1997)	*Technical Communication Quarterly*	Textbooks do not offer suffi-cient or adequate writing instruction.
Catanach and Rhoades (1997)	*Issues in Accounting Education*	Use writing assignments to help students develop expert thinking abilities, learn about current issues, and synthesize information from diverse sources.
Catanach and Golen (1997)	*Accounting Education: A Journal of Theory, Practice and Research*	Surveys should focus on users of accounting writing, not academics or professionals.
Baird, Zelin and Ruggle (1998)	*Issues in Accounting Education*	Use "freewrites." Improvement on some exams, not on others.
Almer, Jones and Moeckel (1998)	*Issues in Accounting Education*	Use "freewrites." Students improved on essay exams, not on other types of exams.
Riordan, Riordan and Sullivan (2000)	*Business Communication Quarterly*	Faculty lecture on "grammar, sentence structure, and word choice." Writing mechanics improve.
Ashbaugh, Johnstone and Warfield (2002)	*Issues in Accounting Education*	Use lectures on writing. Students writing mechanics improve, as do written essays.
Stout and DaCrema (2004)	*Journal of Accounting Education*	Focus on issue of faulty modifiers. Find improvement in student writing.

(continued)

Author(s) and Year	Journal	Thumbnail
Cleaveland and Larkins (2004)	Journal of Accounting Education	Use computer-based training. Students improve in punctuation, use less passive voice and wordiness.
Matherly and Burney (2009)	Issues in Accounting Education	Peer review helps students write better and evaluate written materials better.
Chu and Libby (2010)	Issues in Accounting Education	Students write six mini-cases and multiple-choice answers and keep a journal. Students report improved critical thinking.

Notes

1 Matherly and Burney (2009) report that the portion of time spent writing may be as high as one-third.
2 "Freewrites" are writing exercises in which the writer develops a response to a specific topic without concern for form, structure, or mechanics in order to elaborate and create critical connections with existing knowledge.
3 He later expressed regret over these words.
4 For instance, accounting education was the theme of the entire February/April 1996 issue of *Critical Perspectives on Accounting* (7), edited by Marilyn Neimark.
5 In addition to being called a "generic" or basic skill, writing is also referred to as a "soft" skill. We question this. If writing is so soft, why do so many people continue to find it so difficult —both to learn and to teach?

References

Accounting Education Change Commission (1990) "Objectives of education for accountants: Position statement number one," *Issues in Accounting Education*, 5: 307–312.
Ackerman, J. (1993) "The promise of writing to learn," *Written Communication*, 10.
Albrecht, W.S. and Sack, R.G. (2000) *Charting the Course Through a Perilous Future, Accounting Education Series Volume No. 16*, Sarasota, FL: American Accounting Association.
Almer, E.D., Jones, K. and Moeckel, C.L. (1998) "The impact of one-minute papers on learning in an introductory accounting course," *Issues in Accounting Education* 13: 485–498.
Arum, R. and Roksa, J. (2011) *Academically Adrift: Limited Learning on College Campuses* Chicago, IL: University of Chicago Press.
Ashbaugh, H.K. Johnstone, M. and Warfield, T.D. (2002) "Outcome assessment of a writing-skill improvement initiative: Results and methodological implications," *Issues in Accounting Education*, 17: 123–148.
Baird, J.E., Zelin II, R.C. and Ruggle, L.A. (1998) "Experimental evidence on the benefits of using "writing to learn" activities in accounting courses," *Issues in Accounting Education*, 13,: 259–276.
Bloom, R., Heymann, H.G., Fuglister, J. and Collins, M. (1994) *The Schism in Accounting*, Westport, CT: Quorum Books.
Borthick, A.F. and Clark, R.L. (1987) "Improving accounting majors' writing quality: The role of language analysis in attention directing," *Issues in Accounting Education*, 2: 13–27.
Britton, J. (1970) *Language and Learning*. Portsmouth, NH: Boynton/Cook.

Carnegie, G.D. and West, B. (2011) "A commentary on 'Contextualising the intermediate financial accounting courses in the global financial crisis'", *Accounting Education: An International Journal*, 20: 499–503.

Catanach, Jr, A.H. and Golen, S.P. (1997) "Developing a writing model for accountants," *Accounting Education: A Journal of Theory, Practice and Research*, 2: 41–58.

Catanach, Jr., A.H. and Rhoades, S. (1997) "A practical guide to collaborative writing assignments in financial accounting courses," *Issues in Accounting Education*, 12: 521–536.

Chu, L. and Libby, T. (2010) "Writing mini-cases: An active learning assignment," *Issues in Accounting Education*, 25: 245–266.

Cleaveland, M.C. and Larkins, E.R. (2004) "Web-based practice and feedback improve tax students' written communication skills," *Journal of Accounting Education*, 22: 211–228.

Colomb, G. (1992) "Teaching accountants to write: A guide to developing programs," in T. Frecka (ed) *Critical Thinking, Interactive Learning and Technology: Reaching for Excellence in Business Education*, Chicago, IL: Arthur Andersen & Co.

Condon, W. (2001) "Accommodating complexity: WAC program evaluation in the age of accountability," in S.H. McLeod, E. Miraglia, M. Soven and C. Thaiss (eds) *WAC for the New Millennium: Strategies for Continuing Writing-Across-the-Curriculum Programs*. Urbana, IL: National Council of Teachers of English.

Corman, E.J. (1986) "A writing program for accounting courses," *Journal of Accounting Education*, 4: 85–95.

Deane, P. (2011) *Writing Assessment and Cognition*. Research Report ETS RR-11-14. Princeton, NJ: ETS.

Ezzamel, M. and Hoskin, K. (2002) "Retheorizing accounting, writing and money with evidence from Mesopotamia and ancient Egypt," *Critical Perspectives on Accounting*, 13: 333–367.

Gallagher, K. (2011) *Write Like This: Teaching Real-World Writing through Modeling & Mentor Texts*, Portland, ME: Stenhouse Publishers.

Gelinas, U.J. (1997) "Selection of technical communication concepts for integration into an accounting information systems course: A WAC case study," *Technical Communication Quarterly*, 6: 381–401.

Gingras, R.T. (1987) "Writing and the Certified Public Accountant," *Journal of Accounting Education*, 5: 127–137.

Hermsen, L.M. and Franklin, S.V. (2008) "A new research agenda for writing-to-learn," in Marschark, M. and Hauser, P.C. (eds) *Deaf Cognition: Foundations and Outcomes*, Oxford, UK: Oxford University Press.

Hirsch, Jr., M.L. and Gabriel, S.L. (1995) "Feedback strategies: Critique and evaluation of oral and written assignments," *Journal of Accounting Education*, 13: 259–279.

Jones, C.K. (2011) "Written and computer-mediated accounting communication skills: An employer perspective," *Business Communication Quarterly*, 74: 247–271.

Klein, P. (1999) "Reopening inquiry into cognitive processes in writing-to-learn," *Educational Psychology Review*, 11: 203–270.

Krashen, S. (2003) "We learn to write by reading, but writing can make you smarter," *Ilha do Desterro*, 44: 67–81.

Langer, J. (1986) "Learning through writing: Study skills in the content areas," *Journal of Reading*, 29: 400–406.

Matherly, M. and Burney, L. (2009) "Using peer-reviewed writing in the accounting curriculum: A teaching note," *Issues in Accounting Education*, 24: 393–413.

McIsaac, C.M. and Sepe, J.F. (1996) "Improving the writing of accounting students: A cooperative venture," *Journal of Accounting Education*, 14: 513–533.

McPhail, K. (2001) "The dialectic of accounting education: From role identity to ego identity," *Critical Perspectives on Accounting*, 12: 471–499.

Mohrweis, L.C. (1991) "The impact of writing assignments on accounting students' writing skills," *Journal of Accounting Education*, 9: 309–326.

Newell, G. and Winograd, P. (1989) "The effects of writing on learning from expository text," *Written Communication*, 6: 196–217.

Novin, A.M., Pearson, M.A. and Senge, S.V. (1990) "Improving the curriculum for aspiring management accountants: The practitioner's point of view," *Journal of Accounting Education*, 8: 207–224.

Oechsner, R. and Fowler, J. (2004) Playing devil's advocate: Evaluating the literature of the WAC/WIC movement, *Review of Educational Research*, 74: 117–140.

Rader, M.H. and Wunsch, A.P. (1980) "A survey of communication practices of business school graduates by job category and undergraduate major," *The Journal of Business Communication*, 17: 33–41.

Riordan, D.A., Riordan, M.P. and Sullivan, M.C. (2000) "Writing across the accounting curriculum: An experiment," *Business Communication Quarterly*, 63: 49–58.

Roslender, R. (1992) *Sociological Perspectives on Modern Accountancy*, London, UK: Routledge.

Roy, R.H. and MacNeill, J.H. (1967) *Horizons for a Profession: The Common Body of Knowledge for Certified Public Accountants*, New York, NY: AICPA.

Schmidt, L.A. (1948) "Employers' conference evaluates accounting curriculums, recruitment, placement," *The Journal of Accountancy*, October: 292–296.

Schumacher, G. and Nash, J. (1991) "Conceptualizing and meaning change due to writing," *Research in Teaching of English*, 25: 67–96.

Scofield, B. (1994) "Double entry journals: Writer-based prose in the intermediate accounting curriculum," *Issues in Accounting Education*, 9: 330–352.

Scofield, B. and Combes, L. (1993) "Designing and managing meaningful writing assignments," *Issues in Accounting Education*, 8: 71–85.

Stout, D.E. and DaCrema, J.J. (2004) "A writing intervention for the accounting classroom: Dealing with the problem of faulty modifiers," *Journal of Accounting Education*, 22: 289–323.

Stowers, R.H. and White, G.T. (1999) "Connecting accounting and communication: A survey of public accounting firms," *Business Communication Quarterly*, 62: 23–40.

Subotnik, D. (1987) "What accounting can learn from legal education," *Issues in Accounting Education*, 3: 313–323.

Sullivan, S.M. and Rosin, M.S. (2008) *A New Agenda for Higher Education: Shaping a Life of the Mind for Practice*, San Francisco, CA: Jossey-Bass.

Tinker, T. and Gray, R. (2003) "Beyond a critique of pure reason: From policy to politics to praxis in environmental and social research," *Accounting, Auditing & Accountability Journal*, 16: 727–761.

Van Wyhe, G. (2007) "A history of U.S. higher education in accounting, part I: Situating accounting within the academy," *Issues in Accounting Education*, 22: 165–181.

Williams, J. (1990) *Style: Towards Clarity and Grace*, Chicago, IL: University of Chicago Press.

Wygal, D.E. and Stout, D.E. (1989) "Incorporating writing techniques in the accounting classroom: Experience in financial, managerial and cost courses," *Journal of Accounting Education*, 7: 245–252.

Young, J. (2006) "Making up users," *Accounting, Organizations and Society*, 31, 579–600.

13

Is XBRL a 'killer app'?

Joanne Locke

Introduction

Computers and the Internet are disruptive technologies that have had far-reaching impacts in business and society (Downes, 2009). How these technologies affect accountants' work practices and their communication of accounting information have been the subject of research (for example, Caglio, 2003; Cong et al., 2008; Debreceny et al., 2002; Lymer and Debreceny, 2003; Quattrone and Hopper, 2006; Unerman and Bennett, 2004). The purpose of this chapter is to focus on eXtensible Business Reporting Language (XBRL), which is a digital data standard[1] designed specifically to facilitate the communication of business data on networks.

Originally named eXtensible Financial Reporting Language, XBRL was the brainchild of Charlie Hoffman in 1998. Charlie Hoffman identified eXtensible Markup Language (XML) as potentially capable of automating the exchange of business information on the Internet. He worked with a small group of others to provide an initial use case that showed that XML could be developed to incorporate the key business rules embedded in accounting (such as debit and credit and the requirement that they balance) and definitions of the elements of business reporting (such as revenue and depreciation expense). XBRL as it has been developed to date allows software to add tags containing this accounting information to data so that each data item may be automatically searched and downloaded into analysis software. Attaching the tags to the data means that instead of a user needing to search the web for an annual report and cut and paste data required for analysis, this process can be done automatically by the computer. For example, an investor may wish to compare performance ratios for five companies in a single industry. Tagging data using XBRL allows the investor with the right software to search for the specific companies and the data elements (s)he wants for the years of interest and have the software locate and download those data items into a (spreadsheet) template to calculate the ratios as specified by the investor. Given the capacity of computers there is virtually no constraint on the number of companies that could be automatically analysed at one time (Roth, 2009).

The benefits claimed for XBRL include that it will save time and increase the accuracy of identification and download of data (Apostolou and Nanopoulos, 2009; Cox, 2008). This would allow a greater scrutiny of company reports and therefore potentially an increase in transparency (21st Century Disclosure Initiative Staff, 2009; Roth, 2009). Additionally, some tags are provided in many languages (www.iasb.org/xbrl), so translation of the accounting terms into a preferred language may be available. The increase in speed, accuracy and the potential for language translation all suggest a possible improvement in communication as a result of the adoption of XBRL.

XBRL's success as a communication tool, however, depends on the quality of the software used to implement it, the co-operation of the different groups developing it, the quality of the processes used by companies to tag their reports and the degree of sophistication used by those analysing the data. There is currently a lack of software to allow analysis, but there is no reason why it will not eventually become available given that key groups are now co-operating to achieve the consistency in the high-quality technical elements needed. While there is concern about the quality of the early filings of tagged data to the SEC, there is an expectation that as preparers of the reports gain experience, it will improve (Aguilar, 2009).

The appropriate use of the data poses a more intractable problem for high-quality communication. XBRL tags, if correctly selected and attached, will be accurate for the process of analysis described above. The problem for improved analysis and decision making is that the automation of the process may itself reduce the quality of the analysis. Extracting specific items of data from a report and automating the analysis of an almost unlimited number of companies at a time means that the data are taken out of the context of the companies and their accounting policies so that incorrect conclusions may be drawn (Locke et al., 2010). The tagging of data with the same tag suggests they have a comparability that is actually not supported by the underlying accounting which relies on annual reports being taken as a whole. The benefits and limitations of XBRL are discussed more fully in the next section.

After Hoffman's successful pilot project, the American Institute of Certified Public Accountants sponsored the project (Cover, 2000) and from there an international consortium (XBRL International Inc. – XII) was formed to carry on the development (Kernan, 2009; see also www.xbrl.org) and maintain control of the XBRL specification as a data standard.

Adoption of XBRL is expanding, but in contrast to the expectations that there would be 'grass-roots' demand from investors, it has actually been regulators who have been the driving force for adoption (Locke and Lowe, 2005; Nimmons, 2005). This is because regulators benefit directly from the automation of the transfer and processing of data from the many filing companies they supervise and they have the regulatory authority to require companies to use XBRL. By requiring XBRL, regulators may automate the initial validation of documents submitted for completeness and internal logic and provide an immediate response to submitting entities about the initial acceptability of the submission. Surveillance may also be enhanced and extended by automating the analysis of submissions and checks against benchmarks and red flags. Regulators have also claimed that it will reduce the compliance cost of submitting entities (SEC, 2009; Standard Business Reporting, 2009). The most notable of the regulator adoptions is the Securities and Exchange Commission (SEC) in the U.S., which required companies filing with it to provide documents in XBRL format, commencing in 2009 (SEC, 2009). Internationally many other regulators have either allowed or mandated its use, including China, Netherlands, Belgium, UK, Australia, Singapore, Japan, India and Germany (see www.xbrlplanet.org). XBRL now has a strong foundation of international users as a result of regulatory requirements.

According to many of its proponents, XBRL is not a descriptive or engaging name (Cox, 2006). Important projects adopting XBRL have chosen to 're-brand' themselves as Standard Business Reporting (Australia and the Netherlands) or Interactive Data (USA).[2] This is not auspicious for a data communication standard and masks the extent of XBRL's adoption. However, XBRL is an intriguing development in business communication. The focus of this chapter is to explore the potential for XBRL to be a 'killer app' for business communication. Downes (2009, p. 10) defines a killer application (abbreviated to 'app') as; 'a technological innovation whose introduction disrupts long-standing rules of markets or even whole societies. Killer apps establish new industries and transform existing ones' (see also Downes and Mui, 1998).[3] While killer apps are often rapidly adopted because of their 'cutting edge' functionality, Downes argues that the disruption to the institutional structures related to the domain or industry affected may emerge over a long period of time. Further, once institutional adjustments are made, the 'second-order' effects of the killer app may be more significant than the initial ones (p. 17).

A basic overview of XBRL is provided in the following section. Whether or not XBRL may be a killer app for accounting communication is explored in the third section, initially by evaluating XBRL's progress relative to its developers' early expectations. Evidence of XBRL exhibiting other characteristics of a killer app including its potential for second-order effects is then discussed. Finally, conclusions are drawn and suggestions for future research outlined.

An overview of XBRL

The discussion in this section is divided into three practical perspectives: Why does digital business reporting need standards for the Internet? What benefits does XBRL offer? What are some of the technical elements that make it work?

Why does digital business reporting need standards?

In simple terms, to communicate financial reporting information on the Internet, a report must be created in a digital form, transmitted over the network and 're-materialized' at the destination. This is the same as any communication over the Internet, such as email or web-pages. A standard is needed so that any sender and any receiver have access to a common reference to 'code' and then 'decode' a message. There are many such standards underpinning the Internet; including Hypertext Markup Language (HTML) that is used for web pages; and Simple Mail Transfer Protocol (SMTP) for email (Leiba, 2008). Many of these standards work because all the software and platforms that interact with the Internet have open access to them and so regardless of what computer or software or browser a user is running, they are able (within some constraints) to send and receive data over the Internet. The digital exchange of business reporting information has the same requirement: to ensure that the data are transmitted and received accurately. Along with many other uses and domains, companies providing reports on their websites have adopted Adobe's Portable Document Format (PDF) (Jones and Xiao, 2004). PDF guarantees that what is sent will be presented to the recipient exactly as intended by the sender as long as the recipient uses the Adobe Acrobat reader (or other variations that are now available). By making the PDF reader free to download, Adobe succeeded in dominating the market for a document exchange format on the Internet, despite it being proprietary.

The other standard that became widely used for business reporting was HTML. It is an open standard that allows all web browsers to process the data on a server for presentation as a web page to any user. HTML is a very powerful concept that businesses have used to present their financial statements as web pages and to provide hypertext links to other pages inside and outside of the report (Allam and Lymer, 2003; Ashbaugh et al., 1999; Baker, 2006). Despite being proprietary products, Microsoft's Word and Excel are so widely used that they have become de facto standards for business reporting, but less frequently used than PDF and HTML (Beattie and Pratt, 2003; Jones and Xiao, 2004).

Joanne Locke

What benefits does XBRL offer?

XBRL is an alternative format to those described above. PDF and HTML are powerful in delivering the required web-page or document accurately and almost immediately. However, it was the scope for extending the benefits of digital reporting through semantic tagging using XML (Debreceny and Gray, 2001) that Charlie Hoffman sought to translate into XBRL.

Table 13.1 explains the key additional features of XBRL related to rendering, searchability, automated download and validation.

Table 13.1 Key additional features of XBRL

Feature	PDF and HTML	XBRL	Notes
Rendering: the format in which the recipient may receive the document.	The whole document or web page is presented to the user as designed by the preparer.	The data is 'atomized'; tagged individually to allow any tagged item to be searched for and retrieved automatically in isolation from the rest of the report. The user may choose which data to access and how they will be presented.	iXBRL has been designed as a 'hybrid' approach in which the presentation of the report is controlled through HTML (like any web page) and the data is tagged and so can also be abstracted and searched.
Searchability/ Accessibility: the accessibility of the data depends on being able to find it on the Internet or within longer individual documents.	Searching PDFs on the web is not possible (the terms need to be provided as meta data for the PDF document). Searching within a PDF is possible, but the terms used in the search must match those used in the document (e.g. revenue vs earnings)	Searching for XBRL tagged data on the Internet should soon be facilitated by search engines that can locate an exact data item based on the element from the taxonomy and other (context) data about the company or organization (e.g. the revenue for Apple Inc. of period ending 31 December 2011). The search will return the data item regardless of what the presentation term used is as long as it is tagged in the taxonomy used correctly.	There is a problem with tagging. The user must know which taxonomy is being used because there are quite a number of them. Also there is always the problem that the data item may be either accidently or deliberately incorrectly tagged or tagged using an unnecessarily created 'unique' tag for the company (an extension).

(continued)

Table 13.1 (Continued)

Feature	PDF and HTML	XBRL	Notes
Automated download into other applications: the interoperability of the data format with a range of other applications.	PDF, Excel or Word documents sent internally in an organization or posted on a website require cut and pasting in order to reformat the data for a user's analysis. This can be time intensive and error prone.	With an appropriate software interface/ application XBRL may enable data to be slotted into analysis software (e.g. Excel) according to a template specified by the user based on the tags. This automated population of an analysis tool would speed analysis and increase the accuracy of the placement of the data (as long as the tagging is correct – see above).	There are concerns about the atomizing of the data in this way. It may increase the tendency to view financial data in particular in isolation from the supporting notes in the annual accounts. While users may ignore notes, narratives and other linked aspects of accounting data even when it is presented in the document, with XBRL the user may never even see it or know that a note existed for that data.
Validation: an automated check for internal consistency of the data.	PDFs, Word or Excel documents may or may not be the product of careful processes for checking their accuracy and completeness depending on the degree of formality associated with them (e.g. internal planning estimates vs annual reports for filing).	XBRL tagging permits automated validation against some basic inbuilt rules based on the expected mathematical relationships in the data.	Validation does not mean the document is correct. It just means that some possible basic errors may be picked up automatically.

The additional functionality benefits stakeholders in different ways and presents some with new issues to overcome. For example, regulators such as stock exchanges, tax authorities, banking supervisors and financial services authorities are by far the largest stakeholder group to adopt XBRL (Locke and Lowe, 2005). Their business case is based on savings that accrue to them through the capacity to:

• automate validation, which means they can be confident that the basic business rules inscribed in the XBRL data standard are complied with in the submitted document before they accept it, and

- automatically download the data from the submitted document into databases or other soft-ware for automated exception testing and the generation of benchmarks – this improves the level of surveillance they can undertake with limited resources (Hannon, 2002).

Regulators also claim that there are compliance cost savings for the companies preparing and submitting the documents (SEC, 2009). However, experience in many settings including the Netherlands, Australia and the USA, shows that submitting companies do not perceive that there are any cost savings and only a small percentage of eligible companies participate if filing in XBRL is voluntary (Chung, 2008).

The SEC's Interactive Data[4] project also claims that benefits will accrue to investors who are end users of the data the SEC publishes on its EDGAR[5] website (Cox, 2007). However, despite the geometrically increasing quantity of XBRL tagged data now available, there is very little software available for investors to use to capitalize on the benefits of searchability and automatic download. Software vendors claim that there is not a 'mass market' demand for such applica-tions, so that it is not profitable to invest in the development required. It is important for XBRL that this 'gap' in demand is closed because otherwise the benefits for investors claimed by the SEC and other regulators will not materialize and pressure to remove the mandatory require-ment for XBRL filing will mount.

The technical elements of XBRL

XBRL is an umbrella term for a suite of digital business reporting standards and approaches that include internal reporting at the journal level (XBRL GL), external reporting (XBRL FR) and a variant preferred by some regulators (e.g. HMRC in the UK), iXBRL. Each of these variants aims to provide a means for exchanging business data in a format that allows computers to recognize and process each item based on an attached tag. The metaphor often used is that each item of business data, regardless of whether it is financial, numeric or narrative, is 'barcoded', so that its meaning may be recognized by computers to automate the exchange of information (internally to the organization and/or externally).

Technically, XBRL is a data standard based on XML. It is a grammar which allows the for-mation of *taxonomies* (hierarchical dictionaries of concepts) and *instance documents* (containing data for a specific entity for a specific period/time) in accordance with the *specification* produced and maintained by the consortium – XII.

The specification contains the technical rules that are relevant to those writing software applications or developing XBRL tools. Taxonomies and instance documents are relevant for accountants and so they are discussed in more detail[6] in the following sections.

Taxonomies

To convert a 'barcode' into information about a product, the code must be linked to a list of information about the product (description, price, etc.). An XBRL taxonomy contains a list of accounting and more broadly, business reporting, concepts and a description of each. It is struc-tured in a hierarchical fashion (parent/child) based on the relationships inherent in the financial statements. For example, the balance sheet is broken down into assets, liabilities and equities; and then into sub-categories such as current and non-current. Each element is defined in rela-tion to reference literature, such as accounting standards, or is defined within the taxonomy. The main taxonomies in use for external reporting are national GAAP ones (such as the US and UK GAAP taxonomies) and the IFRS taxonomy.

Figure 13.1 is an extract of one view of the IFRS 2011 taxonomy. It shows some of the elements in the asset section of the balance sheet. It sets out aspects of the element, such as whether or not it has a normal debit or credit balance, and its reference, so that it may be understood conceptually. Other technical elements in the taxonomy specify 'business rules' including what items should total correctly. This is represented simply in Figure 13.1 by underlining the column where the figures are expected to add to the total. The taxonomy is also based on the accounting equation, so it is possible to validate an XBRL-tagged balance sheet to check that it balances.

Figure 13.1 is a re-presentation of the underlying XML code through an application. Very few people would choose to work with a taxonomy using the raw XML; a small extract of which is provided in Figure 13.2. The taxonomy is made up of many folders of zipped files organized by standard. The IFRS taxonomy may be downloaded at no cost from www.ifrs.org/IFRSs/IFRS.htm and national jurisdiction taxonomies are similarly available from the relevant XII jurisdiction or the relevant standard setter's website.

Assets [abstract]		
Non-current assets [abstract]		
Property, plant and equipment	X instant, debit	IAS 1.54 a Disclosure, IAS 16.73 e Disclosure
Investment property	X instant, debit	IAS 1.54 b Disclosure, IAS 40.76 Disclosure, IAS 40.79 d Disclosure
Goodwill	X instant, debit	IAS 1.54 c Disclosure, IAS 36.134 a Disclosure, IAS 36.135 a Disclosure, IFRS 3.B67 d Disclosure
Intangible assets other than goodwill	X instant, debit	IAS 1.54 c Disclosure, IAS 36.134 b Disclosure, IAS 36.135 b Disclosure, IAS 38.118 e Disclosure
Investments accounted for using equity method	X instant, debit	IAS 1.54 e Disclosure, IFRS 5.24 a Disclosure
Investments in subsidiaries, joint ventures and associates	X instant, debit	IAS 1.55 Common practice
Non-current biological assets	X instant, debit	IAS 1.54 f Disclosure
Trade and other non-current receivables	X instant, debit	IAS 1.54 h Disclosure, IAS 1.78 b Disclosure
Non-current inventories	X instant, debit	IAS 1.54 g Disclosure
Deferred tax assets	X instant, debit	IAS 12.81 g (i) Disclosure, IAS 1.54 o Disclosure, IAS 1.56 Disclosure
Current tax assets, non-current	X instant, debit	IAS 1.54 n Disclosure
Other non-current financial assets	X instant, debit	IAS 1.54 d Disclosure
Other non-current non-financial assets	X instant, debit	IAS 1.55 Common practice
Non-current non-cash assets pledged as collateral for which transferee has right by contract or custom to sell or repledge collateral	X instant, debit	Expiry date 2013-01-01 IAS 39.37 a Disclosure, Effective 2013-01-01 IFRS 9.3.2.23 a Disclosure
Total non-current assets	X instant, debit	IAS 1.66 Disclosure, IAS 31.56 Disclosure

Figure 13.1   IFRS Taxonomy 2011 – extract from balance-sheet view

```
<link:referenceArc xlink:type="arc" xlink:to="res_137" xlink:from="loc_29"
    xlink:arcrole="http://www.xbrl.org/2003/arcrole/concept-reference"/>
<link:loc xlink:href="../../ifrs-cor_2011-03-
    25.xsd#ifrs_ReserveOfGainsAndLossesFromInvestmentsInEquityInstruments" xlink:type="locator"
    xlink:label="loc_285"/>
<link:referenceArc xlink:type="arc" xlink:to="res_137" xlink:from="loc_285"
    xlink:arcrole="http://www.xbrl.org/2003/arcrole/concept-reference"/>
<link:loc xlink:href="../../ifrs-cor_2011-03-
    25.xsd#ifrs_ReserveOfChangeInFairValueOfFinancialLiabilityAttributableToChangeInCreditRiskOfLiability"
    xlink:type="locator" xlink:label="loc_325"/>
<link:referenceArc xlink:type="arc" xlink:to="res_137" xlink:from="loc_325"
    xlink:arcrole="http://www.xbrl.org/2003/arcrole/concept-reference"/>
<link:loc xlink:href="../../ifrs-cor_2011-03-
    25.xsd#ifrs_OtherIncomeExpenseFromSubsidiariesJointlyControlledEntitiesAndAssociates" xlink:type="locator"
    xlink:label="loc_332"/>
<link:referenceArc xlink:type="arc" xlink:to="res_148" xlink:from="loc_332"
    xlink:arcrole="http://www.xbrl.org/2003/arcrole/concept-reference"/>
<link:loc xlink:href="../../ifrs-cor_2011-03-25.xsd#ifrs_ReportedIfInComplianceWithRequirementOfIFRSMember"
    xlink:type="locator" xlink:label="loc_154"/>
<link:referenceArc xlink:type="arc" xlink:to="res_178" xlink:from="loc_154"
    xlink:arcrole="http://www.xbrl.org/2003/arcrole/concept-reference"/>
ink:referenceLink>
linkbase>
```

Figure 13.2   Extract – underlying XML for IFRS Taxonomy 2011

The creation and maintenance of taxonomies creates some controversial issues. There are technical issues over their design and structure and their relationship to accounting standards. For example, there are over 15,000 elements in the US GAAP taxonomy because its designers took an inclusive approach. In contrast, the IFRS taxonomy has only about 4,000 elements because of its close alignment with the principles-based IFRS standards.

There are also issues about who should bear the cost of developing and maintaining taxonomies. The usefulness of XBRL-tagged data crucially depends on users being able to 'decode' the data using the correct taxonomy. The implication is that the 2011 IFRS taxonomy not only needs to be created to a high technical standard using an appropriate due process for use now – but needs to be available for the foreseeable future. Since standards change, there is a growing suite of taxonomies, the availability of which must be ensured over time.

Instance documents

If the metaphor of a taxonomy as a data 'dictionary' is extended, then an instance document is an 'essay' written to express a view at a particular time using terms from the dictionary. That is, an instance document combines selected elements from the taxonomy with the data for a set of financial statements to communicate a specific company's business report at a specific date.[7]

Figure 13.3 is an extract of an instance document obtained from XII's website. The XML code is shown but, as can be quickly seen, users would not be interested in the data in this format. The instance documents need to be made useable by intervening software or platforms as is the case for taxonomies (Figures 13.1 and 13.2). Currently, the user can have the data presented as a spreadsheet or web page on platforms such as the SEC's EDGAR and similar platforms in other jurisdictions (see Figure 13.4). However, the technical possibility to access selected individual items of data and download them into analysis software (such as a spreadsheet) formatted for a pre-specified template is not available to average end users because there is no readily available software.[8]

Those with the technical expertise are making use of data in instance documents, however. In particular, some data aggregators are simplifying their data-collection processes by eliminating the need to re-type data into their proprietary databases (Anonymous, 2004). Similarly members of the XBRL consortium demonstrated the potential power of data tagging in financial statements by running a one-week competition in 2011 to see who could identify the fact (reported item) with the largest value in USD in a filed XBRL instance. The winner was the first respondent to find the $US79 trillion notional derivative for JP Morgan. The number of participants in the game was low (about seven) perhaps because it was just for fun (the prize was a t-shirt), but the number of people with the skills to work with raw instance documents and code search queries from scratch is very limited.

Other developments indicate the possibilities for skilled technicians to leverage their expertise and the growing availability of instance documents. XBRL Cloud provides access to EDGAR filings that uses more of the functionality of XBRL than is currently available in EDGAR. Figure 13.5 highlights some of the additional features enabled by the underlying XBRL instance documents. It is still only a platform to provide access to US data on a company-by-company basis rather than web-wide searches. The business behind XBRL Cloud appears to be targeting companies interested in developing their own data warehouses to analyze company filings, rather than individual investors. However, the existence of such an application indicates the possibility that a range of other platforms may emerge. As access to XBRL data is facilitated, further demand may stimulate the development of easy-to-use packages for tagged data analysis.

```
<?xml version="1.0" encoding="UTF-8" ?>
<!-- This instance document is designed to validate when saved in the same folder of the xbrl-us-us-gaap-entryPoint-all-2011-01-
31.xsd entry point in a local copy of the US GAAP 2011 taxonomy. It has been created for demonstrative purposes only, it is based on t
<xbrli:xbrl xmlns:xsi="http://www.w3.org/2001/XMLSchema-instance" xsi:schemaLocation="http://xbrl.org/2006/xbrldi
   http://www.xbrl.org/2006/xbrldi-2006.xsd" xmlns:us-gaap="http://fasb.org/us-gaap/2011-01-31"
   xmlns:link="http://www.xbrl.org/2003/linkbase" xmlns:xbrli="http://www.xbrl.org/2003/instance"
   xmlns:iso4217="http://www.xbrl.org/2003/iso4217" xmlns:xlink="http://www.w3.org/1999/xlink"
   xmlns:xbrldi="http://xbrl.org/2006/xbrldi">
   <link:schemaRef xlink:type="simple" xlink:href="xbrl-us-us-gaap-entryPoint-all-2011-01-31.xsd" />
   <xbrli:context id="c005">
     <xbrli:entity>
       <xbrli:identifier scheme="www.xbrl.org">XII</xbrli:identifier>
       <xbrli:segment>
         <xbrldi:explicitMember dimension="us-gaap:PropertyPlantAndEquipmentByTypeAxis">us-
         gaap:MachineryAndEquipmentMember</xbrldi:explicitMember>
       </xbrli:segment>
     </xbrli:entity>
     <xbrli:period>
       <xbrli:instant>2010-06-30</xbrli:instant>
     </xbrli:period>
   </xbrli:context>
   <xbrli:context id="c001">
     <xbrli:entity>
       <xbrli:identifier scheme="www.xbrl.org">XII</xbrli:identifier>
     </xbrli:entity>
     <xbrli:period>
       <xbrli:instant>2010-06-30</xbrli:instant>
     </xbrli:period>
   </xbrli:context>
   <xbrli:context id="c002">
     <xbrli:entity>
       <xbrli:identifier scheme="www.xbrl.org">XII</xbrli:identifier>
     </xbrli:entity>
     <xbrli:period>
       <xbrli:instant>2011-06-30</xbrli:instant>
     </xbrli:period>
   </xbrli:context>
   <xbrli:context id="c003">
     <xbrli:entity>
       <xbrli:identifier scheme="www.xbrl.org">XII</xbrli:identifier>
     </xbrli:entity>
     <xbrli:period>
       <xbrli:startDate>2009-07-01</xbrli:startDate>
       <xbrli:endDate>2010-06-30</xbrli:endDate>
     </xbrli:period>
   </xbrli:context>
   <xbrli:context id="c004">
     <xbrli:entity>
       <xbrli:identifier scheme="www.xbrl.org">XII</xbrli:identifier>
     </xbrli:entity>
     <xbrli:period>
       <xbrli:startDate>2010-07-01</xbrli:startDate>
       <xbrli:endDate>2011-06-30</xbrli:endDate>
     </xbrli:period>
   </xbrli:context>
   <xbrli:context id="c006">
     <xbrli:entity>
       <xbrli:identifier scheme="www.xbrl.org">XII</xbrli:identifier>
       <xbrli:segment>
         <xbrldi:explicitMember dimension="us-gaap:PropertyPlantAndEquipmentByTypeAxis">us-
         gaap:MachineryAndEquipmentMember</xbrldi:explicitMember>
```

Figure 13.3   Extract of instance document – XII 2011
Source: www.xbrl.org/sites/xbrl.org/files/imce/XII_FS_2011_1_0.xbrl (downloaded 28 May 2012)

XBRL's power to facilitate large scale analysis as XBRL filing becomes widespread internationally is clear. Roth (2009) describes this as the potential for 'radical transparency'. He and
other proponents, such as the past SEC Chairman Christopher Cox, have highlighted the
strength of empowering many people to automate and scale up their analysis while also allowing
automated 'drill down' to detailed disclosures in the footnotes (Cox, 2006; Hodge et al.,
2004; Knight, 2007). However, care should also be taken not to over-emphasize automated
calculation (Lowe et al., 2012).

Is XBRL the 'killer app' for business reporting?

XBRL is an information communication technology and as such it needs wide adoption to be
viable as a standard (Shapiro and Varian, 1999, p. 13; Zhu et al., 2006). For example, a person
in a telephone network that only has one other user has a very limited number of people to call.

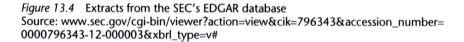

Figure 13.4 Extracts from the SEC's EDGAR database
Source: www.sec.gov/cgi-bin/viewer?action=view&cik=796343&accession_number=
0000796343-12-000003&xbrl_type=v#

The viability of the network and the standard that it is based on increases as more people adopt it (Bonaccorsi and Rossi, 2003). This is the idea referred to as Metcalfe's Law (Downes, 2009, p. 15). XBRL is a data standard and so needs software applications to operationalize it. However, like HTML that has been an important part of the Internet implemented through web browsers, XBRL has the potential to be harnessed in ways that could fundamentally change the communication of accounting information.

Claims for XBRL have equated it to technologies and events that have been disruptive, world or industry-changing. For example, it was said to be as revolutionary as the general ledger (Covaleski, 2000) and to have the impact of colour TV, and the French Revolution (Hughes, 2008; Stuart, 2006). There were also predictions of rapid adoption (Hannon, 2001). In more measured terms, the early catchphrase for XBRL suggests it will have an incremental impact to

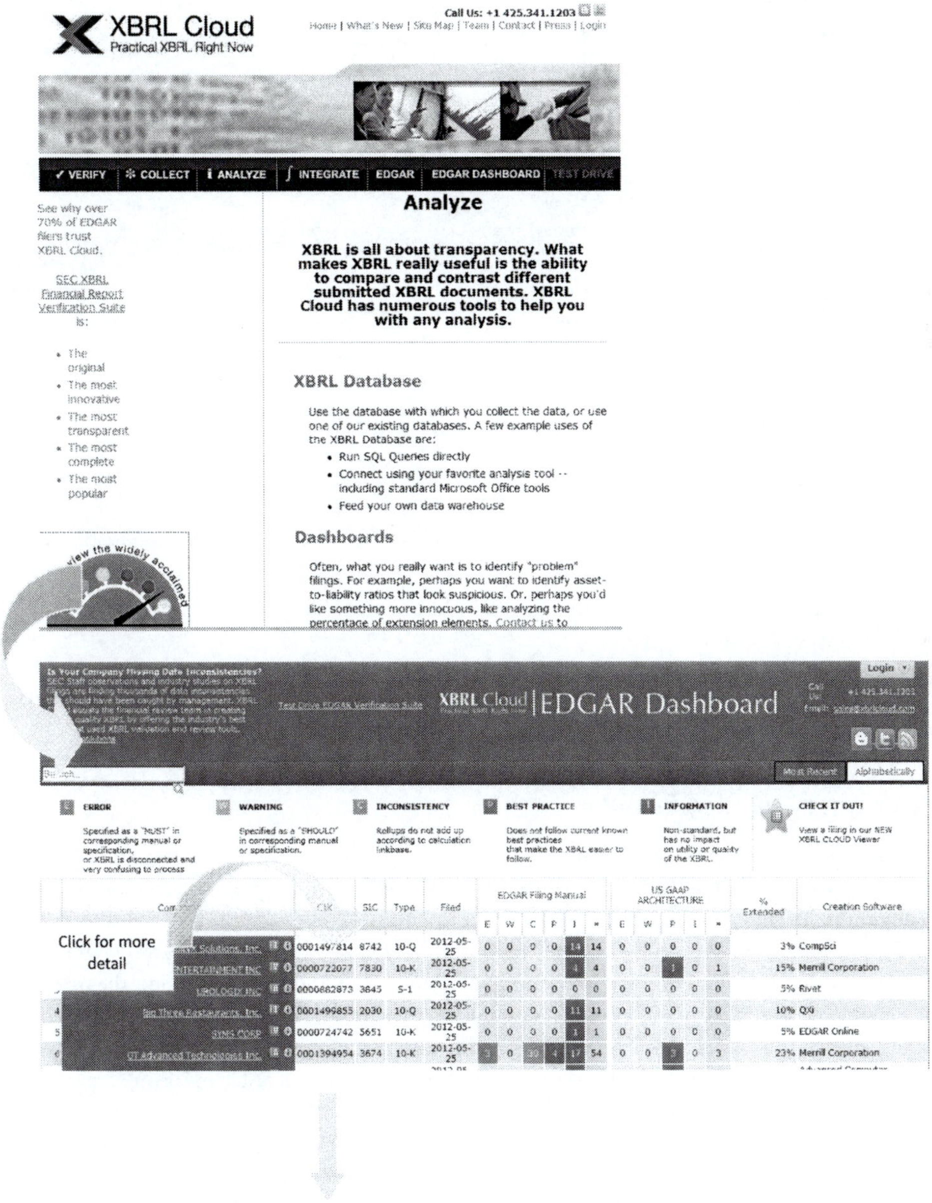

Figure 13.5 XBRL Cloud – demonstration of some of XBRL capabilities
Source: www.xbrlcloud.com/analyze.html

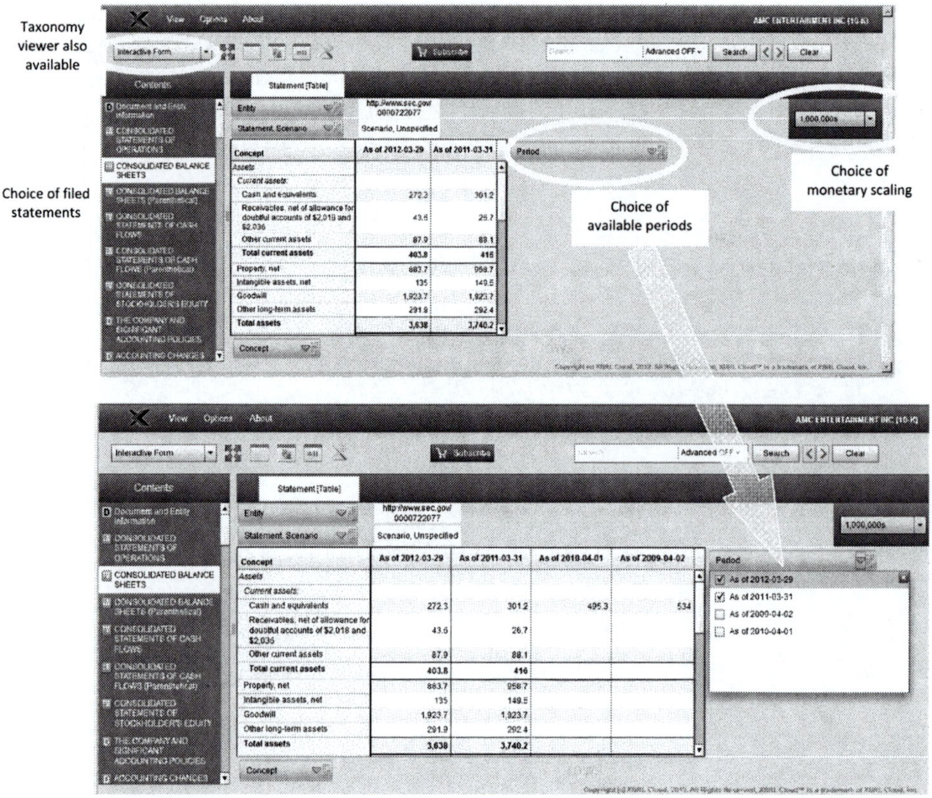

Figure 13.5 (continued)

make business reporting: 'better, cheaper, [and] faster' (Derby, 2005; Hucklesby and Macdonald, 2000; Moyer, 2008).

XBRL: better, cheaper, faster?

This section considers the progress of XBRL against this goal of incremental change and then explores evidence that XBRL has characteristics of a killer app: rapid adoption and industry-changing impacts.

The claim that XBRL provides better reporting has focused on the broad issue of improving 'transparency' for end users and increasing efficiency and reducing costs for the preparers of reports (21st Century Disclosure Initiative Staff, 2009; Bolgiano, 2009; Roth, 2009). Transparency is a widely used term that implies different things to different stakeholders. In particular, it is claimed that XBRL will enable more accurate and faster reporting and that the ease of extracting information from the company's systems could provide a basis for more flexible and therefore relevant reports for users (Derby, 2005; Jones and Xiao, 2004). These advantages are all technically possible; however, the early evidence generated from companies providing tagged data as required by the SEC does not support the claims. XBRL is a communication tool and may be used well or badly. The early concerns have been that preparers have not used the best elements to tag their statements and have made errors in the tagging process[9] leading to the instance documents not being valid (Debreceny et al., 2010; Stewart, 2009). This suggests that the tagged statements may actually be less accurate and reliable than other formats, at least initially. The risk is that rather than improving investor confidence in capital markets (Cuneo, 2002; DiPiazza and Eccles, 2002; Hannon, 2002), the experience will undermine their confidence in tagged data.

The best hope that this will not happen before companies gain experience with creating instance documents is the simple observation that investors and other stakeholders are not using the data directly because there is no software to enable their access. Ironically, this barrier to use may give preparers time to produce 'good-quality' XBRL instance documents. The delay may also provide time for auditors to catch up and address the issues associated with auditing XBRL tagged financial statements (Pawlicki, 2008; Srivastava and Kogan, 2010). To the extent that audit is seen as adding to the reliability of financial statements, the lack of a requirement to have them audited is currently also a weakness. Arguably, such a requirement cannot be introduced until there is audit guidance in place.

Another element of transparency, or 'better' reporting, is the impact on the accessibility of data that XBRL has the potential to provide (Roth, 2009). As discussed earlier, the lack of software is a barrier to this. However, there is also an implicit assumption that such large-scale analysis will be based on standardized data that may be *meaningfully* compared. Communication requires that the sender and the receiver of the message share enough common understanding of the meaning of a term for it to be selected by the sender and reasonably accurately interpreted by the receiver (Austin, 1961; Cooren, 2000). In a technical field like accounting this may be problematic in general purpose reporting. XBRL tags are supposed to reduce the possibility of misunderstanding by linking each element to a definition or references that explain its meaning. To the extent that users have access to the tags and choose to use them this could be a significant improvement in communication of business data. However, if, on the other hand, the hype around XBRL leads users to believe that they can extract and compare data items in isolation from any reference to the context of the financial statements or the meaning of the items in different settings, then poor decision making rather than better decision making is likely to result. Locke et al. (2010) report the result of an experiment that suggests that XBRL tagging does not help decision makers to distinguish the detailed differences contained in footnotes, such as the different treatment of brands purchased rather than internally generated. The effectiveness of communication in financial reporting could actually be reduced if users are encouraged to rely on 'apparently' comparable data from many companies without reference to the footnotes or an understanding of the companies and their industry context.

The second claim is that XBRL would make the production and consumption of accounting data cheaper. There are early indications that this may be true for data aggregators. However, companies preparing reports using XBRL are currently using the simplest method which involves adding the tagging process at the end of all their usual processes (called a 'bolt-on'). Unless preparers invest the time and money to build the tagging process deeper into company reporting systems, it will be an additional requirement and have no cost savings. Once again there is a 'catch-22' – the preparers have to be convinced of the business case to invest more in XBRL even though they were initially only using it because it was made mandatory. So far the key motivator to bring XBRL reporting in-house and deeper into their reporting systems has not been cost savings, but concerns over failure to achieve legal compliance now that the protection from legal liability on XBRL filings in the US is expiring for the first tranche of filers (Starr, 2012; Thomas, 2012).

Similarly, the final claim that reporting could be made faster by XBRL has been stymied by the use of 'bolt-on' systems by companies. As long as XBRL is not built into company-reporting systems, it cannot reduce the time to produce statements, because it is not even being introduced into the process until after all the other steps have been completed. Companies reporting to the SEC using XBRL are given extra time to submit their XBRL filings, so it is slower rather than faster to become available. Starr (2012, p. 20) argues that a study of US filers reporting that '78% of companies surveyed reported a one day (or less) delay in their reporting due to XBRL' is good news. This is clearly not 'faster reporting' from the perspective of users, though. Analysis of instance documents once they are on the Internet should be faster as a result of the improved accessibility and automatic download capability of XBRL tagging, but this relies on software being available for this purpose. It requires a complex series of technical solutions to be in place and organizational acceptance of XBRL in preference to already existing systems for the goal of end-to-end faster reporting to be achieved.

This section has identified the barriers to the achievement of XBRL's three incremental goals in the large-scale implementations in regulator adoptions that have dominated its diffusion. The next section turns to the bigger question of whether or not XBRL has the characteristics of a killer app.

Momentum of adoption

A stable technical standard for XBRL has been available since the end of 2003. The response has been slow and regulator dominated. This suggests that it does not have the dramatic, industry-changing potential of 'killer apps' like the early Visicalc spreadsheet. Gartner's (2010) survey of standards for regulatory requirements moved XBRL out of the 'trough of disillusionment' (which comes after the initial hype) and onto the 'slope of enlightenment' with a projected period to mainstream adoption of less than two years (p. 7). It evaluates the benefits as high and maturity as 'early mainstream' but market penetration is estimated at only between 20 per cent and 50 per cent despite the (then recent) SEC mandate (Gartner, 2010, p. 57). This is a positive evaluation but, given the strong support from regulators, the lack of awareness of preparers of filings and their reliance on third-party publishers (an outsourced 'bolt-on' approach) to produce the instance documents, the Gartner evaluation also suggests only cautious optimism.

XBRL is caught in an uncomfortable hiatus where many companies have been forced to use it to file with regulators, they are not reaping any savings and only a very limited number of end users have access to the full functionality of the tags. A tipping point will soon be reached where the momentum for XBRL use starts cascading out to a range of stakeholders as the instance documents are seen as a valuable resource; otherwise support for the continuing mandatory requirements for XBRL filing will fade.

The next section addresses the question: If XBRL does diffuse to wide and effective use, could it be a 'killer app' with important second-order effects (Downes, 2009)?

'Second-order' effects

An important vision for XBRL tagging of data was that it would enable accountants and accounting standard setters to rethink the 'paper paradigm' underlying business reporting.[10] Accepting a digital approach in which data is atomized and may be produced, accessed and processed as individual elements[11] as the foundation for all accounting communication has implications for accounting at a conceptual level. The annual report is presented as a whole document with the financial statements and notes to the accounts and some form of management discussion and analysis (in most jurisdictions). The documents are audited as a whole. Atomized data accessibility means that some users may never see more than a few extracted numbers from the whole report. How should accountants, educators and auditors respond to this shift in how the 'statements' are disseminated?

Can auditors provide assurance over individual data items? Would all the data items need to be released at once or could there be continuous reporting on some key indicators? Could a choice be offered so that different combinations of elements were 'pre-packaged' for different stakeholder groups? A summary data element could be subdivided in many ways to great levels of granularity and the user could choose which level and perspective they wanted (e.g. factory operating cost in a particular region for a particular product for the last three quarters). Why only provide a single valuation approach when users would have the capacity to select the data item they are interested in (for example, property, plant and equipment at depreciated historic cost or resale value or replacement cost)? Should companies be required to meet any increased demand for such flexible accounting data and would an embedded XBRL system deliver enough efficiency to make it cost neutral? How would it all be secure?

These questions just provide a flavour for the possibilities for re-thinking accounting using a digital paradigm. XBRL has already had less dramatic, but nonetheless potentially important effects on standard setting. In a number of cases, but in particular for the IFRS Foundation, there is a developing relationship between those responsible for writing accounting standards and those creating the taxonomies.[12] Taxonomy creation requires a clear definition of elements and this often raises questions about how a particular element should be defined in relation to another across all standards. An interchange between standard setters and taxonomy developers helps to refine the outputs of both. Companies adopting IFRS for the first time also report that tagging their reports using the IFRS taxonomy helped to highlight omissions and supported their understanding of concepts and requirements in the standards.

Conclusion

So XBRL is not a 'killer app' on the same scale as HTML. XBRL's lack of spontaneous adoption and reliance on being mandated by regulators results from a lack of interest in the innovative functionality it offers. If it survives the pressures it is currently facing, XBRL does have the potential to stimulate a second-order effect in the institutional arrangements surrounding accounting and this will need to happen if the possibilities of digital communication are to be realized. In the meantime, there are barriers to the momentum generated by regulatory requirements. The lack of software for access and analysis, the limited scope of adoption by companies, the proliferation of taxonomies and variation in national accounting standards all reduce the usefulness of XBRL. The next two to five years will be very important. XBRL will not attract the resources needed to maintain it if it does not appeal to investors and creditors, so this is an important focus for market development. Meanwhile there is a strong demand in the US and other jurisdictions with a regulatory requirement for XBRL for accountants and technology people with skills in XBRL and XII has initiated a certification programme (www.xbrl. org/foundations_certificate).

XBRL's impact on the future of accounting communication is likely to be more modest than the initial hype, but even if it is not obvious, it is and will continue to change the way accounting is constructed and communicated for the foreseeable future. On a practical level, further research to identify how the atomization of business reports into digital data affects decision making is needed (Arnold et al., 2012; Ghani et al., 2009; Locke et al., 2010). The accumulated knowledge from such studies should be used as a basis for improving the design of software for analysis and for modifying educational materials. Technical issues related to taxonomy development and comparability are currently important and would benefit from up-to-date independent analysis (compare, Boixo and Flores, 2005; Bovee et al., 2002; Debreceny et al., 2009; Lara et al., 2006). XBRL also poses interesting research questions from the perspective of its development as a sociotechnical object. These studies focus on the impact on its development of the actors and allies brought into its network and those with which it competes and co-operates (Guilloux et al., 2012; Locke and Lowe, 2007; Locke et al., 2010; Piechocki et al., 2009). Research on the implications of XBRL adoption in different contexts such as risk reporting and corporate social responsibility reporting will also be needed (Bonsón et al., 2008; DiPiazza and Eccles, 2002; Garthwaite, 2000). Questions raised above about how the digital paradigm may affect aspects of the institutional infrastructure of accounting requires additional 'blue skies' research to begin framing future possibilities (Ashbaugh et al., 1999; Srivastava and Kogan, 2010; Woodroof and Searcy, 2001). As an emerging innovation in accounting, XBRL is a rich field for future research, even if it is not a killer app.

Notes

1 A data standard for the exchange of information on the Internet is the same in principle as an accounting standard. Spivak and Brenner (2001, p. 16) provide a commonly used definition; 'A standard defines a uniform set of measures, agreements, conditions, or specifications between parties (buyer-user, manufacturer-user, government-industry, or government-governed, etc.)' (cited in Lyytinen and King, 2006, p. 405).

2 Even XII's own magazine is called *Interactive Business Reporting* – iBR (www.ibr-mag.com/).

3 Charlie Hoffman discussed in his blog what applications could be 'killer apps' for XBRL, but does not examine the role of XBRL itself in communication using this lens (http://xbrl.squarespace.com/journal/2009/4/30/xbrl-killer-app-a-radically-tailorable-tool.html; see also Corporate Executive Board, 2012).

4 See www.sec.gov/spotlight/xbrl/what-is-idata.shtml.

5 Electronic Data-Gathering, Analysis, and Retrieval system (see www.sec.gov/edgar/quickedgar.htm).

6 Useful resources include: Hoffman (2006), Weverka and So (2007) and White (2006).

7 The elements included in the instance document also include essential information about the context of the statements including; the company name, date, currency and the scale of the numbers.

8 This is the functionality that would eliminate the need to cut and paste data into the appropriate cells in a spreadsheet or to have to amend formulas to match the cell location of data.

9 These related to a misunderstanding of the implications of the debit/credit attribute assigned to an element in the taxonomy and in some cases companies sought to 'correct' the way elements would appear when rendered into a financial report by their selection of taxonomy element. Experience working with the taxonomy is expected to significantly reduce the number of errors quite quickly (Aguilar, 2009).

10 For early work of this type on the impact of Internet reporting and XBRL see (Wallman, 1996; Ashbaugh et al., 1999; Debreceny and Gray, 2001).

11 For example, a contingent liabilities footnote or revenue for all companies in an industry for a specified period.

12 See www.ifrs.org/The+organisation/About+XBRL/About+XBRL.htm.

References

21st Century Disclosure Initiative Staff. (2009). Towards greater transparency: Modernizing the Securities and Exchange Commission's disclosure system, from www.sec.gov/spotlight/disclosureinitiative/report.pdf.

Aguilar, M. K. (2009). More progress, fewer errors on XBRL filings. *Compliance Week*, 24 November, www.complianceweek.com/pages/login.aspx?returl=/more-progress-fewer-errors-on-xbrl-filings/article/186543/&pagetypeid=28&articleid=186543&accesslevel=2&expireddays=0&accessAndPrice=0.

Allam, A., and Lymer, A. (2003). Developments in internet financial reporting: Review and analysis across five developed countries. *International Journal of Digital Accounting Research*, 3(6), 165–200.

Anonymous. (2004). Edgar online plans product upgrades around XBRL taxonomies. *Electronic Information Report*, 25(36), 1–3.

Apostolou, A. K., and Nanopoulos, K. A. (2009). Interactive financial reporting using XBRL: An overview of the global markets and Europe. *International Journal of Disclosure and Governance, 6*(3), 262–272.

Arnold, V., Bedard, J. C., Phillips, J. R., and Sutton, S. G. (2012). The impact of tagging qualitative financial information on investor decision making: Implications for XBRL. *International Journal of Accounting Information Systems, 13*, 2–20.

Ashbaugh, H., Johnstone, K. M., and Warfield, T. D. (1999). Corporate reporting on the internet. *Accounting Horizons, 13*(3), 241–257.

Austin, J. L. (1961). *Philosophical Papers*. Oxford: Clarendon Press.

Baker, C. R. (2006). Epistemological objectivity in financial reporting: Does internet accounting require a new accounting model? *Accounting, Auditing & Accountability Journal, 19*(5), 663–680.

Beattie, V., and Pratt, K. (2003). Issues concerning web-based business reporting: An analysis of the views of interested parties. *British Accounting Review, 35*(2), 155–187.

Boixo, I., and Flores, F. (2005). New technical and normative challenges for XBRL: Multidimensionality in the COREP taxonomy. *International Journal of Digital Accounting Research, 5*(9), 79–104.

Bolgiano, M. (2009). Using standards for transparency. *XBRL US Testimony to the Domestic Policy Subcommittee: Oversight and Government Reform committee* Retrieved April, 2009, from http://xbrl.us/documents/XBRL_US_Testimony.pdf.

Bonaccorsi, A., and Rossi, C. (2003). Why open source software can succeed. *Research Policy, 32*(7), 1243–1258.

Bonsón, E., Cortijo, V., and Escobar, T. (2008). The role of XBRL in enhanced business reporting. *Journal of Emerging Technologies in Accounting, 5*, 161–173.

Bovee, M., Ettredge, M. L., Srivastava, R. P., and Vasarhelyi, M. A. (2002). Does the year 2000 XBRL taxonomy accommodate current business financial-reporting practice? *Journal of Information Systems, 16*(2), 165–182.

Caglio, A. (2003). Enterprise resource planning systems and accountants: Towards hybridization? *European Accounting Review, 12*(1), 123–153.

Chung, J. (2008, June 29). US companies shun bar code reporting, *Financial Times*. Retrieved from www.ft.com/cms/s/0/992711e2-45fe-11dd-9009-0000779fd2ac.html.

Cong, Y., Du, H., and Feng, J. (2008). Does web syndication technology facilitate investor decision making? *Journal of Emerging Technologies in Accounting, 5*, 143–159.

Cooren, F. o. (2000). *The organizing property of communication*. Amsterdam: John Benjamins Publishing Co.

Corporate Executive Board. (2012). XBRL: Will this ugly duckling ever become a beautiful swan? *CEB Views*. Retrieved from http://cebviews.com/2012/04/20/idti-xbrl-will-this-ugly-duckling-ever-become-a-beautiful-swan/.

Covaleski, J. M. (2000). The five major accounting firms, American Institute of CPAs, others see XBRL (extensible business report markup language) as maybe being the most revolutionary change in financial reporting since the first general ledger. *Accounting Today, 14*(16), 22.

Cover, R. (2000, April 6). AICPA leads global XBRL initiative. Retrieved January 6, 2005, from http://xml.coverpages.org/XBRL-Ann.html.

Cox, C. (2006). Speech by SEC Chairman to the American Enterprise Institute: The interactive data revolution: Improved disclosure for investors, less expensive reporting for companies. Retrieved May 30, 2009, from www.sec.gov/news/speech/2006/spch053006cc.htm

Cox, C. (2007). Speech by SEC Chairman Christopher Cox: Address to the 16th XBRL International Conference. Retrieved January, 2008, from www.sec.gov/news/speech/2007/spch120307cc.htm.

Cox, C. (January 10, 2008). Speech by SEC Chairman: "International Business—An SEC Perspective" Address to the American Institute of Certified Public Accountants' International Issues Conference Retrieved 26 November, 2008, from www.sec.gov/news/speech/2008/spch011008cc.htm.

Cuneo, E. C. (2002). XBRL: Still a ways away from saving the day; but the standard is seen as an important part of restoring consumer and investor confidence in big business. *Information Week* (Dec 17), 1.

Debreceny, R., Farewell, S., Piechocki, M., Felden, C., and Gräning, A. (2010). Does it add up? Early evidence on the data quality of XBRL filings to the SEC. *Journal of Accounting and Public Policy, 29*(3), 296–306.

Debreceny, R., Felden, C., Ochocki, B., Piechocki, M., and Piechocki, M. (2009). *XBRL for Interactive Data: Engineering the Information Value Chain*. Heidelberg: Springer.

Debreceny, R., and Gray, G. L. (2001). The production and use of semantically rich accounting reports on the Internet: XML and XBRL. *International Journal of Accounting Information Systems, 2*(1), 47–74.

Debreceny, R., Gray, G. L., and Rahman, A. (2002). The determinants of Internet financial reporting. *Journal of Accounting and Public Policy, 21*(4–5), 371–394.

Derby, P. (2005). *Remarks Before the 11th XBRL International Conference: "Better, Faster Smarter Business Reporting Using XBRL."* Paper presented at the 11th XBRL International Conference, Boston. www.sec.gov/news/speech/spch042605pd.htm.

DiPiazza, S. A., and Eccles, R. G. (2002). *Building Public Trust: The Future of Corporate Reporting:* Chichester: John Wiley & Sons.

Downes, L. (2009). *The laws of disruption: Harnessing the new forces that govern life and business in the digital age.* Philadelphia, PA: Basic Books.

Downes, L., and Mui, C. (1998). *Unleashing the Killer App: Digital Strategies for Market Dominance.* Cambridge, MA: Harvard Business Press.

Garthwaite, C. (2000). The language of risk: Why the future of risk reporting is spelled XBRL. *Balance Sheet, 8*(4), 18–20.

Gartner. (2010). *Hype cycle for regulations and related standards* (pp. 1–69). Stamford, CT: Gartner.

Ghani, E. K., Laswad, F., and Tooley, S. (2009). Digital reporting formats: Users' perceptions, preferences and performances. *International Journal of Digital Accounting Research, 9,* 45–98. doi: 10.4192/1577-8517/v9_3.pdf.

Guilloux, V., Locke, J., and Lowe, A. (2012). Digital business reporting standards: Mapping the battle in France. *European Journal of Information Systems, Advance Online Publication,* 1–21.

Hannon, N. (2001). XBRL will spread quickly. *Strategic Finance, 82*(12), 68–69.

Hannon, N. (2002). Accounting scandals: Can XBRL help? *Strategic Finance, 84*(2), 61–62.

Hodge, F. D., Kennedy, J. J., and Maines, L. A. (2004). Does search-facilitating technology improve the transparency of financial reporting? *The Accounting Review, 79*(3), 687–703.

Hoffman, C. (2006). *Financial Reporting Using XBRL: IFRS and US GAAP Edition:* UBMatrix.

Hucklesby, M., and Macdonald, J. (2000). XBRL = Better, faster, cheaper. *Chartered Accountants Journal of New Zealand, 79*(8), 34–36.

Hughes, J. (2008). XBRL: Language to transform communications. *Financial Times: Management Accountancy* Retrieved 14 February, 2008, from www.ft.com/reports/manaccfeb2008.

Jones, M. J., and Xiao, J. Z. (2004). Financial reporting on the Internet by 2010: A consensus view. *Accounting Forum, 28*(3), 237–263.

Kernan, K. (2009). The story of our new language: Personalities, cultures, and politics combine to create a common, global language for business. Retrieved June, 2010, from www.aicpa.org/Professional+Resources/Accounting+and+Auditing/BRAAS/downloads/XBRL_09_web_final.pdf.

Knight, R. (2007). SEC fights financial gobbledygook. *Financial Times.* Retrieved May 27, 2007, from www.ft.com/cms/s/db2c9e70-ff5c-11db-aff2-000b5df10621.html.

Lara, R., Cantador, I., and Castells, P. (2006). XBRL taxonomies and OWL ontologies for investment funds. In J.Roddick, V.Benjamins, S.Si-said Cherfi, R.Chiang, C.Claramunt, R.Elmasri, F.Grandi, H.Han, M.Hepp, M.Lytras, V.Mišic, G.Poels, I.-Y.Song, J.Trujillo, and C.Vangenot (eds), *Advances in Conceptual Modeling – Theory and Practice* (Vol. 4231, pp. 271–280). Berlin: Springer.

Leiba, B. (2008). An introduction to internet standards. *Internet Computing, IEEE, 12*(1), 71–74. doi: 10.1109/mic.2008.2.

Locke, J., and Lowe, A. (2005). *XBRL … A Model Open Source Development? The Crucible and the Crux for Financial Reporting.* Paper presented at ECAIS, Gothenburg, Sweden, 17 May.

Locke, J., and Lowe, A. (2007). Researching XBRL as a socio-technical object. In R.Debreceny, M.Piechocki and C.Felden (eds), *New Dimensions of Business Reporting and XBRL* (pp. 19–56). Wiesbaden: DUV-Verlag, Springer.

Locke, J., Lymer, A., and Lowe, A. D. (2010). *Digital reporting options for Europe: A study of interactive data from the perspective of non-professional investors.* London: ICAEW.

Lowe, A., Locke, J., and Lymer, A. (2012). The SEC's retail investor 2.0: Interactive data and the rise of calculative accountability. *Critical Perspectives on Accounting, 23*(3), 183–200.

Lymer, A., and Debreceny, R. (2003). The auditor and corporate reporting on the internet: Challenges and institutional responses. *International Journal of Auditing, 7*(2), 103–120.

Lyytinen, K., and King, J. L. (2006). Standard making: A critical research frontier for information systems research. *MIS Quarterly, 30*(Supplement), 405–411.

Moyer, P. (2008). XBRL: A magic pill? *California CPA Magazine.* Retrieved December, 2008, from www.calcpa.org/Content/25346.aspx.

Nimmons, A. (2005). XBRL catching on with regulators. *CA Magazine,* www.camagazine.com/2/6/5/3/6/index1.shtml.

Pawlicki, A. (2008). AICPA Assurance Services Executive Committee Whitepaper: The shifting paradigm in business reporting and assurance. Retrieved July, 2009, from www.aicpa.org/Research/StudiesandPapers/DownloadableDocuments/AICPA_ASEC_Whitepaper_Final_20082008April_2008.pdf.

Piechocki, M., Felden, C., Gräning, A., and Debreceny, R. (2009). Design and standardisation of XBRL solutions for governance and transparency. *International Journal of Disclosure and Governance, 6*(3), 224–240.

Quattrone, P., and Hopper, T. (2006). What is *IT*? SAP, accounting, and visibility in a multinational organisation. *Information and Organization, 16*(3), 212–250.

Roth, D. (2009). Road map for financial recovery: Radical transparency now! *Wired.* Retrieved December, 2009, from www.wired.com/techbiz/it/magazine/17-03/wp_reboot?currentPage=all.

SEC. (2009). Interactive data to improve financial reporting: Final rule. Retrieved February, 2009, from www.sec.gov/rules/final/2009/33-9002.pdf.

Shapiro, C., and Varian, H. R. (1999). *Information Rules: A Strategic Guide to the Network Economy.* Boston, MA: Harvard Business School Press.

Spivak, S. M., and Brenner, F. C. (2001). *Spivak, S. M., and Brenner, F. C. Standardization Essentials: Principles and Practice.* New York: Marcel Dekker, Inc.

Srivastava, R. P., and Kogan, A. (2010). Assurance on XBRL instance document: A conceptual framework of assertions. *International Journal of Accounting Information Systems, 11*(3), 261–273. doi: 10.1016/j.accinf.2010.07.019.

Standard Business Reporting. (2009). An Australian Government Initiative: Standard Business Reporting. Retrieved February, 2010, from www.sbr.gov.au.

Starr, M. (2012). SEC iInterview: Inside information. *Interactive Business Reporting, 2*(1), 17–20.

Stewart, N. (2009). Few hiccups so far in XBRL earnings season. *IR Magazine,* July 29.

Stuart, A. (2006). XBRL you can't ignore it anymore: XBR-what? *CFO.com,* from www.cfo.com/article.cfm/7239661/1/c_8310234.

Thomas, A. (2012). AICPA Interview. *Interactive Business Reporting, 2*(1), 12–13.

Unerman, J., and Bennett, M. (2004). Increased stakeholder dialogue and the internet: Towards greater corporate accountability or reinforcing capitalist hegemony? *Accounting, Organizations and Society, 29*(7), 685–707.

Wallman, S. M. H. (1996). The future of accounting and financial reporting Part II: The colorized approach. *Accounting Horizons, 10*(2), 138–148.

Weverka, P., and So, W., S. (2007). *XBRL for Dummies* (limited edition). Hoboken, NJ: Wiley.

White, C. E. (2006). *The Accountant's Guide to XBRL:* SkipWhite.com.

Woodroof, J., and Searcy, D. (2001). Continuous audit: Model development and implementation within a debt covenant compliance domain. *International Journal of Accounting Information Systems, 2*(3), 169–191.

Zhu, K., Kraemer, K. L., Gurbaxani, V., and Xin Xu, S. (2006). Migration to open-standard interorganizational systems: Network effects, switching costs, and path dependency. *MIS Quarterly, 30* (Supplement), 515–539.

Part 4

Construction of meaning

14

A Big Four practitioner view

John Hitchins and Laura Taylor[1]

Introduction

Good communication, both internal and external, is critical to a company's success. Financial results are important in understanding the business and form the bedrock of a company's communication with investors and other stakeholders. But it is not just about the numbers. As well as financial information, corporate reporting comprises non-financial and narrative information. Communications that provide a range of information give stakeholders a clearer picture of a company's business and performance than those that focus purely on finance. Clear communications are particularly important in the current economic climate where there is steep competition to secure investment.

In the UK today, we see large quantities of written corporate communication. When we talk of corporate reporting we traditionally think of press releases and the annual report and accounts, a legal document. This chapter focuses on the annual report, arguably the most important written communication for investors at least, and a form of communication in which companies invest very significant time and effort. However, we should not forget the wider picture of corporate communication and the importance of conveying a company's image in modern society, particularly given the growing trend in social media. The way companies pass on information is vitally important and websites, advertisements, and even commentary on Facebook and Twitter are all important mechanisms for communicating.

Different styles and lengths of communication serve different purposes. In modern society, people demand a constant feed of small pieces of information. A 'tweet' of 140 characters gives an instant nugget of information while commentary on the website about a business activity may be one to four pages. Companies should bear this in mind when preparing information that, due to regulatory requirements, needs to be 10 or 100 times more in length. This would include press releases, which could be as many as 14 pages long, and annual reports at, say, 140 pages or more. While investors need a greater level of detail than a simple tweet, the way information is presented in a longer report is critical to ensure that key messages are put across.

Communication in corporate reporting can be categorized into four levels:

1. The first level is disclosure of the 'bare minimum', that is, meeting accounting (GAAP) and statutory requirements. But communication should not simply be an exercise in compliance; rather it should be a means of providing investors and other stakeholders with a clear understanding of and confidence in a company's operations, strategy and performance.
2. Most companies therefore strive to achieve 'good' GAAP, or level 2, by following disclosure requirements in spirit, rather than only by the letter.

3. This can be supplemented, at a third level, with 'corporate' or narrative reporting that brings the numbers to life. Such communication should be clear and concise and help investors and other stakeholders to differentiate good management from bad, and skill from pure luck.
4. Finally, at the fourth level, is reporting that is fully integrated in its approach and which is likely to provide investors with the best all-round understanding of the business.

Many commentators have debated the subject of communication in corporate reporting. This chapter is structured as follows: A consideration of the current UK reporting position; Communication challenges in annual reports; What information should companies communicate?; Why should companies focus on the way they communicate?; What action should be taken by companies, standard setters and regulators?

A consideration of the current UK reporting position

Information overload! In the twenty-first century we have access to so much information – but how useful is it? Annual reports are ever-increasing in length as companies strive to meet an abundance of disclosure requirements. Consider the report lengths of five FTSE 100 household names in Table 14.1.

Accounting standard development in the last decade has steadily increased disclosure requirements, and legislation has added more on governance, remuneration and sustainability issues, significantly increasing the length of annual reports. Length varies greatly according to a company's particular circumstances (reports of US-listed companies or where there is a complex group structure are likely to be longer) and is not in itself an issue. Many companies understandably aim for levels two ('good' GAAP) and three (narrative explanations) of the four communication categories described above. Yet with many annual reports running to well over 100 pages, the quantity of information reported by the majority of listed companies is certainly significant.

Previous annual reports were not available online for every company sampled above, but for Lloyds Banking Group plc (Lloyds) at least, the size of report has increased significantly over the last decade. In 2000, the annual report and accounts was 77 pages long, in 2005 it was 129 pages, more than doubling to 293 pages in 2010 (Lloyds 2001, 2006, 2011). As explained above, there will be many good reasons for this, including the introduction of new accounting standards, increasing regulation, changes in the nature of the business and changing expectations of good practice.

As reports have grown in length, so has concern that the overall picture presented has become less clear, with more and more detailed information being added into reports. Where companies

Table 14.1 Quick survey of FTSE 100 annual report lengths

	Company	Document	Number of pages
1	BAE Systems plc	Annual report 2010	193
2	BP p.l.c.	Annual report and form 20-F 2010	267[i]
3	J Sainsbury plc	Annual report and financial statements 2011	109
4	Lloyds Banking Group plc	Annual report and accounts 2010	293
5	Marks and Spencer Group plc	Annual report and financial statements 2011	113

Note: i Including parent-company financial statements.

are required to, and/or choose to, present a lot of information, key messages can be lost. Many annual reports are hard to navigate and contain immaterial or repetitive disclosures.

Somewhat ironically, material published in recent years on the subject of streamlining and improving the annual report is plentiful. There is demand for change and innovation and PricewaterhouseCoopers (PwC) explains that this is being driven by forward-looking companies, investors, regulators and government (PwC 2011a: 1). Companies are likely to be aware of the debate but because related publications are discussion or consultation papers, many have not invested time in making changes. Higher priority has to be given to new compulsory reporting requirements, of which there are usually a good number every year.

The Financial Reporting Council (FRC) proposed 'cutting clutter' in corporate reports, that is, reducing immaterial and duplicate information, in order to improve quality a few years ago (FRC 2009). Its discussion paper recommended using common sense to reduce complexity. A project team and advisory panel of experts was put together by the FRC to take the matter further, resulting in a consultation paper. 'Cutting clutter: Combating clutter in annual reports' (FRC 2011a) looks at how companies could remove clutter from annual reports and give prominence to the most relevant information.

The paper identifies two main types of clutter: (i) immaterial information and (ii) explanatory disclosures that remain unchanged from previous years. It encourages further debate and communication with shareholders to understand their information needs. It asks for alternatives, such as the location of explanatory information, to be investigated. The FRC's Financial Reporting Lab aims to address this by bringing management and investors together to develop practical solutions to meet users' needs more effectively (see further below).

Currently, the FRC can only encourage preparers to make changes, but it intends to coordinate its work with that of the government, who is also considering the length and complexity of reporting (ASB 2011). If the Department for Business, Innovation and Skills' (BIS') interesting proposal around the future of narrative reporting became legislation, significant information should be easier to find (2011). The annual report would comprise a 'strategic report', providing key messages about the company's strategy, challenges, results and remuneration, and more detailed, supporting information would be published in an online 'annual directors' statement'.

PwC's practical guide (2011a) sets out other recent initiatives in corporate reporting, including:

- a consultation on the development of an international 'integrated reporting framework' by the International Integrated Reporting Council (2011), focusing on 'value creation' through provision of broad information; and
- a two-year pilot allowing companies to experiment and innovate using the IIRC's integrated reporting framework. This should demonstrate the benefits for companies and investors and define best practice.

Having considered a number of reports and discussion papers recently published in this area, PwC (2011a: 2) identifies common themes: improving transparency and connectivity within the annual report; and removing clutter. Both areas need to be considered if all round improvement is to be achieved.

Communication challenges in annual reports

To understand how communication could be improved, we need first to understand the influences on and challenges faced by companies in their reporting. PwC's practical guide (2011a: 3) suggests improving reports by avoiding immaterial disclosures, removing 'boilerplate' disclosure (there is no point in telling users what they already know) and replacing it with company-specific information, and avoiding duplication (use cross-referencing instead). This sounds straightforward. But, as the FRC explains (2011a: 6), behavioural influences are a barrier to cutting clutter. Consider example Multinational plc, a large group with UK and US listings. Different departments (including experts in IFRS, UK Listing Rules, SEC reporting and divisional heads), contribute to the annual report, each to meet different reporting objectives and requirements. Multinational's investor relations and head office reporting teams coordinate and review reporting, ensuring consistency in style. Illustrative accounts and checklists are used to make sure that nothing is left out. After all, management do not want their report to be questioned by a regulator, for example the Financial Reporting Review Panel (FRRP) or Financial Services Authority (FSA). Management heard that the FFRP reviewed 301 sets of accounts in the year to 31 March 2011 and, of these, 141 companies were approached for further information or explanation (FRRP, 2011). Press releases were only issued to four companies but Multinational's management do not want to risk bad publicity or worse.

Information is duplicated, but due to the report's length, reporting requirements and legislation it is difficult to determine what could be removed. Cross-referencing to similar information elsewhere in the report is complicated, especially as some parts of the report are audited, some are not. Every year, new disclosures are required and because competitors and others are including more information and adhering to good practice (communication levels two and three), Multinational's management decide that more narrative and diagrams should be included.

Management think that some of the information in the annual report is immaterial and, given general interest in this area, wonder how they could reduce their report in length. But where should they start? This will take time and resource; it will cost the company money. Would it not be better, especially in the current economic climate, to focus on the business, on performance and strategy, and look at improving the report next year?

Smaller companies face additional problems. Smaller reporting teams mean even less resource flexibility. It is simpler for preparers to repeat a previous year's disclosure than to stop and think whether it is material or repeats information given elsewhere. It is difficult to determine what is and what is not material and lengthy or difficult discussions with auditors (and potentially regulators) might be avoided if disclosure given in previous years is included again. Most of the effort anyway goes into producing the information in the first place before it can be assessed for materiality. Notably, the FRC (2011a: 23) intends to seek further debate on how materiality should be applied to financial statement disclosures.

The many distinct reporting requirements are a barrier to effective communication. Coherent reporting would be facilitated by a more connected regulatory model that helped companies to integrate their reporting, and reach the fourth level of our communication structure. The current model is complex, with different and overlapping requirements from company law, IFRS, listing rules, voluntary codes and good practice. This can lead to information, for example financial risk disclosures, being presented in a disjointed piecemeal way. Even within IFRS there is no overall framework setting out the principles of what makes useful disclosure. The creation of such a framework is one of the projects the IASB has recently consulted on with a view to setting its future agenda priorities but even if completed it would only cover the accounting standards, not other regulation affecting company reporting. Similarly, it is difficult to radically improve structure because the annual report needs to be capable of being printed, for filing at Companies House. Without this requirement, navigation through long reports could be made easier by using links online. A similar problem arises from the auditing regulatory model: to decrease litigation risk, audited and non-audited information needs to be clearly identified.

Many companies say that it would only be worth cutting clutter and improving transparency and connectivity after a fundamental rethink. In many ways this makes sense given that changing behaviour takes time, resource and effort. Companies need to be convinced that they will benefit from changing their communications.

What information should companies communicate?

Corporate ('level 3'), as opposed to purely financial, reporting helps to put the numbers in context and tells us much more about a business. It helps if information can be substantiated so that investors can trust what is presented. Research indicates substantial economic benefit where information is transparent: companies should 'tell it how it is'. To help attract the reader's attention, reports should have a coherent structure and be clear and concise. Companies will gain from providing quality, as opposed to quantity, of information. These principles are broadly similar to the principles of effective communication that the FRC mentions in its report, 'namely that reports should be: open and honest; clear and understandable; and interesting and engaging' (2011a: 31). It is helpful to bear all these principles in mind as we consider what information companies should communicate.

PricewaterhouseCoopers has invested more than a decade of research in this area, performing global industry surveys to question investors, analysts and companies about information that is needed to understand the quality and sustainability of performance. As a result, two models have been developed to encourage transparent, relevant reporting. The models, described by DiPiazza and Eccles (2002) and PwC (2011c), highlight the need for non-financial information and information that is specific to a particular company's circumstances. Working at the third level of our communication categories, PwC's straightforward model of corporate transparency in Figure 14.1 recommends development of communication across three tiers.

By way of example, under tier two, industry-specific metrics for a retail company could be sales per square foot, number of new stores opened, or average footfall, and in the investment property industry could be total property return. Such metrics would provide relevant contextual information for consideration alongside the financial statements themselves.

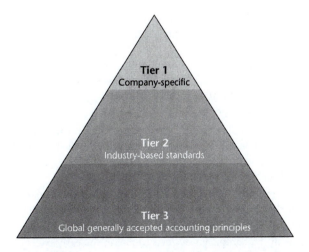

Figure 14.1 PricewaterhouseCoopers' Three-tier model of corporate transparency
Source: DiPiazza and Eccles (2002: 39)

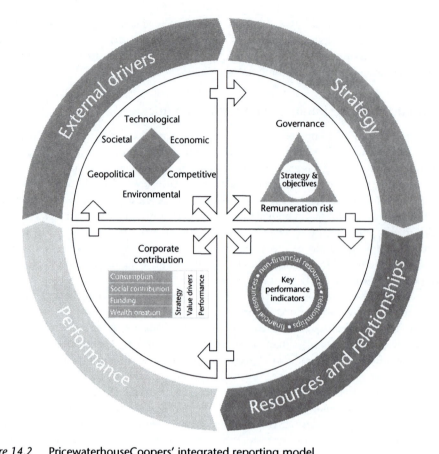

Figure 14.2   PricewaterhouseCoopers' integrated reporting model
Source: PwC (2011c: 5)

As a result of PwC's research over recent years, this three-tier model has evolved considerably. Illustrating the fourth level in our communication structure, PwC's integrated reporting model is shown in Figure 14.2.

The integrated reporting model covers four broad areas: external drivers (including the market, environmental and social issues), corporate strategy, resources and relationships and business and financial results. But, as PwC explains, integrated reporting is more than just a collection of statements covering these areas, an integrated report provides a holistic picture of a company's performance and prospects: 'a strategic picture of the business that explains how a business creates and sustains value now and in the future' (2011c: 5). An integrated report explains stewardship of all major capital in the business (not only financial capital, but also, for example, human and intellectual capital).

We return to our example company, Multinational plc, whose management decide to use the integrated reporting model to help determine what to disclose. The company is a retailer with a broad product base and a reputation for all-round quality. Management decide to give a high-level overview of the company's business model in the early pages of the report.

The overview explains key priorities over the past year and looking forward, including the company's growth strategy, not just for the next three years, but also longer term. This includes specific targets for new stores, store expansions and plans for overseas expansion. There is a summary of external influences on the company, including details of the competitive environment (market share) and the impact of current and expected future economic conditions on the retail market.

The overview explains how the company measures its success, and its progress against strategy. The summary of financial and non-financial key performance indicators (KPIs) includes graphical presentation of results. The overview highlights that a key indicator, revenue, has increased by 5 per cent during the year. This is a couple of percentage points higher than its competitors' results this year, but the report explains that this was driven by a significant acquisition and overseas expansion. The company wants to preserve its brand and reputation for quality and therefore selects its suppliers carefully and is fair in its trading with them. It is also looking to improve its carbon emissions and waste levels. It has non-financial KPIs relating to this. Multinational has a reputation for looking after both its staff and customers, hence the report explains the new staff development programme, staff retention targets and results as well as the results of recent customer satisfaction surveys. The report goes on to explain the impact that the company's strategy and results have had on remuneration.

Only headline information is presented in the overview, but clear references from each part point the reader to the pages where more detail on each subject can be found. Further on in the report, more detailed narrative and financial information explains segment priorities and results. The report is connected and transparent, allowing investors to assess the company's current position as well as its future prospects. Although hypothetical, the Multinational example illustrates how a 'level four', coherent reporting structure will help investors understand what is driving the results.

Why should companies focus on the way they communicate?

Good disclosure is essential if companies are to secure investment in the current economic climate. In 2012, for example, there was intense competition for obtaining investment and also re-financing this year (for example, significant volumes of five-year loans taken out in 2007 (before the credit crunch) matured in 2012). In order to obtain finance, and do so at reasonable cost, companies will do well to provide clear disclosures, particularly in relation to cash and debt (PwC 2012a).

What other benefits are there of good reporting? Phillips and Thomas (2004: 4) describe economic benefits across three areas: better decision making, lower share price volatility and cost of capital; and better stakeholder engagement. Communications that are transparent, credible and relevant should give investors more confidence in their analysis and allow them to take a longer-term view, reducing the risk of short-term share-price volatility. In theory, if investors have more confidence in the quality of performance and have information that gives them confidence in forecasting, they should demand lower returns, thus improving the company's cost of capital. This is illustrated in the case study set out on page 220 (Thomas: 2003/4).

This case study illustrates comprehensive reporting that gives investors confidence in the business and its operations and systems. Coloplast was rewarded by Schroder's investment team for providing substantive evidence of good overall corporate performance. Investors with the full information set were more confident in their forecasts and awarded a higher valuation to the stock, hence the propensity towards 'buy' recommendations. This full information set is what companies should strive towards in corporate reporting.

Phillips and Thomas (2004: 5) explain that users ask consistently for 'better non-financial data that would allow them to set financial performance in context'. The benefits described in the case study above are likely to be of great financial significance but there are other ways in which a company may benefit, for example in being able to attract and retain the best in the workforce or improved customer loyalty. Philips and Thomas (2004) present the results of a number of studies.

Case study: A tale of two reports

In 2003, PricewaterhouseCoopers presented two versions of Danish healthcare company Coloplast A/S's 2001/2002 report and accounts to the investment team at Schroder Asset Management. The investment team was split into two separate groups. One group was given a comprehensive performance report, including the financial reports and the quantified non-financial information that Coloplast voluntarily provides in its report. The other group was given the more typical information found in annual reports: the financial statements, a description of strategy, engagement with stakeholders and the innovation process. Each investor was asked to produce revenue and earnings forecasts, to give a recommendation on the shares and comment on relative risk, explaining their reasons.

Those with the broader range of information generated lower economic estimates than those with the regulatory document. Surprisingly, however, despite the lower economic estimate, over 60 per cent of those with the more comprehensive report would buy the shares. Conversely, over 80 per cent of those who saw only the regulatory document said they would sell them.

Investors who had access to a more comprehensive picture of overall corporate performance, including non-financial information, were far more confident in their forecasts and felt that Coloplast's stock was no more risky than its peers. The group presented with just the financial data perceived Coloplast to be 'above average sector risk'.

PricewaterhouseCoopers' Global Human Capital Survey shows that those companies with a documented, and therefore embedded, human-resources strategy generate 35 per cent more revenues per employee, have 12 per cent lower rates of absenteeism and more efficient performance management systems. Phillips and Thomas (2004: 5) explain that McKinsey & Co demonstrated in 1999 that companies with strong brands generate, on average, returns to shareholders that are 1.9 per cent above the industry average, while weaker brands lag behind the average by 3.1 per cent. They go on to cite a 1999 University of Michigan study that has shown that for a *Business Week* 1000 company with average assets of about US$10 billion, a 1 per cent increase in customer satisfaction was associated with an increase in firm value of about US$275 million (Phillips and Thomas 2004: 5).

What action should be taken by companies, standard setters and regulators?

It is easy to explain the many ways in which reporting could be improved. But achieving widespread change in mindset will not be easy. Indeed, the FRC expects this to be a longer-term undertaking (2009: 12). Some companies, however, are already successfully experimenting with the structure of their reports within the constraints of existing legal and regulatory reporting requirements, and are tackling clutter.

As a forum to debate and experiment with new reporting formats, The Financial Reporting Lab aims to provide evidence and create ideas for more effective communication. Although in the early stages, we should look forward to the results. The FRC (2011b: 2) has indicated that its initial projects could make a significant difference to the usefulness of financial statements and that, at least for some companies, improvements should be at relatively low cost.

Actions for companies

Companies should not be complacent: even small changes can improve reporting. Given current debate, companies should think now about whether and how they meet user needs. Taking the principles of the integrated reporting model and cutting clutter as good practice, information can be presented in a way that is accessible and credible. Companies should initially start experimenting with a clearer structure and greater transparency in their reports. Having achieved this it will be easier to determine how and where to cut clutter.

ARM Holdings plc (2010) won PricewaterhouseCoopers' Building Public Trust Award 2011, 'Excellence in reporting in the FTSE 100'. Its annual report is described as engaging, highly readable and accessible. The front half is well-structured: sections are easy to navigate and the awards brochure states that the 'plain language – "How ARM makes money" – is especially refreshing' (PwC 2011b: 6). The company effectively communicates information around the market and strategy. Graphs and diagrams illustrate results and break up the narrative and the personal perspectives of senior employees help to explain ARM's complex business model. Highly commended in the same awards, National Grid plc's (2011) report uses graphics to help explain and clarify the company's different markets and regulatory environments, with a clear emphasis on strategy and performance against objectives.

Man Group plc has experimented with the structure of financial information. The financial review includes key notes grouped around the related primary statements and aims to give 'salient information.. in a format that explains the relationships between funds under management, margins, profit, cash flow and capital which underpin [the Group's].. sustainable business model' (Man Group plc 2011: 56). Other information (such as cash flow, taxation and discontinued operations notes) is included within 'Additional financial information' and the group states that the information in this latter section could just be stated online because, while important, it is less significant for understanding the business. Readers may initially be unsure about a layout that breaks with tradition, but it gives a clear picture of what directors consider the most significant financial information.

ITV plc (2011: 69) has provided a more straightforward structure, giving readers '… a clearer understanding of what drives financial performance..'. The accounting notes in its 2010 report have been grouped into reporting areas: results for the year, operating assets and liabilities, and capital structure and financing costs. Accounting policies are grouped with relevant notes and text in speech bubbles explains the content in each section. Similarly, other companies, such as ICAP plc (2011) and Schroders plc (2011), have positioned accounting policies with the relevant notes to the accounts. In the coming reporting season we expect more companies to reorder their reports in this way and also to give greater prominence to the more significant accounting policies and notes and relegate others to the end of the annual report.

Cutting clutter describes many areas offering good opportunities to reduce immaterial information, including the directors' report, principal risks, CSR reporting, financial instruments, post-retirement benefits and intangibles. Suggestions include presenting standing statutory information in an appendix and incorporating it into the directors' report by cross-reference. Financial instrument risk disclosures could be reduced by addressing only those risks that are material to the entity, rather than a detailed list of every possible risk (FRC 2011a: 42). Cutting clutter's disclosure aids include further recommendations to make changes clear and highlight significant points (for example, explicitly stating whether or not the adoption of new standards has resulted in a material change to the financial statements).

Clutter can be reduced by signposting to where disclosures that are not significant and not specifically required by legislation can be found, for example, on the company's website.

The back page of The Sage Group plc's (Sage's) 2011 annual report directs readers to a digital version of the report for a 'richer experience and enhanced content' that includes case study videos, page preview and thumbnail views, search tools and quick links (Sage 2011: 124). The front half of the report refers to online videos that supplement case studies showing how priorities are delivered on (Sage 2011: 24–35).

Great Portland Estates plc's (2011) annual report is another example of coherent, well-structured reporting. Pages six and seven give an overview of priorities in action in 2010/2011 and priorities for the coming year with clear cross-referencing through to other parts of the report where more information can be found. Moving with the times, Wolseley plc's (2011) annual report includes quick response (QR) codes to allow users to access extra content online via their smartphone. ICAP plc's (2011) annual report uses a ten point overview of the company, explaining what it does and how it has performed. The information is high level, but with clear signposting to where more information can be found.

The importance of transparent cash and debt disclosure was mentioned above. National Grid plc's annual report goes beyond our 'level 2', or 'good' GAAP in providing additional information not required by financial reporting standards or legislation, in the form of an analysis of changes in net debt (2011: 151). The note is reproduced in Figure 14.3, with annotations illustrating why it is effective (PwC 2012c). Reformatting information can be just as effective in cutting clutter as removing unnecessary data.

PricewaterhouseCoopers (2011c) has identified four ways to take reporting forward now – see Figure 14.4. Companies should be encouraged to get involved in joining the debate, experimenting and innovating in order to influence the future.

Actions for standard setters and regulators

A broad public debate about the corporate reporting model is needed if effective communication, at 'level four', is to become widespread. This chapter has, until now, focussed on UK reporting, but such debate could beneficially take place internationally, with UK involvement. The IIRC has proposed broadening the integrated reporting model such that an organization's strategy, governance and financial performance would be reported in the context of its social, environmental and economic background, thus addressing sustainability in its broadest sense. Such reassessment of the whole model will, however, take time and is likely to necessitate changes to law and other requirements.

Regulators and standard setters should, in the meantime, think about whether the reporting burden could be reduced or simplified and should explore both regulatory and non-regulatory options when considering how to improve the reporting model. It is important to consider what any changes might cost a company, versus any potential benefit.

PricewaterhouseCoopers' response to BIS's consultation on narrative reporting (2011d) says that a consolidated picture of risk, funding and performance, brought together by narrative, financial and non-financial information, should be encouraged. It is not logical, for example, for the different elements that explain how a company is funded to be spread across various parts of the report. The emphasis from regulators and standard setters should therefore be less on where information is located in the report, and more on its quality, accessibility and understandability. A high-level strategic report setting out the directors' key messages, directing readers to all the other elements of information reported, including standing data on a company's website, seems a sensible way to proceed.

(d) Analysis of changes in net debt

	Cash and cash equivalents £m	Bank overdrafts £m	Net cash and cash equivalents £m	Financial investments £m	Borrowings £m	Derivatives £m	Total* £m
At 31 March 2008	174	(10)	164	2,095	(20,993)	1,093	(17,641)
Cash flow	545	(7)	538	(184)	(1,316)	716	(246)
Fair value gains and losses and exchange movements	18	–	18	207	(3,222)	(628)	(3,625)
Interest charges	–	–	–	79	(1,245)	5	(1,161)
At 31 March 2009	737	(17)	720	2,197	(26,776)	1,186	(22,673)
Cash flow	(16)	(12)	(28)	(826)	2,079	(560)	665
Fair value gains and losses and exchange movements	(1)	–	(1)	2	644	220	865
Interest charges	–	–	–	24	(1,042)	22	(996)
At 31 March 2010	720	(29)	(691)	1,397	(25,095)	868	(22,139)
Cash flow	(333)	(13)	(346)	1,551	2,933	(133)	4,005
Fair value gains and losses and exchange movements	(3)	–	(3)	(34)	402	325	690
Interest charges	–	–	–	25	(1,337)	84	(1,228)
Reclassified as held for sale	–	–	–	–	9	–	9
Other non-cash movements	–	–	–	–	(68)	–	(68)
At 31 March 2011	384	(42)	342	2,939	(23,156)	1,144	(18,731)
Balances at 31 March 2011 comprise:							
Non-current assets	–	–	–	–	–	1,270	1,270
Current assets	384	–	384	2,939	–	468	3,791
Current liabilities	–	(42)	(42)	–	(2,910)	(190)	(3,142)
Non-current liabilities	–	–	–	–	(20,246)	(404)	(20,650)
	384	(42)	342	2,939	(23,156)	1,144	(18,731)

(i) Includes accrued interest at 31 March 2011 of £162m (2010: £232m).

Provides a clear breakdown of the components of net debt

Gives a clear analysis of the factors impacting the movement in net debt in the year

Gives a clear breakdown of net debt by asset and liability, current and non-current

Figure 14.3 Extract from Annual Report and Accounts 2010/11, National Grid plc

Sources: Note 27.(d): Analysis of changes in net debt (National Grid plc 2011: 151) and PricewaterhouseCoopers (forthcoming)

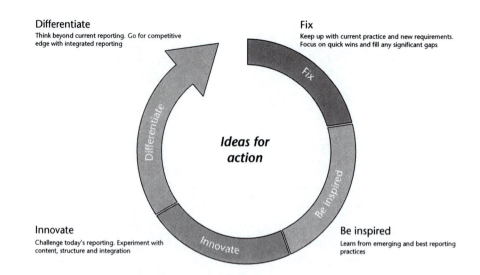

Differentiate
Think beyond current reporting. Go for competitive edge with integrated reporting

Fix
Keep up with current practice and new requirements. Focus on quick wins and fill any significant gaps

Ideas for action

Innovate
Challenge today's reporting. Experiment with content, structure and integration

Be inspired
Learn from emerging and best reporting practices

Figure 14.4 PricewaterhouseCoopers' Ideas for action
Source: PwC (2011c: 10)

Incentives might encourage companies to move forward and experiment in more transparent reporting. Correspondingly, use of benchmarking could be an appropriate way of challenging weak performers to improve their reporting. PwC (2011d) notes that this is already happening in the private equity industry, where the Guidelines Monitoring Group reviews companies applying the Walker Guidelines (2010).

Conclusion

Generally speaking, it is difficult for investors to identify, and therefore reward, well-managed companies because there is considerable room for improvement in corporate reporting. This is not least because of the UK's regulatory framework. But corporate reporting should not be a compliance exercise. In the short term, companies should be encouraged, and rewarded for, taking steps to improve their communications and striving for what we have called 'level four', or integrated reporting. Many improvements in structure and transparency can be made without new regulation.

Commentators agree that good reporting is concise, transparent and provides sufficient detail to demonstrate the quality and sustainability of a company's position and performance. We have seen that good communication can provide economic benefit. Good all-round reporting helps investors to make better informed decisions.

In the longer term, we anticipate the development of a more holistic model for corporate reporting. An improved model will need to be straightforward yet suitable for all, and able to respond to the changing needs of global capital markets.

Note

1 John Hitchins is a Partner at PricewaterhouseCoopers LLP and Laura Taylor is a Senior Manager at PricewaterhouseCoopers LLP. However, this chapter represents the authors' personal opinions only,

and does not necessarily represent the opinion of PricewaterhouseCoopers LLP nor any other firm within the PricewaterhouseCoopers network of firms. This chapter has been prepared for general guidance on matters of interest only, and does not constitute professional advice. You should not act upon the information contained in this publication without obtaining specific professional advice. No representation or warranty (express or implied) is given as to the accuracy or completeness of the information contained in this publication, and, to the extent permitted by law, the author, publishers and PricewaterhouseCoopers firms do not accept or assume any liability, responsibility or duty of care for any consequences of you or anyone else acting, or refraining to act, in reliance on the information contained in this publication or for any decision based on it.

References

Accounting Standards Board (ASB) of the Financial Reporting Council (FRC) (2011) *ASB publishes report on cutting clutter from annual reports. ASB Press Notice 362.* Online. Available HTTP: www.frc.org.uk/asb/press/pub2566.html (accessed 4 January 2012).

Addleshaw Goddard, in assoc. with bvca (2010) *The Walker guidelines for disclosure and transparency in private equity: report and accounts checklist for portfolio companies.* Online. Available HTTP: www.walker-gmg.co.uk/sites/10051/files/The-Walker-Guidelines-June%202010.pdf (accessed 18 January 2012).

ARM Holdings plc (2011) *Annual report and accounts 2010.* Online. Available HTTP: www.media.corporate-ir.net/media_files/irol/19/197211/626-1_ARM_AR_040311.pdf (accessed 17 January 2012).

BAE Systems plc (2011) *Annual report 2010.* Online. Available HTTP: www.bae-systems-investor-relations.production.investis.com/en/media/Files/B/BAE-Systems-Investor-Relations-2009/PDFs/results-and-reports/reports/2011/ar-2010.pdf (accessed 17 January 2012).

BIS (Department for Business, Innovation and Skills) (2011) *The future of narrative reporting: consulting on a new reporting framework.* London: BIS. Online. Available HTTP: www.bis.gov.uk/assets/biscore/business-law/docs/f/11-945-future-of-narrative-reporting-consulting-new-framework.pdf (accessed 12 January 2012).

BP p.l.c. (2011) *Annual report and form 20-F 2010.* Online. Available HTTP: www.bp.com/assets/bp_internet/globalbp/globalbp_uk_english/set_branch/STAGING/common_assets/downloads/pdf/BP_Annual_Report_and_Form_20F.pdf (accessed 17 January 2012).

DiPiazza Jr, S. A. and Eccles, R. G. (2002) *Building public trust: the future of corporate reporting.* New York: John Wiley & Sons, Inc.

Financial Reporting Council (FRC) (2009) *Louder than words: principles and actions for making corporate reports less complex and more relevant.* London: FRC. Online. Available HTTP: www.frc.org.uk/images/uploaded/documents/FRC%20DiscussionPaper%20louder%20than%20words.pdf (accessed 4 January 2012).

Financial Reporting Council (FRC) (2011a) *Cutting clutter: Combating clutter in annual reports.* London: Addison. Online. Available HTTP: www.frc.org.uk/images/uploaded/documents/Cutting%20clutter%20report%20April%2020112.pdf (accessed 4 January 2012).

Financial Reporting Council (FRC) (2011b) *A guide to the Financial Reporting Lab.* London: FRC. Online. Available HTTP: www.frc.org.uk/images/uploaded/documents/frc%20lab%20leaflet%20final1.pdf (accessed 4 January 2012).

Financial Reporting Council (FRC) (2011c) *Update from the Financial Reporting Lab.* London: FRC. Online. Available HTTP: www.frc.org.uk/documents/pagemanager/frc/Financial_Reporting_Lab/201111%20-%20FRL%20Update.pdf (accessed 18 January 2012).

Financial Reporting Review Panel of the Financial Reporting Council (FRRP) (2011) *Annual Report 2011.* London: FRRP. Online. Available HTTP: www.frc.org.uk/images/uploaded/documents/FRRP%20Annual%20Report%202011%20final.pdf (accessed 4 January 2012).

Great Portland Estates plc (2011) *Annual report 2011.* Online. Available HTTP: www.gpe-annualreport.co.uk/ (accessed 17 January 2012).

ICAP plc (2011) *Annual report for the year ended 31 March 2011.* Online. Available HTTP: www.icap.com/investor-relations/annual-reports-and-publications.aspx (accessed 17 January 2012).

International Integrated Reporting Council, 2011. *Towards integrated reporting: communicating value in the 21st century.* Online. Available HTTP: www.theiirc.org/wp-content/uploads/2011/09/IR-Discussion-Paper-2011_spreads.pdf (accessed 6 January 2012).

ITV plc (2011) *Report and accounts 2010*. Online. Available HTTP: www.2010.itv.ar.ry.com/?id=73624 (accessed 18 January 2012).

J Sainsbury plc (2011) *Annual report and financial statements 2011*. Online. Available HTTP: www.annualreport2011.j-sainsbury.co.uk/downloads/pdf/sainsburys_ar11_full.pdf (accessed 17 January 2012).

Lloyds Banking Group plc (2001) *Annual report and accounts 2000*. Online. Available HTTP: www.lloyds-bankinggroup.com/media/pdfs/investors/2000/2000_LTSB_Group_R&A.pdf (accessed 17 January 2012).

Lloyds Banking Group plc (2006) *Annual report and accounts 2005*. Online. Available HTTP: www.lloydsbankinggroup.com/media/pdfs/investors/2005/2005_LTSB_Group_R&A.pdf (accessed 17 January 2012).

Lloyds Banking Group plc (2011) *Annual report and accounts 2010*. Online. Available HTTP: www.report 2011.mangroupplc.com/downloads/pdf/full_report.pdf (accessed 17 January 2012).

Man Group plc (2011) *Annual report for the financial year ended 31 March 2011*. Online. Available HTTP: www.lloydsbankinggroup.com/media/pdfs/investors/2005/2005_LTSB_Group_R&A.pdf (accessed 17 January 2012).

Marks and Spencer Group plc (2011) *Annual report and financial statements 2011*. Online. Available HTTP: www.corporate.marksandspencer.com/documents/publications/2011/annual%20report%202011 (accessed 20 February 2013).

National Grid plc (2011) *Annual report and accounts 2010/11*. Online. Available HTTP: www.nationalgrid.com/NR/rdonlyres/14D2D31C-7F56-4D6F-B661-A762BAB714F7/47190/ng_annualreportandaccounts_201011_Mid12.pdf (accessed 17 January 2012).

Pearsall, J. and Trumble, B. (eds) (1996) *The Oxford English Reference Dictionary*, 2nd edn. Oxford: Oxford University Press.

Phillips, D. M. H. and Thomas, A. (2004) Corporate governance: a reporting perspective, *Global Corporate Governance Guide 2004: best practice in the boardroom,* Global White Page (consulting editor Barry Metzger).

PricewaterhouseCoopers (PwC) (2011a) *Practical Guide to IFRS: streamlining the annual report*. London: PwC. Online. Available HTTP: www.pwcinform.pwc.com/inform2/show?action=informContent&id=1156122112168308&highlighted=yes&pg=sec (accessed 11 January 2012).

PricewaterhouseCoopers (PwC) (2011b) *Building Public Trust: 'Excellence in reporting' awards. Showing the way forward*. London: PwC. Online. Available HTTP: www.bptawards.com/bpta-2011-post-awards-brochure.pdf (accessed 11 January 2012).

PricewaterhouseCoopers (PwC) (2011c) *Corporate reporting: from compliance to competitive edge*. London: PwC. Online. Available HTTP: www.pwc.com/en_GX/gx/corporate-reporting/assets/pdfs/Thought.piece.survey.Competitive.Edge.2011.pdf (accessed 12 January 2012).

PricewaterhouseCoopers (PwC) (2011d) *The future of narrative reporting: consulting on a new reporting framework* (Comment letter in response to the Department of Business, Skills and Innovation consultation on the future of narrative reporting), London: PwC. Online. Available HTTP: www.pwcinform.pwc.com/inform2/show?action=informContent&id=1222274401105680 (accessed 27 January 2012).

PricewaterhouseCoopers (PwC) (2012a) *Technical update: Investor view 20: How to win the competition for capital*. Online. Available HTTP: www.pwcinform.pwc.com/inform2/show?action=informContent&id=1239245501161936&lid=1242194301109360 (accessed 27 January 2012).

PricewaterhouseCoopers (PwC) (2012b) *Investor view 20: How to win the competition for capital*. Online. Available HTTP: www.pwcinform.pwc.com/inform2/show?action=applyInformContentTerritory&id=1242194301109360&tid=1 (accessed 27 January 2012).

PricewaterhouseCoopers (PwC) (forthcoming) extract from National Grid plc (2011), Note 27.(d) Analysis of changes in net debt, *Annual report 2010/11,* annotations by PwC. Available HTTP: www.corporatereporting.pwc.com/uk/trends/trends.nsf/id/BTUR-8TPE8V/$file/NAT%20GRID_net%20debt%20APRIL%202012%20FINAL.pdf (accessed 20 February 2013).

The Sage Group plc (2011) *Annual report and accounts 2011*. Online. Available HTTP: www.asp-gb.secure-zone.net/v2/index.jsp?id=624/1708/4067&lng=en (accessed 17 January 2012).

Schroders plc (2011) *Annual report and accounts 2011*. Online. Available HTTP: www.annualreport2010.schroders.com/servicepages/welcome.html (accessed 17 January 2012).

Thomas, A. (2003) Assessing the benefits of corporate transparency. *International Journal of Business Performance Management,* 5(2/3): 174–187.

Thomas, A. (2003/4) Sounding board: A tale of two reports. *EBF,* 16: 79–81.

Thomas, A. (2005) A perspective on corporate governance reporting. *Professional Investor*, January: 25–28.

Wikipedia (2012) *Communication*. Online. Available HTTP: www.en.wikipedia.org/wiki/Communication (accessed 4 January 2012).

Wolseley plc (2011) *Annual report and accounts 2011*. Online. Available HTTP: www.wolseley.com/files/pdf/reports/annualreport/WOS-AR-2011.pdf (accessed 17 January 2012).

15

Argument, audit and principles-based accounting

Wally Smieliauskas

Introduction

The objective of this chapter is to outline the role of argumentation in justifying fairness of presentation (true and fair presentation) in accounting communication, specifically general purpose financial reporting. This justification is especially important from an independent, external auditing perspective in which fairness of presentation needs to be made auditable. This quality of being auditable is an important consideration because the International Organization of Securities Commissions (IOSCO 2008: 3) has noted, "The independent audit function is a contributor to investor confidence in the capital markets." Since the expressions "present fairly" (or "true and fair") are overriding indicators of financial reporting quality but are not defined in professional standards, I propose a partial definition via a more specific principle of measurement risk as part of the argument that supports the audit opinion on fairness of presentation under principles-based accounting.

An argument is implied by the International Federation of Accountants' (IFAC) International Standard on Auditing (ISA) 700, "Forming an Opinion and Reporting on Financial Statements," when an independent, external auditor claims the opinion is based on sufficient and appropriate audit evidence that has been obtained by the auditor. Argumentation is the chief means of justifying professional judgments with principles-based accounting. Auditors therefore need to provide and document good reasons for fairness of presentation using principles-based accounting. These reasons and the reasoning process are communicated in natural language such as English or Mandarin. The communication can take the form of audit file documentation, verbal defence of professional judgments in courts, in disciplinary hearings, and to regulators. Argumentation is the analysis of a reasoning process in natural language. Argumentation is the basis of the reasoning system in law, the social sciences, the arts, and humanities.

Reasoning in natural language means being able to show or demonstrate that a statement is true. This is achieved by argument. An argument is a series of statements that purport to support the truth of another statement, the conclusion (claim). Statements that purport to establish the conclusion are referred to as the premises of the argument. This is the reasoning process in natural language. This is how one rationally justifies a conclusion or claim in natural language.

Accounting is frequently referred to as the "language of business." This language is intended to facilitate economic decision making and the efficient operation of markets. The global expansion of trade and investment has created unprecedented integration and interdependencies in the world economy. These economic interdependencies have in turn created a virtually irresistible demand for a common, consistent set of accounting concepts on which to base global accounting standards. Such harmonized standards increasingly tend to rely on more general principles than on detailed rules of accounting that have evolved in different countries.

The Institute of Chartered Accountants of Scotland (ICAS 2006) has done more to promote principles-based accounting to serve as a basis of globalized accounting communication than perhaps any other individual accounting organization. In particular, I rely on ICAS (2006) for its excellent review and analysis of the issues and their conclusions. Specifically, I use the following of their conclusions:

1. Principles-based accounting best meets the needs of the public interest.
2. Principles-based accounting requires a clear hierarchy of overarching concepts.
3. Principles-based accounting requires taking more responsibility for auditor judgments.
4. Principles-based judgments need to be documented and disclosed.

The above recommendations assume that their adoption will encourage a new mindset among professionals to make sound and ethical judgments in the overriding interest of fair presentation.

The rest of this chapter reviews in greater detail the nature of argumentation to achieve this objective.

The influence of the concept of principles-based accounting standards can be seen in the International Accounting Standards Board's (IASB) conceptual framework project. This project is explicitly geared to developing principles-based standards:

> Our goal—which we share with our constituents—is for our standards to be based on consistent and appropriate principles. To provide the best foundation for developing principle-based standards, we undertook this project to establish an improved conceptual framework. We have set out to develop a conceptual framework that is rooted in fundamental economic concepts rather than one based on a collection of arbitrary conventions.
>
> *(IASB 2010: 2)*

Interestingly, the U.S. public company accounting standard setter, the Financial Accounting Standards Board (FASB), is also adopting the same conceptual framework as the IASB. Although the FASB does not refer to the conceptual framework as leading to principles-based accounting, it is clear that making the framework authoritative for legal purposes (codification) would over time lead to standards that are principles-based (FASB 2010: 2).

Inherent in the above ICAS principles is the need for an argument to justify a particular accounting treatment in specific circumstances. This is especially important for external independent auditors whose function would be to verify conformity with principles-based accounting. Logically, it is more straightforward to verify the accuracy of factual information such as the count of cash or inventory, or conformity with some detailed accounting rule than it is to verify that the rule is not misleading. Identifying a single-point estimate as a fair presentation of a range of possible future outcomes means that using the estimate is not misleading. How is this done? This issue is becoming increasingly common in global fair-value accounting and is an example of the kinds of accounting communication issues principles-based accounting should be addressing. But are they? At this time, no. The conceptual framework is only partially completed with major controversial issues, such as appropriate accounting measurement and disclosures, still to be addressed. However, with some argumentation concepts it is possible to outline the nature of the reasoning process auditors and preparers of financial information would need to follow in order to justify particular accounting treatments.

The next section reviews relevant general argumentation concepts and issues that can be used by standard setters, regulators, auditors, preparers, and students of accounting communications. The third section then concludes with an outline of the accounting argumentation required in the audit of principles-based accounting communications. The accounting argumentation proposed in this section uses concepts that: highlight the importance of future events in financial reporting (Beaver 1991), have as a central feature the accounting for uncertainty of future events (Savage and Van Allen 2002), and incorporate features of the increasingly influential field of risk or probability management (Hubbard 2009). Smieliauskas et al. (2010) indicate how the acceptable levels of accounting risks associated with future events can affect fairness of presentation. For this reason, I identify it as a specific principle in outlining the argumentation to be used in principles-based financial reporting.

Key concepts of argumentation for accountants

A common example of a conclusion about the quality of accounting communication that an auditor claims is justified is the following standardized opinion wording under ISA 700:

> In our opinion, the financial statements present fairly, in all material respects, the financial position of ABC Company as of December 31, 20XY, and of its financial performance and its cash flows for the year then ended in accordance with an appropriate financial reporting framework (specific framework such as Canadian generally accepted accounting principles needs to be specified).

The above excerpt is the conclusion of an auditor's report. Other parts of the report explain in general terms the nature of the audit process, and management vs. auditor responsibilities. The auditor's responsibility is to express an opinion on the accounting communication, as illustrated above. This opinion needs to be supported by audit evidence, as indicated by the following sentence in the standardized audit report: "We believe that the audit evidence we have obtained is sufficient and appropriate to provide a basis for our audit opinion." Audit evidence that supports the audit opinion as specified in the ISA 700 report includes: "… evaluating the appropriateness of accounting policies used and the reasonableness of accounting estimates made by management, as well as evaluating the overall presentation of financial statements."

Inductive and epistemic probabilites

The written conclusion in an auditor's report, the audit opinion, is justified in statements or "argumentation" in which reasoning actively organizes thoughts to support the conclusion. The truthfulness of an audit opinion is dependent on the truthfulness of other statements (premises). If the premises are acceptable rationally and the argument has logical strength, then there is a sound argument. The strength of the link between the premises and the conclusion can be summarized by the concept of the *inductive probability* of the argument: that is, the probability that the conclusion is true *if* the premises are true (Skyrms 1986, 11). The inductive probability applies to the argument as a whole (similar to the overall evaluation stated in an audit opinion). However, an auditor is interested usually in the *truthfulness* of a conclusion itself, or the *epistemic probability* of the conclusion. The *epistemic probability* of the conclusion is a function of the truthfulness of the premises used in the argument *and* the inductive probability of the argument itself. If the premises are 100 percent true, then the epistemic probability equals the inductive probability (Skyrms 1986: 15–18). Note, however, that only the auditor and those who review the audit file (such as in a court of law or an accounting oversight board) can directly assess the epistemic probability of the auditor's conclusion, the audit report. Most users need to rely on the wording of the report and an implicit appeal to expert opinion (or other authority) argumentation (Walton 1998: 56–57).

Under principles-based accounting standards auditors are expected to take more responsibility for the broader evaluation of the implementation of general principles in specific cases than previously. Under rules-based accounting, auditors' evaluation is considered adequately addressed by mere referencing to conformity with detailed accounting rules that have been accepted and referenced. The increasing responsibility for accounting-communication evaluation contemplated under principles-based accounting is best addressed through the implementation of argumentation concepts and principles in developing the audit and accounting reasoning process.

Key parts of an argument

My argumentation analysis draws upon some aspects of Barnes' (1991) proposed general model of logical argumentation in public-sector auditing: his concepts of "conclusion," "warrants," "data" and "qualifiers," summarized below.

Conclusion is a statement representing the claim of a logical argument. It can be supported either 100 percent by other statements (as with deductive arguments) or less than 100 percent (as with inductive arguments). In auditing engagements, the audit opinion represents a conclusion that is warranted by supporting evidence or other acceptable premises. To be socially justified, an audit opinion needs to be warranted. Mere feelings cannot be the basis for socially justifiable audit opinions. Logical arguments justify professional audit opinions. Such arguments are also, or should be, an integral part of professional judgment.

Warrants are statements in an argument that explain the connection between the data (evidence or facts) and the conclusion. Warrants are the *major premises* of an argument: they include concepts, explanations of data relevance, principles, rules, and definitions. Examples of common warrants in auditing are risk, materiality, management assertions, and the audit risk model. These warrants are combined in audit argumentation with financial accounting concepts, such as the matching principle, going concern assumption, and monetary unit assumption. Warrants determine whether qualitative requirements (such as relevance) are met by the argument, as well as quantitative requirements (such as risk and materiality). The warrants used determine the reasoning process in accounting and auditing justifications.

Data are evidence of the auditors' procedures, including observation, analysis, and knowledge of a client's business and industry. Data are facts on which the financial reporting is based. Data are considered the *minor premises* of an argument because they depend on the warrants (major premises) to determine their relevance for the conclusion. Unreliable or less reliable audit evidence reduces the epistemic probability of the data in an audit argument. This explains why auditors prefer more reliable evidence.

Qualifiers are constraints on warrants, or exceptions with using warrants. Explicitly acknowledging a qualification in an argument helps strengthen the argument. "Your credibility requires that you limit the scope of your arguments by hedging the uncertainty of your claims and evidence with modifying words and phrases" (Booth et al. 1995: 140). A good example of a qualifier in financial reporting is to point out that although "Generally Accepted Accounting Principles" (GAAP) are the most common benchmark for evaluating financial reporting, GAAP do not always result in fair presentation.

Qualifiers sometimes arise because of an exception to a warrant. For example, considering qualitative aspects of misstatements is a qualifier to the warrant that "immaterial misstatements are acceptable." Thus, qualifiers clarify the scope of a warrant. Qualifiers also arise because there may be other warrants that conflict with a given warrant. For example, a famous warrant from the history of ethical philosophy is to never lie or deceive people. But should you be obligated to answer truthfully if a known murderer asked you the location of his/her next victim? Most people would say "no." This can be best explained from an argument perspective by recognizing that there is another warrant that has precedence over not lying. That is the warrant to not facilitate the killing of people. Thus, qualifiers are a way of bringing out the limitations of any warrants one may wish to use in an argument. This is similar to the hierarchy of overarching concepts identified in ICAS (2006).

Syllogisms and standard form of arguments

The logical clarity of an argument is maximized when it is set up in the standard form using the following order: warrants, qualifiers, data, conclusions. Logic has been studied for 24 centuries using simplified arguments called syllogisms. Syllogisms typically use statements where each statement represents one of the four concepts of argumentation summarized above.

Of course, practical arguments can have any number of premises and lots of data. In addition arguments may be incorporated in other arguments or extraneous material. Finally, the above key features of argument may be missing or only implied. Natural language communication is extremely versatile! What matters, however, is the correctness of the completed process of reasoning. This is what is implied by argument analysis.

The simplest argument consists of one premise and a conclusion. For example:

Premise: The Financial Statements Are in Conformity with Generally Accepted Accounting Principles (GAAP)

Conclusion: The Financial Statements Present Fairly.

Some courts have determined that the above argument is incorrect if the financial statements are misleading, and this can arise when GAAP is insufficiently principles-based.

The above argumentation concepts are also based on the pioneering work by Toulmin (1958), who noted that everyday argumentation is socially situated in the sense that the relevance of premises and conclusions changes with the setting and context. Formal logic is insufficient in such settings as "attributes such as level of interest, and argumentation strength, constantly change according to group the dynamics and goals and discourse norms of that specific interaction" (Sillince 2000: 1130). Thus, a variety of contextual factors need to be considered in evaluating persuasiveness in addition to the logic of the argumentation. For example, the auditor should have a different perspective on the audit when the going concern assumption is being violated than when it is not. Or, as the above example illustrates, the auditor should consider whether a knowledgeable user would consider technical conformity with GAAP misleading in the circumstances. The recent financial crisis has shown that many auditors seem to ignore the changed reporting issues for banks whose viability is being questioned (EU Green Paper 2010). The idea behind more principles-based standards is that if the principles are grounded in broad social norms, they are more likely to result in fair presentation accounting.

Social norms and value statements

A very important class of statements are value statements (e.g. financial statements "present fairly"), and the social norms associated with those value judgments. Social norms are essentially a variety of behaviors, and accompanying expectations, shared by a group of individuals. They can be very much dependent on the context of a situation, e.g., what conditions constitute a valid wedding ceremony.

The role of norms is to help regulate and coordinate behavior within a group, whether the group is a professional body such as ICAS, a student club, or an entire country. An important type of norm is symbols and their meanings. Symbolic thinking such as language, writing, and mathematics seem to be at the heart of human intelligence. For example, the value of paper currency is entirely symbolic and has a meaning independent of its physical characteristics. This symbolic meaning and its related social norms are referred to as "social reality," and the entities and relationships so created as regarded to be "socially constructed."

For our purposes the relevance of social reality is that it is the basis of the social sciences, including economics and financial reporting (e.g., see Shapiro 1998: 653). The problem for auditors is that they need to verify social reality and social constructs such as income. This can be difficult because much of social reality is subjective. Auditors use norms in the form of suitable criteria such as GAAP to help deal with subjectivity. Part of the challenge of principles-based accounting is to determine what kind of social reality should be included in the principles of financial reporting. In particular, I propose that a key principle be the acceptability of the risks associated with the estimation uncertainties concept of ISA 540 (Auditing Accounting Estimates, Including Fair Value Estimates, and Related Disclosures)—mainly because these uncertainties are a pervasive problem of financial reporting and greatly influence the nature of the social reality reflected in financial reporting.

Both language and social context can have important roles in influencing the strength of all argumentation, including audit of financial statement arguments. These two factors explain why rhetoric is also important to audit argument evaluation. In its broadest sense, the word *rhetoric* covers the logic, the language, and the context of argumentation. But it is up to the public accountant to use rhetorical principles in effective argumentation and to expose through skepticism and critical analysis any deception that management and other accountable individuals attempt through their own rhetoric. Some have developed an analysis of rhetoric as an economic transaction, using the analogy of "selling" an idea to selling a good. The gist of the analysis is that when information costs are high (the listeners are uneducated or the information is difficult to understand because it is complex), then rhetorical devices, such as appealing to the authority of the speaker or using emotional appeals, become more important (Posner 1995: 501–3).

Young (2003) has suggested that standard setters have improperly used rhetoric to help justify their standard-setting processes. This may help explain the dissatisfaction with current accounting standards and the move to more principles-based accounting standard setting. However, principles-based accounting relies on appropriate identification of the important goals, concepts, and principles of accounting communication; and its implementation requires fluency in good argumentation and accompanying sensitivity to rhetorical issues. Consistent with the ICAS principles above, these are new skills auditors will need to acquire in order to effectively implement principles-based accounting standards.

Soundness of arguments

For an argument to be good it should be "sound" with respect to its subject matter (its contents) and to its form (structure). An argument is sound with respect to its subject matter if all its component statements are true (i.e., epistemic probability of the premises is 1.00). This is dependent on the knowledge of the field that the argument deals with.

An argument is sound with respect to its form (validity) if its logical structure is appropriate for the burden of proof for the situation (i.e., has appropriately high inductive probability). This aspect of soundness is the focus of logic. In some cases deductive logic is required (e.g., mathematical or logical theorems). However, in most practical situations, including auditing, inductive proof (that is, an acceptable level of inductive probability below 1.0) is sufficient. Since accounting and auditing deal with a world of uncertainties, inductive argumentation is the dominant one. But how high or low can the epistemic probability of the audit conclusion (opinion) be in order to appropriately meet the auditor's social role? Audit standards claim that the auditor provides "reasonable" assurance that the financial statements present fairly. From an argument perspective, fair presentation in part means being as precise in the reasoning and statements as the arguer's knowledge allows. If the arguer is the auditor then this would mean that a fairly presented estimate involving forecasts of future events (these types of estimates pervade GAAP accounting) must have sufficiently high epistemic probability of being true (i.e., being measured accurately, or being achieved, or being realized). For an example using this perspective and assuming the acceptable epistemic probability of future event estimates is 80 percent, only accounting estimates which are at least 80 percent sure of being realized should be shown as measurements in the financial statements.

The standard form of an argument as outlined by Barnes/Toulmin makes most prominent the major premise or warrant by listing it first. But what if we have more than one warrant that supports a conclusion? If there are several warrants supporting a conclusion then we need to put a structure on the warrants by setting up a hierarchy of them that most effectively supports the conclusion. This is a very important issue that is implicit in the ISA 200/700 fairness of presentation framework because traditionally there has been a hierarchy of generally accepted accounting principles (GAAP). The big question is whether *any* GAAP hierarchy will suffice for fair presentation, or are some hierarchies more logical in supporting a fair presentation opinion than others? For example, principles-based approaches to accounting theory imply that the broader principles take precedence over more detailed rules.

Argument perspective

An argument follows from a perspective or viewpoint. This can affect the concepts used. Concepts are important in helping us assign meaning to our senses and information that we use. Immanuel Kant's views on this have been very influential in computer science and artificial intelligence. These views can be summarized in the saying that "Concepts without data are empty; and that data without concepts are blind." What this means is that you need concepts and data to make sense of the world. Both are needed in making effective arguments. In other words, concepts provide meaning to our observations and evidence. Without concepts we have no way of knowing how useful or relevant our evidence is, including evidence on which financial reporting is based.

This Kantian view is reflected in arguments by the fact that the most important reasons (major premises) are usually conceptual ones, based on some assumed model, theory, or principles. These major premises determine what data are relevant in an argument. For example, in auditing, the concept of management assertions drives much of the evidence-gathering logic. The assertions of existence, control, valuation, completeness, and presentation are the major points at issue in financial reporting. In turn, they are embedded in the theory and assumptions of accrual accounting, which determine the kind of data needed to verify the assertions. For example, much of financial reporting is based on historical cost. So, to verify assertions related to historical cost, auditors need evidence on what a client actually paid for various items.

This means the relevant evidence the auditor needs to gather is driven by historical cost accounting theory. This illustrates that evidence is less important than the historical cost accounting theory because without the theory we would not know what evidence to gather. For this reason audit evidence is treated as a minor premise in audit argumentation. The historical cost concept is what gives meaning and relevance to audit procedures that involve gathering evidence about records related to what was actually paid. Being aware of this relationship between concepts and evidence is a necessary understanding of effective argumentation.

Fortunately, in argumentation it is neither necessary nor possible to make all your assumptions, concepts, and principles explicit because your audience may accept the vast majority of your reasons. It is only a few contentious reasons that normally are the centre of controversy. Most people will agree with or accept most of your reasons without question. This is because in a society we share much common knowledge (the "obvious" or "common sense") and many social conventions that we often take for granted (such as a shared language and all its conventions for efficient communication).

A good critical thinking auditor or accountant should be able to anticipate which claims or conclusions are going to be controversial (i.e., be able to understand the perspectives of others) and sharpen the argument to explain why a claim is appropriate in a particular case. This is one of the reasons why it is important to know your audience. For example, the auditor must decide on the acceptable level of epistemic probability for an estimate relying on forecasts of future events. This decision would be greatly facilitated if principle-based standard setters could provide guidance on acceptable ranges for epistemic probabilities of various types of "fairly presented" accounting estimates or, equivalently, acceptable risks of failing to achieve the estimates (Smieliauskas et al. 2008 refer to these as accounting risks). Note that without such guidance it can be difficult, if not impossible, to distinguish between reasonable, fairly presented forecasts and unreasonable or fraudulent forecasts in estimates. What is a fraudulent forecast? When is an assumption unreasonable? Current accounting standards say very little about making these distinctions in financial reporting. Yet they are crucial for determining fairness of presentation. These distinctions hinge on principles related to the acceptability of epistemic probabilities of forecasted estimates, and therefore principles-based standards should incorporate such principles, especially given the increasing use of such estimates.

Consistency in argumentation

It is also important to be consistent in argumentation because inconsistency can be shown to be formally equivalent to lying (Rodgers 2000: 205). This is why arguments are put in standard form of the warrants, then the data, followed by the conclusion. It also helps explain why ICAS (2006) recommends a clear hierarchy of concepts. The focus on consistency of judgment (and standards) is crucial for treating similar cases similarly. To get this result, the focus is on the specifics of a particular situation because that is how an auditor decides whether and when two situations are similar enough to be treated consistently. If two similar situations are not treated consistently then the reasoning in professional judgments or the standards is wrong!

The underlying principle of consistency is that if you conclude you should make different decisions, or do different things, in two similar situations then you must be able to point to a morally relevant difference between the two different situations that accounts for the different decisions. Otherwise the auditor is inconsistent or can't think straight. An auditor or accountant who can't think straight may be considered to be perpetrating a "fraud of incompetence" if such thinking is what supports the conclusion of the standard audit report.

An interesting paradox arises from reasoning for consistency that is called the slippery-slope fallacy. This says that once you accept one particular position then it will be extremely difficult, or indeed impossible, not to accept more and more extreme positions. If you do not want to accept more extreme positions you must not accept the original less extreme position.

These types of paradoxes arise because most concepts have a certain vagueness: if a concept applies to one object then it will still apply if there is a very small change in that object.

The way to get around a slippery slope fallacy is to create a barrier or draw a line at some point in the slope. Preferably, the barrier should be justified for some principled reason. But even arbitrary barriers may be necessary to ensure clear policy. The line may be arbitrary but it is not arbitrary that a line is drawn. For example, stopping a car on a red light may be an arbitrary rule but if everyone followed it you get order out of traffic chaos. Creating such a line is the reasoning underlying the setting of overall materiality and levels of acceptable risks that are the basis of risk-based auditing. It is also the logic that is used in developing statistical decision rules.

Philosophers frequently use imaginary cases in testing arguments and in examining concepts. These are called "thought experiments." They, like many scientific experiments, are designed to test a theory. The cases that can be used for making comparisons may be real, hypothetical, ideal, or even unrealistic. Moral imagination can be very useful in these thought experiments as they challenge routine ways of thinking. Lying to a murderer in order to save a life is an example of a thought experiment that qualifies the warrant to never lie. When an auditor identifies assumptions needed to make forecasts in accounting estimates, she essentially will be doing thought experiments with the evidence and using her imagination about future outcomes. Unless guided by some principles as to what is "reasonable" in the context of financial reporting and what constitutes fair presentation in financial reporting, how else can she predict the "reasonable" future that is considered "fairly presented" as an accounting estimate?

For example, a reasonable representation may be defined to be a range of possibilities or future outcomes at a specified probability such as 95 percent. A reasonable range need not capture all possible outcomes, just a "reasonable" number such as 95 percent. This is economic reality about the future. The reporting of this reality is determined by fairness of presentation criteria, such as what size of reasonable range is acceptable for an accounting estimate. In other words fairness criteria should help the auditor decide when the reasonable range is too wide to report as a measurement.

Thought experiments in the form of calibration exercises and related techniques (Hubbard 2009: Ch. 6) are ways to make accounting estimates verifiable. This is a potentially new technique for helping to audit principles-based financial reporting. However, such techniques need to be accompanied by principles of fair presentation accounting for future event uncertainties such as proposed in Smieliauskas et al. (2010). These issues have not yet been addressed in the IASB (2010) conceptual framework as a basis for principles-based standards, but perhaps they should be.

Argumentation as it applies to principles-based accounting and fairness of presentation

Reasoning from principles is like reasoning using the Barnes/Toulmin argumentation framework. A hierarchy of major premises might start with a general moral theory or some assumption about social norms of financial reporting, such as a hierarchy of objectives of financial reporting. A recent objective in ISA is to detect and deter fraudulent financial reporting. An extension of this might be to detect any cheating (including fraud by management incompetence) via financial reporting. Fraud of management incompetence includes any false claim by management of its capabilities. An example of fraud of incompetence in a university is setting is cheating by students on an exam and getting a higher mark than deserved, and as a result perhaps a better job than qualified for. If such cheating were uncontrollably rampant it could undermine the credibility of university degrees and the broader economy.

Similarly, detection and deterrence of all types of cheating by capital users against capital providers may be crucial for preserving trust, and thus the functioning, of capital markets (e.g., see Smieliauskas 2006). Fraud of management incompetence includes such common problems as inability to prepare fairly presented financial statements. Misstatements might be unintentional yet arise because of management incompetence or inability to deal with financial reporting issues. The auditor's traditional role has been to detect such incompetence but it has not been treated as a form of fraud. However, if the concept of cheating were defined to include fraud by management incompetence then cheating would incorporate poor economic performance due to mismanagement, and misleading reporting including all reporting that fails to reflect the economic substance of an entity's activities. Thus detection of cheating via financial reporting can address the goal of reflecting economic substance of principles-based standards (IASB 2010: 2) as well as detection of fraudulent financial reporting. Savage and Van Allen (2002) give good illustrations of how cheating can arise through conformity with traditional GAAP.

Further down the hierarchy are theories such as utilitarianism, widely used in economics theory and business. Since it is unlikely that a monistic ethical theory such as utilitarianism would be sufficient to deal with all moral issues; other theories such as Kant's universal imperatives (e.g., the biblical commandments) may be added as qualifiers. Such an approach results in "top-down" reasoning that is laid out in standard logical form following the Barnes/Toulmin approach, explained earlier, with the major premises in hierarchical order, followed by minor premises that are explained by the major premises, followed by the conclusion.

A good example of top-down or principles-based reasoning in existing professional standards is IFAC's Code of Ethics for public accountants. This code avoids preparing detailed rules or interpretations, as these will be influenced by national laws, culture, and the particular circumstances of the engagement. However, a detailed rule should not conflict with a basic principle. If it did, the system of ethical reasoning would be illogical (inconsistent). Instead, detailed rules should clarify the application of a principle, yet be consistent with it. The principle has conceptual primacy over a detailed rule. This means that if a rule conflicts with a principle, the principle overrides the rule. Principles-based reasoning has always been important in moral philosophy. Principles-based reasoning is also increasingly important in financial reporting and auditing, especially under IFRS.

Part A of the IFAC code provides general concepts and a conceptual framework. Part B illustrates how the framework is applied by public accountants in specific situations. IFAC feels that specific rules can be arbitrary and not represent the public interest in all cases, justifying a conceptual approach. The framework identifies threats against conformity to the general principles, evaluates their significance, and, if warranted, applies safeguards eliminating or reducing them to acceptable levels. Serving the public interest is viewed as the most important principle since the remaining principles and detailed rules are meant to support this objective. Thus, there can be a hierarchy of principles. As accounting and auditing further evolve we can expect more clarification of the principles of financial reporting. For example, how much measurement uncertainty regarding future events should be acceptable in general purpose financial reporting? Or, should there be a priority or hierarchy of user needs that have to be met in serving the goal of meeting the public interest? If the professional standards do not appropriately specify the principles, then there may not be sufficient guidance by standard setters to appropriately implement principles-based financial reporting, thereby resulting in potentially worse account-ing communications than the existing standards.

The reason top-down approaches to argumentation are so useful for auditors and accountants is that they help clarify what is involved in fairness of presentation of financial reporting as required by CAS 200 (Overall Objectives of the Independent Auditor). Top-down or princi-ples-based argumentation clarifies when the accountant should go beyond more specific require-ments of standards and when the accountant should deviate from the detailed standards. The accountant should deviate from detailed rules when they conflict with a general principle. Attempting to consistently implement a coherent, widely accepted system of primary principles (major premises) is a rational way to implement fairness of presentation of accounting commu-nications. The standard setter's task is to articulate such a set of primary principles, and the auditor's and preparer's tasks are to implement the application of the principles.

Below is an outline of a possible conceptual framework of audited financial reporting that incorporates principles-based accounting, and implicitly has embedded within it more detailed guidance consistent with the principles proposed here.

Overall Objective: Serve the Public Interest (social role of auditor and accounting such as detecting cheating of capital providers via financial reporting):

I. First Major Premise: Overriding concepts are moral reasoning and ethical theories that apply to financial reporting. For example, the major underlying objective should be to encourage trust in financial reporting by reducing the risk of cheating in financial reporting to acceptable levels.

A. Moral Responsibilities from Social Norms: Auditors are hired to verify acceptability of management-prepared financial statements consistent with objectives of generally accepted financial reporting.
B. Rules of Professional Ethics:

1. Act in public interest (by effectively detecting cheating against capital providers).
2. Not be associated with misleading information.

- Misleading to whom? Capital providers should be the ones least likely to be misled by the accounting communication.
- Accurately reflect economic substance: this is possible only if cheating of capital providers via financial reporting is appropriately deterred.

II. Second Major Premise: Suitable Criteria for General Purpose Financial Reporting (such as Acceptable Reporting Framework of ISA 200, consistent with a principles-based conceptual framework):

A. Fairness of Presentation Framework (= Principles Based Accounting = True and Fair Override = Top-Down Reasoning)

Conceptual Framework (objectives, principles and related concepts, including auditability) has highest authority. An example of an important fairness of presentation principle is to account for uncertainties of future events in a way that keeps risks associated with measurement uncertainties at acceptable levels (otherwise the reporting may be deemed misleading to capital providers).

1. Allows disclosures beyond specific requirements (detailed rules).
2. Allows departures from specific requirements (detailed rules) when applicable.

B. Compliance Reporting Framework: Detailed accounting rules without reference to generally accepted guiding principles (e.g., cash basis accounting; or tax basis accounting which has no generally accepted principles—the government makes ad hoc decisions about who gets preferential treatment).

III. Third Major Premise: Assurance framework (clarifies conditions of auditability). This premise can be characterized as reducing evidence risks to acceptable levels. The evidence relates to key assertions of accounting communications as reflected in Premises I and II. This means the relevance of the evidence is determined by the applicable reporting framework.

A. Generally Accepted Auditing Standards (ISAs):

1. Provide assurance for, and verify assertions used by, an acceptable financial reporting framework:

- Compliance reporting framework (conformity with II B).
- Fairness of presentation reporting framework (conformity with II A and reduction of measurement risks in accounting estimates to acceptable levels).

B. More detailed guidance via ISAs and audit guidelines (AuGs).
C. Other assurance engagements.

IV. Minor premises: Obtain data (gather sufficient appropriate evidence):

A. Relevance of evidence (must relate to assertions as per III).
B. Hierarchy of reliability of evidence.
C. Sufficiency of appropriate evidence (reduce evidence risk to acceptable levels).
D. Develop well-calibrated ranges to assess accounting estimates.

V. Evaluate data to give an opinion on the appropriateness of the application of an acceptable reporting framework (e.g., fairness of presentation in accordance with principles-based accounting standards).

- This is the justified conclusion in audited financial reporting relying on the above four categories of premises in hierarchical order, and taking appropriate actions consistent with these premises).

The above lays out the general reasoning of principles-based financial reporting and its audits. Principles should be more sophisticated for fairness of presentation reporting than for compliance reporting because of the added complexity associated with claims about fairness.

If the objectives of financial reporting are aligned with user needs, and concepts and principles are aligned with the objectives, then financial reporting should be meeting the public interest. Thus verification of meeting these concepts and principles of reporting should deter fraud of incompetence and fraud due to intentional misstatements by management (i.e., cheating via financial reporting), and meet the objectives of financial reporting. That would mean a high inductive probability to the above argumentation.

But how do we know what is the epistemic probability of the audit opinion? True conclusions follow from true premises. So, this question is answered by looking at the epistemic probabilities of the premises above. If the objectives are widely accepted then the epistemic probability of the objectives is high. Social facts that accounting and auditing deal with depend on general acceptance for their epistemic probabilities—the more generally accepted the higher the epistemic probability. Similarly, it is the relationship of the concepts and principles to such presumed epistemically high probability objectives that determines the epistemic probabilities of the remaining premises. Thus if you believe that the conceptual frameworks of financial reporting and assurance will really help meet the objectives of financial reporting, then you are entitled to assume that they have high epistemic probability. At least that is the way legal reasoning works in the courts and I assume that this is a practical enough approach for auditing and financial reporting.

In conclusion, this chapter notes that argumentation theory aligns quite naturally with ICAS's (2006) principles-based reasoning approach. However, new premises in the form of clarified concepts and principles are needed to achieve fairness of presentation when implementing a principles-based reporting framework. Specifically, new premises related to acceptability of uncertainties in accounting for future events are needed. Such premises relate to the fundamental measurement process of accounting theory and are necessary to make the theory more complete. In addition, premises related to clarification of responsibilities for protecting capital supplier interests in financial reporting are needed, specifically a hierarchy of needs, so that if there is a conflict auditors and preparers know whose needs should take precedence. With such a more complete set of premises, auditors and preparers would be in a better position to justify fairness of presentation in financial reporting using principles-based reasoning.

References

Anderson, T. and W. Twining. 1998. *Analysis of Evidence: How to do Things with Facts Based on Wigmore's Science of Judicial Proof*. Evanston, IL: Northwestern University Press.

Barnes, D.M. 1991. *Value-for-Money Audit Evidence*. Canadian Institute of Chartered Accountants.

Beaver, W.H. 1991. Problems and Paradoxes in the Financial Reporting of Future Events. *Accounting Horizons*. December: 122–134.

Booth, W.C., G.G. Colomb, and J.M. Williams. 1995. *The Craft of Research*. Chicago: University of Chicago Press.

Chomsky, N. 1957. *Syntactic Structures*. The Hague: Mouton.

European Union (EU). 2010. Green paper. *Audit Policy: Lessons from the Crisis*. European Commission. COM (2010) 561 final. Brussels. October 13.

Financial Accounting Standards Board (FASB). 2010. *Conceptual Framework for Financial Reporting*. Norwalk, CT, September.

Hubbard, D.W. 2009. *The Failure of Risk Management*. Hoboken, NJ: John Wiley & Sons.

Institute of Chartered Accountants of Scotland (ICAS). 2006. Principles Not Rules: A Question of Judgment. April.

International Accounting Standards Board (IASB). 2010. Conceptual Framework for Financial Reporting under International Financial Reporting Standards (IFRS). Accessible at www.ifrs.org/NR/rdonlyres/6A6ABF86-D554-4A77-9A4A-E415E09726B6/0/CFFeedbackStmt.pdf.

International Federation of Accountants (IFAC). 2011. Discussion Paper: The Evolving Nature of Financial Reporting: Disclosure and Its Audit Implications. New York, January.

International Organization of Securities Commissioners (IOSCO). 2008. Accessible at www.iosco.org/library/pubdocs/pdf/IOSCOPD269.pdf.

International Standards on Auditing (ISA). 2011. Review Engagements (ISREs), Other Assurance Engagements (ISAEs), and Related Services (ISRSs) promulgated by the International Federation of Accountants (IFAC) in its *Handbook of International Auditing, Assurance, and Ethics Pronouncements*. Accessible at web.ifac.org/publications.

Posner, R.A. 1995. *Overcoming Law*. Harvard, MA: Harvard University Press.

Rodgers, N. 2000. *Learning to Reason*. New York: John Wiley & Sons.

Savage, S. and M. Van Allen. 2002. Accounting for Uncertainty. *Journal of Portfolio Management*, Vol. 29, No. 1: 31–39.

Shapiro, B.P. 1998. Toward a Normative Model of Rational Argumentation for Critical Accounting Discussions. *Accounting Organizations and Society*. Vol. 23, No. 7: 641–663.

Sillince, J.A. 2000. Rhetorical Power, Accountability and Conflict in Committees: An Argumentation Approach. *Journal of Management Studies*. Vol. 37, No. 8: 1125–1156.

Skyrms, B. 1986. *Choice and Chance*. Belmont, CA: Wadsworth.

Smieliauskas, W. 2006. Introduction and Commentary on Forensic Accounting Forum. *Canadian Accounting Perspectives*. Vol. 5, No. 2: 239–256.

Smieliauskas, W.J., R. Craig, and J. Amernic. 2010. Auditing, Reasoning Systems, Reporting Frameworks, and Accounting Policy Risk: A Response to Alexander. *Abacus*. Vol. 46, No. 4: 455–463.

Toulmin, S. 1958. *The Uses of Argument*. Cambridge: Cambridge University Press.

Walton, D. 1998. *The New Dialectic*. Toronto: University of Toronto Press.

Young, J. 2003. Constructing, Persuading and Silencing: The Rhetoric of Accounting Standards. *Accounting, Organizations, and Society*. Vol. 28: 621–638.

16

A critical perspective

Christine Cooper

… We communicate reality: that is the myth; that is what people believe. It is even what most of us believe.

(Hines, 1988a: 254)

Communication is accounting's leitmotiv. Accounting itself takes the form of a wide range of communicative forms including numbers, tables, graphs, written narrative, pictures, photos and cartoons. The roles of accounting changed and expanded in the late twentieth and early twenty-first centuries with, for example, the increasing importance of public-sector performance metrics, which are condensed into league tables, and the now ubiquitous social and environmental accounts, although arguably company financial statements remain a significant form of accounting communication. This chapter considers how the contents of company financial statements are determined in a financialized world from a critical perspective.

'Critical' has many meanings. In this chapter, it means taking a few steps back from the more technical aspects of accounting to think about 'accounting communication' from a social, economic and political context while at the same time drawing from social theory. Of course, the social, economic and political contexts are intertwined; but a very brief exposition of each will be given here to set out the contextualization of the chapter. The contemporary economic context is challenging with financial instability and the recent banking crisis threatening the life chances of a generation. The political context is one in which, in some countries, the finance sector has become dominant over manufacturing. The social context is one in which accounting is deemed to be a profession and, as such, has significant status and social power. Perhaps more importantly, the accounting profession is self-regulated and its rules are set by bodies which are financed by large corporations.

The social theories adopted in this chapter may be new to readers. What they bring to the chapter is a lens through which to view accounting. This lens will enable the reader to critically evaluate whether or not contemporary accounting can communicate neutral, useful information and, if it cannot, what other social functions might accounting fulfil.

Accounting as a social construction

For anyone with an interest in accounting communication I cannot think of a better, more powerful, starting point than Ruth Hines's 1988 seminal research article 'Financial accounting: in communicating reality, we construct reality'. While, from the vantage point of 2013, this paper may not seem so ground-breaking, when Hines began to present her ideas to an academic audience she faced significant hostility from orthodox accounting researchers. In order to set out her ideas as clearly as possible, it is necessary, at this stage, to take a short deviation away from accounting to the theoretical perspective which underpins Hines's work.

The basic premise of Hines's article is that we can only ever understand things from a 'human perspective' and that language is a key element in this. Following a long-established philosophical tradition, Hines argued that the way in which humans understand the world is through language and symbols. Moreover, our languages and symbols are strongly cultural.[1] This means that as very small children acquire language, they don't simply learn the words for things; they also learn the concepts behind the words. So, when a child learns the word 'mummy', she also learns all of the cultural concepts about 'mummies' (they are female, have a certain authority over you, and, depending upon your culture and family circumstances, they are loving and giving). While concepts are sometimes explicitly explained to children, they are also acquired through experience. For example, if a child never sees her father do housework, this will inform her understanding of mothers and fathers. In any case, mothers are conceptually different from fathers. So children learn cultural norms and categorizations through language (for example male/female; father/mother; strong/weak). Children also quickly learn social hierachizations, so, for example, they may learn that one religion or race is better than another or that BMWs are better than Fords. The important point here is that our human understandings are socially constructed – what constitutes a mother can vary across cultures; and our 'realities' are founded upon the concepts, norms, language and behaviour of people. These 'realities' seem very natural and in many cases will be supported by national laws and institutions. Concepts, norms, language, behaviour, laws and institutions are in a constant state of flux, but they feel as if they are concrete.

The theoretical underpinnings of Hines's work on the importance of language and the social construction of reality, alongside other seminal work drawing from diverse social theories are now commonplace in the critical accounting literature. But the norm of academic research in 1988 was to attempt to 'describe things as they are' or 'to look at the facts', as if it were possible to do so in a 'neutral' manner. This was the heyday of positive accounting research which valued empirical observation and large-scale quantitative studies. Hines's concern with this approach was that the facts reported in positivistic research are the product of a socially, culturally and historically mediated human consciousness, although they are reported as if they are not the product of our human understanding,[2] or as if it is possible to see the world, and therefore to report on it, in an unbiased way.

In order to convey this rather new and radical theoretical perspective on accounting, Hines (1988a) set out her article in the form of a dialogue between a master accountant and his apprentice. The two of them are sitting on the top of a hill looking into the valley below. The master asks the apprentice what he can see. The apprentice replies (Hines, 1988, p. 251):

'Well, in the valley, I see buildings of various kinds, spread over a large area, and surrounded by a fence. There are people inside the fence. A river runs through the valley, and through the area enclosed by the fence. And outside the fence there are trees, up the sides of the valley, all around, as far as the eye can see.'

The master asks the apprentice if he knows what it is that he sees. The apprentice replies that the things within the fence are an organization. There is then some discussion about the river from which water is used in the manufacturing process. Is it too part of the organization? The apprentice thinks that it is, but the master says (Hines, 1988, pp. 251–2):

'... the water of the river is not considered to be part of the organization ... Unless of course the organization is sold. If it is sold, then whoever purchases the organization will pay for the water of the river, and, it being thus recognized, will become part of the organization. It will be named "Goodwill".'

The apprentice is stunned by this. He says (Hines, 1988, p. 252):

'The river – the water in it – only becomes an "asset" of the organization, when the whole organization is sold. At that point, the point of sale, it becomes part of the organization's reality. Like a miracle...'

As if by magic, the water of a river can become 'goodwill' – a solid concrete asset. While goodwill can be described as an 'intangible asset', the accounts of a company give goodwill tangibility. The river becomes an asset of the company, and this can influence social practice – investor perceptions, bank lending decisions, bond ratings and so on. This is why Ruth Hines insists that accounting does not communicate 'reality'. *Rather it constructs reality.* Accounting is partial in both senses of the word. It presents an incomplete representation of an organization.[3] And, as will be discussed later in this chapter, it presents a biased representation of an organization in the sense that it is a representation which serves the interests of some people over others.

In short, goodwill serves as an example of a word which has a genuine economic impact, and which therefore affects people's lives. Yet it was socially constructed, in part, by a group of very powerful people, who have an interest in portraying their organizations in a particular way. The important point here is that people tend to forget this 'real' history; they instead tend to accept (for example) that goodwill is *real*. It is an asset, and in the binary opposition system of accounting (debit/credit; asset/liability; profit/loss; realized/unrealized and so on), assets are better than liabilities. Words which have come to take on a certain meaning, like goodwill, have been called 'myths' by French theorist Roland Barthes. Barthes has been used by critical accounting researchers to re-evaluate the fundamentals of communication (Cooper and Puxty, 1994; Davison, 2011); his work will be briefly discussed next.

Accounting and myth

The early work of Roland Barthes (1972) was concerned with the development of a model that would enable social scientists to understand the allure and power of contemporary cultural icons (including brands, logos and so on) which he described as 'myths'. In his fascinating book *Mythologies* he sets out some of what he considers to be the French myths of the 1950s in a series of essays. In one, he writes about soap-powders and detergents, not commodities which would normally be considered to have mythical status. And yet Barthes explains how soap powder in the hands of advertisers becomes 'mythical'. One popular advertisement of the day 'disguised the abrasive function of detergent under the delicious image of a substance at once deep and airy' – *foam* (Barthes, 1972: 37–38). Barthes notes how foam signifies luxury – from the film star in her bubble bath, to the imagery of something airy (like tulle or foie gras). A different brand of detergent appealed to whiteness and called into play vanity and a social concern with appearances. These advertisements were contemporaries of the dish-washing liquid advertisements which promoted the brand as 'mild and gentle' and claimed that 'Now as hands that do dishes can feel soft as your face'. In the case of dish-washing liquid, bubbles signified luxury. Again the harsh abrasive chemical components of dish-washing liquid, and its function of enabling the mundane and never-ending task of dish washing, is hidden. Brands of dish-washing liquid and soap powder become mythical.

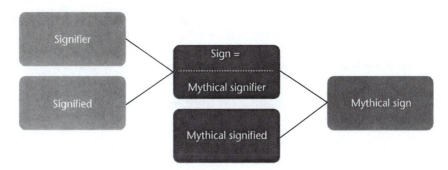

Figure 16.1 A framework for signifiers and myth

One of the strengths of Barthes' work is that he sets out a loose framework to understand the mythical nature of certain forms of communication (Davison, 2011). Barthes wrote about *myth* as a type of speech introduced under special conditions. Rather like the explanation of the word *mummy* above, Barthes, drawing from the work of Saussure (1995), saw language as being composed of three terms: the signifier, which is the empty acoustic image; the signified which is the concept; and the sign which is the associative total of the first two terms (the relation between concept and image). The three terms together form a semiological chain. Myth too contains signifier, signified and sign but is constructed from a pre-existing semiological chain in which the sign in the first system becomes a signifier in the second (see the middle column, top box, in Figure 16.1). Barthes called this second-order semiological system a metalanguage.

In other words, myth is a basic sign (or word) to which something has been added. To Barthes, there is a reason for the addition, for example to encourage people to buy certain products. We know that advertisements do not represent 'the truth'. And yet, we are constantly drawn to the images which they offer us. We buy the washing powder which holds out the hope of having a sparkling white shirt (which makes us or the people wearing the shirts we washed as objects of admiration) rather than a tired grey one.

Accounting, like advertising, can be conceived of as being mythological, as a metalanguage in which signs are appropriated to be 'restored' with 'mythical' meaning. For example the word 'profit' could be conceived as the end result of closing income and revenue accounts and the posting of accrual and prepayments. What can be included as revenue (when we recognize a sale for example) and what must be included as expenses are all determined by rules set by powerful accounting standard setters. However, profit becomes mythical when it is 'robbed' of this technical book-keeping history and instead becomes something 'natural' – a sign of what is important about an organization, its efficiency, its market position and its strong management. Accounting myths are experienced as innocent speech, not because their 'intentions' are hidden – if they were hidden, they could not be efficacious – but because they are 'naturalised' (see Barthes, 1972). *Perhaps the strongest myth in accounting is that it communicates reality.* We don't question accounting communication; we believe that accounts reflect organizations.

In effect what has been argued here is that social power can be gained by those who can influence conceptions of reality, since by influencing conceptions of reality through our norms, hierarchical-structures, myth-making and so on, one can influence social practice. This means that those who can influence 'accounting reality' can also influence social practice for their own personal gain. Accounting standard setters are one of the dominant groups who set out the rules about how things are to be accounted for and they are becoming increasingly powerful.

The next section considers the source of accounting standard setters' legitimacy. It will be argued that standard setters set the rules under which 'the official communicators of organizational reality' operate. But accounting standard setters are part of a large and lucrative industry. The economic context within which they operate is an increasingly financialized one.

Official communicators of reality and their legitimacy in a financialized world

To pursue Hines's goodwill example, the inclusion of goodwill and the form that it takes, the period over which it has to be amortised, and so on, have been the subject of fierce contests. The important point for the general public is that they have very little say in such matters. The contests over if, and/or how, to account for things like goodwill are between the most powerful in society, who are, in the main, unelected. A crucial characteristic of the international accounting standard-setting regime in the twenty-first century is that it is *private* and increasingly *international*. The International Accounting Standards Board (IASB[4]) receives 'voluntary' contributions from private companies with banks being their largest contributor. Such is the IASB's reliance on banks that it has recently been reported that the collapse of Lehman Brothers and Bear Stearns have created significant funding difficulties for the IASB.[5]

The power of private accounting rule makers has been legitimated and ameliorated by nation states. In July 2002, the European Parliament and the Council of the European Union (EU) passed a regulation under which more than 7,000 EU stock-exchange-listed companies are required to account according to the rules set out in International Accounting Standards (IAS) and International Financial Reporting Standards (IFRS). Nölke and Perry (2007) described this as one of the most wide-ranging delegations of public authority to a private, business-funded and business-led body within international politics. The other dominant accounting standard-setting body is the US Financial Accounting Standard Board (FASB). Any country which wishes to engage with the international business community, or attract World Bank or IMF loans, is more or less impelled to adopt IFRS or FASB's accounting standards.[6] Nation states will also adopt IFRS to increase their kudos vis-à-vis other countries and within their own borders. In effect nation states legitimate accounting standards and accounting standard setters legitimate states.

A deeper understanding of legitimation is developed in the work of two sociologists, Peter Berger and Thomas Luckmann.[7] The 'legitimating structures' of society enable the general public to understand what is allowable and what is not allowable (Berger and Luckmann, 1966; Hines, 1988a). Berger and Luckmann (1966) set out a robust and coherent framework for understanding the function of linguistic and social structures through their four levels of legitimation. Their first level of legitimation is linguistic – by having a word (or symbol) for something we must grant its claim to exist, as in the case of goodwill. The second level is 'theoretical propositions in rudimentary form' – this level includes myths, stories and other forms of anecdotal evidence which are used to justify certain social events or relations and could perhaps be seen as akin to the Barthsian myth. The third and fourth levels concern the legitimation of organisations and social structures. Level three consists of explicit theories linked to particular organizational contexts. So for example, there are theories about why it is correct to lock people up in prisons. Finally, the fourth level of legitimation is a 'symbolic universe'. A symbolic universe is where all three levels combine together into a general theory of the cosmos and a general theory of man (although different cultures can have very different symbolic universes). Once a symbolic universe is in place, it needs to be constantly maintained. Legitimation is ongoing.

In order to achieve the strongest level of legitimation possible, accountants require third-level legitimation, which is articulated to the symbolic universe. They need a theory which will support and legitimate their organizational context. In recent times, the way in which the accounting professions have set maintaining their legitimacy is to devise a series of Conceptual Frameworks. Conceptual Framework projects are not functional or technical but a *strategic manoeuvre* for providing legitimacy to standard-setting boards and the accounting profession (Hines, 1989). However, conceptual frameworks also have technical and functional repercussions.

The accounting profession and accounting standard setters in the US, who were arguably the first to begin their search for a Conceptual Framework, started in the late 1960s. Without an 'accounting theory', or strong conceptual basis of their own, accounting standard setters and professionals turned to that of mainstream economics. This was a wise move on their part since by adopting economics they were articulating to the 'symbolic universe' of the day. Interestingly, at this time, mainstream economics was also changing towards a more Chicago School, microeconomic approach which drew its inspiration from a Friedmanite vision. This microeconomic approach was founded upon the principle that the pursuit of individual wealth maximization was entirely natural and also advantageous to society. And that it is possible for individuals to know where to invest their money and efforts in pursuit of wealth maximization since expectations (of future returns from investments) can be reduced to a micro-level domain of knowable outcomes with attached probabilities. The FASB's first Conceptual Framework Project's *Statement of Financial Accounting Concepts, No 1* (1978: viii) states:

> Financial reporting should provide information that is useful to present and potential investors and creditors and other users in assessing the amounts, timing, and uncertainty of prospective cash receipts … Since investors' and creditors' cash flows are related to enterprise cash flows, financial reporting should provide information to help investors, creditors and others assess the amounts, timing, and uncertainty of prospective net cash flows to the related enterprise.

The economic context was that the US economy was beginning to become financialized (Tomaskovic-Devey and Lin, 2011). The *Oxford English Dictionary* describes financialization as 'the process by which financial institutions, markets, etc., increase in size and influence'. Similarly, Epstein (2005: 3) describes financialization as 'the increasing role of financial motives, financial, markets, financial actors and financial institutions in the operation of the domestic and international economies'. More tellingly, Krippner (2005) defines 'financialization as a pattern of accumulation in which profits accrue primarily through financial channels rather than through trade and commodity production' (p. 174). All of these contain important elements of financialization – its international character, the growing importance of the financial sector and the making of profits through financial rather than productive channels. It could be further argued that financialization describes an economic system that attempts to reduce all 'value' that is exchanged (tangible, intangible, future or present) either into a financial instrument[8] (for example a stock or share) or a derivative[9] of a financial instrument (for example an option to buy a stock or share at a future date – see below). Financial instruments or their derivatives can be exchanged in various financial markets. It is this reduction of 'value' to financial instruments or their derivatives that has caused significant problems for accountants as communicators of reality prior to, and since, the banking crisis. Their Friedmanite microeconomic conceptual underpinnings suggested that expected future cash flows from any particular investment can, as stated earlier, be calculated since they can be characterized according to a micro-level domain of knowable outcomes with attached probabilities; typically these are approximated into discounted future cash flows, and then to market (or fair) values.

The difficulty is that future cash flows are not real. In Marxist terms, contracts which involve expected future returns yet to be realised are termed 'fictitious capital'. In accounting terms, they are 'unrealized'. And yet, an accounting profession aligned with an increasingly powerful finance industry can change the rules. And so, in December 1975, the FASB allowed firms, to report unrealized losses and unrealized gains on marketable securities in income when it issued Statement of Financial Accounting Standard No. 12 (FAS12) (Cascini and DelFavero, 2011).

So, three related phenomena coalesced in the symbolic universe at one time – a shift in the dominant form of economic theory, the adoption of this theory by accounting standard setters and financialization. The changes in accounting were at first subtle and could perhaps be best summarized as a move from accounting being concerned with recording past transactions on a historical cost basis for stewardship and taxation purposes, towards an accounting system which is concerned with ways of valuing assets and liabilities as a proxy for their future cash flows, for investors and creditors. This resulted in a gradual change in accounting technologies such that accounting has moved towards a 'balance sheet approach' in which the balance-sheet components have to become meaningful rather than residual values (Power, 2010). The term 'fair value' has been invoked to describe 'useful' asset and liability values. Two generations of 'accounting apprentices' have been taught that the quoted market price in an active market is the best evidence of the fair value of assets and liabilities (*mark-to-market accounting*).

This section has considered accounting standard setters, their knowledge base, their funding and their changing relationship to nation states from a legitimacy perspective. It has been argued that the people who decide the form of financial accounting communication are accounting standard setters who are heavily reliant on funding from large corporations. Although nation states play a role in sanctioning financial-reporting standards, they will feel pressure to ensure that they are competitive with other countries and within their own borders and so are highly likely to endorse these standards. The explicit theoretical underpinnings of accounting standard setters have become articulated to the symbolic universe of financialization, and Chicago School-style economics. Arguably, new accounting technologies have placed accounting on rickety ground – contemporary balance sheets present a way of seeing which is a way of *not* seeing.

The next section considers further the role of accounting communication in the recent financial crisis, since when many people have questioned how it can be that very large financial organizations, with clean audit reports and positive net assets, could have failed so dramatically. It will be argued that we should be concerned that accounting standard-setting bodies, which are funded by banks and other large companies, have set rules, which allow companies (especially banks) to give predicted future cash flows tangibility (by naming them fair-value assets).

Financial communication in a financialized world – accounting for investment gambles

The problem with constructing a reality that is based upon an unknowable future is exacerbated by the fact that there are many extremely complex forms of derivatives which are very similar to investment gambles – they could easily become worthless pieces of paper – even though at some point they may have had a 'market value'. Imagine the example of an option (a derivative), which costs 50 cents on 1 February and which enables the holder to purchase one share (a financial instrument) in 'Hines Corp.' on 1 July for $10. If, on 1 July, Hines Corp. shares are trading for $9, the option would become a worthless piece of paper.[10]

Accounting for derivatives became a significant problem when they increased exponentially in terms of scale and complexity. In the 1970s, the derivatives market was fairly small and domestic, and mainly served the important function of risk hedging.[11] The derivatives' market began to expand around 1995–2008 when it grew at the rate of around 24 per cent per year. In 2008 there were €457 trillion of notional derivatives outstanding,[12] at which time over 1,700 different derivatives were listed on the three major global derivatives exchanges[13] (Deutsche Börse AG, 2008). Krippner (2005) shows that an increasing proportion of company profits in the US came from investing in these markets rather than investing in 'real production'.

While some derivatives can play an important role in risk reduction, many of the forms of derivatives are highly speculative. For example, it is possible for a lender to cover the risk of not being repaid by purchasing a derivative called a Credit Default Swap (CDS), which is essentially an 'insurance policy' taken as a protection against default by a borrower. But, investors can buy (naked) Credit Default Swaps, even if they are not owed any money (for example if they do not own the underlying bond). Naked CDSs account for 80 per cent of the market. Thus it is possible to 'bet' on a company, in which you have absolutely no interest, defaulting on its debt.

The growth of derivatives placed increasing pressure on accounting standard setters to develop new standards and was the catalyst for the expansion of fair-value accounting (FVA) (Power, 2010).[14] The FASB began considering how to account for derivatives around 1992,[15] and took several years to come up with a standard. When large financial institutions did not like their proposal, they tried to have FASB abolished and some withdrew funding from FASB (*The Economist*, 1998[16]). The issues surrounding accounting for derivatives are complex. For example, in the 1990s standard setters (IASB and FASB) seemed to want to distinguish between speculative hedges and risk-removing ones (Bruce, 1994). In practice, accounting standard setters cannot write standards with enough detail sufficient to preclude financial engineering designed to hide more than it reveals.[17] Nor can they write standards which can 'judge' the intentions of companies in terms of whether they are taking risk-avoidance measures or speculating. In any case, standard setters are always a few steps behind an increasingly avaricious, powerful and 'innovative' finance industry (Davenport, 2004).

Accounting came in for much criticism for its roles in the financial crisis (for example, Gup and Lutton, 2009; Krumwiede, 2008; Laux and Leuz, 2009; Sikka, 2009). It is certainly the case that accounting information was unable to communicate the financial position of certain companies. For example, in the weekend before the demise of Lehman Brothers, the bankers and regulators working in the headquarters of the New York Federal Reserve were reportedly told by one of Lehman's bankers, 'We have no idea of the details of our derivatives exposure and neither do you' (Guerrera and Bullock, 2008). One immediate problem with communicating the fair value of derivatives is that their 'value' (as in the case of the option described above) is liable to disappear overnight, and balance sheets are not produced on a daily basis.

There has been much debate about the use of FVA since the banking crisis. As would be expected, the most powerful in society with an economic stake are pushing accounting standard setters to communicate/construct information which is most amenable to them, as well as blaming accounting standard setters for the crisis (Laux and Leuz, 2009). However, while one might question the sagacity of making rules which give tangibility to future values in the run-up to the crisis, it is possible that the rules have now become more tenuous. It has been argued (and accepted) that some markets are too thinly traded to be able to supply information on asset and liability values, or that market prices are fluctuating too wildly to be useful. The US accounting standard, FAS 157, allows some assets and liabilities to be valued according to financial models ('mark-to-model' accounting) rather than market prices.

The models used in mark-to-model accounting are abstract representations based upon the desire to predict future cash flows. So, for example, suppose you wish to know the value of a share which has paid a dividend of $5 every year for the past ten years. If it is assumed that the market price of the share is 'inaccurate', the fair value of the share can be obtained through a model. A very simple model[18] might suggest that the share will continue paying $5 per year for ever. To make the calculations easier, let's also suppose that there is no inflation but that investors would expect a 10 per cent return from shares which are of a similar risk. (Although the risk too would need a financial model to calculate.) A simple model would suggest that the fair value of the share is $50 ($5 per annum discounted at 10 per cent per annum until infinity).

In practice there are various types of financial models which can be used for the purposes of mark-to-model accounting. Some are based upon the capital asset pricing model (CAPM) which was developed in the mid-1960s. After it was developed, researchers set about conducting empirical tests of the CAPM. They found that the CAPM was often inaccurate or unsuitable for predicting asset values.[19] Some crucial theoretical problems with the CAPM were noted as long ago as 1977 by Richard Roll (see also Fama and French, 1992; Hines, 1988b). Roll (1977) explained that the CAPM is tautological and that, consequently, it is impossible to test its viability.

This section has briefly set out the economic context in which mark-to-market and mark-to-model accounting have taken root. A strong case could be argued that we now have liabilities and assets in the accounts of massive corporations which could be described as being based upon unverifiable *mark-to-myth* models. Accounting rules which give tangibility to investment gambles have placed a virus in the system. We now have unverifiable fictitious asset values in financial accounts alongside investors (like those with large naked CDO portfolios) who have a vested interest in perpetuating economic crises. Will the accounting communication produced by mark-to-myth models intensify the next financial crisis?

Conclusion

At the beginning of this chapter, it was stated that the social theories presented in the chapter would enable readers to evaluate whether accounting can communicate neutral information, and if it cannot, perhaps it will enable an alternative perspective of the social purpose(s) of accounting. In order to question accounting's claim to communicate a neutral 'reality', the case was made that it is only possible to understand anything from a human perspective. Human understandings are founded upon the concepts, norms, language and behaviours in our society which are developed within a social, economic and political context. Accounting in *communicating* a social, political and economically determined reality has the power to *construct* a biased reality. But the biased 'reality' which can be found through studying the history of accounting is effaced. In this sense, the language and beliefs which surround accounting and its communicative potential could be considered to be modern myths. Akin to the other myths of our time we are drawn to the images which the accounting profession presents to us. They have a very powerful mystique about them.

A part of this mystique derives from the social categorization which we learn as children that there is a difference between professionals and everyone else. We feel that we can trust professionals since they are experts. The concern of this chapter is that although accountants receive many years of training we cannot trust their neutrality. The accounting profession is subject to economic and political pressure and the theoretical models which underpin their work serves the interests of some groups over others. Accounting work is extremely lucrative. The Big 4 accounting firm revenue in 2011 was $103.6 bn.[20] This is substantially more than the GDP of Iraq.

An alternative perspective of the social purposes of accounting would suggest that:

- accounting legitimates the contemporary economic system;
- creates rules which bring tangibility to the intangible in order for some to profit; and
- communicates the message that financial accounting can render large corporations transparent and accountable, when in reality the information communicated in financial accounts suffers from some serious flaws.

Overall this chapter has argued that the micro-economic underpinning and the paymasters of accounting standard setters have led to subtle changes in the form of accounting towards a system which is designed to enable estimations of expected future cash flows into the balance sheet. Worse, some potentially worthless pieces of paper, which have no underlying values, can be recognized as assets. In the current period of financialization in which profits accrue primarily through financial channels rather than through trade and commodity production, and where there is a massive expansion in derivatives, this is an extremely important concern. Even more concerning is the move from mark-to-market accounting towards mark-to-model accounting. My fear is that when the next crisis comes, as it surely will, there is a level of 'madness' in our system of financial communication such that the whole edifice will come tumbling down.

Notes

1 This perspective sees language as constituting reality rather than being a transparent medium (Barthes, 1967).
2 See Andrew Fagan. 'Theodor Adorno (1903–1969)'. *Internet Encyclopedia of Philosophy*. www.iep.utm. edu/adorno/. Retrieved 24 February 2012.
3 Organizations too are social constructs. They could be described as very complex institutions in which people's goals are varying and disconnected.
4 Of its 15 members, all have an accounting, banking or political background. There is only one woman. The IFRS Foundation, the parent entity of the IASB, was incorporated as a tax-exempt organization in the US state of Delaware.
5 www.accountancyage.com/aa/news/1807831/lehman-collapse-contributed-iasb-funding-issues.
6 The FASB and IASB's standards do not always converge (Baluch et al., 2011); perhaps the differences depend upon the strengths of the various fractional interests who have power over the two bodies.
7 Their writing was strongly influenced by the work of Alfred Schütz.
8 The term 'financial instrument' can be used interchangeably with 'security' or 'financial claim'. A financial instrument can be issued by a company, financial institution or government as a means of borrowing money and raising new capital. In effect, financial instruments are pieces of paper which represent a contractual claim on future income or assets. The most common forms which financial instruments take are stocks and shares, debentures, bonds, treasury bills and bills of exchange (*Collins Dictionary of Economics*).
9 A derivative is a generic term for futures (contracts for the purchase and sale of commodities and financial instruments at a date in the future); options (contracts giving its beneficiary the right to buy or sell a financial instrument or a commodity, at a specified price within a specified period – the option can be freely exercised or disregarded, there being no obligation to transact); or swaps. In other words, derivatives are contracts derived from conventional direct dealings in financial instruments, currencies and commodities (Graham Bannock, and William Manser, *The Penguin International Dictionary of Finance*, 2003).
10 However, if you had bought a share in Hines Corp, even though the share prices might be volatile, at least there will normally be real assets (land, buildings, inventory and so on) which underpin your share.
11 So, for example, international export companies would enter into forward foreign exchange contracts to ensure that they would receive a set home currency amount.
12 The Global Derivatives Market: An Introduction, Deutsche Börse AG (April 2008).

13 Chicago Mercantile Exchange, Eurex and Euronext.Liffe.

14 It is interesting that Hines chose Goodwill as her exemplar of the way in which accounting constructs reality. Accountants (and others) discussed the possibility of putting purchased goodwill onto a balance sheet in the case of an acquisition of one company by another. In order to do this the acquired company assets are revised to their 'fair value' and goodwill is the difference between the amount paid to acquire the company and the fair value of the assets. The 'fair value' of assets was also a contested term, but it came to mean the market value. Fair-value accounting has more recently been called upon to help accounting standard setters, armed with their theoretical underpinnings to come up with a strategy for accounting for derivatives.

15 The first major step towards enforcing fair-value accounting (FVA), in present-day financial account-ing, occurred in December 1975, as the FASB issued Statement of Financial Accounting Standard No. 12 (FAS12) (Cascini and DelFavero, 2011). This was the first time that the FASB allowed firms to report unrealized losses and unrealized gains on marketable securities in income.

16 http://find.galegroup.com/econ/infomark.do?&source=gale&prodId=ECON&userGroupName=ust rath&tabID=T003&docPage=article&docId=GP4100289930&type=multipage&contentSet=LTO&v ersion=1.0 (accessed 1 December 2011); *The Economist*, January 17, 1998: Business: America v the World: Accounting Standards in Dispute.

17 Scott Taub, the deputy chief accountant at the Securities and Exchange Commission, is reported as saying this.

18 For example, the Gordon growth model.

19 http://economics.fundamentalfinance.com/capm.php#footnote3.

20 PricewaterhouseCoopers=$29.2bn(http://press.pwc.com/GLOBAL/News-releases/pwc-reports-fy2011-global-revenues-of-us29.2-billion/s/f2d3a043-5a2c-4293-b59a-0d3744baa9b0), Deloitte Touche Tohmatsu = $28.8bn (www.deloitte.com/view/en_GX/global/press/global-press-releases-en/96616a3cfdc82310V gnVCM1000001a56f00aRCRD.htm), Ernst & Young = $22.9bn (www.ey.com/GL/en/Newsroom/ News-releases/Ernst-and-Young-reports-fiscal-year-2010-global-revenues-of-USD-21-3-billion) and KPMG = $22.7bn (http://www.kpmg.com/Global/en/WhoWeAre/Performance/AnnualReviews/ Documents/kpmg-international-annual-review-2011.pdf).

References

Baluch, C., Cohen, R., Soto, H., Tucker, P., Volkan, A. and Wright, G. (2011) 'Fair value accounting: current status and a proposal for convergence', *International Business & Economics Research Journal*, 10(4): 17–29.

Barthes, R. (1967) *Writing Degree Zero*, trans. A. Lavers and C. Smith, London: Jonathan Cape.

Barthes, R. (1972) *Mythologies*, London : Paladin.

Berger, P. and Luckmann, T. (1966) *The Social Construction of Reality: A Treatise in the Sociology of Knowledge*, Garden City, NY: Anchor Books.

Bruce, R. (1994) 'Learning to play new instruments', *The Times*, 28 July.

Cascini, K.T. and DelFavero, A. (2011) 'An evaluation of the implementation of fair value accounting: impact on financial reporting', *Journal of Business & Economics Research*, 9(1): 1–16.

Cooper, C. and Puxty, A. (1994) 'Reading accounting writing', *Accounting, Organizations and Society*, 19(2): 127–146.

Davenport, T. (2004) 'Accounting reform can only do so much', *The American Banker*, 30 July.

Davison, J. (2011) 'Barthsian perspectives on accounting communication and visual images of professional accountancy', *Accounting, Auditing & Accountability Journal*, 24(2): 250–283.

Deutsche Börse AG, (2008) 'The global derivatives market: an introduction', http://deutsche-boerse.com/ INTERNET/MR/mr_presse.nsf/0/0A4A6E3F8ED836BDC1257457002D5669/$File/2008-04 %20DB_WP%20GlobalDerivativesMarket_e.pdf?OpenElement, (accessed 4 January, 2013).

Epstein, G.A. (2005), 'Financialization and the world economy', Cheltenham: Edward Edgar.

Fama, Eugene F. and French, Kenneth R. (1992) 'The cross-section of expected stock returns', *Journal of Finance*, 47(2): 427–465.

Guerrera, F. and Bullock, N. (2008) 'Struggle to unearth quake's epicentre', *Financial Times*, 31 October, Available www.ft.com/cms/s/0/f2701bcc-a6bb-11dd-95be-000077b07658.html#axzz1ej3P07fG (accessed 1 April 2012).

Gup, B.E. and Lutton, T. (2009) 'Potential effects of fair value accounting on US bank regulatory capital', *Journal of Applied Finance*, 19: 38–48.

Hines, R. (1988a) 'Financial accounting: in communicating reality, we construct reality', *Accounting, Organisations and Society*, 13: 251–262.

Hines, R.D. (1988b) 'A Popper's methodology of falsification and accounting research', *Accounting Review*, October: 657–662.

Hines, R. (1989) 'Financial accounting knowledge, conceptual framework projects and the social construction of the accounting profession', *Accounting, Auditing & Accountability Journal*, 2(2): 72–91.

Krippner, G. (2005) 'The financialization of the American economy', *Socio-Economic Review*, 3: 173–208.

Krumwiede, T. (2008) 'The role of fair-value accounting in the credit-market crisis', *International Journal of Disclosure and Governance*, 5(4): 313–331.

Laux, C. and Leuz, C. (2009) 'The crisis of fair-value accounting: making sense of the recent debate', *Accounting, Organizations and Society*, 34(6/7): 826.

Nölke, A. and Perry, J. (2007) 'The power of transnational private governance: financialization and the IASB', *Business and Politics*, 9(3), www.degruyter.com/view/j/bap.2008.9.3/bap.2008.9.3.1185/bap.2008.9.3.1185.xml, (accessed 4 January, 2013).

Power, M. (2010) 'Fair value accounting, financial economics and the transformation of reliability', *Accounting and Business Research*, 40(3): 197–210.

Roll, R. (1977) 'A critique of the asset pricing theory's tests part I: on past and potential testability of the theory', *Journal of Financial Economics*, 4(2): 129–176.

Saussure, F. de (1995) *Cours de linguistique générale*, Paris: Payot. (Originally published 1916.)

Sikka, P. (2009) 'Financial crisis and the silence of the auditors', *Accounting, Organizations and Society*, 34(6–7): 868–873.

Sikka, P. (2011) Accounting for human rights: the challenge of globalization and foreign investment agreements, *Critical Perspectives on Accounting*, 22(8): 811–827.

Tomaskovic-Devey, D. and Lin, K.-H. (2011) 'Income dynamics, economic rents, and the financialization of the U.S. economy', *American Sociological Review*, 76(4): 538–559.

Index